·2019·

何 梁 何 利 奖

HLHL PRIZE

何梁何利基金评选委员会　编

THE SELECTION BOARD OF HO LEUNG HO LEE FOUNDATION

中国科学技术出版社

·北 京·

图书在版编目（CIP）数据

2019何梁何利奖/何梁何利基金评选委员会编. —
北京：中国科学技术出版社，2020.11
ISBN 978-7-5046-8828-6

Ⅰ.①2… Ⅱ.①何… Ⅲ.①自然科学—科学家—生
平事迹—中国—2019 Ⅳ.①K826.1

中国版本图书馆CIP数据核字（2020）第195654号

责任编辑	韩 颖	
责任校对	焦 宁	
责任印制	李晓霖	

出　　版	中国科学技术出版社
发　　行	中国科学技术出版社有限公司发行部
地　　址	北京市海淀区中关村南大街16号
邮　　编	100081
发行电话	010-62173865
传　　真	010-62173081
网　　址	http://www.cspbooks.com.cn

开　　本	787mm×1092mm　1/16
字　　数	505千字
印　　张	20.5
插　　页	4
印　　数	1—3300册
版　　次	2021年7月第1版
印　　次	2021年7月第1次印刷
印　　刷	北京华联印刷有限公司
书　　号	ISBN 978-7-5046-8828-6 / K·282
定　　价	80.00元

内 容 提 要

本书是何梁何利基金出版物——《何梁何利奖》的第二十六集。书中简要介绍了 2019 年度何梁何利基金 56 位获奖人的生平经历和主要科技成就。为了便于海内外人士了解本奖背景，书中同时收入了反映何梁何利基金及其科技奖励情况的资料，作为附录刊出。

This is the twenty-six collection of the publications of Ho Leung Ho Lee Foundation—*Ho Leung Ho Lee Prize.* In this book, the biographical notes on the 56 awardees of the year 2019 and their main scientific and technological achievements are accounted briefly. This collection includes appendices concerning Ho Leung Ho Lee Foundation and its scientific and technological award in order to help the readers both in China and abroad to understand the background of this prize.

　　2019 年 11 月 18 日，何梁何利基金 2019 年度颁奖大会（第二十六届）在北京钓鱼台国宾馆举行。中共中央政治局委员、国务院副总理刘鹤出席大会并讲话。

　　On November 18, 2019, the 2019 Award Ceremony (26th) of HLHL Foundation is held at Diaoyutai State Guesthouse in Beijing. Liu He, a member of the Political Bureau of the Communist Party of China (CPC) Central Committee and Vice Premier of the State Council, attends and delivers a speech at the 2019 Award Ceremony of HLHL Foundation.

　　中共中央政治局委员、国务院副总理刘鹤，全国人大常委会副委员长张春贤，全国政协副主席万钢，科技部部长王志刚等出席何梁何利基金 2019 年度颁奖大会。国家领导人、各界嘉宾、捐款人代表与何梁何利基金 2019 年度获奖人合影。

　　Liu He, a member of the Political Bureau of the CPC Central Committee and Vice Premier of the State Council, Zhang Chunxian, Vice Chairman of the Standing Committee of National People's Congress, Wan Gang, Vice Chairman of the Chinese People's Political Consultative Conference, and Wang Zhigang, Minister of the Ministry for Science and Technology, attend the Award Ceremony of HLHL Foundation. The state leaders, the honored guests and the representatives of the donors have a group photo taken with the winners of 2019 HLHL Prize.

　　何梁何利基金信托委员会主席、评选委员会主任朱丽兰在何梁何利基金2019年度颁奖大会上做评选委员会工作报告。

　　Zhu Lilan, Chairwoman of the Board of Trustees and Director of the Selection Board of HLHL Foundation, delivers a report on the work of the Selection Board at the 2019 Award Ceremony of HLHL Foundation.

　　何梁何利基金评选委员会秘书长段瑞春宣布获奖人名单。

　　Duan Ruichun, the Secretary-General of the Selection Board of HLHL Foundation, announces the list of the winners of 2019 HLHL Prize.

何梁何利基金捐款人代表梁祥彪先生致辞。

Mr. Thomas Leung Cheung Biu, the representative of the donors of HLHL Foundation, delivers a speech.

中共中央政治局委员、国务院副总理刘鹤为何梁何利基金2019年度科学与技术成就奖获奖科学家吴伟仁颁奖。

Liu He, member of the Political Bureau of the CPC Central Committee and Vice Premier of the State Council, presents prize to Wu Weiren, the winner of 2019 HLHL Prize for Scientific and Technology Achievements.

何梁何利基金 2019 年度科学与技术成就奖获奖者吴伟仁院士在颁奖大会上发言。

Wu Weiren, the winner of 2019 HLHL Prize for Scientific and Technology Achievements and academician of the Chinese Academy of Engineering, delivers a speech at the 2019 Award Ceremony of HLHL Foundation.

何梁何利基金成立 25 周年纪念大会晚宴。

The evening banquet of the meeting celebrating the 25th founding anniversary of the HLHL Foundation.

刘鹤出席何梁何利基金 2019 年度颁奖大会并讲话

2019 年 11 月 18 日，何梁何利基金 2019 年度颁奖大会在京举行。中共中央政治局委员、国务院副总理刘鹤出席大会并讲话，全国人大常委会副委员长张春贤，全国政协副主席、中国科协主席万钢出席大会。

刘鹤强调，党中央、国务院高度重视科技工作。中国经济社会发展正处于极其关键的历史阶段，科技作为第一生产力的作用尤为突出。希望广大科技工作者和各位杰出科学家不忘初心、牢记使命，努力做好各自工作，在各个领域取得更加优异的成绩。科技部门负责人要当好科学家们的后勤部长，为科技创新营造良好环境。

2019 年度何梁何利基金"科学与技术成就奖"授予中国探月工程总设计师吴伟仁，表彰其率先开展深空探测研究，在探月工程总体设计和实施中作出的重要贡献。35 位科技工作者荣获"科学与技术进步奖"；20 位科技工作者荣获"科学与技术创新奖"，其中"产业创新奖"8 人、"青年创新奖"8 人、"区域创新奖"4 人。

何梁何利基金由香港爱国金融家何善衡、梁銶琚、何添、利国伟于 1994 年创立，旨在奖励中国杰出科学家，服务于国家现代化建设。25 年来，共遴选奖励 1362 位杰出科技工作者。

Liu He Attended the 2019 Awarding Ceremony of the HLHL Foundation and Delivered a Speech

On November 18, 2019, the 2019 Awarding Ceremony of the Ho Leung Ho Lee (HLHL) Foundation was held in Beijing. Liu He, member of the Political Bureau of the CPC Central Committee and vice premier of the State Council, attended the Awarding Ceremony and delivered a speech. Zhang Chunxian, Vice Chairman of the Standing Committee of the National People's Congress, and Wan Gang, Vice Chairman of the Chinese People's Political Consultative Conference and Chairman of the China Association for Science and Technology, were also present.

Liu He emphasized that the CPC Central Committee and the State Council have attached great importance to scientific work. China is in a critical historical stage of economic and social development, when science and technology as the primary productive force is playing a prominent role. It is hoped that the broad mass of science and technology workers and all eminent scientists should stay true to their original mission, and do good jobs in their respective work so as to score still better achievements in their respective fields. The persons in charge of science and technology departments should serve as the heads of the logistics departments for scientists, and should also do a good job in this regard so as to create a still better environment for making scientific and technological innovations.

The 2019 HLHL Prize for Scientific and Technological Achievements was granted to Wu Weiren, chief engineer for China Lunar Exploration Program, for he is the pioneer in the field of deep space exploration and has made a significant contribution to the overall design and implementation of the lunar exploration program. The Prize for Scientific and Technological Progress was presented to 35 science and technology workers; and the Prize for Scientific and Technological Innovation was presented to 20 science and technology workers, among which eight people won the Prize for Industrial Innovation, eight people won the Prize for Youth Innovation and four people won the Prize for Regional Innovation.

The Ho Leung Ho Lee Foundation was established in 1994 by four patriotic financial industrialists of Hong Kong, Ho Sin-hang, Leung Kau-kui, Ho Tim and Lee Quo-wei. It aims at rewarding outstanding Chinese scientists and promoting China's modernization. Over the past 25 years, 1362 outstanding science and technology workers have been selected and honored with the HLHL prizes.

序

　　2019 年是何梁何利基金成立第二十五周年。过去四分之一个世纪，在历任信托委员会的无私奉献和基金顾问的指导、投资委员会与评选委员会同仁的努力以及所有义务工作人员的无私奉献中，令何梁何利基金发展成为一个基础稳固、独立性高、获得社会广泛认同和具有影响力的民间科技奖励基金。

　　截至 2019 年，基金奖励的总人数已达到 1362 人，颁发的奖金总额超过港币 2.8 亿元，这方面的成绩有赖历任投资委员会同仁的努力，致力坚守审慎的投资策略，即使经历多次的经济起跌和投资市场波动，仍能克服挑战，令财务状况保持稳固，为基金的长远运作奠下了良好基础。

　　欣逢基金成立二十五周年，基金北京代表处的登记申请也在 2018 年年底得到批准，未来基金在内地的运作受到相关法规的管理，将会更有利于基金的长远健康发展。我们捐款人对于为成立基金北京代表处付出努力的各位参与者，致以衷心感谢。

　　基金自成立以来，一直都得到国家的支持和重视。2018 年 11 月 18 日，基金在北京钓鱼台国宾馆举行了 2019 年度颁奖大会。国务院副总理刘鹤更亲临担任主礼嘉宾并颁奖，并发表了重要讲话，基金同仁都感到非常荣幸。

　　国务院总理李克强在 2019 年 1 月初举行的 2020 年度国家科学技术奖励大会上发表讲话，重申"要深入实施创新驱动发展战略，加快促进科技与经济深度融合，为保持经济运行在合理区间、推动高质量发展提供强大动力"。李克强总理指出"要筑牢基础研究这一科技创新的根基，加大财政稳定支持，引导企业等社会力量增加投入，完善经费保障、成果评价和人才激励机制"，强调科技创新和激励科研人才都是推动国家经济发展的关键。

最近，中美关系紧张、贸易纠纷扩大，更在多个领域中角力，中国科技产业的发展也受到打压。科技开拓需要资源与人才，中国市场庞大，有利于吸引高新科技的发展。因此，我们期望基金能够发挥最大作用，鼓励更多年轻人积极研发高新科技，更好地推动中国科技的自主和创新发展。

我们捐款人都深信，基金同仁定会继续努力，带领基金向前发展，配合国家的科研方针和路线，为奖励人才和促进科技发展发挥最大作用。

何梁何利基金捐款人

何善衡慈善基金会有限公司　　梁铱琚慈善基金会有限公司
何添基金有限公司　　　　　　伟伦基金有限公司

2020 年 5 月于香港

Preface

The Ho Leung Ho Lee Foundation ("the Foundation") celebrated its 25th anniversary in 2019. In the time that has passed since its establishment, the Foundation has developed into a stable, independent, impactful and widely recognised non-government science and technology award. This growth is due to the tireless dedication of the many individuals—past and present—who have provided their support, guidance and expertise to the Foundation: the current and past members of our trustee committee, investment committee and selection committee; those who have served as consultants; and our deeply committed volunteers.

As at the end of 2019, the Foundation had awarded a total of more than HK$280 million to 1362 outstanding scientists. This significant achievement is a great testament to the outstanding efforts of all the members of the Foundation's investment committee over the years. Their skill and determination in consistently adhering to a prudent investment policy has not only enabled the Foundation to successfully weather a broad range of economic cycles and market volatilities, but has also continued to strengthen the solid operational framework that has supported the Foundation's long-term development and growth.

Alongside the landmark event of the Foundation's 25th anniversary, we are delighted to report that our application to establish a Beijing Representative Office was officially approved last year. We are certain that this will greatly facilitate the Foundation as it strives to continue expanding the positive impact of its activities. The Donors wish to express their utmost appreciation to all those involved in the preparation for and establishment of the Beijing Representative Office.

Since its inception, the Foundation has been fortunate enough to enjoy the strong support and the high regard of our Central Government. In November 2019, the Foundation hosted its awards presentation ceremony at the historic Diaoyutai State Guesthouse in Beijing. The Foundation was greatly honoured to have Vice Premier of the State Council, Mr Liu He, officiate at the ceremony, present the awards and deliver the Keynote Speech as Guest of Honour.

At the National Science and Technology Award Conference in January 2020, the Premier of the State Council, Mr Li Ke-qiang, delivered a speech in which he reiterated the importance of and need to "implement firmly the innovation-driven development strategy and accelerate the in-depth integration of technology and economic progress, while at the same time providing a strong impetus for maintaining the level of economic activities within a reasonable range and promoting high-quality development".

Premier Li also highlighted "the importance of firmly establishing the foundation of technological innovation with the augmentation of financial support and channelling the staunch support of enterprises in order to enhance the systems of security of funding, assessment of achievement and incentives for talents", emphasising that scientific and technological innovation, and inspiring and motivating scientific research talent are twin pillars in the promotion of national economic development.

With the recent rise in tensions between China and the United States, primarily over trade but also in other areas, the development of China's technology industries has been set back. The development and advancement of technology requires significant resources and talent. There is huge potential in the Chinese market, which embodies many characteristics that are greatly conducive to the nurturing of high-end technological developments. Our wish is for the Foundation to continue to fully exert its influence and resources to encourage more young people to actively participate in the development of high-tech industries in China, with the continued flourishing of innovation and home-grown, ground-breaking creativity.

Backed by the support of our committee members, advisers, volunteers and the people of China, the Donors firmly believe that the Foundation will continue to reach new heights in recognising and rewarding scientific and technological talent in China and in helping to focus research and development on moving the country forward as a leading international player in the fields of science and technology.

Donors of Ho Leung Ho Lee Foundation

S. H. Ho Foundation Limited   Leung Kau Kui Foundation Limited

Ho Tim Foundation Limited   Wei Lun Foundation Limited

May 2020, Hong Kong

何梁何利基金评选委员会 2019 年度工作报告

信托委员会主席、评选委员会主任　朱丽兰

（2019 年 11 月 18 日）

尊敬的刘鹤副总理，

尊敬的张春贤副委员长，

尊敬的万钢副主席，

各位领导，各位嘉宾，同志们，朋友们：

今天，在举国上下欢庆伟大祖国成立 70 周年、学习贯彻党的十九届四中全会重要决定的热潮中，我们相聚北京钓鱼台国宾馆，隆重举行何梁何利基金 2019 年度颁奖大会暨何梁何利基金创立 25 周年纪念大会，向 56 位杰出科技工作者授予何梁何利科学与技术奖励的崇高荣誉。这是我国科技界、教育界和社会各界的一大盛事。中共中央政治局委员、国务院副总理刘鹤同志，全国人大常委会副委员长张春贤，全国政协副主席万钢，科技部党组书记、部长王志刚同志以及各部门领导亲临大会指导，给予我们莫大鼓舞。在此，我谨代表基金全体同仁，对党和国家领导同志的亲切关怀和悉心指导表示衷心感谢，对捐款人代表、内地和香港科技界、教育界和社会各界嘉宾和代表光临本次盛典表示热烈的欢迎！

下面，我代表基金评选委员会做工作报告。

一、关于 2019 年基金信托委员会会议的有关决定

今年 5 月 27 日，何梁何利基金信托委员会在中银（香港）大厦举行全体会议。会上，基金捐款人代表梁祥彪先生致辞，热情赞扬在信托委员会、评选委员会、投资委员会协同努力下，基金稳步发

展，评选工作卓有成效，何梁何利奖权威性与公信力与日俱增。全体捐款人十分满意，向基金评选委员会和各位志愿者同仁表示衷心感谢。

信托委员会会议在和谐务实的氛围中审议并接受投资委员会截至 2018 年 12 月 31 日和 2019 年 3 月 31 日的投资情况报告；审议并通过评选委员会 2018 年度工作总结和 2019 年工作设想；批准和通过有关信托委员会成员、评选委员会委员更替的决定以及继续聘请毕马威会计师事务所担任基金稽核师，并感谢毕马威会计师事务所多年免费承担基金审计工作，保障基金财务管理规范运行。

需要说明的是，2018 年全球投资市场异常波动，第四季度美股下跌近 15%，欧洲市场也出现债务危机以来最大跌幅。受全球经济环境影响，2018 年年底基金市值跌落到 7.05 亿港元。2019 年第一季度，经投资委员会把握形势、积极应对，基金获得 6.6% 的投资收益，基金市值回升至 7.49 亿港元的高位。考虑到基金未来收益尚存不明朗因素，信托委员会确定今年的授奖金额为 1200 万港元，与 2018 年持平。这笔资金来之不易，我们要感谢投资委员会面对复杂环境付出的艰苦努力。

二、关于今年何梁何利基金评选工作

今年是何梁何利基金成立 25 周年。年初，评选委员会办公室向国内外有效提名人共发出提名推荐书 2300 多份。在规定期限内收到提名推荐材料 862 份，有效被提名人 836 人，再创历史新高。这反映出何梁何利奖在科技人员心目中的分量与日俱增，也对我们做好评审工作提出了更高要求。

今年 7 月 9—12 日，何梁何利基金专业评审会在北京铁道大厦举行。经过 4 天紧张工作，从 492 位被提名人中，按 6.5∶1 的入选率初评产生 "科学与技术进步奖" 候选人 76 名；从 344 位被提名人中，按 10∶1 的入选率初评产生 "科学与技术创新奖" 候选人 34 名。"科学与技术成就奖" 是何梁何利基金的大奖，是评选工作的重中之重。根据《评选章程》规定，评选委员会由段瑞春秘书长牵头、部分评选委员会委员和专业评委组成预审小组，经过考察、听证和综合评议，产生"科学与技术成就奖"候选人1名。上述候选人一并提请评选委员会全体会议审议。

8月27—28日，何梁何利基金评选委员会在北京友谊宾馆举行全体会议，经过科学评价、优中选优、无记名投票表决，评选产生"科学与技术成就奖"1名、"科学与技术进步奖"35名、"科学与技术创新奖"20名，圆满完成了今年三大奖项的评选工作。

三、关于今年获奖科学家总体情况

今年是我们伟大祖国成立70周年。何梁何利基金最高奖项——"科学与技术成就奖"授予我国著名航天测控通信与航天工程技术专家、中国探月工程总设计师吴伟仁。他是我国深空探测领域的主要开拓者和航天战略科学家。他牵头研制我国第二代、第三代航天测控通信系统，使我国深空测控通信能力达到国际先进水平；他先后担任我国嫦娥二号、三号、四号总设计师，实现国际首次月球背面着陆探测，使我国无人月球探测从跟跑、并跑迈向领跑，并带动了我国空间科学跨越发展。他的卓越科学成就获得评选委员会的一致认可，高票荣获基金最高奖项的殊荣。

在习近平新时代中国特色社会主义思想指导下，在建设创新型国家的征程中，我国科学技术事业步入历史跃升期。今年，何梁何利基金评选委员会优中选优，评选出的35位"科学与技术进步奖"、20位"科学与技术创新奖"获奖人科技成果丰硕、创新业绩喜人，人人都有一张十分亮丽的成绩单。他们是我国优秀科技人才、战略科技人才、领军科技人才、青年科技人才的缩影。

第一，基础研究原创性成果突出。有的在力学领域破解了三维弹塑和蠕变裂纹求解的数学难题，其理论创新已在国际上以其名字命名；有的在量子计算领域使自旋量子调控实验技术和装备达到国际领先水平，量子计算机取得重要进展；有的在世界上首次实现单分子磁共振、提升顺磁共振分辨率百万倍、灵敏度百亿倍，被《科学》杂志评价为"重要里程碑"。

第二，生命科学领域硕果累累。例如，基于全基因组的脱靶检测技术，成功构建新一代高保真单碱基编辑工具，获国内和国际专利，使我国基因编辑核心技术居于世界前列；又如，首次建立非人灵长类体细胞核转移技术，攻克体细胞克隆猴的世界公认难题，这项重大成果被 Cell 出版社首席执行官称为"一个新的生命科学里程碑"。

第三，医学、药学领域群英荟萃，成绩斐然。今年从 117 名候选人中产生的 6 名获奖人均是我国医学药学领域的领军人物。其中，有坚持 22 年不懈努力、研发成功了寡糖抗阿尔茨海默病新药 GV-971 并已获准上市；还有发现牙发育新机制，成功实现生物性牙周组织、牙根和全牙再生，并提出实现"生物牙根再生"新理念。

第四，重大技术创新，提升国家整体实力水平。例如，基于微纳米结构研发成功新型热防护关键技术，为重型火箭发动机、涡轮冲压组合发动机等研制提供了重要技术支撑；又如，首创可见光响应光催化水分解产氢材料，将太阳能可利用范围从 4% 提升至 47% 的国际最高效率；再如，攻克轨道交通电力牵引与控制关键技术，创造了高速动车组时速 486.1 千米的世界商业运营最高速和时速 605 千米的滚动台试验最高速，二者均居于国际领先地位。

第五，区域创新全面服务地方经济发展。例如，40 余年从事青藏高原地质研究工作，发现现今全球规模最大的新型热泉型铯硅华矿床，为青藏高原地质理论创新与找矿实践做出了突出贡献；还有扎根新疆 26 年，研发突破大容量风电机组功率调节技术，研制成功具有自主知识产权的大型风力发电机组电控系统，其成果可圈可点。

第六，国防建设和国家战略安全领域捷报频传。例如，持续研究 20 多年，攻克水下发射导弹技术瓶颈，研制成功国际领先水平的水下巡航导弹；又如，成功研制我国新一代反舰导弹，攻克超低空掠海飞行技术等关键技术，支撑我国由"近海防御"走向"远洋护卫"战略；再如，研制成功我国第一型、全国产化的专用武装直升机直-10，成为我国直升机工业跨越发展的重大标志。

第七，获奖人结构合理，青年优秀人才脱颖而出。今年获奖人最年长的为 85 岁，最年轻的为 30 岁，平均年龄 55.2 岁，较前两年有所降低。两院院士获奖人占总数的 34%，非两院院士获奖人占总数的 66%，中青年科学家成为主体。"青年创新奖"获奖人数占创新奖总数的 40%，其中有本土成长的青年科学人，其成果被列为"中国科学十大进展"；有 35 岁以下"海归博士"回国创业，提出深度残差学习的框架，其成果攻克了世界难题。

第八，自主知识产权和总体创新能力显著跃升。今年获奖人共在国际期刊发表论文 8618 篇，人均 156.7 篇；拥有发明专利 1408 项，人均 25.14 项，总数较 2018 年有较大提高。不少获奖科学家注重整合知识产权、实施品牌战略、抢占国家标准或行业标准的高地，折射出我国知识产权强国战略进入进行时。经过初步评估，今年获奖人的主要科技成果均达到国际先进水平，相当多的获奖人已在国际竞争中从"并跑"进入"领跑"方阵。

各位嘉宾，同志们，朋友们，奖励杰出科技人才是国家和全社会的神圣使命，是一项功在当代、泽被永远的崇高事业。1994 年 3 月，香港爱国金融实业家何善衡、梁铢琚、何添、利国伟先生共同捐资创立了何梁何利基金。当时，香港还属于港英政府管辖，四位捐款人宣布这个基金只用于奖励为祖国科技事业做出杰出贡献的中华人民共和国公民。他们的这段宣言情真意切，表达了历经百年沧桑的香港有识之士爱祖国、爱科学、爱人才的拳拳之心。25 年过去，四位基金创立者都已在九旬高龄离世。我们深深地怀念他们。今天，四位捐款人的家属、子女、孙子女秉承爱国先驱的志向，一如既往地推进这项崇高的奖励事业，薪火传承，续写老一辈的创举、善举和义举。在此，我谨向年轻一代捐款人代表表达由衷的敬意，并致以亲切的问候。

1999 年，在国家科委、中国科学院的建议下，经中国科学院紫金山天文台申请，由我国天文学家发现的 4431 号小行星获得国际批准，被命名为"何梁何利星"。为纪念何梁何利基金成立 25 周年，我们将根据最新观测数据制作的"何梁何利星"运行光盘和模型赠送基金捐款人代表，祝愿"何梁何利星"承载着基金创立者的崇高精神永耀星空。

同志们、朋友们，在中央人民政府和香港特别行政区政府的关心和支持下，何梁何利基金已经走过 25 年的历程。我们将不忘初心、牢记使命，进一步健全评审机制、提高评选质量，把基金梦、创新梦、强国梦融为一体，朝着创建国际一流奖励基金的方向砥砺前行。

让我们站在新的历史起点上，以习近平新时代中国特色社会主义思想为指导，大力实施创新驱动发展战略，为实现"两个一百年"奋斗目标、实现中华民族伟大复兴的中国梦而努力奋斗！

谢谢大家！

2019 work Report of the Selection Board of Ho Leung Ho Lee Foundation

Zhu Lilan, Chairperson of the Trust Board and Director of the Selection Board

(November 18, 2019)

Dear Vice Premier Liu He,

Dear Mr. Zhang Chunxian, Vice Chairman of the Standing Committee of the National People's Congress,

Dear Mr. Wan Gang, Vice Chairman of the Chinese People's Political Consultative Conference,

Dear leaders, guests, comrades and friends:

Today, when people all over the country celebrate the 70th anniversary of the founding of the People's Republic of China and learn and implement the important decision made at the 4th plenary session of the 19th CPC Central Committee, we gather at the Diaoyutai State Guesthouse in Beijing to hold the 2019 Awarding Ceremony of the Ho Leung Ho Lee (HLHL) Foundation and the meeting commemorating the 25th anniversary of the founding of the HLHL Foundation. At this ceremony the science and technology prizes of the HLHL Foundation will be granted to 56 outstanding science and technology workers. The granting of prizes is a grand event for the education circle, science and technology circle and all other walks of life.

Comrade Liu He, member of the Political Bureau of the CPC Central Committee and vice premier of the State Council, Zhang Chunxian, vice chairman of the Standing Committee of the National People's Congress, Mr. Wan Gang, vice chairman of the Chinese People's Political Consultative Conference, Mr. Wang Zhigang, Secretary of the Leading Party Members' Group of the Ministry of Science and Technology and Minister of Science and Technology, and leaders of many other departments attend the meeting to give their guidance. Their arrival brings great joy and encouragement to us. On behalf of all my colleagues at the Foundation, I would express my heartfelt thanks to the leaders of the CPC and the State for their care and guidance, and extend my warmest welcome to the distinguished guests from the education circle, science and technology circle and all other walks of life on the Chinese mainland and Hong Kong for their presence at this ceremony.

Next, I will deliver the work report on behalf of the Selection Board.

I. About the Decisions Made at the Meeting of the Trust Board of HLHL Foundation in 2019

On May 27, 2019, the Trust Board of HLHL Foundation held the plenary meeting at Bank of China Tower in Hong Kong. At the meeting, Mr. Leung Cheung Biu, representative of donors, delivered a speech, in which he warmly praised the HLHL Foundation for its steady development under the concerted efforts of the Trust Board, the Selection Board and the Investment Board, the effective work of selecting prize winners and the steadily increased authority and public credibility of the HLHL prizes. As all donors are fully satisfied with the work of the HLHL Foundation, they expressed their heartfelt thanks to the Selection Board and all other volunteers and colleagues.

In a harmonious and pragmatic atmosphere, the meeting of the Trust Board deliberated and approved the investment reports made by the Investment Board up to the following two dates: December 31, 2018 and March 31, 2019. It deliberated and approved the 2018 work report and the 2019 work plan of the Selection Board. It approved and adopted the decisions about the personnel replacement in the Trust Board and the Selection Board. It also decided to continue to engage KPMG LLP as the Fund Auditor, and expressed thanks to KPMG LLP for its free-of-charge auditing over the years to ensure the normal financial operation and management of the HLHL Foundation.

It should be noted here that the global investment market underwent abnormal fluctuations in 2018. The fourth quarter of 2018 saw a drop of nearly 15 percent in the US stock market and the biggest drop in the European market since the occurrence of the sovereign debt crisis. Affected by the global economic situation, the market value of the HLHL Foundation dropped to 705 million HK dollars at the end of 2018. Such a market value returned to 749 million HK dollars with the income on investment standing at 6.6 percent after the Investment Board actively responded to the situation in the first quarter of 2019. Considering the uncertainties in the future income of the HLHL Foundation, the Trust Board decided that the total amount of prizes this year would remain 12 million HK dollars, which is equivalent to that of 2018. It is hard to get this sum of money. We express our thanks to the Investment Board for its considerable efforts to deal with the complicated situation.

II. The Work of Selecting the Winners of the HLHL Prize in 2019

This year marks the 25th anniversary of the founding of the HLHL Foundation. Early this year, the office of the Selection Board sent more than 2,300 nomination forms to effective proposers at both home and abroad. Within the prescribed period of time, the Board received 862 recommendation materials. There were 836 effective nominees, hitting a record high. Such a new record reflects the enhancement in the prestige and influences of the HLHL Prize in the eyes of science and technology workers. It also raises higher requirements for us to do a good job in evaluation.

On July 9–12 this year, the special review meeting of the HLHL Foundation was held at Beijing Railway Hotel. After four days of tough work of preliminary evaluation, the meeting selected a total of 76 candidates for the "Prize for Scientific and Technological Progress" from among 492 nominees at a selection rate of 6.5 : 1, and selected 34 candidates for the "Prize for Scientific and Technological Innovation" from among 344 nominees at a selection rate of 10 : 1. As the "Prize for Scientific and Technological Achievements" is the highest prize of the HLHL Foundation, selecting the prize winner is of primary importance in the evaluation work. In accordance with the Selection Regulation, a preliminary review team composed of some members of the Selection Board and special judges was established under the leadership of Duan Ruichun, the Secretary–general of the Selection Board. After examining the candidates, holding a hearing and making a comprehensive appraisal, the preliminary review team selected one candidate for the "Prize for Scientific and Technological Achievements." The meeting submitted the list of all the above–mentioned candidates to the plenary meeting of the Selection Board for final evaluation.

On August 27–28 this year, the Selection Board of HLHL Foundation held a plenary meeting at Beijing Friendship Hotel. Based on scientific evaluation following the principle of selecting the top from among the excellent candidates and voting by secret ballot, the Board selected one winner of the "Prize for Scientific and Technological Achievements", 35 winners of the "Prize for Scientific and Technological Progress", and 20 winners of the "Prize for Scientific and Technological Innovation", satisfactorily completing the work of selecting the prize winners this year.

III. Overall Situation of Prize-winning Scientists This Year

This year marks the 70th anniversary of the founding of the People's Republic of China. The "Prize for Scientific and Technological Achievements" which is the highest prize of the HLHL Foundation is granted to a renowned expert in space telemetry, tracking, command (TTC) and communication and astronautic engineering technology, and the chief engineer for China Lunar Exploration Program. He is the main pioneer in the field of deep space exploration and a strategic astronautic scientist. China occupies a world–leading position in terms of deep space TTC and communication capability with the second and the third generation of space TTC and communication systems developed under his leadership. He served as the chief designer of Chang'e–2, 3 and 4 lunar probes which realized the first landing and exploration on the Moon's far side. Due to such a success, China is running ahead of its competitors instead of running behind or running along with them in the field of unmanned lunar exploration. Such a success also drives the leap–frog development of China's space science. As he has been unanimously recognized by the Selection Board for his remarkable scientific achievements, he is granted the special honor of wining the highest HLHL prize with most judges voting in his favor.

Under the guidance of Xi Jinping Thought on Socialism with Chinese Characteristics for a New Era, China is undergoing a historical period of marked development in science and technology in the process of building itself into an innovative country. Following the principle of selecting the top from among the excellent candidates, this year the Selection Board of HLHL Foundation selected 35 winners of "Prize for Scientific and Technological Progress" and 20 winners of "Prize for Scientific and Technological Innovation." Having a series of noticeable accomplishments to his or her credit, each of these prize winners has scored fruitful scientific achievements and delivered gratifying performances in making innovations. They are the epitome of excellent scientific talents, strategic scientific talents, leading scientific talents and young scientific talents in China.

First, outstanding original achievements have been scored.

A winner specializing in the field of mechanics has cracked tough mathematical problems of finding solutions to 3D elastic–plasticity and creep rupture, with his theoretical innovation named after his own name in the world.

Another winner specializing in quantum computation has become a world leader in the field of spin quantum manipulation experimental technology and equipment, contributing to the important progress in the development and research of quantum computers.

Still another winner has realized single-molecule magnetic resonance for the first time in the world, and increased the resolution ratio of electron paramagnetic resonance (EPR) by one million times and the sensitivity of EPR by ten billion times. Such achievements are rated by journal Science as "important milestones."

Second, great success has been achieved in the field of life science.

For instance, a prize winner has successfully developed the new-generation high-fidelity single base editing tool based on genome-wide off-target detection methods, an achievement having been granted domestic and international patents. China occupies a world-leading position in the core technology of genome editing with such a success.

Another prize winner has successfully developed the somatic cell nuclear transfer (SCNT) of non-human primates for the first time, cracking a worldwide recognized tough problem in producing monkey clones using SCNT. Such a significant achievement was called by the CEO of Cell Press a new milestone in life science.

Third, splendid results have been achieved by a galaxy of talents in medicine and pharmacy.

Six prize winners out of the 117 candidates are all leading experts in the field of medicine and pharmacy. Among them there is a prize winner who, after 22 years of efforts, has successfully developed a new drug GV-971 against Alzheimer's Disease by using oligosaccharide, and GV-971 has been approved to be provided on the market.

Another prize winner has discovered the new mechanism of the growth of teeth, successfully realized the regeneration of biological periodontal tissues, roots of teeth and whole teeth, and proposed the new concept of "regeneration of biological roots of teeth."

Fourth, significant technological innovations have improved the overall national strength.

For instance, a prize winner has successfully developed a new-type key thermal protection technology based on micro-nanostructure. Such an achievement provides important technical support for the development and manufacturing of heavy rocket engine and turbo-ramjet combined engine.

Another prize winner has developed the technology of visible light response photocatalyst materials for water splitting for hydrogen production. This is the first of its kind that can increase the usable scope of solar energy from 4 percent to 47 percent, which represents the highest efficiency in the world.

Still another prize winner cracked a key technology in electric traction and control in rail transit. Supported by such a technology, the speed per hour of the high-speed train reaches 486.1 km, which is the highest speed in the commercial rail operation in the world, and the speed per hour of the train running on the experimental rolling rig reaches 605 km, one of the fastest speeds in the world.

Fifth, regional innovations serve regional economic development in all respects.

For instance, a prize winner having been engaged in geological research on Qinghai-Tibet Plateau for 40-plus years has discovered the largest ever new-type hot spring cesium-bearing geyserite deposit in the world, making outstanding contributions to the innovation of geological theory of Qinghai-Tibet Plateau and the practices of finding deposits.

Another prize winner having worked in Xinjiang for 26 years has made a breakthrough in developing the technology of power regulation for large capacity wind turbine generator system, and has successfully developed the electric control system for large wind turbine generator system that has proprietary intellectual property rights. His contributions are praise—worthy.

Sixth, news of success keeps pouring in the fields of national defense construction and national strategy security.

For instance, after 20—plus years of research, a prize winner has cracked the bottleneck in the technology concerning underwater launched missiles and successfully developed submarine cruise missile that reaches world—leading level.

Another prize winner has successfully developed China's new generation of anti—ship missile, and resolved difficulties in developing key technologies such as sea skimming flying at the minimum altitude, thus supporting China's efforts to shift from implementing the strategy of "offshore defense" to implementing the strategy of "ocean escorting."

Still another prize winner has successfully developed China's first homemade special armed helicopter "Z—10", which has become a significant mark of China's frog—leap development in the helicopter industry.

Seventh, the prize winners are characterized by a reasonable distribution of age, with young excellent talents coming to the fore.

The oldest prize winner this year is 85 years old, and the youngest one is only 30 years old. The average age of prize winners is 55.2 years which is lower than that of the prize winners in the previous two years. Academicians from the Chinese Academy of Sciences and the Chinese Academy of Engineering account for 34 percent of the total number of prize winners, while non—academicians account for 66 percent of the total. Middle—aged and young scientists account for the larger part of prize winners, and the number of young winners of the "Prize for Scientific and Technological Innovation" accounts for 40 percent of the total number of winners of the prize.

One of these young prize winners is trained and works at home and his achievement has been listed as one of "China's ten major scientific advances" . Another one is a holder of doctoral degree from a foreign university who returned to China before he was 35 years old and started his own businesses. He proposed the framework of deep residual learning, overcoming a world-class difficulty.

Eighth, prize winners have demonstrated a marked improvement in terms of proprietary intellectual property rights and the overall capacity of making innovation.

This year, the prize winners have published 8,618 academic papers in international periodicals, or 156.7 papers for each person. They possess 1,408 invention patents, or 25.14 invention patents for each person. Such numbers are markedly increased when compared with those of 2018.

Many prize-winning scientists attach importance to integrating intellectual property rights by implementing brand strategy and racing to control commanding points in formulating national standards or industrial standards. These efforts reflect that China is implementing the strategy of becoming a major country in terms of intellectual property rights.

According to preliminary evaluation, the major scientific achievements obtained by prize winners this year have all reached the world advanced level. Many prize winners who used to "run along with" their international competitors gradually "run ahead of" their international competitors.

Guests, comrades and friends, rewarding excellent scientific talents represents both a sacred mission for the State and the society at large and a glorious undertaking that contributes to the present age and benefits people of future generations.

In March 1994, four patriotic financial industrialists in Hong Kong—Mr. Ho Sin-Hang, Mr. Leung Kau-kui, Mr. Ho Tim and Mr. Lee Quo-Wei—jointly donated money to establish the Ho Leung Ho Lee Foundation. Despite the fact that Hong Kong was still under the jurisdiction of British Hong Kong government at that time, four donors announced that HLHL Foundation would reward only the citizens of the People's Republic of China who make outstanding contributions to the scientific and technological development of the motherland. These words reveal true sentiments and sincerity of the men of insight in Hong Kong— a city which witnessed vicissitudes for more than one century, and express their love for motherland, science and talents.

We still cherish the memory of these four founders of the HLHL Foundation who all passed away at the age of over 90 during the past 25 years. Upholding the ideal of their patriotic fathers and grandfathers, the relatives, children and grand–children of these four donors promote this pioneering, benevolent and virtuous act as always by continuing the glorious undertaking. Here I would express my heartfelt thanks and give my kind regards to all the representatives of the donors of a younger generation.

In 1999, at the suggestions of State Science and Technology Commission and the Chinese Academy of Sciences, the Purple Mountain Observatory under the Chinese Academy of Sciences named the No. 4431 asteroid discovered by Chinese scientists "HLHL Star" after tendering an application and obtaining international approval.

To commemorate the 25th anniversary of the founding of the HLHL Foundation, a compact disk recording the moving of "HLHL Star" based on the latest observation data and a model would be presented to representatives of the donors of the HLHL Foundation, to express our wish that the "HLHL Star" which reflects the lofty spirit of the founders of the HLHL Foundation will always shine in the starry sky.

Comrades and friends, ever since its establishment 25 years ago, the HLHL Foundation has grown under the care and with the support of the Central People's Government and the government of the Hong Kong Special Administrative Region. We will stay true to our founding mission, further improve the evaluation mechanism and improve the evaluation quality, help scientists regard "winning the prizes of the HLHL Foundation, making innovation and rejuvenating the country" as an integrated dream, and forge ahead towards the goal of making the HLHL Prize an internationally first-class prize.

Standing at the new historical starting point, let's vigorously implement the innovation-driven development strategy under the guidance of Xi Jinping Thought on Socialism with Chinese Characteristics for a New Era, and work still harder towards the Two Centennial Goals and fulfill the Chinese Dream of rejuvenating the Chinese nation!

Thank you!

目　录

何梁何利基金科学与技术创新奖获得者传略

附　　录

CONTENTS

PROFILES OF THE AWARDEES OF PRIZE FOR SCIENTIFIC AND

TECHNOLOGICAL INNOVATION OF HO LEUNG HO LEE FOUNDATION

APPENDICES

何梁何利基金科学与技术成就奖获得者传略

PROFILES OF THE AWARDEES OF PRIZE FOR
SCIENTIFIC AND TECHNOLOGICAL ACHIEVEMENTS OF
HO LEUNG HO LEE FOUNDATION

吴 伟 仁

吴伟仁，1953年10月出生于四川省平昌县。中国探月工程总设计师，航天测控通信和深空探测工程总体技术专家。中国工程院院士，国际宇航科学院院士，全国政协常委，中国科协常委。毕业于中国科技大学，长期在航天部北京遥测技术研究所、国防科工委、国家航天局探月与航天工程中心等单位从事科研工作，是中国深空探测领域的主要开拓者之一和战略科学家。负责研制中国第一代计算机遥测系统；推动研制建设了与美、欧并列的中国深空测控网；负责探月工程研制，提出并实现嫦娥二号"一探三"、嫦娥三号首次自主月面软着陆、嫦娥四号国际首次月球背面着陆探测，为主提出月面无人采样返回和月球科研站实施方案，实现中国月球探测由跟跑、并跑走向部分领跑。获国家科学技术进步奖特等奖2项、一等奖2项、二等奖1项、三等奖1项，首届全国创新争先奖，国防科技工业杰出人才奖等。发表论文70余篇，出版专著10余部。

吴伟仁，1978 年毕业于中国科学技术大学无线电系，后在华中科技大学、西北工业大学分别获工学博士、管理学博士学位。先后在航天部北京遥测技术研究所、中国运载火箭技术研究院 210 厂和国防科工委等单位工作，历任工程组长、研究室主任、副所长、厂长等职；现任国防科工局探月与航天工程中心研究员、中国探月工程总设计师兼二期工程总设计师、嫦娥四号工程总设计师。四十年来，主要从事航天测控通信系统研制、探月工程总体设计与实施以及深空探测发展战略研究。

一、航天测控通信系统研制

1. 负责研制我国首套 S 频段计算机遥测遥控系统

20 世纪 80 年代，针对我国第一代 P 频段航天测控系统码率低、精度差、严重制约航天型号研制和定型的难题，率先提出以灵活性为核心、开放式体系架构的思想，负责研制了第二代 S 频段计算机遥测遥控系统，并成功应用于载人航天工程、长征系列火箭等，使我国航天测控跻身世界先进行列。该成果于 1995 年获国家科技进步奖一等奖。

2. 创建了一种远程运载火箭遥测新体制

针对远程火箭飞行距离远、测控参数多、飞行效果评估难的特点，攻克了飞行过程中实时变状态、天地一体特征码生成与实时快速识别等关键技术，被后续型号广泛应用。该成果于 2003 年获国家科技进步奖特等奖。

3. 率先开展深空测控通信研究

在探月工程中制订了 X 频段统一载波＋差分单向测距的天地一体测量试验方案，并首先在嫦娥二号工程中试验验证；推动研制建设了全球布局、S/X/Ka 三频段兼容的 35 米、66 米天线口径深空测控网，使测控通信距离由数万千米提升至数十亿千米；推动改造升级传统天文观测的甚长基线干涉测量系统（VLBI），使航天器定轨定位精度得到数量级的提高。不仅为未来太阳系探测奠定了测控通信基础，也带动了我国多个天文台站对地外天体探测能力与水平的大幅提升。

二、探月工程总体设计与实施

1. 提出嫦娥二号"一探三"技术方案并成功实施

针对月表 ±10 千米高起伏地形、嫦娥二号变轨控制点处于月球背面无法测控的难题，创新了一种控制点偏置的非对称降轨控制方法，使发动机关机点从月球背面延至月球正面，可测可控，避免了低轨撞月风险，实现了距月面 15 千米高精度探测，为获取嫦娥三号预选着陆区 1.5 米高分辨率立体图奠定了重要基础。在圆满实现既定的"环月探测"目标基础上，创新提出对日-地拉格朗日 L2 点和"4179"号小行星拓展探测的技术方案。采用低能量转移和双向流形拼接轨道设计方法，解决了日-地-月-星四体环境下双端点参数敏感的轨道设计难题，在国际上首次实现从月球轨道出发逃逸至 150 万千米处的日-地 L2 点探测，获得了太阳耀斑爆发等珍贵原始数据，实现了我国科学界多年的夙愿。针对潜在威胁地球安全的"4179"号小行星轨道不稳定和轨道数据被国外封锁的难题，组织相关天文台站协同攻关，指导建立了轨道递推模型，实现了对该小行星的高精度测轨；提出了近距离目标逼近交会方法，实现在距地球 700 万千米处以 3 千米超近距离的交会飞越探测，在国际上首次实现对该小行星 3 米分辨率高清成像。嫦娥二号"一探三"的实现使我国成为第三个对日-地拉格朗日 L2 点和小行星探测的国家，并至少节省了一箭一星约 20 亿元。嫦娥二号成为国际上唯一一个绕太阳运行的人造行星。上述有关成果于 2012 年获国家科技进步奖特等奖。

2. 创新设计嫦娥三号"三自主"着陆方案并成功实施

针对形貌复杂、下降过程地面无法实时控制和着陆过程不可逆等月面着陆难题，制订了基于自主导航、自主控制、自主避障的主减速、快调整、粗避障、悬停六段式着陆方案。创新了惯性导航辅以多波束微波测距测速与激光测距相结合的自主导航方法，实现速度精度优于 0.1 米 / 秒的高精度导航。针对着陆区形貌复杂和光照变化影响地形识别的难题，提出粗避障与精避障相结合的接力避障方法；制定了机器视觉、多敏感器融合等自主避障策略，主持攻克了激光三维图像高度 / 坡度障碍快速识别技术，实现控制精度优于 1.5 米的精确避障，使嫦娥三号创造了一次即实现成功着陆的先例。有关成果于 2016 年获国家科技进步奖一等奖。

3. 制定了嫦娥四号国际首次月球背面着陆探测实施方案并成功实施

针对月球背面与地球无法直接通信的难题，提出充分利用地-月 L2 点解决月背与地球中继的方案。主持攻克了地-月 L2 点 Halo 使命轨道构型设计、多约束耦合条件下的轨道控制等关键技术，指导研制了首个用于深空的轻小型、长寿命中继星和长时间工作在 -235℃低温环境下的轻质、高增益、大口径、可展开中继天线，实现了高可靠中继通信。针对月夜 -190℃低温生存及国外核电源引进的难题，牵头开展其空间安全应用技术研究，制订了极端环境条件下的四大类 19 项试验项目的技术规范和试验方案，推动研制了我国首个同位素电源产品，成功应用于嫦娥四号任务，并在国际上首次精确测量出月夜温度。使我国成为继美、苏之后第三个实现同位素电源在月球上成功应用的国家，牵引了我国空间核动力研究和应用的发展。嫦娥四号的成功在国际上引起了强烈反响。探月十五年来，美、俄、欧、日、德首次来电来函祝贺。

在工程研制与实施中，吴伟仁始终坚持自主创新和自主可控原则，带领研制团队先后获得发明专利 1000 多项、软件著作权上百项，涵盖了特种材料、动力、信息技术、试验验证规范等技术链，填补了一系列空白，带动了我国基础工业的进步。

在抓空间技术突破的同时，吴伟仁高度重视空间科学发展，每次任务都瞄准科学前沿，合理配置各种科学仪器设备，取得多项国际首次的科学成果，如最高分辨率 7 米全月图、地球周围等离子体层图、月球正面和背面局部深度 300 米地质剖面图等，并获得大量月球地质、环境、形貌等原始科学数据，改变了我国科学家过去长期依赖他国二手、三手数据进行研究的困境，使我国空间物理、空间天文、行星科学等学科研究迈入世界前列。

三、深空探测发展战略研究

1. 牵头制定月球无人采样返回（三期工程）实施方案

作为论证组长，吴伟仁立足当代水平、着眼长远发展，主持论证提出探月工程三期（嫦娥五号、六号）实施方案。该方案已于 2011 年经中央批准实施，于 2020 年前实现月球采样返回，将为载人登月验证一系列关键技术奠定重要基础。

2. 牵头论证制定月球科研站基本型（四期工程）实施方案

作为论证组长，吴伟仁为主提出基于月球南极资源开发与利用的探月工程四期（嫦娥七号、八号）实施方案。该方案拟于 2030 年前建成月球科研站基本型，目前已进入国家立项程序。

同时，作为论证组长，他还提出了 2050 年前我国深空探测发展战略规划、重大项目和技术路线。拟在新中国成立 100 周年之际实现我国航天器飞至距地球 100 个天文单位（即 150 亿千米），具备星际探测的能力。

Profile of Wu Weiren

Wu Weiren was born in Pingchang County of Sichuan Province in 1953. He received a Bachelor's Degree in Radio Science degree from the University of Science and Technology of China in 1978, and the Ph.D in Electrical Engineering from Huazhong University of Science and Technology. He then completed another Ph.D degree in Management Science from Northwestern Polytechnical University.

He has served as the project group leader, director of research division, deputy director of BRIT（Beijing Research Institute of Telemetry）of the Ministry of Aerospace, and the director of the 210 Plant of CALT（China Academy of Launch Vehicle Technology）. He then moved to The Commission of Science, Technology and Industry for National Defense of the PRC. Currently, he is a Lead research fellow at the Lunar Exploration and Aerospace Project Center of State Administration of Science, Technology and Industry for National Defence. He also serves as the chief designer of China Lunar Exploration Project and the chief designer of Chang'E-2 project and Chang'E-4 project. He is an expert in the field of TT&C and aerospace project design, an academician of the Chinese Academy of Engineering, an academician of the International Academy of Astronautics, a Standing Committee member of CPPCC（the Chinese People's Political Consultative Conference）and CASF（China Association for Science and Technology）. He is one of the main pioneers in the field of deep space exploration of China.

He has won several National Scientific and Technological Progress Award, including two special prizes, two first prizes, one second prize and one third prize. He also received the first

National Innovation Medal, the outstanding talent award of national defense science and technology industry, and etc. He is the author of over 70 articles and 10 books. During the last 40 years, he has been mainly engaged in three fields: firstly, the development of aerospace TT&C system, in which he was in charge of the development of China's first S-band TT&C system and a new telemetry system for long-range launch vehicle, as well as taking the lead research in deep space TT&C system. Secondly, the general design and implementation of the lunar exploration project, in which he proposed and successfully implemented the "One mission, Three Exploration" technical schemes for Chang'E-2, the innovative "Three-Autonomy" landing schemes for Chang'E-3, and the lunar farside landing scheme for Chang'E-4. Thirdly, the development strategy of deep space exploration in China, in which he took the lead in formulating the implementation scheme of the third Phase of China's Lunar Exploration Program and the lunar unmanned sampling return mission. He also leaded the basic implementation plan of lunar base, which is the fourth Phase of China's Lunar Exploration Program.

何梁何利基金科学与技术进步奖获得者传略

PROFILES OF THE AWARDEES OF PRIZE FOR
SCIENTIFIC AND TECHNOLOGICAL PROGRESS OF
HO LEUNG HO LEE FOUNDATION

数学力学奖获得者

郭 万 林

郭万林，1960年10月出生于陕西省眉县。1991年毕业于西北工业大学飞行器系，获固体力学博士学位。1992—2000年任西安交通大学副教授、教授。其中，1995年9月—1996年1月在澳大利亚Monash大学机械工程系做客访教授。1996年获国家杰出青年基金资助。1997年4月—1998年4月，作为特邀专家，在澳大利亚国防科学技术组织墨尔本专家中心工作。1999年受聘为教育部"长江学者"特聘教授。2000年至今任南京航空航天大学特聘教授，创建南京航空航天大学纳米科学研究所、纳米力学硕士与博士点、纳智能材料器件教育部重点实验室、"纳智能材料器件"工信部重点学科、纳智能材料结构与仿生工程国防重点学科，共同创建机械结构力学及控制国家重点实验室。2004年入选新世纪百千万人才工程国家级人选，2005年作为学术带头人的"纳尺度物理力学"团队入选教育部"长江学者创新团队"计划，2012年获全国优秀科技工作者称号，2013年获徐芝纶力学一等奖，2017年增选为中国科学院院士。

郭万林面向飞行器安全和智能化的需求，长期从事飞机结构三维损伤容限、低维功能材料力电磁耦合和流固耦合的力学理论与关键技术研究。

一、建立三维疲劳断裂理论，攻克了飞机结构三维损伤容限设计关键技术

20世纪80年代以来，针对三维疲劳断裂难题开展了近30年的系统研究，建立了三维约束下的弹塑性和蠕变断裂理论，被国际上以其名命名，称为"郭因子""郭解""郭理论"，并被编入多部飞机设计手册、收入NASA报告、编入美国空军等国内外飞机结构疲劳断裂分析软件，被40多个国家和地区的450多位学者大篇幅引用和应用。成果系统地应用于我国新歼等多种型号飞机的研制，被研制方肯定为"该领域的重大技术创新，使我国三维损伤容限分析达到国际领先水平"。

二、提出低维体系局域场和外场耦合的概念，构建了低维纳米材料结构力-电-磁-热耦合的物理力学理论体系

提出了低维体系局域场和外场耦合的概念，预测了纳米结构的巨电致伸缩效应、与温度和结构关联的能量耗散、碳材料软硬相变、弯曲泊松效应以及应变梯度和外场显著调控的柔性光电效应与磁电效应等重要新性质和规律，主要预测结果被美国洛斯阿拉莫斯、阿贡、劳伦斯国家实验室等国内外著名研究机构实验严格证实，建立了低维纳米材料结构力-电-磁-热耦合的物理力学理论体系。开辟了利用电子束刻蚀和亚纳米尺度的自发相变耦合制造亚纳米结构的新途径，被橡树岭国家实验室等机构学者称为"先驱性的结果"。

三、发现流-固耦合发电的新效应和流体传感新方法，拓展了经典动电效应理论，揭示了水伏效应，创导了水伏学研究

在宏观工程环境中发现了流-固界面边界运动生电的拽势和波动势、气流生电效应，突破了经典双电层理论，被《国家科学评论》和英国皇家物理学会评为"拓展了动电效应两百年的理论"；发现水的自然蒸发能在碳黑等薄膜中引起伏级的电压、直接驱动商用电子器件，揭示了水伏效应，并创导水伏技术和水伏学研究。

在 *Nature Nanotech*、*Nature Commun*、*Phys. Rev. Lett*、*J. Am. Chem. Soc*、*Adv. Mater*、*Nano Lett* 等国际一流学术刊物上发表 SCI 论文 300 余篇，被 SCI 源刊物引用 6500 多次，2014—2018 年连续入选爱思唯尔中国高被引学者榜单，获授权国家发明专利 10 余项。部分成果获 2012 年度国家自然科学奖二等奖 1 项（第一完成人）。已培养博士生 44 名、硕士生 32 名。

Awardee of Mathematics and Mechanics Prize, Guo Wanlin

GUO Wanlin was born in Mei County of Shaanxi Province in October 1960. He is, Chair Professor in mechanics and nanoscience, founder and director of the Key Laboratory of Intelligent Nano Materials and Devices of Ministry of Education and the Institute of Nanoscience of Nanjing University of Aeronautics and Astronautics. In 1981—1991, he studied aerospace engineering and solid mechanics in Northwestern Ploytechnical University and obtained his Master and PhD degrees in solids mechanics. In 1991—2000, he worked as a postdoc researcher, an associate professor and a full professor in Xi'an Jiaotong University. In 1995—1998, he worked as a research scientist in the Center-of-Expertise of Australian Defense Science and Technology Organization at Monash University, Australia. He received the National Science Foundation of China for Distinguished

Young Scholars in 1996 and the honor of Cheung Kong Scholars of the Education Ministry of China in 1999. Since 2000, he is a chair professor in Nanjing University of Aeronautics and Astronautics. In 2017, Dr. Guo was elected as an academician of Chinese Academy of Sciences.

Guo Wanlin has been engaged in fatigue fracture mechanics and structural damage tolerance durability design, physical mechanics, nano-intelligent material and devices and new energy conversion technology for a long time. He established the three-dimensional theory for crack-tip fields in elastic-plastic and creeping solids, which has been named "Guo's theory". He also established the method of predicting the damage tolerance of three-dimensional aircraft structure by using material standard test data, and a relatively complete three-dimensional fatigue fracture theory system of aircraft structures. These achievements have been systematically applied to aircraft structure damage tolerance design and full size aircraft structure tests. He proposed the concepts of local field and field coupling in low-dimensional systems, constructed the theoretical system of physical mechanics of mechanical-electro-magnetic-thermal coupling in low-dimensional materials, discovered new effects of current-electric coupling and new methods of fluid sensing, and proposed a new way to manufacture sub-nanostructures from top to bottom.

His current research focuses on intelligent nano materials and devices, novel conception and technology for efficient energy conversion, molecular physical mechanics for neuronal signaling and molecular biomimics, as well as strength and safety of aircraft and engine. He has published more than 400 peer-reviewed journal papers on *Nature* series, *Phys. Rev. Lett.*, *J. Am. Chem. Soc.*, *Adv. Mater.*, *J. Mech. Phys. Solids*, *Nano Lett.*, etc. He obtained the National Nature Science Prize of China in 2012 for his contribution to physics mechanics, and the first prize of Xu Zhilun Mechanics in 2013, and the ICCES Eric Reissner Award in 2019 for his sustained contributions to the integrity and durability of aerospace structures, and to nano-mechanics.

数学力学奖获得者

江 松

江松，1963年1月出生于四川省达州市。1988年毕业于德国波恩大学数学系，获理学博士学位；1989—1996年在德国波恩大学进行博士后研究，并担任数学系的 Assistant Professor；1996年年底获得德国教授（授课）资格 Habilitation。1997年年初回国至今在北京应用物理与计算数学研究所工作，任研究员。1998—2018年先后担任北京应用物理与计算数学研究所研究室主任、科技委副主任/主任、副所长、党委书记，中国工程物理研究院某重大任务数值模拟子项目副总设计师。2011年至今担任国家自然科学基金委重大研究计划指导专家组组长，2018年起兼任国家自然科学基金委数理学部主任。曾获国家自然科学奖二等奖、军队科技进步奖一等奖等。2015年当选中国科学院院士。

主要从事可压缩流体力学方程的数学理论、计算方法及应用研究，在可压缩纳维-斯托克斯（CNS）方程的适定性理论、磁流体瑞利-泰勒不稳定性和小马赫数极限的数学分析、武器物理数值模拟方法研究和重大型号软件平台研制等方面开展了系统、深入的研究，取得了一系列重要的理论与应用成果。

一、高维 CNS 方程的适定性与磁瑞利-泰勒不稳定性的数学分析

通过建立一个新的压力动能耦合势估计和发展脱靴（即循环和封闭估计）技术，江松与合作者证明了对任意大于1的绝热指数和在任意大外力作用下，高维定常 CNS 方程存在弱解，基本解决了具有大外力的三维定常问题弱解的存在性这一重要的公开问题（仅剩绝热指数=1未解决）。所发展的新技术被同行所采用和充分肯定。

通过建立描述密度振荡的一个全新可积性估计和发展处理解的新技术，江松与合作者率先对球、轴、螺旋对称初值在二、三维情形将菲尔兹奖得主 Lions 的整体弱解的存在性工作推进到任意大于1的绝热指数情形，部分解决了重要的公开问题，从本质上推进

了该方面研究。研究成果受到同行充分肯定和广泛引用，并引发了后续研究。

在磁流体力学瑞利-泰勒（RT）不稳定性的数学理论以及高维 CNS 方程的小马赫数极限研究方面取得多项重要成果。例如，与合作者一起研究了外加磁场对不可压非均匀 / 可压缩分层导电流体力学 RT 不稳定性的影响。通过分析相应的线性化谱问题，并利用修正变分方法及细致的先验估计，建立了在外加垂直磁场条件下磁 RT 定态解稳定 / 不稳定的判别准则，证明了磁 RT 定态解的非线性稳定性 / 不稳定性，揭示了垂直磁场对 RT 不稳定性的非线性致稳作用，即垂直磁场的强度越大、稳定性越高。发现了水平磁场与垂直磁场一样对有界域上磁流体 RT 不稳定性的致稳作用。运用修正的变分方法并充分利用边界效应，建立了有界区域上非均匀磁流体 RT 定态解线性和非线性稳定 / 不稳定性的一个准则，证明了水平磁场与垂直磁场一样能抑制磁流体 RT 不稳定性的增长，更新了知名学者 Kruskal 和 Schwarzschild 关于水平磁场无致稳作用的论断。

二、武器物理数值模拟计算方法研究与软件平台研制

建立能很好描述武器型号物理性能的数值模拟软件平台是国家安全的重大战略需求，而建立软件平台必不可少的条件之一在于设计出能够高精度计算多种物理性质差别极大的轻重介质大变形运动界面以及后期界面两侧介质混合状态的计算方法，这一直是武器物理数值模拟计算方法研究的难题。

十余年来，江松先后作为所级技术负责人，直接负责了国防重大高性能计算项目的实施、国防某重大型号软件平台的研制任务等。在软件平台研制任务中，他与同事针对软件平台研制中的上述计算方法难题，提出了多种实用的算法以克服计算难题。例如，通过引入多介质拉氏混合网格并利用欧拉界面捕捉方法，提出了一种拉氏欧氏自然耦合方法，此方法充分结合了传统 ALE 方法和高精度欧拉方法的各自优点，适合于多介质大变形流体运动的高精度计算；为提高计算多介质大变形运动精度，构造了一种适用于一般状态方程的自适应近似黎曼解法器，它吸收了文献中三种常用近似黎曼解法器的优点，对激波和接触间断都具有很好的分辨效果；为提高拉氏格式重分重映精度，构造了一种基于多目标优化的网格重分方法，该方法综合兼顾了网格的几何品质与随流场变化的自适应，克服了一些常用的网格重分方法不能处理复杂非凸区域的弱点。

此外，江松还带领团队将所发展的方法应用于软件平台的研制和重大型号的实际数值模拟，解决了以前方法和程序有时算不下去、算不准确的困难，取得了显著的应用成效（用软件平台计算了一系列试验，计算与试验结果高度符合），圆满完成了该重大型号软件平台的研制任务，为武器物理数值模拟能力的提高和持续发展做出了重要贡献。

Awardee of Mathematics and Mechanics Prize, Jiang Song

Jiang Song, was born in Dazhou City of Sichuan Province in January 1963. He is Professor at the Institute of Applied Physics and Computational Mathematics (IAPCM) in Beijing, After his PhD degree at the University of Bonn, Germany in 1988, he was an Assistant Professor at the same University (1991—1996), and received the German Habitation at the end of 1996. He joined the Institute of Applied Physics and Computational Mathematics in Beijing in 1997. From 2001 to 2018, he served as vice-chairman/chairman of the Science and Technology Committee at IAPCM, vice director of IAPCM, etc.

His main research interests are in the mathematical theory and numerical methods for models from fluid dynamics, in particular, the well-posedness and qualitative behavior, including dynamic stability/ instability, of solutions to hyperbolic-parabolic coupled systems, such as the compressible Navier-Stokes equations, the magnetohydrodynamic equations, and the equations of radiation hydrodynamics. He has made a series of contributions to these fields.

In 2011, Jiang received the Second Prize in China's State Natural Science Award, and in 2014 the First Prize in China's Military Science and Technology Progress Award. He was elected as an Academician of Chinese Academy of Sciences in 2015.

物理学奖获得者

杜 江 峰

杜江峰，1969年6月出生于江苏省无锡市。1985—1990年在中国科学技术大学少年班和近代物理系学习，获得学士学位；1997年和2000年分别获得中国科学技术大学理学硕士学位和理学博士学位。1990年起留校任教，2004年起任中国科学技术大学教授，同年获得国家自然科学基金委杰出青年科学基金资助，2005—2007年任德国多特蒙德大学玛丽·居里研究员，2008—2013年任教育部"长江学者奖励计划"特聘教授，2013年入选国家高层次人才特殊支持计划（万人计划）"科技创新领军人才"，2015年当选中国科学院院士。

主要从事量子物理及其应用的实验研究，基于在自旋量子调控领域的长期积累作出了大量原创性工作，取得了实验装备、技术、前瞻性应用方面的突破性进展，赢得了国际学术界的广泛认可，引领和推动了相关领域的研究和发展。

一、系统发展国际领先的固态自旋量子调控实验装备和技术

量子调控实验研究首先要解决的是实验装备和技术方面的挑战。固态体系因内部存在多种复杂的相互作用，对其实施量子调控更为艰巨。面对这一挑战，杜江峰带领团队研发了系列高性能磁共振实验装备和高精度固态自旋量子调控实验技术，将自旋量子调控的灵敏度和分辨率提升到国际领先水平。

在实验装备方面，研制成功用于系统自旋量子调控的国内首台自主知识产权脉冲X波段顺磁共振谱仪，打破了国外在X波段高功率放大器上对我国的禁运限制，实现了当时国际商用谱仪不具备的微波幅度相位连续可调的功能，并将相位稳定度提升两个数量级、脉冲时间精度提高一倍，指标全面领先；研制成功用于单自旋量子调控的系列光/力探测磁共振实验装备，并研发成功原始创新的国际首台具备单核自旋探测灵敏度的多波段脉冲单自旋磁共振谱仪。凭借自制谱仪的优越性能，通过与商用谱仪实验比对，指出

法、德、美联合小组在其 *Nature* 论文中单分子磁体自旋基态信号的错误观测（得到原作者承认，但他们认为真实信号太弱，难以在实验上观测），并实验观测到真正的自旋基态信号，被 PRL 作为亮点文章发表，被《英国皇家化学会评论》综述文章引用并承认这是首次观测。

在实验技术方面，发展了核与电子自旋的高精度脉冲调控技术和动力学解耦实验技术，在国际上率先实现真实噪声环境下固态电子自旋量子相干时间三个数量级的提升，厘清了此类固态体系中各种退相干机制对自旋量子相干性的影响，被 *Nature* 评价为"朝实现量子计算迈出重要的一步"。在此基础上，系统性地发展了有效抑制金刚石固态单自旋体系各种主要噪声的方法，在抵抗噪声的高精度室温固态量子逻辑门控制研究上取得系列重要进展，保持着这一体系最高精度水平量子控制的世界纪录。此外，将量子调控从厄米体系推广到非厄米体系，建立了在量子系统中实现非厄米哈密顿量量子调控的普适理论，并借此首次在单自旋体系中实验观测到宇称时间对称性破缺，开启了实验研究非厄米量子力学的新篇章。

二、开创自旋量子精密测量研究新领域

量子精密测量研究利用量子力学原理实现对物理量的高灵敏度和高分辨率测量。杜江峰基于自主发展的高精度自旋量子调控技术和实验装备，在国际上首次测得单个蛋白分子的顺磁共振谱，开启了单分子磁共振谱学与成像的新领域。

磁共振是重要的学科领域和物质科学研究手段，从其发现到应用已获得五次诺贝尔奖。然而，传统磁共振通常只能测量毫米尺度上百亿个分子的统计平均性质，无法实现对单个分子的直接测量。杜江峰瞄准单分子磁共振这一物质科学研究的重大前沿，通过金刚石固态单自旋量子调控的途径，解决了其中的若干关键问题：①利用高阶动力学解耦技术有效抑制噪声影响，显著提升了金刚石单自旋磁量子传感器的性能，达到了单分子的探测灵敏度；②发展了高精度的自旋量子干涉仪测量方法，将被测单分子自旋的极微弱磁信号转化为传感器上自旋量子干涉仪的相位信息并逐级放大读出；③在自主研制的磁共振实验装备上实现了所有功能的高性能集成。基于上述突破，在室温大气下测得首张单蛋白分子的顺磁共振谱，成功将电子顺磁共振技术分辨率从毫米推进到纳米、灵敏度从百亿分子推进到单个分子。与超高分辨荧光显微技术（获 2014 年诺贝尔物理学奖）相比，这项新技术不仅同样能够提供纳米分辨率的空间定位信息，还可进一步解析出单个分子的结构信息和构象变化，可用于在单分子层面认识物质科学和生命科学的机理，将在物理、化学及生命科学等多个领域有广泛的应用前景。杜江峰带领其团队进一步取得了在室温水溶液环境中探测单个 DNA 分子磁共振谱、细胞原位铁蛋白分子的纳米级磁成像等多个重要进展，为推动单分子磁共振谱学与成像的最终应用作出了卓越贡献。

利用自旋量子精密测量原理，杜江峰及其团队还原创提出并实验实现基于固态自旋搜寻超越标准模型新粒子的新方法。该方法受到国际学术界高度重视，被评为在实验室

尺度寻找新粒子的四个重要方法之一。意大利国家核物理研究所举办的 SPIN 2018 国际会议、2019 年美国物理学会年会、2019 年美国能源部核科学咨询委员会会议均邀请其作特邀报告。

三、取得量子计算重要进展

量子计算研究是基于量子力学原理的新型计算，被认为是下一代革命性的信息处理技术。杜江峰在基于自旋的量子计算研究上取得了一系列重要研究成果：首次从理论上提出并实验实现了量子博弈算法的全过程，指出博弈结果随量子纠缠的增加存在对抗、过渡和合作三个区域，从实验角度验证了量子计算可以解决经典计算所无法解决的难题；采用绝热量子计算这一新型量子计算模式实现了 Shor 算法，有效降低了实验难度，连续保持着使用量子算法完成质因数分解的世界纪录；首次实现压缩量子模拟，将原本需要 2^{32} 的经典比特资源压缩到只需要 5 个量子比特资源来实现，朝着超越经典计算能力的实用化量子模拟迈出重要一步；实验实现氢分子、水分子及化学反应动力学的量子模拟，是国际上量子化学模拟的先驱性工作，受邀在国际学术期刊撰写综述文章；研制成功首个工作在室温大气条件下的可编程固态自旋量子处理器。

杜江峰所取得的成就标志着中国在自旋量子技术领域达到世界领先行列，对推动世界量子科技发展起到了重要作用。发表研究论文 200 余篇，成果多次入选国内十大科技进展，并获得国家自然科学奖二等奖等奖励。因其突出贡献，杜江峰受邀成为国际著名的高登研究会议"金刚石色心量子调控"主题 2019 年大会共同主席和 2021 年大会主席。

Awardee of Physics Prize, Du Jiangfeng

Du Jiangfeng was born in Wuxi City of Jiangsu Province in June 1969. He received undergraduate education and further pursed his mater and doctoral degree in University of Science and Technology of China（USTC）. Since the year 2004，he works as a professor in the Department of Modern Physics of USTC. In 2015，he was elected as the academician of Chinese Academy of Sciences. Du is an expert in the area of quantum physics and its applications.

1. Development of spin magnetic resonance spectrometers and spin quantum control techniques

Du and his team developed a series of advanced spin magnetic resonance spectrometers and pulsed spin control techniques to precisely manipulate both the ensemble spins and single-spin. Especially，they developed the dynamical decoupling technique with which they successfully prolonged the spin coherence time by near three orders of magnitudes. Based on the spectrometers and techniques，they accomplished the most accurate logic gates so far performed on solid-state spins in the world, and further realized the universal quantum control of spins under non-Hermitian Hamiltonians. These represent the leading level of the spin quantum control in the world.

2. Breakthroughs in spin quantum metrology

The progresses in the quantum control of single-spin in diamonds opened the way for single-molecule magnetic resonance, which is a long-standing dream in the field of magnetic resonance. Du and his team obtained the first single-protein spin resonance spectroscopy under ambient conditions, in which the magnetic resonance sensitivity was increased by ten billion times and the resolution increased by a million times compared to the conventional magnetic resonance. Further, they realized the single-DNA electron spin resonance spectroscopy in aqueous solutions, and the nanoscale magnetic imaging of ferritins in a single cell. These milestone works represent solid breakthroughs toward single-molecule magnetic resonance spectroscopy and imaging. Besides, they proposed and experimentally realized a diamond sensor-based route to search for the exotic spin-dependent interactions. Their method was soon recognized as a new method to search for new particles beyond the standard model.

3. Important progresses in spin-based quantum computation

Towards the goal of building a spin-based quantum computer, Du and his team have made several important progresses: the first experimental verification of quantum game; the largest integer numbers ever factorized by quantum computation with their own proposed adiabatic quantum algorithm; the first experiment of compressed quantum simulation in which a 32-spin Ising chain is simulated by only 5 qubits; the first programmable solid-state quantum processor which works under ambient conditions, etc.

化学奖获得者

冯 小 明

冯小明，1963 年 10 月出生于四川省武胜县。1981—1988 年就读于兰州大学，获得理学学士和硕士学位；1996 年毕业于中国科学院化学研究所，获理学博士学位；1998—1999 年在美国科罗拉多州立大学进行博士后研究。2000 年至今任四川大学化学学院教授、博士生导师。2002 年获国家自然科学基金委杰出青年科学基金项目资助，2005 年入选教育部"长江学者奖励计划"特聘教授，2013 年当选中国科学院院士，2014 年当选英国皇家化学会会士。他是国家创新研究群体学术带头人，人事部等七部委"新世纪百千万人才工程"国家级人选，教育部"长江学者和创新团队发展计划"创新团队学术带头人，教育部《跨世纪优秀人才培养计划》入选者。兼任国务院学位委员会学科评议组成员，中国化学会常务理事、手性专业委员会主任委员、有机化学学科委员。政协第十三届全国委员会委员，中国致公党第十五届中央委员会委员。同时，担任 3 个学术刊物编委和 7 个学术刊物顾问编委。

主要从事不对称合成方法学及手性医药、农药和具有生理活性化合物的合成研究，在新催化剂、新反应、新方法、新策略以及手性生物活性分子的高效高选择性精准合成等方面作出了一系列开创性研究工作。

其原创性、创新性、引领性和有用性的研究工作在国内外同行中产生了重要影响，为手性科学的快速发展提供了重要基础，对提升我国在不对称合成领域的国际地位作出了重要贡献。

一、新型优势手性双氮氧催化剂和配体的设计合成

基于手性配体设计中的双功能和 C_2-对称性等设计策略，冯小明发展了一类全新的具有柔性骨架的手性双氮氧酰胺化合物，这是具有自主知识产权的标签性催化剂，被公认为新"优势"手性配体和催化剂，突破了传统优势配体刚性骨架的要求，证实了具柔

性骨架配体的优异性能和发展潜力，为新手性催化剂和配体的设计提供了新思路。该类手性配体可与 20 多种金属离子配位，包括主族金属 Mg（Ⅱ）、In（Ⅲ）和过渡金属 Ti（Ⅳ）、Cu（Ⅰ）、Cu（Ⅱ）、Zn（Ⅱ）、Ni（Ⅱ）、Fe（Ⅱ）、Fe（Ⅲ）、Co（Ⅱ）、Ag（Ⅰ）以及稀土金属 Sc（Ⅲ）、Y（Ⅲ）、La（Ⅲ）、Pr（Ⅲ）、Eu（Ⅲ）、Dy（Ⅲ）、Gd（Ⅲ）、Yb（Ⅲ）等，形成的手性双氮氧-金属配合物催化剂能够与底物实现"手性配体—金属—底物"之间立体、电子效应的完美匹配，彰显了催化剂的强自适应性，并展现出优异的手性诱导和催化能力。该类催化剂和配体原料价廉易得、合成简便、结构高度可调、稳定性好，对水和空气具有容忍性，已作为商品化催化剂向全世界销售，被国内外多个课题组和公司成功应用于研究和产品开发中，如美国芝加哥大学 Yamamoto 课题组、德国莱比锡大学 Schneider 课题组、德国马普所 Kumar 课题组和 Waldmann 课题组、日本东京大学 Kobayashi 课题组、北京大学贾彦兴课题组、厦门大学黄培强课题组、武汉大学王春江课题组及浙江九州药业等。

二、高效高选择性不对称催化新反应、新方法、新策略

冯小明利用自己发展的催化剂和配体建立了手性双氮氧-金属配合物催化剂库，在温和条件下高效高选择性实现了 40 多类重要的不对称反应，包括 10 多类具有挑战性和以前无法实现的不对称催化新反应，更新了对反应和化合物性质的认识。

利用自主研发的手性双氮氧-钪（Ⅲ）配合物催化剂解决了 α-重氮酯与羰基化合物不对称催化反应中化学和立体选择性难控制的问题，首次实现了高效高选择性催化不对称 Roskamp 反应，催化剂用量可降至万分之五，被 Elsevier 公司出版的有机人名反应专著 Organic Synthesis Based on Name Reactions 收录并被冠名为"Roskamp-Feng 反应"，这是中国学者在中国本土所做工作被冠以中国人名的反应。同时，该研究工作纠正了美国通用有机化学教材中"不能制备手性中心位于两个羰基之间光学活性 β-酮酯"的片面结论。α-重氮酯与芳基烷基酮发生的不对称 α-胺化反应丰富了重氮化学的研究内容，为碳-氮键形成提供了一条新途径。以手性双氮氧-钪（Ⅲ）配合物催化剂首次实现了烯酮的区域专一性和高立体选择性的不对称溴胺化反应，温和条件下以万分之五的催化剂用量高收率、高区域和立体选择性地得到了 α-溴代-β-氨基酮类化合物，被评为 *Angew. Chem. Int. Ed.* 的 VIP 论文。该研究工作也被 2001 年诺贝尔化学奖得主 Ryoji Noyori 教授写入德国 Wiley 公司出版的有机化学专著《有机化学——突破和展望》。

基于手性双氮氧-金属配合物催化体系发展了对映选择性发散型合成新方法和双金属接力催化新策略。在使用同一个手性双氮氧配体情况下，通过改变中心金属的种类催化吡唑啉酮对烯酮的不对称 Michael 反应，实现了吡唑啉酮衍生物的对映选择性发散型合成，有效解决了因手性源匮乏而难以获得两种相反构型催化剂的难题。利用金（Ⅰ）/手性双氮氧-镍（Ⅱ）双金属协同催化剂实现了炔醇/胺与 β，γ-不饱和 α-酮酸酯的高效高选择性环化/反电子需求杂-Diels-Alder 串联反应和烯丙醇与炔酮/酯的烷氧化/Claisen

重排串联反应。

三、重要生物活性分子的精准合成

冯小明利用发展的新催化剂、新反应、新方法和新策略，为超过 20 个药物分子、候选药物、天然产物及其合成中间体的高效高选择性合成提供了核心技术，如药物普瑞巴林、帕罗西汀、非罗西汀、巴氯芬、中风神经保护剂 Maxipost、治疗老年痴呆症药物 Coerulescine、治疗青光眼药物毒扁豆碱 Physostigmine 等。发展的不对称催化方法以 71% 的收率、94% ee 的对映选择性一步得到抗癌细胞增生剂，大大缩短了原有七步的合成路线；手性双氮氧-镍（Ⅱ）配合物催化的 Diels–Alder 反应能够简洁高效合成具有抗恶性疟原虫活性的手性候选药物 KAE609。

自 1999 年独立工作以来，冯小明已发表高水平 SCI 论文 380 多篇，其中 *J. Am. Chem. Soc.* 12 篇、*Angew. Chem.* 48 篇、*Acc. Chem. Res.* 和 *Chem. Rev.* 各 2 篇，论文累计 SCI 他引 10700 余次，H 因子 65；应邀撰写综述 12 篇、国内外专著 17 个章节；授权中国发明专利 5 项。研究工作入选 2011 年"中国高等学校十大科技进展"、中国科学院《2012 科学发展报告》《国家自然科学基金资助项目优秀成果选编》和多部专著及教材中。获得国家自然科学奖二等奖、教育部自然科学一等奖、未来科学大奖——物质科学奖、SCIFinder 有机合成创造奖、全国优秀教师和宝钢优秀教师奖、中国化学会手性化学奖、中国化学会黄耀曾金属有机化学奖、全国优秀博士生学位论文指导教师等荣誉。迄今为止，已培养 91 名博士生和 25 名硕士生，其中 1 人获中国青年女科学家奖、2 人获国家杰出青年基金项目资助、2 人获国家优秀青年基金资助、20 人在"双一流"高校任（副）教授、3 人入选国家"青年千人"计划、3 人入选四川省"青年千人"计划、4 人获德国洪堡奖学金。

Awardee of Chemistry Prize, Feng Xiaoming

Feng Xiaoming was born in Wusheng County of Sichuan Province in October 1963. He studied in Lanzhou University from 1981 to 1988 and obtained the Bachelor's and master's degrees. In 1996, he got his Ph.D degree from Institute of Chemistry, Chinese Academy of Science. Then he did the postdoctoral research for one year. In 1999, he got back to China and joined Sichuan University as a full professor. He achieved the National Science Fund for Distinguished Young Scholars in 2002, and was appointed as the Distinguished Professor of the Yangtze River Scholars Program by the Ministry of Education of China in 2005. He was elected as an academician of the Chinese Academy of Sciences in 2013 and a fellow of the Royal Society of Chemistry in the next year. He is the academic leader of national innovation research group and innovation team of "the Program for the Yangtze River Scholars and Innovative Research Plan" as well as the national person for "New Century Talents Project" of seven ministries including ministry of personnel. He is the winner of "trans—century excellent talents cultivation plan" of ministry of education. He is the member of discipline evaluation group of academic degree committee of the state council. Currently, Feng is appointed as the standing director of Chinese Chemical Society, and chairman of the chiral committee, and was also elected as the member of the 13th national committee of the CPPCC and 15th central committee of the Zhigong party of China. He serves as the editorial committee of 3 academic journals and the advisory editorial committee of 7 academic journals.

Feng Xiaoming dedicates himself to develop novel chiral catalysts, catalytic asymmetric reactions, as well as the application of them to synthesize chiral pharmaceutical molecules and so on.

天文学奖获得者

史 生 才

史生才，1964年12月出生于江苏省南京市。1985年毕业于南京工学院（现东南大学）无线电工程系，1989年于紫金山天文台获硕士学位，1996年于日本综合研究大学院大学天文系获工学博士学位。1992—1998年留学日本国立天文台，其间先后任NRO和COE研究员。1998年回国至今在中科院紫金山天文台工作，任毫米波和亚毫米波技术实验室主任及研究员。2008年起任"国际空间太赫兹技术年会"科学委员会委员，2011年5月起任中科院射电天文重点实验室主任，2014年4月起任中科院紫金山天文台学术委员会主任，2019年起任东亚天文台/JCMT望远镜理事和中国天文学会射电天文专业委员会主任。先后担任欧盟下一代远红外空间干涉阵FISICA计划国际咨询专家、日本宇宙开发事业团JAXA客座研究员、中国电子学会射电天文分会副主任等。

主要从事太赫兹超导探测器技术及应用研究，创建和领导了有国际影响力的太赫兹超导探测器研究团队，在太赫兹波段超导隧道结量子混频、超导热电子混频、大规模阵列超导探测器等方面作出了一系列开创性研究工作，实现了我国太赫兹天文探测器芯片技术的自主可控。

一、超导隧道结量子混频技术

超导隧道结具有极低暗电流、超强非线性（量子特性）以及毫电子伏特能隙（比半导体低三个量级）等显著特征，诞生之初就被认为是理想的微波至远红外波段高灵敏度探测器。但早期发展存在两大瓶颈——隧道结自身电容对高频电磁信号的阻断，金属波导腔中电磁信号的高效传输需借助机械调谐（难以应用于干涉阵）。超导隧道结片上集成谐振和无调谐波导混频腔两项关键技术的突破，使得超导隧道结混频器灵敏度逼近测不准原理制约的量子极限，得以广泛应用于毫米波亚毫米波射电天文望远镜及干涉阵，推动了20世纪90年代至今毫米波亚毫米波天文的快速发展。在超导隧道结量子混频的两大关键技术方面，史生才与日本国立天文台合作者共同提出了三种国际主流片上集成谐振技术之一的并联双子超导隧道结（PCTJ），构建了其量子混频模型；提出了分布式超导隧道结阵概念，突破了低临界电流密度超导隧道结在高频段应用的障碍；此外，提出了一种片上集成中频/直流回路的新型无调谐波导混频腔，率先实现了高性能无调谐超宽带超导隧道结混频器。基于发展的 PCTJ 和无调谐波导混频腔技术，研制了 0.1～1 THz 频段系列超导隧道结混频器，灵敏度突破 5 倍量子极限。研制的超导隧道结混频器应用于两项国际天文大科学装置 ALMA 和 SMA，提升了我国在太赫兹探测器领域的国际影响力；应用于我国 13.7 米毫米波望远镜（是超导探测器在我国的首次应用，也是我国超导领域的一项重大突破），使其灵敏度得到大幅提升，成为国际上最具竞争力的毫米波望远镜之一，为我国毫米波天文发展作出了重要贡献。

经典铌（Nb）超导隧道结需工作在液氦温区。对于空间应用，一方面深低温制冷技术是一项挑战，另一方面可工作在更高温区的高能隙（如氮化铌 NbN）超导隧道结灵敏度长期滞后于经典 Nb 超导隧道结。通过解明 NbN 超导隧道结散粒噪声机理，史生才突破芯片设计、制备（与日本 NiCT 研究所合作）及封装等关键技术，成功研制灵敏度率先突破 5 倍量子极限的 NbN 超导隧道结混频器，并实现国际首次天文应用。此外，首次实验证认了高能隙 NbN 超导隧道结可在 10K 温区工作的独特优势，突破了空间液氦温区制冷技术的制约。基于 NbN 超导隧道结混频器的太赫兹装置将搭载我国载人航天工程，有望实现我国空间太赫兹天文观测"零"的突破。

二、太赫兹超导热电子混频技术

较之于超导隧道结混频器，超导热电子混频器特性与频率弱相关，特别在 1 THz 以上频段具有丰富应用前景。超导热电子混频器的核心是一个纳米尺度厚超导微桥，其电阻具有强非线性温度转变特性，在吸收太赫兹光子或被电流加热状态下，其电子及声子温度分布呈非平衡态。尽管经典的"热点"模型可以解释超导热电子混频的基本物理特征，但其电子及声子输运物理机制尚未完全解明，导致其灵敏度和瞬时带宽性能的改善遭遇瓶颈。史生才通过解明超导热电子混频器的若干物理机制，包括超导微桥太赫兹波非均匀吸收机制及电子声子输运特性、超导热电子混频器灵敏度温变特性普适规律以及超导微桥电极区噪声等，构建了首个频率相关"热点"模型，并成功研制迄今 1.4 THz 频段灵敏度最高的超导热电子混频器。此外，与荷兰空间研究所合作研制了迄今频率最高的 5.3 THz 天线耦合超导热电子混频器。研制的太赫兹超导热电子混频器将应用于国家重大科技基础设施建设项目"中国南极天文台"。

基于外差混频的相干探测需要一个高频率稳定度的泵浦信号源。近年来，量子级联激光器成为一种非常有前景的太赫兹泵浦光源，但针对实际应用的光源锁相稳幅、低温集成等问题仍亟待解决。史生才与荷兰 SRON 和美国 MIT 等团队合作，首次实现了同时稳频稳幅的太赫兹量子级联激光器光源。此外，与法国 IEF 和上海技物所等团队合作，首次实现了同一低温环境下太赫兹量子级联激光器与超导热电子混频器的集成。上述成果为实现太赫兹及远红外高光谱分辨天文探测器奠定了重要基础。

国家重大科技基础设施建设项目"中国南极天文台"将建于南极冰穹 A，史生才为此研制了国际上首例无人值守的太赫兹超宽带傅里叶光谱仪，获得南极冰穹 A 太赫兹大气透过率长周期精确实测数据。全新结果揭示了南极冰穹 A 观测宇宙的太赫兹远红外新窗口，并给出了新的大气辐射模型约束条件，相关研究发表于 *Nature Astronomy* 创刊号。

三、大规模阵列超导探测器技术

长期以来，毫米波至太赫兹波段射电天文观测缺乏类似光学红外波段 CCD 的大规模阵列成像探测器。超导相变边缘探测器（TES）和超导动态电感探测器（KID）的出现推动了太赫兹波段大规模阵列成像探测器技术的快速发展与应用。在国家基金委首批重大科研仪器设备研制专项的支持下，史生才在我国率先开展了大规模阵列超导探测器技术的自主研发。通过突破超导动态电感探测器多参数协同仿真设计、大规模二维阵列芯片制备、频分复用读出等关键技术，自主研制了 32 × 32 像元超导 KID 探测器阵列芯片及成像系统，灵敏度及像素达国际同类探测器前沿水平，实现了我国超导探测器技术新突破，使我国太赫兹天文观测迈入相机时代。该系统将是南极 5 米太赫兹望远镜下一代主观测设备，为星系和宇宙学等研究提供太赫兹波段巡天"传世"数据库，还有望应用于 JCMT、LCT 和 GLT 等国际亚毫米波望远镜及其他领域。

Awardee of Astronomy Prize, Shi Shengcai

Shi Shengcai was born in Nanjing City of Jiangsu Province in December 1964. He graduated from the Department of Radio Engineering of Nanjing Institute of Technology（now Southeast University）in 1985, received his MSc degree from the Purple Mountain Observatory in 1989 and PhD degree in engineering from the Department of Astronomical Science of the Graduate University for Advanced Studies（Japan）in 1996. He was with the National Astronomical Observatory of Japan from 1992 to 1998 as an NRO and COE researcher. Since 1998, he has been with the Purple Mountain Observatory（PMO）of the Chinese Academy of Sciences（CAS）, serving as a lab head and a professor.

Shi Shengcai has been engaged in the research and development of superconducting mixers and detectors at THz wavelengths mainly for astronomical applications.

（1）Co-inventing single-feed parallel-connected twin junctions and a fixed-tuned broadband waveguide cavity for the development of high-sensitivity superconducting SIS mixers for ALMA and SMA, which are the most advanced mm-and submm-wave interferometers in the world.

(2) Developing three generations of superconducting SIS receivers for the PMO's 14-m mm-wave radio telescope, including the first superconducting receiver ever developed in China. With the upgraded SIS receivers, this radio telescope has become a world-class single-dish telescope at the 3-mm band.

(3) Developing an all-NbN superconducting SIS mixer, which can work at higher frequencies and at higher temperatures, and demonstrating its use for the first time on a telescope. This technology has been selected for a THz instrument to be deployed onto the China's space station.

(4) Measuring the atmospheric radiation from Dome A in Antarctic with an unattended FTS instrument across the whole THz/FIR band for the first time. The measurements — regarded as a technical and logistical tour de force — unveil the value of this unique site to both astronomy and atmospheric science.

(5) Developing the state-of-the-art THz superconducting hot-electron-bolometer (HEB) mixers, THz HEB/quantum cascade laser (QCL) integrated receivers, and a THz superconducting imaging array with the most advanced detector technologies (MKIDs and TES) for China's Antarctic astronomical project.

地球科学奖获得者

何 继 善

何继善，1934年9月出生于湖南省浏阳市。1960年毕业于长春地质学院物探系。1994年当选为中国工程院首批院士。曾任中南工业大学校长、中国有色金属学会副理事长、中国地球物理学会副理事长、中国工程院能源与矿业工程学部主任、湖南省科协主席。现任湖南省科协名誉主席、美国勘探地球物理学家协会终身会员。

他提出了三元素群的自封闭加法，实现了$2n$系列伪随机信号的快速递推编码，创立了伪随机信号电法体系；创立了高分辨率检测堤坝管涌渗漏入水口的"流场法"，为病险水库隐患探测和汛期堤坝查险提供了必不可少的技术支撑和科学抢险决策依据；统一了频率域电磁法全区电阻率的定义和算法，创立了广域电磁法，为电磁勘探开辟了崭新的研究领域；创建了中国第一个以地电场与观测系统为特色的国家级重点学科；发明了一系列具有国际先进水平和自主知识产权的地电场观测仪器和装备，为中国资源勘探和工程勘察事业作出了重大贡献。他创立和发展的以伪随机信号电磁法和双频激电法为特色的勘探地球物理理论体系被国际上誉为应用地球物理界的一重大事件。他的研究成果和学术思想对中国地球物理学的发展有重要指导意义。

一、广域电磁法为深地探测提供了中国范本

"深地探测"战略是为了拓展中华民族生存空间和资源与能源供给、加速中华民族复兴伟业进程，在国家层面组织实施的重大战略举措；同时也是世界各大强国竞相抢占的学科制高点。

何继善针对传统电磁法"探不深—探不精—探不准"，无法满足"深地探测"战略需求的问题，从理论—方法—技术—装备—应用全链条开展研究，发明了广域电磁法，研发了具有完全自主知识产权的大深度高精度探测技术与装备，实现了电磁法由粗放到精细的跨越，实现了电磁法勘探"探得深—探得精—探得准"，有力支撑了面向国家重大需

求的深地探测战略。该技术在中石油、中石化、地调局等 50 多家单位成功应用，提交页岩气资源量或地质储量 4641.22 亿立方米；获得常规油气地质储量 1.86 亿吨；获得生物气储量 80 亿立方米；释放了 2000 多万吨煤炭；潜在经济价值超过 15000 亿元。

广域电磁法被誉为"绿色、高效、低成本"的勘探技术，为油气勘探、深部找矿、煤矿水害探测、地质灾害防治、压裂监测、城市物探、潜艇探测等提供了全新的技术手段。"大深度高精度广域电磁勘探技术与装备"获 2018 年国家技术发明奖一等奖。

二、伪随机信号电法为中国矿产资源可持续供给开辟新路

我国的矿产资源保有储量严重不足，许多老矿山因资源枯竭而面临破产关闭，因此必须尽快寻找新的有效勘探方法和技术，在生产矿山深边部和西部中高山地区寻找新的接替资源，走资源自给之路。这就要求勘探方法技术具有抗干扰能力强、勘探深度大、分辨率高、观测参数多，勘探设备具有轻便、能耗低、机动性好、能快速进行矿与非矿区分等特点。

何继善早在"八五"末期，针对原有电磁法"变频"方案工作效率低、不能实现一发多收、观测精度难以保证；"奇次谐波"方案设备笨重、机动性差、不适应在西部中高山区开展面积性工作；常规激电法测量参数单一、不能有效区分异常源性质等缺点，发明并提出了"2 的 n 次幂系列均匀广谱伪随机电磁法的主动源方法技术"，并研制了相应的观测系统。伪随机信号方法只需供电一次，便可以完成所有频率的测量，具有快速、高效、电源利用率高、仪器轻便、抗干扰能力强、相对观测精度高、异常可靠等优点。该方法为生产矿山深边部隐伏资源的勘探和西部中高山区的资源勘探提供了一种轻便、快速、观测精度高的新方法和一种异常源性质快速评价的新技术和评价指标。

该技术在国内外成功应用，据不完全统计，到目前为止所找到的矿产资源潜在经济价值达 3000 多亿元，解决或缓解了多个矿山的资源危机状况，为资源增储和国民经济的可持续发展提供了技术保障，为中国矿产资源可持续供给作出了突出贡献。

三、双频道激发极化法成为金属矿勘探和工程勘察的利器

20 世纪 60 年代后期，国内学者开始对频率域激电方法开展研究，所应用的方法技术是国外引进的变频法或奇次谐波法。这两种方法由于理论缺陷，在我国的应用并不成功。何继善于 70 年代初期开始激电法研究，并在 80 年代初期正式提出双频道激发极化法。

双频激电法的中心思想是把两种频率的方波电流叠加起来形成双频组合电流，同时供入地下，接收来自地下的含有两个主频率（也含其他频率成分）的激电总场的电位差信息，一次同时得到低频电位差和高频电位差，计算视幅频率，也可根据需要测多组双频信号以形成频谱测量。

双频激电法经过多年的发展形成了系列产品，成为了金属矿勘探和工程探测利器。双频激电法在各种地质环境、各种气候条件、不同矿种上进行了大量工作，找到了一大

批工业矿体，创造了巨大的经济价值和社会效益。

四、"流场法"准确探测堤坝管涌渗漏，保障人民生命财产安全

水患自古以来就是中华民族的"切肤之患"，1998 年长江发生了全流域性特大洪水，而溃堤是汛期的最大灾害，其中 90% 以上的溃堤是由管涌渗漏造成的。国内外当时都没有查找管涌的科学方法和仪器，只能人工拉网式沿堤巡查或派潜水员水下摸探，不仅效率低、危险性大，而且探测结果不精确，对深水处的管涌无法查找。因此，快速准确查明管涌渗漏的进水部位是汛期处险的关键。

何继善根据电流密度场和水流场的相似性原理，创立了全新的探测堤坝管涌渗漏隐患的"流场法"理论，研制出了世界上第一台能在汛期恶劣环境下快速准确探测堤坝管涌渗漏入水口的仪器设备——普及型堤坝管涌渗漏检测仪，该仪器具有灵敏度高、分辨率高、抗干扰能力强、操作简便、工作高效、可靠性强的特点。十几年来，堤坝管涌渗漏检测仪先后在湖南、湖北等 10 多个省市探测发现 110 多处堤防险情和 20 多处水库大坝渗漏点，准确率超过 90%，为这些地方及时准确地排除重大险情提供了极其重要的依据。

2002 年，堤坝管涌渗漏检测仪被列为国家防汛抗旱储备物资，并列入"国家火炬计划项目"；2005 年被国家发改委列为重点产业化示范项目；2006 年被评为"国家重点新产品"；2008 年列入国家"堤防隐患探测规程"。科技部、水利部还召开堤坝隐患探测技术交流大会，重点向全国洪涝灾害地区推广堤坝管涌渗漏检测仪，并装备了中国主要省份的水利技术单位和防汛管理部门。

Awardee of Earth Sciences Prize, He Jishan

He Jishan, born in Liuyang City of Hunan Province in September 1934, studied at the Department of Applied Geophysics of the former Changchun Geologic Institute (now renamed as Jilin University). After graduation in 1960, he joined the former Central South Institute of Mining and Metallurgy (now renamed as Central South University, CSU). Since then, he devoted himself to the development of geophysics in China and made outstanding achievements in the field. He proposed the closed addition in a three-element set, which realized the fast recursive coding of 2^n sequence pseudo-random signals, and created a pseudo-random signal electrical system. He developed the flow field fitting method for locating the dam piping and leakage with high accuracy, providing essential technical supports for detecting the hidden dangers of reservoirs and levees in the flood season, as well as for the scientific rescue decision making. He unified both the definition and algorithm of the all-field apparent resistivity of the frequency domain electromagnetic method, and developed the wide field electromagnetic system, opening a new field for the electromagnetic exploration. He established China's first national key discipline of geoelectric field and observation system. He also invented a series of internationally advanced geoelectric field observation equipment with independent intellectual property rights, which has made significant contributions to China's resource exploration and geophysical engineering. He developed and established the exploration geophysical theory system featured by the pseudo-random signal electromagnetic method and the dual-frequency IP method, which was regarded as a major event in the applied geophysics in the world. His theory and research results provide indispensible guidance for the development of geophysics in China. He is a founding member of the Chinese Academy of Engineering (CAE) established in 1994. He once served as the president of the former Central South University of Technology (now CSU), vice chairman of the Nonferrous Metals Society of China, vice chairman of Chinese Geophysical Society, director of the Energy and Mining Engineering Department of CAE, chairman of Hunan Association of Science and Technology. Now he is a professor of geophysics in CSU, an honorary chairman of Hunan Association of Science and Technology, and a lifetime member of the US Society of Exploration Geophysicists.

His main contribution includes the wide field electromagnetic method sets up a "China Model" for deep earth exploration, the pseudo-random signal electrical method brings a new way for achieving sustainable supply of mineral resources in China, the dual-frequency IP method has become a powerful tool for metal ore exploration and geophysical engineering, the flow field fitting method for accurately detecting the leakage of dams and levees to protect people from the loss of lives and property.

地球科学奖获得者

周 卫 健

周卫健，女，1953年3月出生于贵州省贵阳市。中国科学院院士，发展中国家科学院院士，美国地球物理联合会会士。1995年在西北大学地质系获地质学博士学位。1976—1985年在中国科学院地球化学所工作；1985年至今在中国科学院地球环境研究所工作，任西安加速器质谱中心主任；2000—2010年任黄土与第四纪地质国家重点实验室主任，现为学术委员会主任；2004—2017年先后任中国科学院地球环境研究所副所长、所长。现任中国第四纪科学研究会副理事长，中国矿物岩石地球化学学会副理事长，国际地球科学计划理事会理事，美国地球物理联合会会士委员会、Lal奖与Simpson奖评选委员会委员，发展中国家科学院咨询委员会委员，国际放射性碳学术刊物副编辑。1997年获国家基金委"杰出青年科学基金"，2002年获基金委"优秀青年科学家群体"带头人。作为首席科学家，先后负责国家攀登计划和"973"计划项目、中科院知识创新工程重大项目。获国家自然科学奖二等奖2项、三等奖1项，省部级一等奖5项，获全国首届百篇优秀博士学位论文。

周卫健从事宇宙成因核素与全球环境变化研究，在^{14}C年代学、宇宙成因核素示踪全球环境变化领域获享国际声誉的系统创新成果，是活跃在国际舞台上的卓越女科学家，主持建成的多核素加速器质谱中心成为亚洲顶尖的实验室。

一、开拓我国^{14}C、^{10}Be等多核素示踪区域和全球环境变化研究新方向

应用^{14}C示踪化石能源对大气CO_2和雾霾的贡献，为我国CO_2减排提供定量数据；开启^{129}I示踪我国核环境安全新领域，推动了我国加速器质谱应用研究学科的发展。

开拓了黄土^{10}Be示踪地磁场变化和重建古降水的新方向，提出多变量地学系统的线性回归分析中的"平均值概念"，首次提出了分离黄土^{10}Be记录中的地磁场影响与气候影响的思路和方法，解决了从复杂黄土^{10}Be记录示踪和重建全球地磁场和黄土高原季风降水变化的学术难题，带领团队成功定量重建了最近13万年黄土^{10}Be记录的地磁场强度和

古季风降水变化历史。根据黄土 ^{10}Be 和葫芦洞记录，提出氧同位素阶段 3 时期的季风降水显著增加是受控于南北半球太阳辐射梯度变化，显著不同于高纬太阳辐射驱动季风变化的概念。通过 ^{10}Be 示踪，明确了布容/松山界线位于第七层古土壤中（S7），解决了布容/松山极性倒转界线在黄土和海洋记录中不同步的长期争论，为建立中国黄土可靠年代标尺和古气候记录的全球对比作出重要贡献。国外科学家认为"她解决了长达 20 多年的争议，是创新且及时的工作"。Granger 教授指出"^{10}Be 记录对干旱-半干旱的沉积物的降水变化具有高度的敏感性，其研究具有重要意义"。

二、发展 ^{14}C 测年技术，基于高精度 ^{14}C 测年和黄土 ^{10}Be，揭示季风突变事件及东亚季风变迁的新机制

率先建立了小样品-微量样品 ^{14}C 测年方法序列，解决了 20 世纪 80 年代考古和地质小样品测年难题，为兵马俑提供了可靠年代。小样品装置被悉尼大学测年中心主任 Barbetti 评价为"提供了高质量数据，对 ^{14}C 测年方法序列作出重要和有价值贡献"。较早建立不同类型样品的化学前处理方法，最早开展我国风积物花粉测年，保证了 ^{14}C 测年的可靠性。经十年艰苦努力，主持建成西安加速器质谱中心，成为国家十大科学仪器中心之一，各项性能指标均达国际先进水平。国际著名 AMS 专家 Raisbeck 评价道，"我在西安测量所获得的 ^{10}Be/^{9}Be 本底 1×10^{-15} 比现有国际上 AMS 实验室水平更好，你们的加速器是当前最高水平"。发展超微量样品 ^{14}C 测年技术，参加国际比对成绩优秀，应邀在 *Radiocarbon* 上撰写综述论文，引领我国 ^{14}C 年代学发展。

在我国首先开展精确的高分辨率 ^{14}C 测年，重建最近 13000 年东亚季风区十余个湖沼和风积物剖面碳同位素、生物标记化合物等季风代用指标时间序列，首先发现了 12.6 千年—11.5 千年东亚季风 YD 突变事件的可靠证据，指出其具有半球寒冷性质和季风降水增加的特点。较早提出高低纬气候相互作用对过去季风突变事件的影响机制，为我国乃至东亚的气候环境预测提供了历史相似型。当时的 QR 主编 Porter 认为"东亚季风区揭示的 YD 颤动特征在非洲湖泊中也有类似记录"。*Radiocarbon* 主编 Jull 认同周卫健提出的"区域气候变化同全球特征一样具有重要意义"。当时的 PAGES 主席 Bradley 在 Paleoclimatology 一书中赞赏"仔细的 ^{14}C 测年揭示了 YD 温度很低，却更湿润"并来信祝贺"你的成果对试图解释过去气候变化和原因所付出的国际科学努力与贡献是十分重要和有意义的"，后来他在 EOS 又引用周卫健的论点。根据青海湖 ^{14}C 年代异常的系列数据，揭示冰消期冰川消融全球升温的气候事件，为研究 CO_2 与温度谁先影响气候变化这一难题提供科学依据。在 2007 年首次揭示并随后在 Science 上论证了南北半球低纬夏季太阳辐射梯度是驱动亚洲季风气候变迁的重要机制，在一定程度上对经典的米兰科维奇理论提出了挑战。

三、提出重霾研究建议并论证重霾成因

周卫健研究证明距今 3000 年来人类无序活动基本造就了今天的毛乌素沙地，在 2001

年全国两会期间提出了我国西北干旱区生态环境建设的建议，受到国家领导的重视，关于会后向中央呈递了《自然过程和人类活动对我国西北地区生态环境的影响》报告，提出我国西部现今自然面貌是自然环境长期历史演变的结果，半干旱区应视为西部生态环境和沙尘暴治理的重点地区。

在陕西省首先提出了"低碳经济"理念，组织调研"低碳经济发展"，完成了《陕西省实施低碳经济战略的对策与建议》调研报告，并为陕西省委中心组做低碳经济专题报告，得到省委领导的好评。

带领团队并组织院士专家队伍在黄土高原开展观测和试验研究，系统评估了治沟造地工程的科学性、可行性和生态环境效应，并向国务院提出了"积极实施与退耕还林还草并重的治沟造地重大方针的建议"，得到刘延东副总理的批示支持。2018年在全国两会上提出了黄土高原综合治理的"26字方略（塬区固沟保塬，坡面退耕还林草，沟壑拦蓄整地，沙区固沙还灌草）"，受到广泛关注；同年9月，向中共中央、国务院提交了《关于新时代黄土高原生态环境综合治理方略的建议》咨询报告，获领导批示，并受到水利部、陕西省的高度重视。

2017年春，向李克强总理建议重点研究我国北方雾霾，明确提出氨排放重要性，指出重霾是人类排放物与大气过程相互作用的结果，获得总理的肯定和批示，为"大气重污染成因与治理攻关项目"这一总理基金立项作出重要贡献。2019年在 *PNAS* 参与发表文章，详细论证重霾事件的成因。

Awardee of Earth Sciences Prize，Zhou Weijian

Zhou Weijian，female，was born in Guiyang City of Guizhou Province in March 1953. She earned her PhD in Geology in 1995，from Northwest University. She worked at the Institute of Geochemistry，Chinese Academy of Sciences（CAS）from 1976 to 1985. Since 1985，she has worked at the Institute of Earth Environment，CAS（IEECAS）and was promoted to professor in 1995. She is currently the director of the Xi'an Accelerator Mass Spectrometry Center. She served as the director of the State Key Laboratory of Loess and Quaternary Geology（SKLLQG）from 2000 to 2010，and she is currently the director of the SKLLQG Academic Committee. From 2004 to 2017，she served as vice director and director of IEECAS. She was awarded the "Outstanding Youth Science Fund" by the National Natural Science Foundation of China（NSFC）and elected as leading scientist of the NSFC Innovative Scientific Research Young Group Scholarship. As chief scientist，she directed the National 973 Program and CAS major knowledge innovation project. She received two National Natural Sciences second-class rewards and a third-class reward，and five provincial first-class rewards. In 1999 her PhD thesis was awarded "The First National reward for the One Hundred Most Outstanding PhD Theses in China." She made key contributions to

SKLLQG, which achieved excellence ratings seven times. She is currently the council member of the International Geoscience Program responsible for global change research, member of the Union Fellows Committee of the American Geophysical Union (AGU), and associate editor of Radiocarbon. She is Academician of CAS, TWAS Academician, and AGU Fellow.

Dr. Zhou pioneered a new direction for tracing global environmental change, by using several cosmogenic isotopes including ^{14}C and ^{10}Be. Her ^{10}Be measurements have greatly improved quantitative reconstructions of the histories of global palaeogeomagnetic intensity and palaeo-precipitationfrom the Chinese loess. As a result she has settled a long-standing question about the apparent asynchronous position of the B/M reversal boundary in terrestrial and marine sediments, and provided a critical time marker in loess chronology which enables robust correlation between the Chinese loess and other global palaeoclimate records. On the basis of high precision^{14}C dating and loess ^{10}Be, she published a new model for the dynamics of monsoon systems, and showed that the summer solar insolation gradient between the Northern and Southern Hemispheres drives the Asian Monsoon. She identified the Younger Dryas abrupt event in China, with its characteristic variability in cooling and humidity, thus providing a historic analogue to understand possible future trends resulting from global warming. She proposed, headed, and oversaw the construction of the Multi-nuclide Accelerator Mass Spectrometry Center in Xi'an. This is a world leader of its type and has become one of the 'Ten National Large Scientific Instrument Centres' in China.

生命科学奖获得者

胡 海 岚

胡海岚，女，1973年9月出生于浙江省杭州市。1996年毕业于北京大学，2002年在美国加州大学伯克利分校获得博士学位，2003—2008年在美国冷泉港实验室进行博士后研究。2008—2015年在中国科学院神经科学研究所担任研究员，2015年至今为浙江大学医学院教授、浙江大学神经科学中心执行主任。先后担任美国神经科学学会SFN议程委员会委员、Julius Axelrod Prize委员会委员，中国科学技术协会第九届全国委员会委员，国际分子和细胞认知学会委员会理事。先后获得中国青年女科学家奖（2015）、中国青年科技奖（2016）、谈家桢生命科学创新奖（2016）、中国科学十大进展奖（2018）、"臻溪生命学者"奖（2018）及IBRO–Kemali神经科学国际奖（2019）等。

胡海岚，在抑郁症的分子机制、社会竞争的神经调控及情绪的神经编码等脑科学前沿作出了创造性、系统性的贡献。

一、揭示抑郁症发生及氯胺酮快速抗抑郁的脑机制

抑郁症严重损害身心健康，是全球疾病负担的榜首病种，也是自杀问题的重要诱因。传统的抗抑郁药物起效缓慢（>6～8周），获益患者有限（<30%），提示这些药物可能只是间接靶向，也反映出抑郁症的机制研究还未触及核心。近年来，在临床上意外发现麻醉剂氯胺酮在低剂量下具有快速（1小时内）、高效（在70%难治患者中起效）的抗抑郁作用，被认为是精神病领域半世纪来最重要的发现。剖析氯胺酮的作用机理成为探知抑郁症脑机制的方便门径。然而，氯胺酮的成瘾性导致其不可能安全地长期使用，因此亟须明确抑郁症机制，为下一代药物提供新靶点。

胡海岚在这一领域建立了以大脑外侧缰核为核心的学术体系并取得了一系列引领性进展。利用蛋白质谱技术，其团队首次建立了缰核活动与抑郁情绪的分子联系，发现钙调蛋白激酶在大脑的"反奖赏中心"缰核内过度表达，改变突触可塑性，导致缰核过

度兴奋，从而引发抑郁。在环路机制上，胡海岚发现缰核神经元是通过特征性的高频密集的簇状放电抑制大脑中产生愉悦感的"奖赏中心"。在系统层面，直接证明了簇状放电是诱发动物产生绝望和快感缺失等行为的充分条件。在分子层面，发现簇状放电是由 NMDAR 受体介导。作为 NMDAR 阻断剂，氯胺酮正是通过抑制簇状放电，快速高效地解除其对下游奖赏中心的抑制，从而在短时间内改善情绪。胡海岚进一步对产生簇状放电的细胞及分子机制作出了深入阐释，发现了崭新的神经元—胶质细胞相互作用。她发现在组织学层面，缰核中胶质细胞对神经元成致密包裹。抑郁的形成伴随着胶质细胞中的钾离子通道 Kir 4.1 的过量表达。在神经元—胶质细胞相互作用的狭小界面中，Kir 4.1 在胶质细胞上的过表达引发神经元胞外的钾离子降低，从而诱发神经元细胞的超极化，导致簇状放电。

这一系列研究超越了流行的"单胺假说"，对抑郁症核心机制作出了系统阐释。在应用上，鉴定出 β CaMKII、NMDAR、Kir 4.1、T 型钙通道等多个具成药性的靶点，为研发氯胺酮的替代药物提供了科学依据，已申请国内发明专利 5 项；以 T 型钙通道为新靶点，创造性地将抗癫痫药物乙琥胺"标签外使用"快速抗抑郁的策略，已在浙江大学医学院附属第一医院启动临床试验。相关工作以两篇长文形式在 *Nature* 同期背靠背发表，体现了该研究的原创性、突破性和完整性；被 *Nature*、*Science*、*Nat Rev Neurosci* 等专文报道，被 F1000 评为 exceptional 和 seminal，并入选"中国科学十大进展"。

二、破解社会竞争及"胜利者效应"的神经调控机制

竞争是动物世界最显著的社会行为之一，也是等级这一基本社会组织方式的成因。对群体而言，稳定的等级结构可限制族群内的耗散性冲突，节约总体能量，与社会稳定、种群延续息息相关；对个体而言，社会等级深刻影响其生活质量，被认为是健康的最佳风向标。社会竞争行为的神经环路机制是胡海岚的另一研究重点。

长期以来，缺乏等级行为的实验范式是这一领域研究的瓶颈。胡海岚首先在方法学上突破，首次建立了研究动物社会竞争和线性量化等级的行为学范式，以钻管对抗的结果来反映小鼠的竞争能力，因测量的直观与稳定性而获广泛采用，被誉为动物社会行为研究的 3 个经典范式之一。基于此范式，她发现社会等级的高低与内侧前额叶皮层中神经元的活动强度正相关，对这组神经元活动进行增强与抑制的操作，可即刻改变动物的竞争行为与获胜概率。进一步研究揭示了这一神经环路的可塑性，即反复获胜会对环路的活动产生长期增强效应；环路可塑性又构成行为可塑性的物质基础，使动物在今后竞争中的获胜概率增加，并确立其在团体中的强势地位。由此，胡海岚团队完成了对"胜利者效应"这一重大脑机制的破解。

这一系列工作为研究竞争行为和社会层级建立了研究方法、开辟了思路，也为神经经济学、社会行为学等研究提供了靶点脑区，并为研究社会行为相关疾病奠定了理论框架。*Science*、*Nat Rev Neurosci* 等发表专文对此成果进行特别推介，肯定该工作在神经环路及细胞学层面作出的原创性突破。

三、揭示正常情绪的神经编码

近一个世纪，神经生物学在对外在感觉系统的神经编码方面已取得长足进展。然而，内在情绪在大脑中怎样被表征和编码仍不明确。胡海岚的博士后工作原创性地阐述了情绪增强记忆的分子细胞学机制，相关工作入选神经科学最有影响力的教科书。回国后，胡海岚开发了 TAI-FISH 技术，实现了在单细胞分辨率下在同一大脑中标记正面与负面两种相反情绪所激活的神经环路，使后续功能研究成为可能。

胡海岚热心学术服务，担任 *Science Advances* 和 *Science China* 的编委以及数十家顶级国际期刊的特邀审稿人；培养的博士生获得国家级最高奖学金高达 12 人次，包括 3 次中国科学院院长特别奖和 2 次吴瑞奖。

Awardee of Life Sciences Prize, Hu Hailan

Hu Hailan, female, was born in Hangzhou City of Zhejiang Province in September 1973. She graduated from Beijing University in 1996 and received her Ph.D. from university of California Berkeley in 2002. She conducted postdoctoral research in Cold Spring Harbor Laboratory. In 2008, she returned to China and worked as a principal investigator at the Institute of Neuroscience, Chinese Academy of Sciences. Since 2015, she has been a professor at the School of Medicine, Zhejiang University and the executive director of the Center for Neuroscience, Zhejiang University. She has served on the Program Committee and the Julius Axelrod Prize Selection Committee of Society for Neuroscience, and the Molecular and Cellular Cognition Society (MCCS) Council. She is recipient of the L'Oreal Women Scientist Award of China (2015), Chinese Young Scientist Award (2016), Tan Jia Zhen Life Science Award (2016), Top10 Science Advances Prize of China (2018), Fountain-Valley Life Sciences Award (2018) and IBRO-Kemali International Prize for Basic and Clinical Neurosciences (2019).

1. Molecular and circuit mechanism of depression and rapid antidepressants

Hu's group systematically characterized the molecular and cellular changes in the lateral habenula (LHb) using animal models of depression. They identified several key molecules critically involved in depression by a quantitative proteomics screen in the habenula of congenitally learned helpless rats. They first demonstrated that upregulated β CaMKII strengthens synapses in the LHb by inserting AMPARs into synapses, leading to increased spike output and multiple depression-like phenotypes. Next, they found that upregulation of Kir4.1 in astrocytes leads to excessive buffering of extracellular potassium, causing hyperpolarization and enhanced burst firing of LHb neurons. LHb burst firing is necessary and sufficient to induce depression–like behaviors. Finally, they found that LHb burst firing critically depends on NMDAR, a prominent target of ketamine, as well as a hyperpolarized membrane potential, and low–voltage activated T–type calcium channel.

2. Neural circuit mechanism of social hierarchy

Hu's group adopted an old "tube test" assay and established it as a paradigm in social hierarchy study. They demonstrated that the hierarchy ranking is positively correlated with and causatively regulated by synaptic strength of neurons in the dorsal medial prefrontal cortex (dmPFC). Furthermore, they unveiled the neural mechanism of the "winner effect", where animals increase their probability of victory after prior winning, a prominent phenomenon reinforcing the establishment of social hierarchies in nature. Through this series of work, Hu's group established the MDT–dmPFC circuit as an important neural substrate integrating both the intrinsic (mental strength) and extrinsic (history of winning) factors for social hierarchy determination.

3. Neural coding of emotional valence

Hu's group developed a method, tyramide amplified immunohistochemistry–fluorescence in situ hybridization (TAI–FISH), which enables mapping of both reward–and punishment–activated neuronal ensembles in the same animal brain, and at single–cell resolution. Using this method, Hu's group mapped the limbic forebrain and identified neuronal ensembles encoding positive and negative emotional valences. These results provide novel insights into the coding of emotional valence and act as a proof of principle of a powerful methodology for simultaneous functional mapping of two distinct behaviors.

生命科学奖获得者

季 维 智

季维智，1950年6月出生于云南省昆明市。1978—1982年就读于云南大学生物系。1983—2012年任中国科学院昆明动物研究所研究员，其间（1987—1989年）赴美国俄勒冈国家灵长类研究中心做访问学者；1995—1997年任美国威斯康星大学动物医学与生物化学系客座教授；1996—2005年任中国科学院昆明动物研究所所长；2005—2008年任中国科学院昆明灵长类研究中心主任；2012年至今任云南省灵长类生物医学动物重点实验室理事长、生物医学动物模型国家地方联合工程研究中心主任；2014年起任昆明理工大学特聘教授、灵长类转化医学研究院院长。先后担任世界经济论坛全球未来理事会理事（2016—2018）、国家干细胞研究指导协调委员会专家、国家重大科学研究计划生殖与发育专家组成员（2006—2014）、国家实验动物研究委员会专家组成员和"973"项目首席科学家。2017年当选中国科学院院士。

季维智长期坚持灵长类研究，围绕灵长类早期胚胎发育调控、干细胞多能性和人类疾病的猴模型及致病机理等科学问题，形成了体外受精、胚胎早期发育、基因编辑以及干细胞等系统研究体系。在灵长类生殖和发育分子机制、干细胞的自我更新和分化调控等方面都有新的发现，在国际上首次获得了猴多能性干细胞，开启了靶向基因编辑建立灵长类动物模型的研发和应用。季维智长期为国家生殖发育、干细胞专家组服务，为中国生殖与干细胞研究作出了突出贡献，也为中国灵长类研究的国际化并跻身于世界先进行列发挥了重要作用。

一、优化非人灵长类体外研究技术体系，发现了胚胎早期发育调控的新机制

建立了完善的灵长类辅助生殖技术，并揭示了胚胎的发育调控机制，首次报道了季节、激素、年龄以及胚胎培养成分对胚胎发育的机制；首次揭示了猴早期着床前胚胎发育过程是去甲基化的同时发生了再甲基化的动态过程。相关工作发表49篇研究论文，为灵长类动物的生殖发育研究奠定了基础。

二、首次证明猴胚胎干细胞的发育多能性，优化了灵长类干细胞分离、规模化培养技术体系

首次获得嵌合体和早期生殖细胞嵌合的食蟹猴胚胎干细胞系；建立了规模化三维悬浮培养体系和规模化三维心肌细胞分化体系；构建了灵长类多能干细胞的神经细胞分化技术体系；建立了猴胚胎干细胞和体细胞核移植胚胎干细胞资源库。相关工作发表 19 篇研究论文，为灵长类多能干细胞系的分离、应用和相关研究奠定了重要基础。

三、灵长类基因编辑取得重大突破，创制了多种复杂疾病灵长类动物模型

获得中国首例表达 GFP 蛋白的转基因猕猴，为后续的靶向基因编辑技术在灵长类的应用打下了坚实基础；进行靶向基因编辑技术建立灵长类动物模型研究，在国际上首次成功获得了食蟹猴和猕猴的基因编辑模型，被 *Nature* 评价为里程碑式的突破，*MIT Technology Review* 评为 2014 十大科技突破。获得首例转基因帕金森病猴模型及首批基因敲除的杜氏肌营养不良症猴模型；2017 年首次建立基因编辑瑞特综合征猴模型；2018 年获得基因敲入食蟹猴，使得在灵长类水平研究获得性基因的功能成为可能。相关工作发表 12 篇研究论文，为人类疾病致病机理和探索治疗新方法提供了重要基础。

Awardee of Life Sciences Prize, Ji Weizhi

Ji Weizhi was born in kunming City of Yunnan Province in June 1950. He currently is Member of Chinese Academy of Sciences, Professor and Director of Yunnan Key Laboratory of Primate Biomedical Research/Institute of Primate Translational Medicine, Kunming University of Science and Technology. Ji Weizhi has been engaged in primate reproductive biology research since 1980s and regarded as one of the most influential scholars of this field in China. Prof. Ji's lab has scored remarkable achievements and published a range of important findings in nonhuman primate basic and biomedical research. He has established the in vitro culture system of nonhuman primate germ cells and embryos, and has brought forward the idea of superovulation which has increased the effective use of the precious monkey resources. Building on that, Ji's lab has been able to proceed an extensive research on epigenetics, regulation of embryonic development, stem cell pluripotency, nonhuman primate disease models & diseases mechanism and genome editing. He elaborated the interrelations between DNA methylation variation and embryonic development, and revealed the difference of methylation pattern between primates and rodents which modifies the traditional theory that early embryonic development only involves demethylation without subsequent methylation. More importantly, he has successfully obtained the pluripotent embryonic stem cells and proved the feasibility of generating chimeric monkeys using embryonic stem cells, which has been long regarded as mission impossible by US scientists. In 2014, Ji reported the first target gene-edited monkeys via CRISPR/Cas9 system. This research marks as a milestone in human disease models study, commented by Nature, and it also listed as top 10 technology breakthrough of year 2014 by MIT Review. Theses successful attempts of Prof. Ji Weizhi have greatly facilitated the progress of the transition from basic science to clinical applications, and also posed China as a leading force in nonhuman primate research in the world.

生命科学奖获得者

杨　辉

　　杨辉，1985年8月出生于江西省南昌市。现任中国科学院脑科学与智能技术卓越创新中心/神经科学研究所研究员。2012年6月于中科院生物化学与细胞生物学研究所获博士学位，2012—2014年在美国麻省理工学院从事博士后研究工作。2014入选青年千人计划；2015获优秀青年科学基金资助，同年入选"上海市青年拔尖人才"；2018年获上海市自然科技技术一等奖、中科院上海分院"杰出青年科技创新人才奖"；2019年获杰出青年科学基金资助，近期又荣获中源协和生命医学创新突破奖。

　　杨辉聚焦于新型基因编辑技术的开发、脱靶效应检测以及在疾病治疗中的应用研究，取得了一系列原创性成果，具有极大的应用价值。

一、发现单碱基基因编辑存在脱靶效应并开发了解决方法

　　目前已知的遗传性疾病有7000余种，但绝大部分缺乏有效的治疗药物和方法，如先天性黑蒙症、先天性耳聋、神经退行性疾病等。新型基因编辑技术CRISPR/Cas9的出现和快速发展为这些疾病的治疗带来了曙光。然而，基因编辑技术应用于临床最大的问题在于其引起的脱靶效应。所谓脱靶，是指基因编辑工具编辑目标位点的时候造成非靶标位点的基因序列改变。开发出既高效又特异的基因编辑工具一直是基因编辑领域内最重要的科学问题之一，也是基因编辑技术应用于临床的关键。现有的新型基因编辑技术主要包括CRISPR/Cas9技术以及单碱基编辑技术。但由于之前的脱靶检测技术都不能灵敏地检测单碱基突变造成的脱靶且受遗传背景影响很大，因而基因编辑工具的真实脱靶效应一直存在争议。

　　针对上述问题，杨辉开发出一种遗传背景完全一致、不需要基因组体外扩增、没有偏向性的全基因组脱靶检测技术，简称GOTI。通过编辑小鼠二细胞胚胎的一个卵裂球并标记为红色，再利用全基因组测序比较经编辑的红色细胞子细胞群和未编辑细胞子细胞群差异，不仅避免了单细胞体外扩增带来的噪音问题，而且基因背景完全一致。相对于之前的脱靶检测技术，GOTI在脱靶检测的精度、广度和准确性上都得到极大提高。采用GOTI，杨辉首次证实单碱基编辑技术并不安全，存在严重的DNA脱靶问题，目前不适合用于临床基因治疗。进一步发现单碱基编辑技术不仅会造成DNA脱靶，而且还会产生大量的RNA脱靶，RNA脱靶位点广泛存在于癌基因和抑癌基因上，具有较强的致癌风险。通过对混合细胞和单细胞水平的RNA突变位点进行分析，发现RNA脱靶位点和目的靶向序列没有相关性，是由脱氨酶产生的随机脱靶位点。通过进一步对单碱基编辑工具进行改造建立一系列突变库，最终筛选到既保留高效的单碱基编辑活性又不会造成额外脱靶的新一代高保真单碱基编辑工具。更为重要的是，开发的ABE（F148A）突变体还能够缩小编辑窗口，实现更加精准的DNA编辑。这些研究为单碱基编辑应用于临床治疗奠定了重要基础。

二、CRISPR/Cas9介导的单条染色体特异性敲除

除去对单碱基编辑工具的优化与改造外，杨辉还使用CRISPR/Cas9工具成功特异性敲除了一条染色体。增加或缺失一条染色体可导致妊娠期流产或出生缺陷等非整倍体疾病，目前尚无有效治疗手段。随着CRISPR/Cas9基因编辑技术的出现和快速发展，该技术已经应用于制备精确的基因突变、重组和染色体大片段敲除的细胞或动物。然而，对于该技术是否可用于整条染色体的消除、进而为非整倍体疾病治疗提供新的途径，仍是未知。杨辉发现应用CRISPR/Cas9在Y染色体上进行多位点DNA切割，可以有效敲除小鼠胚胎及胚胎干细胞中的Y染色体；进一步研究发现小鼠X染色体、人的7号和14号染色体都可以通过这种方法敲除。更为重要的是，唐氏综合征患者的iPS细胞中多余的一条21号染色体也可以通过这种方法特异性敲除，且不会造成额外的脱靶和基因组异常。

Awardee of Life Sciences Prize, Yang Hui

Yang Hui was born in Nanchang, City of Jiangxi Province in August 1985. Currently, he is holding a principal investigator position at the Center for Excellence in Brain Science and Intelligent Technology. In 2012, Yang received his PhD from the Shanghai Institute of Biochemistry and Cell Biology of the Chinese Academy of Sciences. From 2012 to 2014, he carried out the postdoctoral research in the Massachusetts Institute of Technology（MIT）. In 2014, he was selected by the Youth Thousand Talents Program in order to come back to China to join the Laboratory of Disease Model in Non-human Primates in the Institute of Neuroscience of Shanghai, a research institute affiliated to the Chinese Academy of Sciences.

Among his numerous awards, we must underline the National Science Found for Excellent

Young Scholars Award he received in 2015 and his selection as one of the Shanghai Young Talents in the same year. In 2018, he won the First Prize of Shanghai Natural Science and Technology and the Outstanding Youth Science and Technology Innovation Talent Award of the Chinese Academy of Sciences, Shanghai Branch. In 2019, he was awarded with the National Science Found for Distinguished Young Scholars and he has recently garnered the VCANBIO Award for Biosciences and Medicine.

Gene editing, Yang's field, aims to correct genetic diseases at a molecular level changing its gene expression. Nowadays, the main bottleneck for clinical application is concerned to safety problems, due to the off-target activity of the system. Therefore, efficient and high-fidelity editing tools have become one of the most urgent issues in the field of gene editing. However, single-nucleotide polymorphisms among individuals and defects in existing off-target detection methods make off-target detection impossible to quantify clearly. Yang focuses on the development of new gene editing tools and their off-target issues, as well as their applications on diseases treatments. During his research, a series of original and important results were achieved, which has great application value.

1. DNA&RNA Off-target mutation induced by DNA Base Editing and its elimination by mutagenesis

Genome editing tools hold great promise for correcting pathogenic mutations. However, it is difficult to determine off-target effects of editing due to the existence of single nucleotide polymorphisms (SNPs) in different individuals. Here, Yang developed a method named GOTI (Genome-wide Off-target analysis by Two-cell embryo Injection) to detect off-target mutations by editing one blastomere of two-cell mouse embryos using either CRISPR-Cas9 or base editor BE3. Comparison of the whole genome sequences of progeny cells of edited vs. non-edited blastomeres atE14.5 showed that off-target single nucleotide variants (SNVs) were rare in Cas9-edited embryos, with a frequency close to the spontaneous mutation rate. In contrast, BE3 editing induced SNVs with over 20-fold higher frequencies, requiring a solution to address the fidelity of base editors. However, any potential RNA mutations caused by DNA base editors have not been evaluated. Adeno-associated viruses are the most common delivery system for gene therapies that involve DNA editing; these viruses can sustain long-term gene expression in vivo, so the extent of potential RNA mutations induced by DNA base editors is of great concern. Here we quantitatively evaluated RNA single nucleotide variations (SNVs) that were induced by CBEs or ABEs. Both the cytosine base editor BE3 and the adenine base editor ABE7.10 generated tens of thousands of off-target RNA SNVs. Subsequently, by engineering deaminases, we found that three CBE variants and one ABE variant showed a reduction in off-target RNA SNVs to the baseline while maintaining efficient DNA on-target activity. This study reveals a previously overlooked aspect of off-target effects in DNA editing and also demonstrates that such effects can be eliminated by engineering deaminases.

2. CRISPR/Cas9-mediated targeted chromosome elimination

Yang's team demonstrates the use of the CRISPR/Cas9 system to eliminate targeted chromosomes. Using either multiple cleavages induced by a single-guide RNA (sgRNA) that targets multiple chromosome-specific sites or a cocktail of multiple sgRNAs, each targeting one specific site, they found that a sex chromosome could be selectively eliminated in cultured cells, embryos, and tissues in vivo. Furthermore, this approach was able to produce a targeted autosome loss in aneuploid mouse embryonic stem cells with an extra human chromosome and human induced pluripotent stem cells with trisomy 21, as well as cancer cells. CRISPR/Cas9-mediated targeted chromosome elimination offers a new approach to develop animal models with chromosome deletions, and a potential therapeutic strategy for human aneuploidy diseases involving additional chromosomes.

农学奖获得者

刘 仲 华

刘仲华，1965 年 3 月出生于湖南省衡阳县。1988 年毕业于湖南农业大学茶学系，获农学硕士学位；2014 年毕业于清华大学化学系，获理学博士学位。1999 年晋升教授，一直在湖南农业大学茶学系从事科研教学工作。现任湖南农业大学学术委员会副主任、茶学学科带头人，国家植物功能成分利用工程技术研究中心主任，茶学教育部重点实验室主任，国家茶叶产业技术体系加工研究室主任，浙江大学兼职教授。先后兼任中国茶叶学会副理事长、中国茶叶流通协会副会长、中国国际茶文化研究会副会长等。围绕茶叶加工与资源高效利用，主持国家和部省级项目 30 多项，以第一完成人获国家科技进步奖二等奖 2 项、湖南省科技进步奖一等奖 3 项及首届湖南省十大科技创新奖、湖南省光召科技奖等；获授权发明专利 57 件，制定国家标准 5 项；以第一作者或通讯作者发表 SCI 论文 60 多篇，主编或参编学术专著与高校教材 13 部。

刘仲华一直从事茶叶加工与资源高效利用研究，致力于创新茶叶加工理论技术、提高茶叶资源利用率和产业综合效益，开展了一系列创新性研究工作。

一、创新黑茶加工理论与技术，强力推进我国黑茶产业提质增效与快速发展

我国有绿茶、黑茶、乌龙茶、红茶、白茶、黄茶六大茶类。然而，传统黑茶产业由于品质形成机理不清，面临质量不稳、工艺装备落后、产品规格单一等发展瓶颈。刘仲华率团队系统揭示了黑茶加工中优势微生物菌群及其演变规律，明确了黑茶初制中优势微生物菌群是假丝酵母菌、黑曲霉、芽孢细菌等，黑茶（茯砖茶）压制发酵中的优势微生物为冠突散囊菌；明确了湿热作用与微生物释放胞外酶的交互作用是黑茶加工中生化成分变化的主要动力，揭示了多酚类、氨基酸、生物碱、色素类、黄酮类、糖类物质的变化动态与途径及其在色香味形成中的作用，发现 4 种新的黄酮苷类物质。

揭示了黑茶的主要生物活性及作用机理，为饮用黑茶与健康提供了理论依据。明确了黑茶缩小小鼠脂肪细胞体积、抑制前脂肪细胞分化、上调脂肪分解酶和下调脂肪合成酶基因表达、提高胰岛素敏感性、加速葡萄糖转运等调节糖脂代谢生物活性的作用机制；发现黑茶可有效改善肠道菌群结构，使双歧杆菌、乳酸杆菌等有益菌群丰度提高 20% 以上，使大肠杆菌、金色葡萄球菌等有害菌群丰度下降 30% 以上。

发明了黑茶优质高效加工关键新技术。通过纯化冠突散囊菌优异菌种、精准调控不同茶叶基质中发花（冠突散囊菌为优势菌的固态发酵）温度、湿度、氧气等环境因子，发明了诱导调控发花、散茶发花、砖面发花、快速醇化系列新技术，降低了黑茶加工成本 30% 以上，提高品质 2～3 个等级，综合效益提高 50% 以上，并为黑茶产品多元化提供了技术支撑，突破了传统黑茶品类单一的发展瓶颈。通过融合低氟茶树品种筛选、不同嫩度原料拼配、微生物发酵富集氟、茶菌分离去除氟等技术，发明了高效综合控氟技术，可在相对较低成本下控制茯砖茶含氟量符合国家标准（<300mg/kg），有效保障了黑茶质量安全。

构建了标准化的现代黑茶生产技术体系。制定黑茶国家标准 4 项、地方标准 13 项，规范了黑茶品类构成、原料要求、加工技术、加工装备、品质指标、储运条件、品饮方法等全产业链的技术要素，推进了黑茶从传统手工作业向标准化现代生产跨越，综合效率显著提高，直接加工成本大幅度降低。

这些创新成果的推广应用和标准引领助推湖南黑茶与广西六堡茶、陕西茯茶、湖北青砖茶、浙江茯砖茶协同发展，推进黑茶成为近十年我国六大茶类中规模与效益增长之最。强力支撑了湖南黑茶近十多年规模和效益增长近 100 倍、综合规模达 200 多亿元，产生了显著的经济社会效益。

二、创新茶叶深加工核心技术体系，促进茶叶资源高效利用和产业转型升级

我国夏秋茶资源占比达 50% 以上，因品质相对较低且利用率不高，严重影响茶叶产业效益。20 世纪 90 年代，我国茶叶深加工由于技术水平限制，在功能成分提制纯度、速溶茶品质、提制效率、安全性等方面存在诸多技术瓶颈，缺乏国际竞争力。刘仲华带领团队采用动态逆流提取、膜浓缩与分离、大孔树脂分离、逆流旋风低温喷雾等先进技术组合，创建了仅以水和酒精为溶剂的茶叶功能成分和速溶茶绿色高效提制技术体系，不仅解决了传统技术中采用氯仿、甲醇、金属离子等有害分离介质的安全性问题，而且提高产品收率 5 个百分点、产品纯度 8 个百分点以上。针对茶叶原料中可能存在农药残留的现实问题，采用膜分离与特种树脂吸附、离子交换技术融合，发明了茶叶提取物中农药残留的高效去除技术，实现了低成本生产脱农残茶叶提取物的技术突破。

针对我国儿茶素单体制备一直处在实验室阶段、未能实现产业化的问题，发明了 EGCG、EGC、ECG 单体分离制备新技术，使我国儿茶素单体产量实现 60 吨级的全球最大规模，并填补出口空白；针对从红茶中提制茶黄素的成本太高这一问题，发明了儿茶

素酶促氧化制备茶黄素及其高效分离纯化新技术，使茶黄素规模化制备成本降低 70% 以上，为我国儿茶素单体和茶黄素制备技术引领国际提供了强力支撑。

利用茶浓缩液自身的起泡特性，在不使用任何添加剂的情况下发明了中空颗粒速溶茶提制新技术，解决了传统速溶茶流动性、溶解性、抗潮性差的技术难题，为速溶茶的大众化消费提供了技术支撑。

采用细胞模型、基因模型、线虫模型和动物模型，从细胞和分子水平揭示了儿茶素、茶黄素、茶氨酸及茶叶提取物的抑菌、抗氧化、抵御环境胁迫、改善肠道菌群、调节糖脂代谢的生物活性及作用机理，为茶叶功能成分在大健康产品中应用提供了理论依据。

创制的茶叶提取物制品催生了一批国际主流健康产品，引领我国茶叶功能成分提制技术由追踪日本等发达国家上升到领跑国际水平。研制的儿茶素 GTC-80 成为日本厚生省批准的第一个降脂减肥茶饮料的原料，且十多年来保持最热销；与美国 P&G 研究院合作研制的脱苦味速溶绿茶广泛应用于全球茶制品开发；研制的高纯儿茶素 Polyphenon E 成为 1962 年以来美国 FDA 批准的第一个纯植物药 Veregen 的活性制药原料。

上述研究成果在 10 多个省市推广，助推我国 20 多万吨夏秋茶（约占茶叶总产量 8%）加工成茶叶功能成分提取物，应用于茶饮料、茶食品、茶化妆品等终端产品开发和出口国际市场，为千亿级茶叶深加工产业提供了技术支撑，取得了显著的经济社会效益，引领我国茶叶产业向大健康产业延伸拓展。

Awardee of Agronomy Prize，Liu Zhonghua

Liu Zhonghua was born in Hengyang County of Hunan Province in March 1965. He got Ph. D degree from Chemistry Department of Tsinghua University，works as full-time professor in department of tea science，college of horticulture in Hunan Agricultural University since and part-time professor in Zhejiang University since 2018. At present，professor Liu is the deputy director of Academic Committee in Hunan Agricultural University and leader for tea science discipline. He is also the director of the National Research Center of Engineering and Technology for Utilization of Botanical Functional Ingredients，director of Tea Processing Laboratory of National Technical Research System for Tea Industry. Successively serve as the vice president of China Tea Science Society，China Tea Marketing Association and China International Tea Culture Institute. Professor Liuis a leading expert in tea science and has been undergoing more than 30 national，ministerial and provincial research projects. He has been winning two second prize for National Science and Technology Progress Award，three first prize for Scientific and Technological Progress in Hunan Province as the First Completed. He has been authorized 57 invention patents，formulated five national standards for tea and published more than 60 SCI papers as first author or corresponding author.

1. Innovating the theory and technology of dark tea processing, and strongly promoting the quality and efficiency of dark tea in China

Dark tea is one of the six categories of Chinese tea. But the development of dark tea industry is slowly, because of the underdeveloped processing technology. Professor Liu revealed the change of microbial community, mainly chemical components and the formation mechanism of characteristic flavor during the processing of dark tea and the characteristic of chemical composition of functional components in dark tea. Four of new flavonoid glycosides were found in dark tea by Prof. Liu's team. The health benefits of dark tea were also revealed, including improve the gastrointestinal function and the glycolipid metabolism.Several key processing technologies of dark tea, such as *Regulated Fungal Fermentation*, *Fungal Fermentation of Loose Tea*, *Rapid Mellowing*, *High efficiency fluorine reduction*, were invented.The clean, mechanized and standardized modern dark tea processing technology system was established. More than 20 new dark tea products were developed. Four national standards for dark tea were formulated. The industrial scales of dark tea in Hunan, Shanxi, Guangxi, Hubei and Zhejiang province were rapid and collectively development by using above new technologies and standards. Especially in Hunan province, the scale and benefits of dark tea industry have increased by nearly 100 times in the last decade with Significant economic benefits.

2. Innovating the core technology system of tea comprehensive processing, promoting the utilization level of tea resources and upgrading tea industry in China

Tea comprehensive processing is an important value-added approach for enhancing the utilization level of tea resource in summer and autumn season.Professor Liu established green and efficient technology system for extraction and isolation offunctional components from tea and instant tea processing. Key technologies of tea comprehensive processing, including extraction and purification of catechinmonomers and L-theanine, theaflavinspreparation by catechins enzymatic oxidation, hollow particles instant tea processing, pesticides removal technology in tea extracts, were invented. The quality, cost and safety of products were improved signally by using these new technologies during tea comprehensive processing. Created new products of tea functional ingredients have spawned a number of mainstream health products in global market. Research achievement of Prof. Liu and his group, has been leading China's tea active ingredient extraction technology from tracking developed countries such as Japan to leading international counterparts, significantly improving the utilization rate of resources, scale and economic efficiency of tea industry, and boosting the development of the 100 billion tea comprehensive processing industry.

农学奖获得者

印 遇 龙

印遇龙，1956年1月出生于湖南省桃源县。1978年本科毕业于湖南师范学院生物系，1997年获英国女皇大学哲学博士学位。现任中国科学院亚热带农业生态研究所畜禽健康养殖研究中心负责人，畜禽养殖污染控制与资源化技术国家工程实验室主任，国家生猪产业技术创业战略联盟理事长，一级研究员。中国工程院院士。以第一完成人获国家科技进步奖二等奖2项、三等奖1项和国家自然科学奖二等奖一项；发表论文300余篇，被引用9000余次，入选汤森路透2014年和2015年全球高被引科学家和中国引文桂冠奖；出版专著12部。兼任湖南省科学技术协会副主席和湖南省政协常委，中国农学会微量元素与食物链分会理事长，国家新饲料评审委员会副主任和中国饲料工业协会副会长。先后获全国创新争先奖状、全国五一劳动奖章、湖南省科学技术"杰出贡献奖"、中国科学人2017年年度人物、2014年World Animal Nutrition奖、2018年Asia-Pacific Nutrition Award（APNA）奖、九三学社全国优秀社员、中国科学院创新文化先进奖和优秀共产党员等殊荣。

长期从事生猪营养学研究，在生猪健康养殖领域取得了系统性的重要成果，是国际生猪营养与健康领域有影响的中国学者之一。部分成果在生产中获得应用，经济、社会和生态效益显著。

一、建立猪饲料高品质、低残留、低排放的生态养殖技术体系，解决了国内外传统饲料配制不当技术难题

创新了肠T型瘘管、桥型和血插管技术，攻克了不能实时定量检测肠道内容物和血液养分变化的国际难题；发现猪饲料中营养物质（干物质、有机物质、能量、蛋白质、氨基酸和纤维类物质等）在猪消化道不同部位的消化代谢规律；建立了40多种饲料原料中磷、氮、氨基酸、淀粉等营养素利用率数据库，开发的系列猪饲料中蛋白质和磷的利用率提高 20% 以上；建立猪饲料有效氨基酸等配方参数体系，解决了氮过剩或不足的难题。有关方法和技术参数在国内外发表后被广泛应用。

揭示了制约猪日粮氮高效利用的关键因素，揭示了氨基酸、磷、葡萄糖和非淀粉多糖等在猪肝门静脉回流组织吸收利用的规律，研究成果为提高猪饲料氮利用率提供了新的理论。在此基础上，带领团队发明了半乳甘露寡糖等生物活性物质调控氨基酸、能量、磷等营养物质代谢和改善猪肉品质调控技术，将营养物质的代谢与调控从消化道层次提升到组织器官层次、从机体水平提升到分子水平。

二、发现饲料中氨基酸新的生理功能，创建了仔猪肠道健康调控关键技术

发现了氨基酸的多种新的生理功能（促进多胺和一氧化氮合成、增强免疫和抗氧化能力、调控蛋白质和脂质代谢等），提出了功能性氨基酸概念。该项研究改变了既有的将氨基酸仅作为蛋白质合成原料的认识，不仅丰富了猪氨基酸营养理论，还促进了猪氨基酸营养调控技术的研发，推动了氨基酸作为饲料添加剂在养猪生产中的科学应用。该研究发现精氨酸和精氨酸生素可通过调控 miRNA 表达，促进胎盘发育，提高母猪繁殖性能；精氨酸还可以通过 NO 途径促进猪胚胎滋养外胚层细胞生长和蛋白质合成，其机制为激活 mTOR 信号通路；精氨酸对圆环病毒感染动物繁殖障碍存在干预作用，并阐明了其营养生化机制；功能性氨基酸（精氨酸、谷氨酸、支链氨基酸）通过促进蛋白质翻译，提高机体蛋白质的合成；精氨酸还可通过差异调控肥育猪肌肉和脂肪组织脂肪代谢相关酶活性和基因表达，从而降低机体脂肪率、提高肌内脂肪含量、促进蛋白质沉积和、降低和重新分配体脂，达到改善动物肉质、风味和营养价值的目的。

探明了影响仔猪肠道健康的重要分子生物学机理，并揭示了仔猪肠道健康调控的关键作用机制。研究发现，N-乙酰谷氨酸合成酶表达下降导致肠道内源性精氨酸合成不足，是造成肠黏膜萎缩的主要原因；断奶应激显著改变肠道代谢功能关键基因和蛋白的表达；日龄和断奶都是改变仔猪肠道菌群结构的主要诱因。据此，首次建立了预测仔猪肠黏膜发育和关键性功能基因 mRNA 表达量随日龄变化的数学模型。发现精氨酸家族类物质调控肠道抗氧化和黏膜免疫功能的机制，可促进肠黏膜蛋白合成和血管生长，缓解断奶仔猪肠道损伤；植物提取物等活性物质通过改善肠道微生态，增强肠道健康；不同碳水化合物通过其消化利用的特异性、非淀粉多糖（NSP）酶通过加速肠道中 NSP 水解影响仔猪肠道健康和生长性能；建立了仔猪肠道健康调控关键技术——精氨酸家族类物质调控肠道健康技术，以改善肠道吸收功能、抗氧化能力和黏膜免疫功能；建立了以植物提取物、合生素和甘露聚糖酶等专利技术为主的调控技术，优化了肠道微生物区系，提高了营养物质的消化率。此外，还开发了仔猪碳水化合物和脂肪的高效利用技术，在大大提高生产性能的同时，开发出调控仔猪肠道健康的关键性产品——新型饲料添加剂和系列化乳仔猪饲料产品。此项技术结合应用双圆柱连体颗粒饲料技术和一种特殊的饲料模具，开发出了膨化乳猪配合饲料等系列产品。与传统产品相比，使用该类产品，仔猪日增重

提高 12%～20%，饲料利用率改善 10%～15%，腹泻率下降 25%～35%，极大地提高了养猪生产效率，产生了巨大的社会经济效益和生态效益。

三、发明生猪低矿和无抗饲料技术

在解决老百姓吃肉难问题的同时，印遇龙前瞻性地看到了我国畜禽养殖业接踵出现的养殖粪便污染环境、猪肉品质下降、药物抗生素超标等问题，率先提出"管好猪屁股，养猪才有前途"的科学论断，即从养殖源头着手减少畜禽养殖废弃物排放、又结合末端处理资源化利用的思想。为从根本上解决这一问题，印遇龙从全产业链着手，先后开发了生猪微量元素和氮减排技术、生猪双低日粮调制技术、抗生素替代技术和木本饲料等卓有成效的应用技术。减少猪粪尿中 20% 以上的氮磷排放，重金属元素铜、铁、锌、锰的排放量减少 50% 以上。解决了长期以来猪粪资源化利用率低、造成严重环境污染的难题，技术应用和减排成果获国际好评，并获国家领导和各省政府的认可推广。

Awardee of Agronomy Prize, Yin Yulong

Yin Yulong was born in Taoyuan County of Hunan Province in January 1956. He graduated from biology department of Hunan normal university in 1978. In 1997, he received his PhD from queen's university in the United Kingdom. Now, he is and the First-Class professor, the director of livestock and poultry health breeding research center of the Institute of Subtropical Agriculture, Chinese Academy of Sciences, director of National Engineering Laboratory for Pollution Control and Waste Utilization in Livestock and Poultry Production, chairman of the the National Swine Industry Technology Innovation Strategic Alliance. He was elected as an academician of Chinese academy of engineering in 2013. Since 1978, after he was assigned to the Institute of Subtropical Agriculture, Chinese Academy of Sciences, he has set up research platforms such as livestock and poultry health breeding research center, national engineering laboratory of livestock and poultry breeding pollution control and resource recovery technology, and key laboratory of animal nutrition, physiology and metabolism of Hunan province. As the first accomplisher, he has won two second prizes, one third prize of national science and technology progress, and one second prize of national natural science. He has published more than 300 papers and 12 monographs, which were cited more than 9000 times, H index 51. He was selected into the Thomson Reuters 2014 and 2015 global highly cited scientists and China citation laurel award. He was elected as vice chairman of hunan association of science and technology, standing committee of hunan CPPCC, chairman of trace elements and food chain branch of Chinese agricultural association, vice chairman of national new feed appraisal committee and vice chairman of China feed industry association. He has won the national innovation Award, the national May Day labor medal, the Outstanding contribution Award of Hunan province for science and technology, the 2017 person of the year of Chinese scientists, the 2014 World Animal Nutrition Award, the 2018 Asia-pacific Nutrition Award (APNA) Award.

Yin Yulong has been engaged in the study of pig nutrition for a long time, and has made important systematic achievements in the field of healthy pig breeding. He is one of the influential Chinese scholars in the field of international pig nutrition and health. Some of the achievements have been applied in production, with remarkable economic, social and ecological benefits.

He established an ecological breeding technology system with high quality, low residue and low emission of pig feed to solve the technical problems of improper preparation of traditional feed at home and abroad. He discovered new physiological functions of amino acids in feed and established key technologies for regulating intestinal health of piglets. He also developed feeding techniques with low mineral element and no antibiotics adding.

农学奖获得者

张 献 龙

张献龙，1963年3月出生于河南省上蔡县。1990年毕业于华中农业大学农学系，获农学博士学位。1990年7月入职华中农业大学。1993—1994年在加拿大曼尼托巴大学从事访问研究一年。1992年至今在作物遗传改良国家重点实验室工作，2002年始任重点实验室副主任；2002年6月—2008年2月任华中农业大学植物科学技术学院院长；2008年3月—2018年8月任华中农业大学副校长。兼任中国农学会棉花分会副理事长、中国作物学会常务理事、中国遗传学会理事、作物学报副主编。获国家科技进步奖二等奖1项、省科技进步奖一等奖2项；入选国家"万人计划"领军人才，获"全国创新争先奖状""国家教学名师""全国优秀科技工作者"等荣誉称号；连续5年入选爱思唯尔中国高被引学者，SCI论文被引6200多次。

主要从事作物科学研究，在棉花遗传育种理论和应用技术创新方面作出了一系列开创性研究。

一、创新遗传育种理论，增强育种针对性

完成了四倍体栽培种陆地棉和海岛棉参考基因组的组装，阐述了四倍体棉种A、D两个亚基因组的不对称选择和进化，定位了一批控制纤维品质的QTL位点。阐述了纤维发育过程中的甲基化调控，揭示了棉花3D基因组与基因表达的关系，丰富了棉花优质纤维形成的理论。初步明确了棉花纤维发育的基因调控网络并发现一批关键调控基因，为纤维品质改良提供了基因资源。探明了基因SSN调控棉花抗病性的新机制，发现广谱抗性基因*GhLac1*，阐述了棉花抗病响应机制的多样性。发现了甲基化调控高温不育的模式，研究了高温导致棉花蕾铃脱落而造成减产的理论机制，定位了一批耐高温基因。

这些遗传机理的阐述提高了对棉花各个性状遗传基础的认识，增强了育种针对性。

30 年来，在棉花遗传育种理论研究方面发表研究论文 300 多篇，其中 SCI 论文 160 多篇，SCI 论文被引 6200 多次，在国际上彰显了我国棉花科研领域的成就。

二、创新棉花资源，丰富育种材料

针对棉花资源来源单一、突破性品种少的问题，把种质创新作为棉花育种的核心问题。利用远缘杂交和胚抢救技术，获得栽培陆地棉与 7 个野生棉的杂交后代，并人工合成 1 个四倍体；利用栽培陆地棉与远缘杂交种不断回交，培育出优质、抗病、抗虫、耐旱的材料 100 余份。发展了分子标记辅助远缘杂交技术，构建了陆地棉背景的海岛棉、黄褐棉、毛棉、达尔文棉导入系。这些导入系不仅为抗性、优质基因提供了遗传背景不同的材料群体，还为筛选优质、抗病和抗虫材料提供了新途径，同时这些导入系为研究棉花两个亚基因组的进化选择提供了材料。先后收集评价各类材料 3000 余份，筛选出优质材料 160 份、抗虫材料 32 份、高抗枯萎材料 20 份、抗黄萎材料 12 份、耐高温材料 29 份、极耐高温材料 7 份。克隆功能基因 30 多个，创新各类材料 400 余份。这些研究工作将为突破性品种选育奠定了材料基础。

三、创新育种方法，提高育种效率

有性杂交只能在有限的栽培种与野生棉之间实现，为了更广泛地引进野生棉的有益基因，必须突破远缘杂交方法。张献龙带领团队首次从野生种原生质体再生植株，首次利用体细胞杂交获得栽培种与野生种细胞对称、非对称融合材料，并通过获杂交种回交转育获取含有目标性状基因转移的有育种价值的材料。

棉花是我国唯一释放的转基因大田作物，但只在抗虫方面有成功应用。为提高转基因育种效率，张献龙带领团队建立了年产万株以上转基因苗的棉花高效转基因技术体系，将体细胞再生周期缩短到 5 ～ 6 个月，转基因技术和受体材料被国内外 10 余家科研单位使用。最近，在 CRISPR/Cas9 棉花基因编辑技术上获得重要突破，在单个基因编辑基础上建立了高通量基因编辑技术，一次载体构建可以编辑 100 个以上的基因，同时可以对一个基因家族所有成员进行编辑；建立了单碱基的基因编辑技术及高通量检测编辑效率的技术。高效的基因编辑技术对于阐述棉花的复杂生物学问题、提升育种效率、创造新材料、验证基因功能等具有重要应用价值，该技术已提供给美国、澳大利亚等 100 多个国内外科研机构使用，并被 *Trends in Plant Science* 和 *Advanced Sciences* 两个国际著名综述期刊邀请撰写该方面进展的综述文章。

四、培育突破性品种，服务棉花产业

针对我国棉花品种在产量、品质和抗性方面难以同步改良的突出问题，提出引进外来材料、多地多环境筛选评价资源、分子标记区分遗传差异、确定性状互补的骨干材料、利用遗传差异大的材料组建轮回选择群体，选育自交系；通过大群体测配、大概率淘汰，在高选择压下培育综合性状优良新品种的育种策略，在育种实践中证明了这一育种策略的有效性，先后培育出棉花新品种 11 个。其中，华杂棉 H318 在 2009 年长江流域国家审定品种中综合指数居第一位，增产极显著、稳产性好、综合抗性强、纤维品质优、早熟性好，突破了长江流域棉花品种长期存在的多性状难以同步改良的难题。培育的棉花新品种已累计推广 2000 余万亩，产生了显著的经济和社会效益，成果获湖北省科技进步奖一等奖和国家科技进步奖二等奖。

Awardee of Agronomy Prize, Zhang Xianlong

Zhang Xianlong was born in Shangcai County of Henan Province in March 1963. Zhang graduated in 1990 from Huazhong Agricultural University where he also obtained his doctoral degree(Ph.D.). In July 1990, he was appointed as a faculty member of Huazhong Agricultural University, when he started his teaching and research career. He was a visiting researcher for one year(1993—1994)in the Department of Plant Science, University of Manitoba, and then he come back to his position, and was promoted as a full professor in January 1997. Zhang is a faculty of the College of Plant Science and Technology, also a PI of the National Key Laboratory for Crop Genetic Improvement since 1992. He has worked as an associate director of the National Key Laboratory since 2002. From June 2002 to February 2008, he was the Dean of College of Plant Science and Technology, and then took the position of Vice President of Huazhong Agricultural University from March 2008 to August 2018. Zhang is Vice-President of the Cotton Association, Agronomy Society of China, standing director of the Crop Society of China, and senior editor of both *Acta Agronomica Sinica* and *Plants*, *People*, *Planet*. He has been awarded a National Science Progress Prize(second class)and twice awarded a Hubei Provincial Science Progress Prize(first class)for his contributions to agriculture. Zhang and his colleagues have published more than 300 papers, of which 160 papers are published by international journals, giving him an H index of 43, and his SCI papers have been cited more than 6200 times. He has been a recognized highly cited Chinese scholar by Elsevier continuously for recent 5 years. He was honored as a leading talent by the National "Ten Thousand Talent Plan", the National "Creation and Glory" Prize and a National "Excellent Teacher in Education". Zhang is also honored as a "National Outstanding Scientist" and "Hubei Provincial Ten Best Ethical Teacher".

Zhang Xianlong's research focuses on Crop Science. He has made great achievements in developing genetics and creating technologies in cotton breeding, and his cotton varieties are broadly used in cotton production.

(1) Developing genetics and genomics, unveiling the regulatory mechanisms underpinning key characters, laying a solid basis for cotton genetic improvement.

（2）Creating and developing cotton germplasm to enrich the genetic background for breeding elite varieties.

（3）Developing novel breeding tools for improving breeding efficiency in cotton.

（4）Breeding elite varieties to serve cotton production.

医学药学奖获得者

范 先 群

范先群，1964年6月出生于安徽省寿县。长江学者特聘教授，上海交通大学医学院附属第九人民医院眼科学科带头人。范先群从事眼科临床和科研32年，主攻眼眶病和眼肿瘤，牵头组建中华眼科学会眼整形眼眶病学组和中国抗癌协会眼肿瘤专业委员会，并担任组长和主任委员。此外，还担任亚太眼整形外科学会主席、亚太眼肿瘤眼病理学会主席，英国皇家眼科学院 Fellow 和爱丁堡皇家外科学院 Fellow Ad Hominem，引领我国眼眶病眼肿瘤专业走向国际。主持"863"和国家重点研发计划等国家级项目14项；以第一和通讯作者发表 SCI 论文159篇；获授权专利17项；以第一完成人获国家科技进步奖二等奖2项、上海市科技进步奖一等奖3项、教育部高等学校科技进步奖一等奖等。

一、创建眼眶外科内镜导航手术系统，开创精准手术模式，攻克眼眶手术难题

眼眶病是致盲、致残、造成颅面畸形的跨学科疑难眼病，主要依赖手术治疗。眼眶内含眼球和视神经等重要组织，与颅内和颌面相通，空间狭小，手术难度大、风险高，提高手术成功率是世界性难题。范先群师从张涤生院士，实现学科交叉融合，研发眼眶外科新技术，研制内镜导航手术系统，创建了眼眶外科修复重建关键技术体系。

（1）建立眼眶外科新技术，制订规范化诊疗方案。率先建立我国眼眶正常值数据库，创建数字化眼眶模型和虚拟手术、眼球突出度测量新方法、修复材料定制技术等，实现了眼眶手术从经验到精准的跨越；提出眼眶骨折3型12类分类方法，开展整复治疗新术式，建立规范化诊疗方案，主持制定我国首个眼眶骨折诊疗专家共识。

（2）研发眼眶手术导航技术，引领眼眶内镜手术发展。率先建立眼眶手术术前模拟、术中引导、术后评估等技术，研发眼眶手术导航系统并应用于眼眶骨折修复术，精度从4～6毫米提高至1毫米，复视改善率和眼球内陷矫正率显著提高，实现了精准整复；率先开展眼眶内镜手术，解决了眶尖狭小和病变难以暴露的难题，推动了眼眶微创外科的发展。

（3）首创内镜导航手术系统，攻克眼眶手术难题。导航可精确定位，但看不到深部结构；内镜可看到深部结构，但无空间定位功能。首次提出"内镜导航"新理念，将内镜和导航相融合，建立具有自主知识产权的内镜导航手术系统，实现了"图像影像对称匹配、深部组织可视可知、重要结构实时预警"。该系统可用于眼眶减压和畸形矫正等疑难手术，修复眼眶、重建视路，提高成功率，降低并发症，使眼眶巨大神经纤维瘤等成为可治之症。成果入选"中国眼科近五年十大进展"，并获 2015 年国家科技进步奖二等奖（排名第一）。

二、创建眼恶性肿瘤手术新模式，建立综合序列治疗新方案，提高生存率和保眼率

眼恶性肿瘤严重危害视力和生命，是亟待解决的世界性难题。我国晚期患者多、病情重，死亡率和眼球摘除率居高不下。范先群探索视网膜母细胞瘤等常见眼恶性肿瘤的介入化疗，创新手术模式，建立了关键诊疗技术体系。

（1）开展介入化疗新技术，提高保眼率。开展视网膜母细胞瘤眼动脉超选择介入化疗，主持全球首个视网膜母细胞瘤介入化疗多中心 RCT 研究，显著提高患者保眼率；开展泪腺腺样囊性癌介入化疗，改变了眶内容物以剜除为主的手术方式。

（2）创建手术新模式，提高生存率。开展睑板腺癌显微控制切除和即期修复术，显著降低复发率和死亡率。主持国际最大规模睑板腺癌多中心队列研究，降低复发率，提高生存率，建立其预后预测模型；牵头制定我国首个睑板腺癌诊疗专家共识。

（3）建立综合序列治疗新方案，提高整体治疗水平。完成全国视网膜母细胞瘤回顾性队列研究，开展多中心 RCT 研究，建立综合序列治疗新方案，使晚期视网膜母细胞瘤和结膜黑色素瘤生存率显著提高。成果获 2018 年国家科技进步奖二等奖（排名第一）。

三、研制眼眶修复新材料，发现甲状腺眼病免疫新机制，建立眼恶性肿瘤多靶点治疗新方法

（1）研制生物活性新材料，实现眼眶骨再生。针对现有材料不可降解、无生物活性等问题，研制氧化石墨烯活性材料等 9 种功能化材料，获 CMA 资质认证；应用间充质干细胞复合新型眼眶功能化材料，实现原位骨再生。

（2）揭示甲状腺眼病免疫调控新机制。甲状腺眼病是严重危害视功能的最常见眼眶病，发病机制不清。首次阐明 Th17 细胞在该病中的免疫调节作用，发现 Th17 细胞 / Treg 细胞失衡导致疾病发生，并筛选出靶向 Th17 细胞的天然化合物 Vialinin A，绘制了免疫微环境图谱。研究成果被 F1000 评价为"为甲状腺眼病发病机制研究开辟了新方向"。

（3）发现眼内恶性肿瘤发生新机制，创建多靶点治疗新方法。建立国际最大的眼肿瘤生物样本库。发现视网膜母细胞瘤新致病区 GAU1，提出葡萄膜黑色素瘤发生的"RNA 级联反应"和"陷阱修饰"学说，被 F1000 评价为"揭示肿瘤发生新机制，是肿瘤研究的范例"。靶向葡萄膜黑色素瘤 lncRNA ANRIL，同时激活抑癌基因 INK4A、INK4B 和

ARF，建立了多靶点治疗新方法。

范先群带领学科入选国家临床重点专科，并建立了我国最大的眼眶病眼肿瘤医教研中心，为我国 32 个省、市、自治区 503 家医院培养眼眶病眼肿瘤医师。同时，主编"十三五"规划教材《眼科学》。在世界眼科大会等作专题报告 32 次，在美国眼科年会连续多次开设"眼眶手术新进展"课程，荣获亚太眼科杰出贡献奖、中华眼科杰出成就奖、全国优秀科技工作者、全国卫生系统先进工作者等荣誉。

Awardee of Medical Sciences and Materia Medica Prize, Fan Xianqun

Fan Xianqun was born in Shou County of Anhui Province in June 1964. He is a distinguished professor of changjiang scholars. He has been engaged in clinical and scientific research of ophthalmology for 32 years, mainly focusing on orbital diseases and ocular tumors. He has led the establishment of Oculoplastic Surgery and Orbital Disease Group of Chinese Ophthalmology Society and Ocular Tumor Committee of China Anti-cancer Association. He has successively served as the President of Asia Pacific Society of Ophthalmic Plastic & Reconstructive Surgery, the President of Asia Pacific Society of Ocular Oncology and Pathology. He has also been entitled as the Fellow of Royal College of Ophthalmologists and the Fellow Ad Hominem of Royal College of Surgeons of Edinburgh.

As the first or corresponding author, he has published 159 SCI papers on Cell Stem Cell, Genome Biology, Nucleic Acids Res et al. Among which 8 papers' IF is greater than 10, and the total IF is 538. He has also obtained 17 patents. Owing to his clinical and scientific achievements, he has won two second prizes of Chinese National Science and Technology Progress Award, three first prizes of Shanghai Science and Technology Progress Award and the first prize of High Education Science and Technology Progress Award.

He has made 32 keynote speeches at national and international ophthalmic conferences, and established the course of "new progress in orbital surgery" at American Academy of Ophthalmology's annual meeting. He has won the award for outstanding contribution to Asia Pacific ophthalmology, and the award for outstanding achievement in Chinese ophthalmology.

医学药学奖获得者

耿 美 玉

耿美玉，女，1963年8月出生于山东省威海市。1986年和1989年于山东医科大学（现山东大学医学院）分别获得学士和硕士学位，1997年获日本东京大学药学博士学位。1989—2006年在中国海洋大学工作，历任助教、讲师、教授；2006年5月加入中国科学院上海药物研究所，历任副所长、党委副书记、党委书记等职。现任上海药物研究所研究员、学术所长，兼任中国抗癌协会抗癌药物专业委员会副主任委员、中国药理学会肿瘤药理学专业委员会副理事长、国家自然科学基金委员会医学部"十三五战略规划"专家组副组长。获中国工程院光华工程科技奖、吴阶平·保罗杨森医学药学奖等。

耿美玉长期致力于重大复杂疾病的创新药物研发，在抗阿尔茨海默病（AD）和抗肿瘤创新药物研发及生物标志物研究工作方面取得了系列有重大国际影响力的创新性成果，为我国重大新药创制和个性化治疗作出了突出贡献。

一、研发国际首个抗 AD 病程改变和症状改善药物 GV-971，有望突破 AD 领域 17 年无新药上市的困境

AD 治疗是医学领域的世界性难题，抗 AD 药物研发尤为艰难。300 余个进入临床研究的候选药物均以失败告终，造成 17 年无抗 AD 新药问世的窘境。耿美玉潜心研究 22 年，成功研发抗 AD 原创新药 GV-971，被业界誉为 AD 药物研发领域近十余年来的重大突破。

针对 AD 病程进展关键分子 β 淀粉样蛋白（Aβ）聚集及其神经毒性产生均需内源性糖链参与这一病理基础，耿美玉建立了"Aβ 多位点拮抗–神经元保护–血脑屏障突破"一体化的抗 AD 药物筛选体系，从海藻多糖降解产物中发现寡糖分子 GV-971 具有显著的抗 AD 药效。818 例轻 / 中度 AD 患者随机双盲、安慰剂对照、为期 36 周的 3 期临床研究表明，GV-971 可明显改善轻 / 中度 AD 患者认知功能障碍，显著阻止病程恶化，且能持续改善症状；与安慰剂组相比，认知功能障碍改善 2.54 分（$p < 0.0001$），疗效明显优于上市药物

（临床上最好药物多奈哌齐认知功能障碍改善得分仅为 1.9），安全性良好。该研究结果于 2018 年 10 月在第 11 届国际 AD 临床试验大会（CTAD）作为主旨报告首次披露后，引起业界广泛好评。大会执行主席 Schindler 评价"这是继胆碱酯酶抑制剂之后十余年来领域最振奋人心的结果"。国际 AD 临床研究终身成就奖获得者、美国克利夫兰诊所 Cummings 评价"GV-971 的 3 期临床研究展示出坚实、持续的认知功能改善作用，有望成为 AD 治疗新方案"。美国班纳 AD 研究所所长 Reiman 评价"GV-971 独特的作用机理和令人鼓舞的认知功能改善作用将为 AD 患者提供多元化选择"。该成果入选中国科学院改革开放四十周年标志性重大科技成果。

耿美玉还对 GV-971 的治疗机制进行了深入研究，发现在 AD 进程中，肠道菌群失衡导致外周血中苯丙氨酸和异亮氨酸的异常增加，进而诱导外周促炎性 Th1 细胞的分化、增殖及向脑内侵润。侵润入脑的 Th1 细胞和脑内固有的 M1 型小胶质细胞共同活化，导致 AD 相关神经炎症的发生。GV-971 可重塑肠道菌群平衡、降低外周促炎氨基酸的累积、减轻脑内神经炎症，进而改善认知障碍、达到治疗 AD 的效果。据此，耿美玉提出 AD 整体治疗策略，为突破 AD 治疗提供了原创方案。国际著名专家美国神经学协会主席、华盛顿大学 David M. Holtzman 教授等撰文同期发表题为 The microbiome：A target for Alzheimer disease? 评述，认为"这项新的工作证明了 GV-971 可通过重塑肠道菌群，减弱 Aβ 相关病理特征，为靶向肠道菌群的 AD 治疗新策略提供了更进一步的证据""毫无疑问，该数据为新近涌现的靶向肠道菌群的 AD 治疗新策略提供了进一步的支持，可通过 GV-971 或进一步探索其他新策略减慢 AD 疾病进程"。

二、紧密结合肿瘤临床治疗需求，研发原创抗肿瘤新药，实现临床转化

20 世纪 90 年代，靶向激酶抗肿瘤药物的临床成功开启了肿瘤靶向治疗的新时代。然而，由于肿瘤的高度异质性，药物临床治疗有效率低、临床转化困难。针对这一困境，耿美玉以提高临床有效率为目标，建立了贴近临床病理特征的药物研究技术体系，针对敏感群体布局新药研发，并将此研究策略拓展到表观遗传、肿瘤免疫和肿瘤代谢领域，极大提升了个性化药物的研发效率，加速了原创新药的研发进程。

应用这一策略，她成功研发了 10 余个抗肿瘤候选新药，5 个已进入临床研究。其中，我国首个 ALK 二代抑制剂丁二酸复瑞替尼（SAF-189s）临床研究取得重大突破。I 期临床研究结果表明，对 37 例 ALK 阳性的非小细胞肺癌患者治疗有效率达 89.5%，疾病控制率达 100%，且对一代上市药物 Crizotinib、二代抑制剂 Ceritinib 耐药患者及脑转移患者疗效显著（脑转移控制率 100%），有望成为同类产品中的优势品种。高选择性 c-Met 抑制剂 SCC244 避免了多靶点抑制剂的潜在毒性，在联合用药方面具有鲜明的竞争优势，能增敏肿瘤免疫治疗，即将完成临床 I 期研究。新型 FGFR/CSF1R 抑制剂 3D185（HH185）与现有 FGFR 抑制剂相比，具有重塑微环境、协同拮抗肿瘤的特性，已启动临床 I 期研究，截至 2019 年 5 月已完成三个剂量组的安全性评估，耐受性良好。

三、针对肿瘤临床治疗瓶颈，开展新机制和新生物标志物研究，指导药物的精准治疗

临床实践证明，即使针对敏感群体进行治疗，多数抗肿瘤药物的治疗效果依然有限且极易产生耐药。耿美玉深度挖掘靶点自身特性，结合多维组学开展基于靶点功能机制的标志物研究，发现了一批指示疗效响应、监控耐药发生的生物标志物，并提出针对性的联合用药策略。特别是在拓展表观遗传抗肿瘤药物用于实体瘤的治疗方面取得了基础性突破。

她以组蛋白甲基转移酶 EZH2 抑制剂为切入点，发现抑制 EZH2 导致组蛋白 H3K27 位甲基化向乙酰化修饰转换是该类抑制剂治疗实体瘤无效的原因。进一步研究揭示了 MLL1 表达水平是调控该修饰转换的核心机制，并证实 EZH2 和 BRD4、ERK 抑制剂联用对 EZH2 高表达的广大实体瘤，特别是肝癌、胰腺癌等难治性肿瘤疗效显著。*Cancer Discovery* 杂志发表评述认为"该工作揭示了 MLL 指导 EZH2 高表达肿瘤分层治疗的意义，指出表观遗传与 MAPK 激酶通路联合抑制，有望突破难治性肿瘤治疗困境"。

研究进一步发现白血病抑制因子受体（LIFR）反馈激活是组蛋白去乙酰化酶 HDAC 抑制剂治疗三阴乳腺癌失败的原因，并证实联合 JAK 抑制剂能增强其抗肿瘤疗效。相关论文被 Sci Signal 选为推荐文章，被评价为"该工作揭示通过联合用药有望增加 HDAC 抑制剂在三阴乳腺癌的临床应用"。

耿美玉还发现细胞毒类药物通过激活 AIM2 炎症小体导致肠道毒性；证明 pIgR/p-Yes 能预测 MEK 抑制剂的敏感性；揭示 c-Myc 是 c-Met 和 FGFR 抑制剂治疗的疗效监控标志物。上述研究成果为抗肿瘤药物的精准治疗提供了科学指导。

Awardee of Medical Sciences and Materia Medica Prize, Geng Meiyu

Geng Meiyu, female, was born in Weihai City of Shandong Province in August 1963. She received her B.S and M.S. degrees at Shandong Medical University (currently known as Medical School of Shandong University), and her Ph.D. degree at Tokyo University in 1997. She is currently a professor at Shanghai Institute of Materia Medica, Chinese Academy of Sciences, and serves as the Academic Director General. Dr. Geng has dedicated to innovative drug discovery and development to promote conceptual breakthroughs in Alzheimer's disease (AD) and cancer.

1. Discovery of the first oligosaccharide drug being marked as a clinical breakthrough in anti-AD therapy

Through 22 years of audacious efforts, Dr. Geng spearheaded the discovery and pre-clinical-to-clinical development of sodium oligomannate (GV-971), a marine-derived oligosaccharide for

AD treatment. GV–971 is the first anti–AD drug that has successfully met the primary endpoint of phase 3 clinical trials in the past nearly two decades. It was well received by the renowned experts in AD fields including Dr. Jeffrey Cummings who stated that "the trial of GV–971 consistently showed a cognitive benefit and it has promised as a new therapy for Alzheimer's disease". GV–971 has filed NDA to China NMPA for approval as the first–line therapy for patients with mild–to–moderate AD.

Using GV–971 as a probe, Dr. Geng discovered that the imbalance in microbiota facilitates peripheral immune cells to infiltrate the brain, resulting in enhanced microglial activation that contributes to AD pathogenesis. GV–971 decreases Aβ–related pathologies by reconditioning the gut microbiota. The findings were highlighted by Dr. David M. Holtzman, who commented "this data further supports the emerging idea that modulation of the gut microbiome via treatments such as GV–971 or other strategies should be further explored as novel strategies to slow the progression of AD".

2. The translational research promoting conceptual progress in drug innovation and personalized cancer therapy

Dr. Geng has led the development of 11 targeted anticancer drugs, with 5 undergoing clinical trials in China. Among them, a novel anaplastic lymphoma kinase (ALK) inhibitor SAF–189s achieves a disease control rate of 100% and is responded in patients resistant to approved ALK inhibitors in phase I study, suggesting the potential as the best–in–class.

Dr. Geng's research has made conceptual progress in personalized cancer therapy. A highlight is the personalized therapeutic solutions for epigenetic therapeutics, including methyltransferase EZH2 and histone deacetylases (HDAC) inhibitors. She discovered that the intrinsic status of MLL1 informs precision therapy of a combinational regimen with robust efficacy in a broad spectrum of EZH2–aberrant solid tumors. She also discovered that combining JAK inhibitions expands the benefit of HDAC inhibitors to solid tumors like triple–negative breast cancer.

医学药学奖获得者

刘中民

刘中民，1956 年 11 月出生于江苏省南京市。1992 年毕业于上海第二医科大学，获医学博士学位。1992—1997 年在上海第二医科大学附属仁济医院任心胸外科常务主任、主任医师、教授，对复杂、疑难心胸外科疾病的诊断和手术治疗以及危重患者的抢救积累了独到的经验，其间分别赴美国旧金山圣玛利医院、德国心脏中心访问学习。1997 年至今，先后担任同济大学附属东方医院副院长、院长，同济大学医学院临床三系主任，同济大学创伤医学研究所所长，同济大学医学院急诊与灾难医学系主任，同济大学东方临床医学院院长等职。兼任中华医学会灾难医学分会和中华预防医学会灾难预防医学分会创始主任委员，世界急诊与灾难医学会唯一中国理事，亚太灾难医学会副主席，中华医师协会心血管外科学医师分会会长，中华预防医学会伤害预防与控制分会副主任委员等职。

刘中民长期从事心胸外科学、急诊与灾难医学、干细胞研究，取得了一系列系统性成果。主持国家级科研项目 10 项；发表学术论文 392 篇，其中 SCI 论文 97 篇（第一或通讯作者 60 篇），总引用 1000 余次；获国家授权专利 7 项、软件著作权 2 项；主编教材和专著 7 部；获国家科技进步奖 1 项、省市级科技奖等 14 项。

一、灾难医学方向

20 世纪 90 年代中期，刘中民把满足浦东百姓"看病不过江"的需求作为目标，结合浦东开发与城市疾病谱的变化，优先发展急救医学。在国内率先创造了一体化急救医学模式，创建同济大学急诊与灾害医学系，并常年组织医护人员向社会普及急救常识。在汶川地震、玉树地震及上海历次群体性突发公共卫生事件中，刘中民都身先士卒，带领上海市医疗队或组织东方医院医务人员奔赴抗震救灾及应急救援第一线。急诊抢救已成为东方医院乃至上海的一张名片，为此，上海市卫生应急救援队落户东方医院。作为汶川地震上海医疗队队长，2008 年创立了我国第一个急诊与灾难医学系，主编我国第一部规划教材《急诊与灾难医学》并获批 2018 年国家精品在线开放课程；主编了我国研究生规划教材《灾难医学》，并编写国内第一套科普动漫读物《图说灾难逃生自救丛书》；建立国家紧急医学救援队，并成为 WHO 第一支认证的国际应急医疗队。创立中华医学会灾难医学分会、中华预防医学会灾难预防医学分会并担任主任委员，通过规范灾难医学救援共识、建立灾难现场批量伤急救原则和标准，引领我国灾难应急医疗救援的发展方向，并逐步与国际灾难医学救援接轨。针对国内民众普遍缺少灾难防范和逃生知识的现状，推广灾难逃生科普新模式，创立居民小区"卫生应急平安屋"作为普及、培训民众灾难逃生自救技术的基地；通过融媒体形式培训和普及 200 余万人，推动灾难逃生科普进社区、进农村、进学校、进楼宇。成果获国家科技进步奖二等奖、上海市教学成果一等奖等。

二、干细胞方向

针对心力衰竭 5 年存活率低，刘中民开展了干细胞治疗心衰的研究，先后主持干细胞领域的科技部重点研发计划项目、张江国家自主创新示范区重大专项等。负责上海市 Ⅳ 类高峰学科"干细胞与转化"学科建设，是国家首批干细胞临床研究备案机构和上海市首批"四新"基地负责人。牵头成立上海和长三角干细胞产业联盟。率先在国内打造集干细胞基础研究、临床前研究、临床研究、制备质检、转化与应用于一体的全流程创新服务平台——张江国家自主创新示范区干细胞转化医学产业基地。为规范干细胞生产制备和加速干细胞技术及成果转化，牵头起草并发布国内首部干细胞制备与质检的行业标准，并推动上海科创中心干细胞战略资源库和临床研究功能平台建设由国际"并跑"向"领跑"转变。作为中国干细胞研发的倡导、推动和实践者，因成就突出被授予上海市张江杰出创新创业人才奖。

三、心胸外科方向

刘中民擅长各种复杂、疑难先天性心脏病、风湿性瓣膜病、冠心病、大血管病的外科手术治疗，多项手术达到国内先进水平，如应用德国先进技术自制的异种无支架带瓣管道用于治疗复杂先心病、采用异种无支架主动脉瓣和生物二尖瓣治疗风湿性联合瓣膜病变等。

作为国内最早开展人工心脏和心肺移植治疗终末期心衰的医生，刘中民以解决临床问题为导向，致力于心脏病相关机制和器械研究。1998 年，他在德国心脏中心进修时，学习心室辅助装置的相关知识和技术，并开始临床应用和研发。1999 年引进人工心脏技术，探讨人工心脏在国内应用的适应证、辅助循环期间凝血功能的变化、减少并发症的途径、终止辅助循环的时机。2007 年获得科技部"863"计划支持，历经 3 年，研制出具有完全自主知识产权的国产化可植入式心室辅助装置样机，实现无级调速、转速、流量、压力达到植入实时同步测量。在流体动力性能方面的指标已优于国外同类产品，达到国内领先水平，相关成果成功转让给企业，为从根本上解决器官移植供体不足问题奠定了基础。成果获中华医学科技奖二等奖、上海市医学科技奖二等奖等。

Awardee of Medical Sciences and Materia Medica Prize, Liu Zhongmin

Liu Zhongmin was born in Nanjing City of Jiangsu Province in November 1956. In 1992, he graduated from Shanghai Second Medical University with a medical doctor degree. From 1992 to 1997, he served as the executive director, chief physician and professor in Thoracic Surgery Department at Renji Hospital of Shanghai Second Medical University, where he accumulated unique experience in the diagnosis and surgical treatment of complicated and difficult thoracic surgery diseases and the rescue of critical patients. During that time, he visited the St. Mary's Hospital in San Francisco, USA, and the Heart Center in German to improve himself. Since 1997, he has been serving as vice president and then president of Shanghai Eastern Hospital of Tongji University, Department chair of the 3rd Clinical College of Tongji University School of Medicine, Director of the Trauma Medical Institute of Tongji University, Department chair of the Emergency and Disaster Medicine of Tongji University. He also serves concurrently as Director of the Disaster Medical Branch of the Chinese Medical Association and the Disaster Prevention Medicine Branch of the Chinese Preventive Medicine Association, the only Chinese committee of the World Emergency and Disaster Medicine Association, Vice chairman of the Asia Pacific Disaster Medicine Association, Chairman of the Cardiovascular Surgery Branch of the Chinese Medical Association, Member of the Health Emergency Expert Advisory Committee of the Emergency Department, and Director of the Injury Prevention and Control Branch of the Chinese Preventive Medicine Association.

Professor Zhongmin Liu has been engaged in cardiothoracic surgery, emergency and disaster medicine, stem cell research, in which he achieved a series of systematic results and pioneering work. He has been in charge of 10 national scientific research projects and published 392 academic papers, including 97 SCI papers (60 first or corresponding authored papers), over 1000 total citations, 7 national authorized patents, 2 software copyright patents, 7 scientific books; 1 national award for science and technology achievement, and 14 science and technology awards at provincial and/or municipal levels.

医学药学奖获得者

王 松 灵

王松灵，1962年11月出生于湖南省湘乡市。1989年毕业于北京医科大学口腔医学系，获医学博士学位。1991—1992年在日本东京医科齿科大学做访问学者；1996—1998年在美国国立卫生研究院牙颅颌研究所做高级访问学者。现任首都医科大学副校长，全国政协委员，中华口腔医学会副会长，北京医学会副会长，中国高等教育学会口腔医学教育学组组长；*Oral Diseases* 及 *JOR* 副主编，《中华口腔医学杂志》等6本期刊副主编。发表论文209篇，其中以通讯作者发表在 *PNAS*、*Blood*、*Nat Commun* 等英文论文117篇，英文 review article 11篇；以第一完成人获2003年及2010年国家科技进步奖二等奖2项、2018年北京市科技进步奖一等奖；获国际口腔权威的威廉盖茨（William J. Gies）奖、吴阶平医药创新奖、中源协和生命医学奖——成就奖、干细胞转化成果奖；入围Elsevier "中国高被引学者"榜，当选英国皇家外科学院（爱丁堡）杰出 fellow。口腔医学界首位获国家杰出青年科学基金学者，首批入选北京学者。

王松灵研究方向为唾液腺疾病、牙发育和再生研究，他提出慢性腮腺炎性疾病新分类并创建新疗法；揭示腮腺是硝酸盐转运的关键器官，发现人细胞膜硝酸盐转运通道及硝酸盐对人体组织器官的重要保护作用；揭示牙发育新机制，研发牙髓干细胞新药，成功实现生物性牙齿再生，在以上方面作出了一系列开创性研究工作。

一、提出慢性腮腺炎性疾病新分类并创建新疗法

传统观点认为儿童复发性腮腺炎可能是自身免疫病，而王松灵研究表明其与儿童腮腺保护性免疫低下有关，该病大多可自愈或转归为腺体良性肥大，并非自身免疫病。采用腮腺局部碘油灌注取得良好疗效，并规范其治疗，避免了腮腺毁坏性治疗，保存该病的腮腺功能。根据病因学特点，首次命名"慢性阻塞性腮腺炎"。按照治疗原则，提出腮腺慢性炎性疾病新分类，解决了传统分类命名混乱而难以指导治疗的临床难题。该分类

被教科书及专著采用，在国内外广泛应用，获 2003 年国家科技进步奖二等奖。应用唾液腺内镜微创技术，发现导管腔内纤维样阻塞物为慢性阻塞性腮腺炎新病因，内镜微创介入技术剔除纤维样阻塞物具有较好临床疗效。主持制定我国《内镜诊断治疗唾液腺疾病操作指南（试行）》，推动我国唾液腺内镜微创技术应用。

王松灵还发现干燥综合征骨髓间充质干细胞功能明显受损，首次用异体间充质干细胞移植使机体免疫重新取得平衡，临床疗效良好。研究成果被 F1000 推荐，专家评述该研究建立了治疗干燥综合征新的有效方法。

二、发现哺乳动物细胞膜硝酸盐转运通道，揭示硝酸盐器官保护新功能

一般认为，硝酸盐及亚硝酸盐对人体健康的不利影响较大，而人的唾液中硝酸盐含量比血液高约 10 倍，其生理意义不明。王松灵通过对唾液中硝酸盐转运来源、机制及功能等进行系列研究，发现转运硝酸盐的关键器官并揭示硝酸盐有利于人体健康的新功能。

1. 发现腮腺是硝酸盐转运的关键器官

发现腮腺主动转运体内约 25% 的硝酸盐至唾液中，进而发现首个哺乳动物细胞膜硝酸盐转运通道（Sialin，SLC17A5）。Sialin 在腮腺、脑、肝、肾等重要脏器中高表达，是负责转运硝酸盐进入细胞的关键第一步，硝酸盐进入细胞内转化为一氧化氮，进而发挥相应功能（*PNAS* 2012）。同期 *PNAS* 发表专题述评，认为该研究为硝酸盐在人类各组织器官的功能研究及全身性疾病的防治提供了关键性科学依据。相关成果获 2018 年北京市科学技术奖一等奖。

由于 SLC17A5 基因是出生后致死基因（敲除该基因的小鼠在出生后 3 周内即死亡），王松灵随后研究建立了基于 CRISPR/Cas9 的二细胞胚胎一步显微注射法构建致死基因敲除小鼠模型的新方法，以进一步研究该基因在硝酸盐转运及维持生理功能中发挥的作用。

2. 揭示硝酸盐保护器官新功能

明确唾液中亚硝酸盐抑制口腔致病菌的作用；发现应激时唾液腺可主动分泌硝酸盐进入胃肠道，以减少胃溃疡、出血等，发挥胃肠道保护功能。*Curr Opin Gastroen* 发表的综述将该成果列为胃十二指肠主要防御机制之一。研究还表明口服硝酸盐通过抑制细胞凋亡来保护唾液腺功能，降低活性氧水平预防全身放射损伤以及预防肝脏衰老。

三、发现牙发育新机制，成功实现生物性牙周组织、牙根和全牙再生

1. 创建小型猪牙发育研究平台，发现牙发育新机制

针对啮齿类动物无乳恒牙替换等缺陷，率先建立具有乳恒牙替换的小型猪牙发育研究平台，揭示小型猪乳恒牙发育各时相形态学特点及时空关系，发现颌骨通过外泌体调控牙冠形成的新机制，为研究乳恒牙替换及全牙再生奠定了坚实的学理基础。

2. 首次在体内构建出牙周组织、生物牙根和全牙

（1）牙周组织再生：针对牙周炎发病率高、致病机制不清、无有效再生手段等棘手

问题，首次提出牙周膜干细胞受损是该病发生的重要机制；揭示异体牙源性干细胞对宿主 T、B 细胞的免疫调节机制，并率先利用牙源性干细胞成功再生小型猪牙周炎所致牙周缺损组织。根据临床转化需求，建立人牙齿干细胞库；发现牙髓干细胞在来源、增殖、抗衰老等方面有明显优势，进而研发出"牙髓间充质干细胞注射液"新药，是我国新的干细胞管理条例颁布以来首个被国家受理的干细胞新药（受理号：CXSL700137）。前期临床研究表明，局部应用该注射液，可有效治疗牙周炎，此药有望成为治疗牙周炎的新方法。

（2）生物牙根和全牙：与合作者提出"生物牙根再生"新理念，利用干细胞复合支架材料在小型猪颌骨中成功再生具有咀嚼功能的生物牙根，且与种植牙相比有明显生物学优势。该生物牙根被美国国立牙科博物馆永久收藏，展览注释为"牙齿缺失修复提供全新的生物性修复方法"。还发现 C-kit 阳性骨髓细胞是全牙再生新的种子细胞，相关论文获得 *JDR* 最佳封面论文奖及国际口腔权威奖 William Gies Award；并成功实现了小型猪颌骨原位全牙再生。有关成果获 2010 年国家科技进步奖二等奖。

Awardee of Medical Sciences and Materia Medica Prize, Wang Songling

Wang Songling was born in Xiangxiang City of Hunan Province in November 1962. He graduated as phD from the Department of Stomatology, Beijing Medical University in 1989. From 1991 to 1992, he worked as a visiting scholar at Tokyo Medical and Dental University. From 1996 to 1998, he worked as a visiting scientist at the National Institute of Dentistry and Craniofacial Research, National Institutes of Health. He is currently Vice President of Capital Medical University and member of the CPPCC National Committee, Vice President of Chinese Stomatological Association, Vice President of Beijing Medical Association and Head of Stomatological Education Group of Chinese Higher Education Association. He is assoicate editor for Oral Diseases, JOR, China Journal of Stomatology and other six journals. He has published 209 papers, including 117 in PNAS, Blood, Nat Commun and 11 other review articles in English. As the first principal investigator, he won second grade prizes for national scientific and technological award twice in 2003 and 2010, and the first grade prize for Beijing scientific and technological award in 2018; the William J. Gies award, Wu Jieping Prize Medical Innovation Award, VCANBIO Award for Bioscience and Medicine-Achievement Award, Stem Cell Translation study Prize. He is included in Elsevier 2018 Most Cited Chinese Researcher. He has been selected as fellow *ad hominem* of the Royal College of Surgery (Edinburgh). He was the first scholar who achieve The National Science Fund for Distinguished Young Scholars in China dentistry research field, and one of the first batch of Beijing scholars.

Wang Songling mainly investigates salivary gland diseases, tooth development and regeneration. He established new classification and treatment standard of chronic parotid gland diseases, revealed parotid gland is the critical organ of nitrate transportation, nitrate transporter of human cell membrane and important protective effect of nitrate on human tissues and organs, new mechanism of tooth development, developed dental pulp stem cells as a new drug and constructed bio-root tooth regeneration successfully. He has achieved series of excellent research work in scientific fields, such as establishing new classification of chronic parotid gland diseases and new therapies, discovery of nitrate transporter in mammalian cell membranes and reveal new functions of nitrate organ protection, and discover new mechanism of tooth development and successfully regeneration of biological periodontal tissue, root and whole teeth.

医学药学奖获得者

吴 效 科

　　吴效科，1966年12月出生于江苏省滨海县。1988年获徐州医学院学士学位；1994年获第二军医大学妇产科学硕士学位；1996年获南京大学医学院生理学博士学位；1998—2001年在芬兰图尔库大学进行博士后（西医妇产科学）研究；2005—2008年在黑龙江中医药大学进行博士后（中医妇科学）研究；2009—2012年在中国中医科学院进行博士后（科研方法学）研究。现任黑龙江中医药大学附属第一医院妇科主任、博士生导师、黑龙江中医药大学中医妇科学国家重点学科（教育部、国家局等）带头人、中医妇产科国家临床重点专科（卫计委）继承人，世界中医药学会联合会生殖医学专业委员会会长和围产学会副会长，国家中医药管理局妇科重点实验室和研究室主任，是全国妇产科领域唯一"国家中医临床研究基地"首席专家。2019年9月起兼任哈尔滨工业大学附属黑龙江省医院院长。国家卫计委"十三五"规划教材《中医妇科学》英文版主编和《中西医结合妇产科学》主编，为2015年度和2019年度中国工程院院士有效候选人。

　　吴效科从事中西医结合妇科相关领域工作近30年，作出了一系列开创性研究成果。

　　1. 发现疾病新机理

　　在系统梳理历代中医文献、结合多囊卵巢综合征（PCOS）中医临床实践、传承学科韩百灵和王秀霞等老一代妇科名家学术思想的基础上，探索提出PCOS"痰壅胞宫"中医原创理论，并进一步研究发现PCOS"痰壅胞宫"现代生物学基础为卵巢胰岛素抵抗，在国际上首次发现PCOS卵巢胰岛素抵抗病理新机制，引发国外学者的强烈反响和关注，认为该研究是"揭示生殖与代谢偶联的原创性发现"。传承创新"天癸失序、冲任停滞"生殖藏象病机及其"卵巢代谢性核受体失衡和性腺轴生殖-代谢信号传导障碍"等现代分子表征的中医机制，并发表在美国科学院院刊等国际学术期刊上，增强了中医妇科的国际影响力。相关成果获2014年度国家科技进步奖二等奖1项、省部级一等奖8项，授权发明专利9项，填补了国家奖制度设立至今本学科专科领域奖获奖空白。

2. 制定行业新标准

近 10 年来，吴效科多次进行对外交流并密切跟踪学术进步及其专家队伍，主办承办 6 次不孕症国际学术交流会，遴选国内外顶级学者 31 位，依托世中联生殖学会、美国生殖医学会、欧洲人类胚胎与生殖学会和亚太妇产科学会，牵头制定不孕症临床试验报告的技术新标准——哈尔滨国际共识，获本学科顶级杂志 *Hum Reprod* 和 *Fertil Steril* 授权发表，成为目前我国医学界主导制定的唯一国际标准技术规范，该国际共识被《新英格兰医学杂志》《美国医学会杂志》《英国医学杂志》等世界顶级临床期刊等广泛引用。此外，他还参与制定其他中西医国际、国内和行业标准、规范和指南 6 项，并发表于美国《内科年鉴》，首次将中医生殖带入国际舞台，彰显了中医妇科国际地位的提升及话语权，该研究获得第 15 届吴阶平医药奖。

3. 中医协作创新

依托临床基地、重点学科、专科、实验室、研究室、GCP 等 8 个卓越平台，领导国内外同行开展不孕症临床试验和基础研究，组建中医生殖协作网。其中，黄连素的研究入选 2016 年度具有世界影响力的中国十大临床研究。

目前，已发表论文 400 余篇，其中 SCI 论文 120 余篇，论文被《新英格兰医学杂志》《柳叶刀》《自然系列杂志》等引用 6000 余次。

培养博士生 24 名、硕士生百余名；其带领的中医学科团队成员包括"千人计划"外籍学者 2 名、"长江学者""龙江学者"讲座和特聘教授 5 名、国家中医名师 5 名、妇科博士生导师 6 名、二级教授 5 名。作为团队带头人，吴效科荣获了 2010 年度和 2014 年度的"美国生殖医学会"杰出贡献奖，并于 2015 年入选国家"百千万"人才工程计划，被授予"有突出贡献"的中青年专家。

Awardee of Medical Sciences and Materia Medica Prize, Wu Xiaoke

Wu Xiaoke, born in Binhai County of Jiangsu Province in December 1966, graduated from Xuzhou Medical College in 1988 with a bachelor's degree, a master's degree in obstetrics and gynecology from the Second Military Medical University in 1994, a doctor's degree in physiology from the Medical College of Nanjing University in 1996, a postdoctoral degree in Turku University, Finland, 1998—2001 (Obstetrics and Gynecology of Western Medicine), and a postdoctoral degree in Heilongjiang University of Traditional Chinese Medicine (gynecology of Traditional Chinese Medicine), Postdoctoral Research Methodology, Chinese Academy of Traditional Chinese Medicine, 2009—2012. He is currently the director of gynecology and doctoral supervisor of the First Affiliated Hospital of Heilongjiang University of Traditional Chinese Medicine, the leader of the national key disciplines of Gynecology of traditional Chinese medicine (Ministry of Education, State Bureau, etc.) of Heilongjiang University of Traditional

Chinese Medicine, the heir of the national key clinical specialty of gynecology and obstetrics of traditional Chinese medicine (Health Planning Commission), the chairman of the Reproductive Medicine Committee of the World Federation of Traditional Chinese Medicine Associations and the Vice President of Society of Perinatal Obstetrics, Director of the Key Laboratory and Research Laboratory of Gynecology of the State Administration of Traditional Chinese Medicine, is the only Chief Expert of the National Clinical Research Base of Traditional Chinese Medicine in the field of Obstetrics and gynecology in China.As the editor-in-chief of the English edition of the 13th Five-Year Plan textbook "Gynecology of Traditional Chinese Medicine" and the editor-in-chief of "Gynecology and Obstetrics of Integrated Traditional Chinese and Western Medicine" of the National Health Planning Commission, he is an effective candidate for academicians of the Chinese Academy of Engineering in 2015 and 2019. Since September 2019, he has also been the president of Heilongjiang Hospital affiliated to Harbin University of Technology. Professor Wu has been engaged in gynecology related fields of integrated Chinese and Western medicine for nearly 30 years, and has made a series of pioneering research results. The main contributions included discovering the new mechanism of disease, establishing new industry standards, and collaborative innovation of TCM.

医学药学奖获得者

庾石山

庾石山，1962年8月出生于广西壮族自治区全州县。博士，研究员，博士生导师。1993年毕业于中国协和医科大学药物化学专业，获理学博士学位；1995—1996年在奥地利维也纳大学作博士后研究。1996年回国后在中国医学科学院药物研究所工作，先后任副研究员、研究员。现任中国医学科学院药物研究所副所长、"天然药物活性物质与功能"国家重点实验室主任。国家杰出青年科学基金获得者，教育部"长江学者"特聘教授，国家卫生计生委"有突出贡献的中青年专家"。兼任国家药典委员会委员和 *Journal of Asian Natural Products Research* 副主编。

庾石山一直从事天然药物化学和创新药物研究，在活性物质发现、新药创制和成果转化等方面取得了系统性和原创性成果。

一、攻克中草药新活性物质识别与获取的技术难关，创建新的研究模式，发现310个新的高活性化合物，为中草药活性物质的阐明和新药创制奠定基础

针对中草药复杂体系中新活性成分"难识别、难获取"等瓶颈，集成利用色谱与波谱联用及活性测定等多种新方法，攻克新活性物质的识别、锁定和定向获取等技术难关，创建排除已知化合物的新型研究模式，并应用该模式从46种中草药中获取760余个新化合物，发现310个用传统研究模式难以得到的高活性化合物。如从闹羊花中发现镇痛作用比吗啡强5～6倍的二萜化合物，从娃儿藤中发现能透过血脑屏障、具有显著抗肿瘤作用的右旋去氧娃儿藤宁等，充分显示了新研究模式的先进性和实用性，显著提升了我国在该领域的研究水平和能力。部分成果在化学顶级期刊 *Angew. Chem. Int. Ed.* 和 TOP5 期刊 *Org. Lett.*，*J. Med. Chem.* 发表论文140余篇，其中14个新骨架化合物被本领域国际最权威期刊 *Nat. Prod. Rep.* 遴选为国际天然产物研究的重要进展。尤其是发表在 *Org. Lett.* 的伸筋草素A和B的生源途径假说被美国科学院院士（化学领域）K. N. Houk 教授评价为"提出的独特 1，3-偶极环加成反应生物合成机理引领并激起寻找首个 1，3-偶极环加成合成酶的研究热点"，同时 K. N. Houk 教授通过量子计算研究从理论上证实该假说。部分成果以第一完成人获得国家科技进步奖二等奖 1 项。

二、首次全面揭示了野生熊胆和引流熊胆粉的成分构成，阐明活性物质的比例与药效的关系，创制出人工熊胆粉

熊胆具有清热、平肝、明目的功效，用于惊风抽搐、外治目赤肿痛、咽喉肿痛等症，为中国临床常用的名贵药材之一。一方面，目前市场上使用的引流熊胆粉由于动物伦理问题饱受质疑与诟病；另一方面，由于熊的生存状况、身体状态、地域与饲养管理条件存在差异，引流熊胆粉的质量参差不齐。因此，亟须研制新的熊胆药材代用品。

经与王晓良课题组合作，在充分研究野生熊胆和引流熊胆粉的基础上，全面揭示了熊胆和引流熊胆粉的成分构成，阐明了其中的药效物质，为人工熊胆粉的研制提供了坚实的科学依据，并研制出熊胆和熊胆粉的药效物质或药效物质的代用品（包括 5 种结合胆酸、2 种游离胆酸以及包括牛磺酸在内的 16 种以上的氨基酸、各种微量元素等）。同时，筛选出最佳配方，并以此配方研制出人工熊胆粉。人工熊胆粉有效成分的组成及比例与熊胆基本一致。临床前的研究结果表明，产品质量稳定、可控，药效等同于目前使用的引流熊胆粉且安全性良好，已获得国家药监局新药临床试验批件（批件号：2018L02735）。

人工熊胆粉的研制成功有望解决熊胆不能供应、引流熊胆粉质量不稳定的重大难题，同时为促进国家中药事业的可持续发展和保护濒危动物作出了贡献。

三、主持我国重大原创药物的成果转化，成功实现规模化生产，带动创新药物研究领域的产学研结合

领导团队攻克了我国重大原创新药双环醇和人工麝香规模化生产的关键技术，两个药物近三年的产值超过 40 亿元，产生了显著的社会和经济效益。以主要完成人获得国家科技进步奖一等奖和国家科技进步奖二等奖各 1 项。

领导团队创建"天然药物活性物质与功能"国家重点实验室并入选教育部"创新团队"，推动了天然药物化学学科的发展。二十年来，共培养博士生 44 名、硕士生 10 名。研究成果以通讯作者或共同通讯作者发表论文 166 篇，包括国际上化学领域的著名期刊 *Angew. Chem. Int. Ed.*，*Org. Lett.* 等 SCI 论文 146 篇；获授权发明专利 12 项（其中 2 项分别获得美国、欧洲、日本等授权）；获国家科技进步奖一等奖 1 项、二等奖 2 项；主编专著 2 部。

Awardee of Medical Sciences and Materia Medica Prize, Yu Shishan

Yu Shishan was born in Quanzhou County of Guangxi Zhuang Autonomous Region in August 1962. He is a full professor and a doctoral supervisor at the Institute of Materia Medica, Chinese Academy of Medical Sciences & Peking Union Medical College (IMM, CAMS & PUMC) . He received his Ph.D. in Medicinal Chemistry in 1993 from Peking Union Medical College. After the postdoctoral research at University of Vienna, Austria (1995—1996), he joined the IMM, CAMS & PUMC as an associate professor in 1995 and was promoted to full professor in 1998. He is the deputy director of IMM, CAMS & PUMC and the chairman of the State Key Laboratory of Bioactive Substance and Function of Natural Medicines. He has won the National Science Fund for Distinguished Young Scholars, and been titled the Chair Professor of Cheung Kong Scholars Programme of Ministry of education, etc. He is a committee member of Chinese Pharmacopeia Commission and the associate editor in chief of Journal of Asian Natural Products Research. His main research interests focus on the discovery, structures and functions of bioactive substances from natural medicines, and the development of innovative drugs based on natural products, and his perseverance for scientific research has him make a series of achievements.

Firstly, he invented a new research model to break through the technical bottleneck in identifying and obtaining new bioactive substances from Chinese medicinal plants, and more than 760 new compounds were isolated from 46 Chinese medicinal plants, including 310 compounds exhibited significant bioactivities. For example, two diterpenoids from *Rhododendron molle* were found to be more potent than morphine for both acute and inflammatory pain models, which provides more source for innovative drug research. Moreover, 14 compounds with novel structure were reported as highlights on the famous international journal of *Nat. Prod. Rep.*, and gain highly respect from many international colleagues.

Secondly, he developed the substitute of bear bile — "Artificial Bear Bile Powder", whose results of Phase I clinical trial showed that it was safe and ready for Phase II clinical trial. This research will availably solve the historical supply problem of bear bile as drug substance, and is of great significance for protection of endangered animals and sustainable development of traditional Chinese medicine.

Thirdly, he also made creative contributions towards the transformation of science and technology achievements of Bicyclol Tablets and Muoschus Artifactus, which are two major innovative drugs in our country, used for treating hepatitis and replacing for natural musk, respectively. Their output value had more than 4 billion RMB over the past three years, resulting in enormous social and economic benefits.

He has published 146 research papers in peer-reviewed/reputed international SCI journals such as *Angew. Chem. Int. Ed.*, *Org. Lett.*, *J. Med. Chem.*, etc., twelve licensed patents and two monographs. His research achievement won the first prize of National Science and Technology Progress Award one time, the second prize of National Science and Technology Progress Award two times.

For over 20 years, he has had more than 50 postgraduate students, and he has dedicated all his effort to cultivating outstanding young scientists in pharmaceutical fields, such as Prof. You-Cai Hu, who has won the National Science Fund of China for Excellent Young Scholars, and been titled the Young and Middle-aged Science and Technology Innovation Leading Talents of Ministry of Science and Technology, etc. As the chairman of the State Key Laboratory, he has introduced many young talents from overseas to support the laboratory with advanced technologies, valuable expertise and outstanding human resources.

机械电力技术奖获得者

姜 培 学

姜培学，1964年9月出生于山东省烟台市。1986年毕业于清华大学热能工程系（现能源与动力工程系），获学士学位；同年十月赴苏联莫斯科动力学院攻读博士学位；1991年2月回国，在清华大学能源与动力工程系做博士后。1993年起在清华大学能源与动力工程系任教，其间1998—1999年在英国曼彻斯特大学工学院做访问学者。现任清华大学能源与动力工程系主任、能源与动力工程系工程热物理所所长、清华大学校务委员会委员、清华大学山西清洁能源研究院院长、英国诺丁汉大学名誉教授、俄罗斯国立技术大学名誉教授、英国谢菲尔德大学客座教授、北京国际传热会议主席、国际超临界压力流体传热与流动专家会议4位发起人之一和2019年会议主席。曾任清华大学科研院常务副院长、清华大学学术委员会秘书长。先后担任教育部科技委委员及能源与交通学部委员、国家"863"计划先进能源技术领域可再生能源技术主题专家、国家重点研发计划"可再生能源与氢能技术"重点专项总体专家组组长、中国工程热物理学会常务理事及传热传质学专委会副主任、中国可再生能源学会太阳能热发电专委会副主任。

姜培学长期从事能源动力领域中极端条件能质传递理论、方法与关键技术的研究，在极端条件多孔介质局部非热平衡传热理论、微/纳结构与超临界流体传热调控与计算方法和新型热防护关键技术等方面作出了一系列创新性研究工作。以第一完成人获国家自然科学奖二等奖、教育部自然科学奖一等奖和技术发明奖一等奖各1项，其他部级科技奖5项。自2014年连续5年入选爱思唯尔中国高被引学者榜。

一、多孔介质中流动传热与局部非热平衡传热理论

经典多孔介质流动传热理论基于常规尺度和局部热平衡假设，不能准确描述极端条件下流体与固体间的能质传递规律。姜培学深入研究了固体骨架的连接状态和尺度对多孔介质传热过程产生非单调性影响的现象，阐明了多孔介质流动传热过程的内在

多因素竞争机制和规律，澄清了国际上对结构和尺度如何影响传热的模糊认识，提出了"热桥"概念，定量描述了多孔介质壁面上的非平衡热分流规律，并建立了包含黏性耗散及局部热渗透的多孔介质局部非热平衡传热模型；针对微纳尺度多孔介质中的流动传热，实验发现摩擦阻力及传热系数比经典理论值显著减小，提出包含尺度效应的三维直接数值模拟方法，揭示了微纳尺度和界面热阻等对传热的影响规律，建立了含微尺度效应的局部非热平衡传热模型、纳米孔吸附气体准确表征和计量方法；获得了多孔介质中超临界压力流体的流动传热规律，建立了强变物性影响下多孔介质局部非热平衡传热模型。

上述成果形成了极端条件下多孔介质局部非热平衡传热理论，该理论能准确描述从微纳尺度到大尺度、高速、剧烈变物性等条件下多孔介质中局部非热平衡传热规律，被国际传热学界诸多学者引用和评述，并被应用于研究多孔换热器、强化传热、太阳能利用、发汗冷却、燃料电池等。将该理论应用于页岩渗透率测试及含气量评估，研发出了低渗页岩储层渗透率/扩散系数测量仪，测试下限从国外垄断设备的10nD（纳达西）扩至1nD；成功解决了极低湿条件下高速飞行器天线罩微孔结构中湿分迁移定量描述的难题，指导了天线罩的改进设计，确保了高超声速飞行器飞行试验的成功。

成果获2014年国家自然科学奖二等奖（排名第一）。

二、微/纳结构强化传热与超临界压力流体对流传热

传统强化传热和传热计算模型不适用于以超高热流密度、超临界压力及微纳尺度为特征的新一代能源动力系统。在成果一的基础上，姜培学发现多孔结构壁面上的大孔隙率是限制传热能力提高的瓶颈，提出了调控孔隙率以强化传热的方法，并研发出性能优异的微板翅强化传热结构和微型换热器，进而提出了微纳米混合结构强化喷雾冷却、超临界压力流体冲击冷却等方法，解决了超高热流密度冷却难题；揭示了超临界压力流体在微细通道中湍流传热的强化与恶化机理及规律，提出了消除传热非稳定和恶化的方法，构建了微细通道中超临界压力流体流动传热计算模型，实现了高压下微尺度两相界面的实时追踪和定量测量，揭示出化学反应与多孔多相流动的耦合作用产生自密封的机制，以解决超临界压力能源动力系统热设计与安全性分析难题；发明了基于超临界压力二氧化碳的新型供热与发电系统，实现了跨临界二氧化碳喷射器流场的可视化并建立了计算模型，构建并研发出性能优异的跨临界二氧化碳喷射-压缩制冷与供热系统。

研发的微型换热器被国外知名学者作为最优换热性能的代表予以引用，提出的微纳结构强化喷雾冷却方法被认为是强化传热最新技术的代表和未来发展方向，建立的超临界压力热设计方法被国外学者应用于商用跨临界二氧化碳热泵换热器的设计。研究成果被应用于我国首个二氧化碳地质封存示范项目、干热岩开发、超临界二氧化碳热泵及太阳能发电系统等。

三、高温 / 高热流条件的新型主动冷却热防护

热防护技术是发展超高声速航天器的关键技术之一，缺少可靠的主动冷却技术和设计软件是热防护技术发展的瓶颈。在成果一、二的基础上，姜培学发明了发汗 / 气膜 / 冲击 / 逆喷复合冷却、自抽吸自适应且可重复使用的发汗冷却等新方法，被 *Physics World* 专题报道；研发出高温燃烧室燃料喷注部件的发汗冷却技术，通过了高速飞行条件的试验考核，使前缘冷却效率提高 1 倍，解决了燃料加注部件在高温火焰中的热防护难题；研发出飞行器前缘强激波引起的极高热流密度的主动冷却热防护技术，冷却能力提高 6 倍，实现了几十 MW/m² 的高冷却能力；率先获得了旋转条件下超临界压力正癸烷流动传热规律并建立了计算模型和方法，开发出超临界吸热型碳氢燃料主动冷却与热裂解、超临界氢发汗冷却的计算模型与设计软件。

研究成果被应用于更高参数液体冷却涡轮设计，并被应用于液氢液氧重型火箭发动机和某飞行器国家重大专项的热防护结构设计与研制，发挥了重要的技术支撑作用。

成果获 2017 年教育部技术发明奖一等奖（排名第一）。

姜培学是国家自然科学基金委杰出青年科学基金获得者和创新群体学术带头人、教育部长江学者特聘教授和创新团队带头人、新世纪百千万人才工程国家级人选、我国工程热物理领域的学术带头人之一、北京市教学名师。已培养毕业博士生 28 人、硕士生 27 人、博士后 15 人，为我国能质传递理论与技术的发展、人才培养和国际地位的提升作出了突出贡献。

Awardee of Machinery and Electric Technology Prize，Jiang Peixue

Jiang Peixue was born in Yantai City of Shandong Province in September 1964. He graduated from the Department of Thermal Engineering（now the Department of Energy and Power Engineering）of Tsinghua University in 1986 with a bachelor's degree. In October of 1986，he was sent by the Chinese government to the Moscow Power Engineering Institute of the former Soviet Union for his Ph. D. degree. He returned home in February 1991 and worked as a postdoctoral research associate in the Department of Energy and Power Engineering of Tsinghua University. He has been a faculty member in the Department of Energy and Power Engineering of Tsinghua University since 1993. From 1998 to 1999，he was a visiting scholar at the School of Engineering，University of Manchester，UK. He is currently the dean of the Department of Energy and Power Engineering of Tsinghua University，the director of the Institute of Engineering Thermophysics of the Department of Energy and Power Engineering，the director of the Shanxi Institute of Clean Energy of Tsinghua University，an honorary professor of Nottingham University，an honorary professor of the Russian National University of Technology（Moscow Power Engineering Institute）， and a guest professor of Sheffield University. He is chairman of the Beijing International Symposium on Heat Transfer (ISHT), one of the four founders of the International Meeting of Specialists on Heat Transfer and Fluid Dynamics at Supercritical Pressure (HFSCP) and chairman of HFSCP 2019. He was the executive deputy director of the Scientific R&D Office of Tsinghua University and the Secretary-General of the academic committee of Tsinghua University. He has served as a member of the Science and Technology Committee of the Ministry of Education of China, a member of the Division of Energy and Transportation of the Science and Technology Committee of the Ministry of Education of China, a leader of the expert group of the national key research and development program "Renewable Energy and Hydrogen Energy Technology", a standing council member of the China Society of Engineering Thermophysics and a vice director of the Committee on Heat and Mass Transfer, and a vice director of the Special Committee on Solar Thermal Power Generation of the China Renewable Energy Society.

Jiang Peixue has been engaged in research on heat and mass transfer theories, methods and key technologies in energy and power for extreme conditions for a long time. He has conducted a series of innovative studies on local thermal non-equilibrium heat transfer theory for extreme conditions in porous media, on heat transfer control, on calculational methods for micro/nanostructures and supercritical fluids, and on new key technologies of thermal protection of high temperature fluid streams. He won a second prize National Natural Science Award, a first prize Natural Science Award and a first prize Technology Invention Award of the Ministry of Education, along with five other ministerial science and technology awards. He has been one of the most cited scholars in China for five consecutive years since 2014.

机械电力技术奖获得者

王 秋 良

王秋良，1965年8月出生于湖北省浠水县。1986年毕业于湖北大学物理系，获学士学位；1991年毕业于中国科学院等离子所，获硕士学位；1994年毕业于中国科学院研究生院，获博士学位；1996年赴日本九州大学做博士后研究；之后，分别在韩国电气研究所做STEPI访问学者、韩国三星高等技术研究院任高级研究员、英国牛津仪器公司任高级工程师、德国重离子加速器研究中心任访问教授、澳大利亚伍龙贡大学和昆士兰大学任访问教授、美国麻省理工学院核物理实验室任客座教授。现任中国科学院电工所研究员，中国科学院大学教授。国家杰出青年基金、中组部"万人计划"和中国科学院"百人计划"获得者。

王秋良长期致力于极端强电磁装备的基础理论与工程技术研究，在强电磁装备的构造理论、设计方法与成套技术等方面作出了系统性、创新性成果。以第一完成人获国家奖3项、省部级奖励18项；出版论文498篇、专著6部（含英文2部）；获发明专利授权175件，其中美国授权11项。

一、构建了极端电磁装备非线性跨尺度多场耦合理论体系和求解方法

复杂结构的大规模极端电磁装备是我国装备工业的重要组成部分，在国家高技术领域中占有重要的战略地位。其运行接近材料的极限，研制中普遍存在非线性多场耦合、多类异性构件并存、因冷收缩导致结构参数的不确定性及制造精度难以控制等难题，传统的设计理论通常是采用远离材料与结构的极限点的平均结构模型，不能准确反映装备中非线性多场耦合的本质，严重制约了极端强磁电磁装备的整机性能，成为我国在重大电工装备等领域的技术瓶颈。针对传统理论模型的局限性，王秋良创造性地建立了极端条件下电磁装备设计的多尺度非线性多场耦合理论和开域逆问题混合求解算法，揭示了在极低温与强电磁场作用下超导体的电机械效应和磁热不稳定性等规律，建立了完整的稳健设计理论模型，发明了设计方法和关键制造技术，研制成功可以挑战材料与结构极限的多种类型的电磁装备；研制出突破地磁场约60万倍的世界领先水平高精度强磁系统，欧洲超导期刊 *SNF* 连续以 *highlight* 报道，认为是"耀眼的新进展"；研制出的用于超导托卡马克聚变装置研制软件已在多国研制的聚变堆工程实践中得到应用。

二、建立强磁共振系统的电磁理论与成像方法，突破了系统的精密制造与快速清晰成像技术瓶颈

高性能强磁共振作为一种高清晰的成像方法，可获得研究对象的丰富结构和功能信息。但我国高端磁共振核心技术长期被跨国公司垄断，而高端诊疗磁共振技术是国际上尚未解决的难题。针对强磁共振成像领域的技术瓶颈，王秋良攻克了极端条件下异形非稳态机械结构的强磁共振磁体、（非）对称匀场与梯度、多通道射频和高性能的图像重构方法等国际公认的技术难题，研制成功高性价比的强磁共振设备。发明了超大分裂与短腔宽孔等构形的强磁共振主磁体及其制造技术，获得的成像空间高度开放，建造与运行成本大幅度减少。上述技术实现了装备的高性能、低成本、产业化，不仅改变了我国重大强磁装备完全依赖国外进口的局面，而且系列化产品还被多家整机厂使用。

三、突破无液氦超导磁体系统制造关键技术，解决了其运行长期依赖稀缺氦资源的难题，开拓出新应用领域

液氦是稀缺资源，也是传统超导磁体运行的唯一冷源，保持液氦冷却磁体系统的长期稳定运行是世界性难题。我国液氦长期依赖进口，导致超导磁体的工程化应用受到极大制约。王秋良建立了无液氦超导磁体稳定化理论，提出了无液氦超导磁体的制造技术及稀土纳米掺杂工艺；解决了整机复杂热管理和制造难题，研发出无液氦超导磁体新技术，促进了磁体技术的升级换代。

Awardee of Machinery and Electric Technology Prize, Wang Qiuliang

Wang Qiuliang was born in Xishui County of Hubei Province in August 1965. He got the bachelor's degree from the Department of Physics, Hubei University in 1986, master's degree from the Institute of Plasma Physics, CAS in 1991 and doctor's degree from the Graduate School of the CAS in 1994, and then he was a postdoctoral fellow in the Kyushu University in 1996. Afterwards, he worked as a visiting scholar in the Korea Electro-technology Research Institute, a senior research fellow at the Samsung Advanced Technology Institute, a senior engineer at UK Oxford Instruments, a visiting professor in the GSI Helmholtz zentrum für Schwerionenforschung GmbH, Germany, University of Wollongong and University of Queensland Australia, and a guest professor at the Nuclear Physics Laboratory, Massachusetts Institute of Technology. Now, he is the professor at the Institute of Electrical Engineering CAS and the University of Chinese Academy of Sciences.

Wang Qiuliang has studied the high electromagnetic field technologies for many years. He has breakthrough contributed to the design theories and methods, fabricating technologies for the high electromagnetic field system, especially ultrahigh magnetic field superconducting magnet. He won three National awards and 18 provincial and ministerial awards, published 498 peer review papers, 6 monographs (including 2 English versions) and175 patents (including 11 US) . Because of his distinguished work, he has been granted the "National Natural Science Foundation for Distinguished Young Scientists", "National High Level Talents Special Support Plan" and "CAS Hundred Talents Program" .

(1) The large-scale high field electromagnetic equipment technologies are the important technologies for the national industries, which plays an important strategic position in the national high-tech fields. Due to electromagnetic equipment operated near to the limits of the critical parameters in the material and structure, the development of high electromagnetic field equipment is facing numerous problems, such as the nonlinear multi-field coupling, coexistence of multi-type heterogeneous components, uncertainty of structural parameters and difficulty in the manufacturing accuracy control. A traditional design theories usually adopt an average models that are far from the critical parameters of materials and structures, which cannot accurately calculate the nonlinear multi-field coupling feature and severely restricts the performance of the high electromagnetic field equipment, resulting in technical bottlenecks in the R &D. In order to overcome the drawbacks with the traditional theoretical models, he proposed a multi-scale, nonlinear, multi-field coupling theories and an open-domain hybrid algorithm of inverse problem for electromagnetic field, it is revealing the characteristics of superconductivity in the extremely ultralow temperature and ultrahigh electromagnetic field. A set of robust theoretical models, innovative design methods and key manufacturing techniques has been developed, and successfully applied in the various types of electromagnetic equipment that can challenge the operating threshold of the material and structure. A electromagnetic system with magnetic field intensity over than 600, 000 times higher than the Geomagnetic field has been developed, which was reported as "highlight" by European superconducting journal "SNF" . For the large-scale fusion devices with the supercritical helium cooling, Professor Wang developed a porous medium-electric-network model and obtained the exact solutions of the thermal, electromagnetic, fluid, and force during the coupling between the superconducting state and the normal state. The software has been applied in the engineering of the fusion reactors in many countries.

(2) The Nuclear Magnetic Resonance is a high-resolution imaging methods which can obtain rich structural and functional information of the material. However, high-quality MRI technologies have been controlled by the some foreign high-tech companies. In order to breakthrough the technological bottleneck of high field MRI with very short length and large bore-size, shimming and gradient, multi-channel RF system and high-performance imaging reconstruction software were developed by Professor Wang. He invented a large-gap open MRI, short-cavity and wide-bore size MRI magnet technology. The imaging space is highly open, and the fabricating and operating costs are greatly reduced. The MRI technologies have realized the high-performance and low-cost industrialization of equipment, which not only changed the situation that MRI was completely dependent on foreign companies in China, but also exported to other countries.

(3) The Liquid helium is a scarce resource in all over the word and the only cold-down source for the superconducting magnets. It is very difficult for the liquid helium cooling magnet system to operate stably for long time. The liquid helium in China depends on the import from the Unite State, which has led to great restrictions on the R&D and applications of superconducting magnets. Professor Wang developed the design, manufacturing and thermal management technologies for conduction-cooled superconducting magnet applied in the Instruments and special electromagnetic equipments. The new technology has promoted the electro-magnetic equipment quality used in the many fields.

电子信息技术奖获得者

管晓宏

管晓宏，1955 年 11 月出生于四川省泸州市。1982 年和 1985 年分别获得清华大学自动化系学士与硕士学位；1993 年获美国康涅狄格大学电气工程系博士学位。1993—1995 年任美国 PG&E 公司高级顾问工程师，1999—2000 年访问哈佛大学。1995 年起先后任西安交通大学教授、系统工程研究所所长、电子与信息工程学院院长、电子与信息学部主任；1999—2009 年任机械制造系统工程国家重点实验室主任；自 2001 年起先后任清华大学讲席教授组成员、双聘教授；2003—2008 年任清华大学自动化系主任。1997 年获国家杰出青年科学基金，2000 年任长江学者特聘教授。2007 年当选 IEEE Fellow，2017 年当选中国科学院院士。目前担任 *IEEE Transactions on Smart Grid* 编辑，国务院学位委员会学科评议组成员，教育部网络空间安全专业教指委副主任委员等学术职务。

管晓宏长期从事系统工程理论与应用研究，针对能源、电力和互联网等网络化系统提出了系统优化、物理安全与信息安全的新理论与新方法，解决了多个公认难题，取得了系统性创新成果，为能源、电力等系统的提效节能和保障安全作出了重要贡献。

一、提出网络化系统优化新理论与新方法，解决了非凸及混合动态求解、同构奇异、博弈分析等公认难题，取得重大社会经济效益

优化能源、电力、制造等网络化系统运行能够取得提高效率和节能减排的重大效益，但必须面对有限时间无法求解的 NP 复杂性问题。基于拉氏松弛的优化框架能够将复杂优化问题分解为子问题求解，降低计算复杂性，但面临子问题复杂混合动态、同构奇异和解振荡等公认难题，缺乏系统化解决方案。而近年来可再生新能源供应和高耗能能源需求更增加了高不确定性的新挑战。

管晓宏团队提出了基于拉氏松弛优化的新理论和新方法，主要包括精确求解混合动态、时空耦合和非凸目标函数对偶问题最优解的新模型和新方法，避免连续变量离散化而造成指数计算复杂性；非线性逼近和子问题序贯求解 SSS 法，解决了同构奇异和解振荡问题，证明收敛性且保持原问题解下界，成为精确高效求解拉氏松弛对偶问题及获原问题可行解的系统化方法；提出随机优化新方法，保证不确定场景下的安全性。成果被认为是最系统全面的成果之一，被应用于国网、宝钢、NU、PG&E 等国内外企业，取得了节能增效的重大社会经济效益。

二、提出网络化系统优化安全性的系统化方法，发现安全可行性解析判定条件和充分等价约束，为新标准奠定了理论基础

安全性和可行性是网络化系统优化的前提条件，满足数量可达数十万个网络化安全约束具有重大挑战。快速识别冗余安全约束、发现安全瓶颈并进行 N-k（k 个故障）安全性评估极其重要，但同样具有 NP 复杂性，实际系统进行 k >2 的安全评估基本不可行。

管晓宏团队发现了网络化系统安全约束冗余性判定解析条件，成数量级约简冗余电网安全约束，大大提高了优化求解效率；发现了安全约束的等效充分条件，提出 N-k 安全性评估新方法，降低计算复杂性 2 ~ 3 个数量级；发现了可行性解析判定条件，建立了有效不等式及割平面，大幅加速算法收敛；提出了优化调度的能量可实现性理论，建立了能量交付可实现性的充要解析条件，提出了含积分约束的优化模型和求解方法，解决了保证最优解能量可实现性难题。成果应用于国网西北电网，为论证建设第二输电通道必要性奠定了理论基础。能量可实现性理论与含积分约束优化方法应用于宝钢能源系统关口平衡等问题的优化调度，取得节能减排显著效益。

三、提出基于系统理论的信息安全监控新方法，解决了流量异常解析定位、无流量数据估计僵尸网络全球分布问题

大规模网络化基础设施（互联网、智能电网、物联网等）的网络信息安全和系统综合安全涉及国家安全，但面临海量数据无标定、安全监控误报率高、僵尸网络分布隐蔽、安全防卫缺少协同等重大挑战。

管晓宏团队提出了动态分析与估计的网络安全监控新方法，包括基于区域流模型的互信息熵分析法，能够动态监控网络流量异常，并通过可逆解析计算高效获得 sketch 流量异常定位，解决了高速海量数据下网络异常定位难题；通过多源关联分析，大大减少了误报；通过主动周期量测 DNS 缓存中的域名请求，建立了规模估计模型，提出了僵尸网络检测和规模估计方法，解决了无流量数据估计僵尸网络全球分布的难题；基于信息物理关联分析的智能电网和人机系统的安全监控方法，有望成为保障信息物理融合基础设施信息安全的系统化解决方案。由其主持的"863"项目"集成化网络安全防卫系统"获 Aa 最高评价（2%课题组获得），成果转化并研发成功的网络安全监控与防卫系统在近千个政府部门和企事业单位部署，发现僵尸网络域 400 余万个，协助主管部门清除了多个威胁严重的僵尸网络。

以上研究成果获 2005 年、2018 年国家自然科学奖二等奖，1996 年美国李氏基金杰出成就奖和 5 项国际最佳论文奖；发表 SCI 期刊论文 150 余篇，包括 60 余篇 IEEE 汇刊论文；获发明专利授权 30 余项，连续五年被 Elsevier 列为中国高被引学者。

Awardee of Electronics and Information Technology Prize，Guan Xiaohong

Guan Xiaohong was born in Luzhou City of Sichuan Province November 1955. He received his B.S. and M.S. degrees in Control Engineering from Tsinghua University in 1982 and 1985 respectively, and his Ph.D. degree in Electrical and Systems Engineering from the University of Connecticut in 1993. He was a senior consulting engineer with Pacific Gas and Electric from 1993 to 1995. He visited the Division of Engineering and Applied Science, Harvard University from Jan. 1999 to Feb. 2000. Since 1995, he has been with Xian Jiaotong University, and has been as the Cheung Kong Professor of Systems Engineering since 1999, was the director of the State Key Lab for Manufacturing Systems 1999—2009 and Dean of School of Electronic and Information Engineering 2008—2018. He is currently the Dean of Faculty of Electronic and Information Engineering. From 2001 he has also been with the Center for Intelligent and Networked Systems, Tsinghua University, Beijing, China, and severed the Head of Department of Automation, Tsinghua University, 2003—2008. His research interests include economics and security of networked systems, optimization based planning and scheduling of power and energy systems, manufacturing systems, etc., and cyber-physical systems including smart grid, etc.

Professor Guan and his team developed new theories and methods for optimization of networked systems, solved the well-recognized difficulties such as and non-convexity, homogenous singularity, gaming analysis etc., with great social and economic impact. They discovered the analytical conditions and sufficient equivalent constraints and developed the systematic method for the security constrained optimization problems of a class of networked systems. These methods establish the theoretic foundation of the new industrial standard. They also developed the new methods for network security monitoring and defense, solved the difficult issues of positioning abnormal network flows, and the global distribution of a botnet without flow data, etc.

Professor Guan is the member of Chinese Academy of Science, the Fellow of IEEE, and the Editor of *IEEE Transactions on Smart Grid*.

电子信息技术奖获得者

陆 贵 文

陆贵文，1958 年 6 月出生于中国香港。1985 年毕业于香港大学电机工程学系，获哲学博士学位。1992 年至今在香港城市大学工作，先后担任电子工程学系系主任和毫米波国家重点实验室主任，现为电机工程学系讲座教授、电子科技大学和西安电子科技大学荣誉教授、北京大学兼职教授，*Proceedings of the IEEE* 客座主编，IEEE 天线及传播学会最佳论文奖评审委员会主席、IEEE 天线及传播学会领域奖评审委员会主席。IEEE、IET、CIE、HKIE 会士，英国皇家工程院院士。

陆贵文长期致力于天线理论及实验研究，在微带天线、介质天线和偶极子天线等小型天线领域作出了系统性和创造性贡献，推动了无线通信技术的发展。

一、在国际上领先开展微带天线的理论与实验研究，提出了多种新型频谱展宽技术和小型化技术，推动了微带天线广泛应用于现代无线通信系统上

微带天线的主要优点是低剖面结构、体积少、易于载体共形，已被广泛应用于现代无线通信网络和手持机中。陆贵文在国际上是微带天线的开拓者之一，早在 1989 年，他就率先提出了运用腔模理论有效分析载体曲面对微带天线各种参数的影响，引发分析共形微带天线的热潮。

微带天线的主要缺点是频宽较窄（只有几个百分点），得不到广泛应用。1990 年，提出频带达 38% 的偏移双贴片微带天线，成为当代最宽频的微带天线，并因此获得1994 年亚太微波会议最佳论文奖。1997 年，率先研究 U 形槽微带天线理论，推动了研发宽带单贴片微带天线的热潮，这种天线结构简单、性能良好、频宽可达 35%，已被广泛应用。

1998 年，发明 L 形探针微带天线，该天线具有超过 35% 的带宽及 7dBi 的增益，该项技术获得多项发明专利；证明了 L 形探针微带天线能以圆极化和双极化的方式工作，更可以全向的辐射方向工作，或实现大于 90°的波束宽度工作；此外，L 形探针微带天线也可发展成 MIMO 天线。L 形探针微带天线技术已成为天线典范，并被推广到如移动通信基站、手持机、Wifi 路由器和射频读卡机等实际应用中。陆贵文因此荣获了 2001 年香港裘槎基金会优秀科研者奖。

为了在缩小圆极化微带天线体积的同时，保持有效频宽和稳定的方向图，他发明了在微带天线上开槽附加尾线技术和垂直贴片微带天线技术，前者获得中国实用新型专利，后者获 2008 年国际天线及传播年会最佳论文奖。此外，陆贵文基于开槽附加尾线技术，成功研发了应用于中国北斗卫星定位系统接收机中的天线，在 2008 年汶川地震后，这项技术首次得到应用，帮助武警官兵稳定反馈灾情和准确救援定位。基于上述多种微带天线的发明，陆贵文获得了 2011 年国家技术发明奖二等奖（排名第一）。

二、提出了创新的宽带偶极子天线，为 5G 无线通信技术发展提供支撑

2006 年，陆贵文提出将一个电偶极子天线和一个短路微带天线集成，研发了一个名为磁电偶极子的互补天线。这种新型天线不仅拥有近 50% 的带宽，更具有低交叉极化、稳定的增益和辐射方向图以及低后向辐射，远优于其他同类设计。此外，它还可以被设计成双极极化天线或全向天线，并可以设计成高效率宽带毫米波天线和超宽带定向天线。此技术已取得中国及美国发明专利，并已应用于设计新型移动通信基站天线和 5G 毫米波手机天线。基于磁电偶极子天线和 L 形探针馈电微带天线的发明，陆贵文获得了 2017 年 IEEE 天线及传播学会 John Kraus 天线大奖。

三、在国际上率先开展介质谐振器天线的分析和研究，推动了非金属天线和液体天线的发展

介质谐振器天线（DRA）因其频带宽、体积小，特别适用于相控天线阵列。陆贵文是当今世界分析 DRA 的先驱者。为提高 DRA 性能，他研发了多种新技术，如用双层介质片提高带宽、用附载金属片激发圆极化辐射以及用高介电常数物质减少体积，这些成果对 DRA 的发展和应用发挥了极大的带动作用。2003 年，他主编了世界上第一本关于 DRA 的专著《介质谐振器天线》。

与此同时，陆贵文还成功把 DRA 与微带天线结合，发明了高介电常数介质片天线，继而提出水贴片天线，并获得了 2015 年亚太区天线会议最佳论文奖，推动了液体天线的研究。

攻读博士学位期间，陆贵文成功地修正了经典开腔谐振器的工作理论，已故国际资深微波专家 A.L.Cullen 评价其博士论文为最佳博士论文之一。目前，陆贵文已先后指导 25 位哲学博士生和 10 位哲学硕士生，如今他们多供职于国内外知名的学府或天线生产商。他曾领导的毫米波国家重点实验室（香港城市大学）已成为国际天线及微波研究的交流枢纽，为国内外学者和学生提供服务。

Awardee of Electronics and Information Technology Prize, Kwai Man LUK

Kwai Man LUK was born in Hong Kong in June 1958. He received his PhD degree from the Department of Electrical Engineering at the University of Hong Kong in 1985. Since joining City University of Hong Kong in 1992, he was Head of the Electronic Engineering Department from, and Director of the State Key Laboratory of Millimeter Waves. He is honorary professor of University of Electronic Science and Technology of China and Xidian University. He was Chairman of IEEE APS Best Paper Award Committee and IEEE APS Field Award Committee. He is Fellow of IEEE, IET, CIE and HKIE. He was elected as Fellow of the UK Royal Academy of Engineering.

In modern wireless communications, stringent requirements are imposed on the antenna characteristics. Professor Luk has made significant contributions on the design and analysis of microstrip antennas, magneto-electric dipole antennas, and dielectric resonator antennas.

1. Microstrip Antennas

He generalized the cavity model to the analysis of microstrip antennas mounted on curved structures. This efficient classical method was widely used to study the curvature effect on the characteristics of microstrip antennas. He invented the offset stacked patch antenna with over 38% impedance bandwidth, for which he received the Japan Microwave Prize at the 1994 Asia Pacific Microwave Conference. He proposed the principle of operation of the U-slot patch antenna in 1997, which promoted the applications of this wideband antenna in various modern wireless systems. He invented the patented L-probe fed patch antenna in 1998. By replacing the conventional coaxially fed straight probe with an L-shaped probe and increasing the thickness of the antenna to about 10% free-space wavelength, a bandwidth of 35% and a gain of 7 dBi were achieved. He successfully demonstrated that the antenna can be enhanced with dual polarization with high input/output port isolation, circular polarization with wideband and dual band operation, omnidirectional radiation pattern, over 90 degree beamwidth, or pattern and polarization diversity for MIMO systems. This technology has been applied in various countries to base stations, portable phones, notebooks, RFIDs, radars, etc.

He also invented several compact circularly polarized microstrip antennas including the vertical patch antenna and the slot-loaded microstrip antenna with tails. The former design resulted in a best paper award at the 2008 International Symposium on Antennas and Propagation and the latter design was applied to Beidou mobile terminals. Based on the significant contributions in developing various microstrip antennas, he received the 2011 State Technological Invention Award of China (2nd honor, as leading researcher).

2. Magneto-electric dipoles

Modern wireless communication systems require unidirectional antennas not only wide in bandwidth but also low in cross-polarization, low in back radiation and stable in radiation pattern and gain. Conventional antennas such as directed dipoles and microstrip antennas cannot fulfil this requirement. Based on the complementary antenna approach of combining an electric dipole with a magnetic dipole orthogonally, a new antenna—the magneto-electric dipole—was invented in 2006. The basic linearly polarized magneto-electric dipole exhibits 50% bandwidth, about 8 dBi gain and better than 20dB front-to-back ratio. More importantly, the gain, beamwidth and radiation patterns vary only slightly over the wide frequency band, which are attractive features for cellular mobile communications. The wideband magneto-electric dipole provides dual polarization, ultra-wide bandwidth, and circular polarization. It was also successfully adapted to millimeter wave frequencies with excellent performance. This patented technology has been applied to develop base station antennas and portable devices for 5G and beyond.

3. Dielectric resonator antennas

Due to the advantages of wide bandwidth, wide beamwidth, small size, and multi-mode operation, the dielectric resonator antenna (DRA) has been widely investigated in the last decade. As a pioneer of on the analysis and design of DRA, he successfully developed methods to enhance the bandwidth and to reduce the size of the antenna, enabling them for applications in portable wireless devices and phased arrays. His edited book: "Dielectric Resonator Antennas" was the first in this area.

Considering the characteristics of the dielectric resonator antenna and the microstrip antenna, he invented the dense dielectric patch antenna and particularly the water patch antenna which is transparent antennas that can be integrated with other devices such as light sources or solar cells. This success motivated the investigation on liquid antennas in recent years.

Professor Luk has made substantial enhancement on the classical theory of open resonator in his postgraduate study. Over the years, he has successfully graduated 25 PhD and 10 MPhil students. Most of them are now working in universities as professors or in antenna industries as research engineers. The State Key Laboratory of Millimeter Waves that he served as founding Director before has become a national hub for promoting international research collaborations.

电子信息技术奖获得者

龙　腾

　　龙腾，1968 年 1 月出生于福建省福州市。1989 年本科毕业于中国科学技术大学，1995 年毕业于北京理工大学，获工学博士学位。1995 年至今在北京理工大学工作，先后任北京理工大学电子工程系雷达技术研究所副所长、所长，信息与电子学院院长，校长助理，副校长。1999 年和 2002 年分别在美国斯坦福大学和英国伦敦大学学院担任高级访问学者。龙腾为国务院学位委员会第七届学科评议组员；教育部长江学者特聘教授、国家杰出青年科学基金项目获得者、第二批国家"万人计划"领军人才、国家百千万人才工程"有突出贡献中青年专家"；担任"973"项目技术首席、国家"863"重点项目首席专家、某武器系统副总设计师、某卫星副总设计师。兼任中国指挥与控制学会副理事长，中国电子学会常务理事，中国仪器仪表学会常务理事，中国电子学会、中国仪器仪表学会信号处理分会主任委员，并入选 IEEE Fellow、IET Fellow、中国电子学会会士。曾担任 IET 2009 国际雷达会议主席、IET 2013/2015/2018 国际雷达会议荣誉主席；于 2019 年创办 IEEE 国际信号、信息与数据处理会议并担任大会主席。

　　龙腾是我国雷达信号与信息处理领域学术带头人之一，在空天（星、机、弹载）对地探测雷达实时信号与信息处理等方面作出了一系列开创性研究工作。

一、发明"综合单节点处理"和"保质、精简成像"等高效实时处理新技术，研制成功世界上首个星上 SAR 成像处理系统，成果应用于 8 型 10 颗 SAR 卫星及多种机、弹载雷达，实现空天对地探测"响应快"

　　SAR 是距离-方位二维高分辨成像的雷达系统，是空天对地探测的重要雷达体制，其成像处理需对雷达回波的二维相关数据矩阵进行多次傅里叶变换，矩阵数据粒度大、运算时间长，处理系统体积、重量、功耗大。因此，传统的 SAR 卫星不能进行星上处理，需将数据传输到地面进行处理、分发和应用。相比之下，星上在轨实时处理是在星上完成 SAR 成像和图像目标检测等处理，将处理结果直接分发到用户，可大幅减少数据传输量和传输环节，实现空天对地探测系统"响应快"。为此，龙腾发明了"综合单节点处理"技术，通过综合多个处理节点的存储和处理资源，实现大粒度数据短延迟处理；主要创新是在多个处理节点之间构建对称交换网络和精细时间控制，实现各节点处理器对各节点存储器同时对等访问。实测 64 处理节点的并行扩展效率可高于 90%，在单位体积、单位功耗的持续处理能力等方面超过国外同类产品指标。

进一步发明了"保质、精简成像"处理技术，以减少 SAR 成像运算复杂度。即采用二维聚焦深度替代传统的一维聚焦深度，采用优化的定点字长运算替代传统的浮点运算，并给出成像质量与聚焦深度、运算字长关系的解析表达。在保证成像质量的前提下，实测在轨成像处理系统体积、重量、功耗比传统方法减小 25% ～ 40%。

基于以上发明，研制成功世界上首个 SAR 卫星在轨实时处理系统，已在 KX SAR 卫星在轨运行；相关成果在我国 8 型 10 颗 SAR 卫星研制中应用，突破星地数传瓶颈，开创了我国航天成像探测星上处理、实时分发的新模式，实现卫星对地探测"响应快"。

以上发明还应用于我国多种机、弹载雷达：在轰 6K 首次研制成功轰炸机载雷达二维高分辨实时成像，实时处理系统已装机上百套并巡航飞行；使东风 ×× 首次实现弹载环扫 SAR 雷达景象匹配制导，为导弹立项研制提供了关键核心技术支撑。成果获 2011 年国家技术发明奖二等奖（排名第一）。

二、提出"复杂轨迹 SAR 成像"和"广域图像多维处理"新算法，为世界上首个高轨 SAR 卫星提供了理论基础，并研制成功世界上首个星上海洋目标检测处理芯片及系统，成果应用于 10 型 14 颗海洋目标探测卫星，实现空天对地探测"范围广"

平台高度是空天对地 SAR 探测幅宽的决定因素之一。对于轨道高度为 36000 千米的高轨星载 SAR，经典 SAR 成像理论的三个基本假设（"停-走"信号模型、直线轨迹平台运动、正侧视成像）均已不再成立。针对以上难题，建立了"复杂轨迹 SAR 成像"处理算法体系：提出 SAR 回波信号距离-方位联合建模方法，实现了非"停-走"模型下高精度信号建模；提出二维非线性自适应频域成像算法，推导出复杂轨迹 SAR 的二维频谱解析表达，实现了弯曲轨迹、大前斜视 SAR 成像。采用北斗高轨导航卫星作为辐射源进行了实验验证，成功获得高轨卫星照射的双基地 SAR 图像，实测点目标成像方位分辨率与理论值误差小于 1.2%。

针对卫星获取的 SAR 图像和光学图像，进一步提出"广域图像多维处理"新算法，实现了广域图像舰船目标高效率、低漏检、低虚警检测。主要创新是采用分级（像素级、对象级）、分层（直观特征、抽象特征）、分域（目标自身、目标周域）虚警剔除和目标分类鉴别（普通、重点、易漏重点目标）。与国际最新公开报道相比，算法检测率提高 15%，运算速度提高 10 倍以上。

"复杂轨迹 SAR 成像"处理算法为世界上首颗高轨 SAR 卫星立项研制提供了理论基

础，雷达探测幅宽可达 3000 千米；基于"广域图像目标检测"处理算法，研制成功世界上首个星上舰船目标检测专用处理芯片和系统，已在 KX SAR 卫星和 3 颗超大幅宽对地观测卫星（中国遥感卫星 19 号、22 号、27 号）在轨运行。相关成果在我国 10 型 14 颗海洋目标探测卫星研制中应用，使我国具备大范围、快速发现确认海上机动目标能力，实现空天对地探测"范围广"，成果获 2018 年国家技术发明奖二等奖（排名第一）。

三、理论证明调频步进信号波形的高分辨性能，为我国高分辨率 SAR 卫星和雷达导引头提供了理论基础；提出基于高分辨率波形的检测、识别、跟踪系列化处理新方法，研制成功我国首个空地反装甲雷达导引头，实现雷达探测"分辨清"

空天对地、海目标探测存在植被、建筑物、起伏地形及海浪等杂波干扰，必须采用高分辨率雷达进行检测、识别、跟踪。但是传统的高分辨率雷达采用瞬时大带宽信号波形，硬件资源开销大，在星、弹载环境下难以实现分米级高分辨率。针对以上难题，理论证明了调频步进信号波形的高分辨性能，解析推导了信号处理过程和结果，为该信号波形实用化提供了理论基础；该信号采用多个较低瞬时带宽信号合成大带宽，可在星、弹载雷达硬件资源约束下实现分米级高分辨率成像。

对于导弹末制导雷达导引头，高分辨率目标模型是一维扩展目标，其检测、识别、跟踪是雷达领域尚未解决的基础理论难题。为此，提出距离高分辨率雷达检测、识别、跟踪系列化处理新方法，包括双门限目标检测方法，实现扩展目标的高概率鲁棒检测；二叉树级联集成学习的目标分类识别方法，实现目标与强杂波、电磁干扰准确分类；高分辨特征辅助跟踪方法，实现扩展目标稳健跟踪。

研究成果为我国高分辨率星载 SAR 和高分辨率雷达导引头研制提供了理论基础，实现空天对地探测"分辨清"；并作为武器系统副总设计师，研制成功我国首个空地反装甲雷达导引头，距离分辨率、探测距离等关键指标超过国外同类装备水平，实现导弹"发射后不管"换代提升。基于上述研究成果，出版学术专著《宽带雷达》，并"因为在高分辨率雷达系统的贡献"入选 IEEE Fellow。

Awardee of Electronics and Information Technology Prize, Long Teng

Long Teng was born in Fuzhou City of Fujian Province in January 1968. He has been engaged in real-time signal and information processing technology in space-borne, airborne and missile-borne radar. Under the strictly constrained size, weight and power dissipation of satellite, bombers and air-to-ground guided missile, new technologies for high efficient and real-time data processing, new algorithms for high-performance processing and new waveforms for high-resolution signals have been exploited to solve the problems about the radar imaging as well as target detection, identification and tracking in complex ground or sea clutter conditions. He has succeeded in developing the world's first space-borne synthetic aperture radar (SAR) imaging system, space-borne processing chip and system for marine target detection. The achievements have been applied to the development of China's 12-type 16 satellites and China's first air-to-ground guided missile radar seeker which realizes the upgrading of air-to-ground missiles. The proposed new algorithm and new waveforms provide the theoretical basis for the world's first geosynchronous SAR and China's high resolution SAR satellite. The team led by him has a significant influence in the international radar and signal processing society.

电子信息技术奖获得者

吕跃广

吕跃广，1964年5月出生于山东省广饶县。1990年毕业于哈尔滨工业大学应用物理系，获理学博士学位。1990—2017年在中国北方电子设备研究所工作，历任研究室副主任、副总工程师、副所长兼总工程师、科技委主任等；其间，2001—2002年在英国伦敦大学UCL做访问学者。现为中央军委科学技术委员会常任委员，清华大学、哈尔滨工业大学、西安电子科技大学兼职教授和博士生导师，国家人工智能科技重大专项战略咨询委员会委员，中国光学工程学会副理事长。作为主要完成人，获国家科技进步奖一等奖1项、国家技术发明奖二等奖1项、国家科技进步奖二等奖4项；2008年获中国科协"求是"杰出青年实用工程奖，2010年被授予全国优秀科技工作者称号。2011年当选中国工程院院士。

吕跃广长期从事光电信息处理和电磁信号测量等方面的研究工作，主持完成了我国多型科学实验卫星系统的研制和多项国家重大科研项目攻关，有力推进了我国空间对地观测、电磁频谱控制等相关领域的发展。

一、射频前端设计及微弱光电信号感知测量

射频前端是传感系统的耳目和触角，其性能好坏直接决定了电磁测量能力的强弱。多年来，随着设计手段和水平的不断提高，射频前端特别是天线系统的设计指标已经接近传统电磁波理论的极限，新型亚波长电磁材料的出现为射频前端性能提高带来了曙光。从2000年开始，吕跃广带领课题组开展了基于亚波长电磁材料的天线技术研究，提出了多种拓展天线带宽、改善系统性能的技术途径，有效提高了应用系统的探测测量能力。

在深入分析电磁波与亚波长尺度人工结构材料相互作用的机制与规律基础上，构建了多种典型结构的亚波长人工电磁材料对电磁波的调控模型；提出了新颖的高增益宽带微带阵列天线设计方案，通过疏导天线基底的表面波，使其产生二次辐射，提高了能量辐射效率，压缩了单元天线尺寸，更好地满足了阵列天线组阵要求；设计了金属网格结构低折射率人工电磁材料，通过散射参数（S 参数）反演计算，获得了人工电磁材料等效折射率和介电常数，以此为基础设计的高增益小型化波导天线的方向增益较传统设计提高了 15dB 以上。

创新开展了电控可重构射频前端理论研究和设计，针对可重构天线瞬时带宽过窄问题，提出了纵向寄生耦合的频率重构模型，通过在 BST 材料上方加载独立的 FP 腔，引入了额外的谐振频段，使其中心频率可随 BST 介电常数的改变而同步移动，拓展了可重构天线的瞬时带宽，并使其可通过外加电场的控制进行重构。

提出了基于电磁场相位突变的天线频率重构方法，通过对反射型超表面的理论分析和设计，在目标频点得到了任意范围的电磁突变反射相位，通过各个单元的拼接和各层的级联调制色散相位，利用不同结构超表面的切换实现了天线工作频率的重构；采用这一思路设计的可重构天线其中心工作频率可实现跨越式大范围改变，调谐范围达到工作频率的 24%，远大于单纯基于材料调谐的可重构天线的调谐范围。

开展了利用光霍尔效应实现高精度感知理论和实验研究，突破了石墨烯调制光霍尔效应理论建模、石墨烯超表面对光霍尔效应调制分析等关键技术，实现了基于光霍尔效应的高精度界面传感测量，该技术在超分辨率成像等方面有重要应用前景。

以上研究成果发表在 *IEEE*、*Optics Express*、*Optics Letters*、*Applied Physics* 等杂志上。射频前端设计和应用成果获国家技术发明奖二等奖。

二、高精度高灵敏度空间对地观测系统设计研制

在空间科学与技术工程方面，主持完成了多型"实践"系列科学试验卫星系统的综合论证、总体设计和试验测试等工作，提出了星载探测测量载荷的技术体制和主要指标，完成了总体技术方案拟制，制定了工程标准，组织了综合星地对接试验，有力推进了我国空间对地观测、空间电磁环境测量等领域的技术进步。

针对卫星探测覆盖区域大和信号环境复杂密集等特点，提出了对多种微弱电磁辐射信号监测测量技术体制，开发了动态聚类多参数联合分选、模糊识别和智能模板动态跟踪等算法，提高了测量精度和速度，保证了在空间密集复杂信号环境中对测量目标和参数的快速提取和监测；提出了利用空时协同的高精度电磁测量方法，研制了高性能射频前端和星上处理系统，大大降低了对测量基线的要求，提高了测量精度和速度，节省了载荷成本；提出了计划与数据驱动相结合的控制流程，优化了系统设计，实现了不同地区的各种数据信息按需交换，降低了对传输系统的要求，提升了服务质量。星地工程和关键技术研究获国家科技进步奖一等奖、二等奖各 1 项。

三、国家重大基础研究

超高速飞行器在再入大气过程中由于与周围空气剧烈摩擦，导致空气温度升高，高

温气体与飞行器表面材料发生复杂的热化学反应，会产生一层包裹飞行器表面的鞘套层，该鞘套层对通信产生了衰减和阻断，即"黑障"现象。"黑障"对载人航天、临近空间飞行器应用造成了极大威胁。

作为首席科学家，吕跃广带领团队完成了国家科技部"高速飞行器等离子鞘套通信"重大基础研究，在低频磁场波穿透"黑障"通信机理、激光与等离子体鞘套相互作用建模、高动态环境下信道模拟计算以及时空频联合协同通信等方面取得重要进展，为载人航天等领域有效突破"黑障"通信提供了有力支撑。相关研究成果发表在 *IEEE*、*Optics Letters*、*Physics of Plasmas* 等杂志上。

Awardee of Electronics and Information Technology Prize, Lyu Yueguang

Lyu Yueguang, born in Guangrao County of Shandong Province in May 1964, specialized in electronic information technology in China, is academician of Chinese Academy of Engineering and professor of Harbin Institute of Technology. He obtained his PhD in Harbin Institute of Technology 1990, and was a Visiting Scholar in University College London from 2001 to 2002. He was Deputy Chief Engineer/Professor, North China Institute of Electronic Equipment from 2004 to 2017.

Hc has made great contributions to the research and development of multi-type scientific experimental satellite systems and has accomplished many significant projects which effectively led to the promotion and progress of China's earth observation capabilities, space science as well as other related fields. As the chief designer of Global Remote Sensing Monitoring Satellite project, he insisted on innovation and led his team to develope the first network system of remote sensing satellites in China. Because of his endeavour and contributions, he has been awarded many national prizes and honorary titles, including one first class and two second class of National Awards for Science and Technology Progress, one second class of National Award for Technological Invention, the honorary titles of National Outstanding Scientific and Technological Professionals in 2010.

Prof. Lyu has supervised 10 postdocs and 20 doctors, who became the core academic human resource of the most creative and leading teams in the field of electronic information technology in China.

交通运输技术奖获得者

丁荣军

丁荣军，1961 年 11 月出生于江苏省宜兴市。1984 年毕业于西南交通大学电力机车专业，1998 年获长沙铁道学院交通信息工程及控制专业硕士学位，2008 年获中南大学智能控制与模式识别专业博士学位。2000 年在中车株洲电力机车研究所有限公司工作，历任应用技术研究部主任、副总工程师、副总经理、总工程师、总经理、董事长、党委书记等职务。2011 年当选中国工程院院士。现任南车株洲电力机车研究所有限公司首席科学家。

丁荣军长期致力于轨道交通电力牵引及控制、大功率半导体器件的研究与应用，多项技术填补"国内空白"，达到"行业领先"甚至"世界水平"，为中国铁路从普载、常速到重载、高速的跨越以及大功率半导体技术和产业发展作出重大贡献，创造了显著的社会经济效益。30 多年来，他主持和参与国家、省部级重大科研项目 30 多项，获得国家科技进步奖二等奖 2 项，国家技术发明二等奖 1 项，省部级特等奖 3 项、一等奖 7 项、二等奖 6 项；获得变流器的试验电路 27 件授权专利，其中发明专利 24 件；累计在《机车电传动》《中国铁道科学》等期刊上发表学术论文 37 篇，带领团队主持制订了 9 项国际标准及逾百项国家标准、行业标准。其个人先后获得詹天佑铁道科技奖成就奖、茅以升科学技术奖、新世纪百千万人才工程国家级人选和全国劳动模范等多项荣誉称号。

一、攻克轨道交通电力牵引及控制关键技术

交流牵引传动和网络控制系统被喻为机车、动车组的"心脏"和"大脑"，是一个国家轨道交通装备水平高低的重要标志之一，也是重载和高速牵引的基础。但在 20 世纪 80 年代，该关键技术仅为西门子、阿尔斯通、庞巴迪等少数公司所掌握。为了改变受制于人的局面，丁荣军带领团队在资料和开发手段匮乏的情况下潜心研究，探索适合国情的大功率牵引传动系统技术模式，全力突破国外技术封锁，攻克了多数字处理器实时协同控制、自适应粘着控制等关键核心技术，开发了自主知识产权的牵引与控制系统产品。

该系统创造了高速动车组时速 486.1 千米的世界商业运营最高速和时速 605 千米的滚动台试验最高速，技术水平国际领先，是目前全球轨道交通装备领域产品型谱最全、应用最广、业绩最多的电传动核心系统之一，在国内轨道交通市场占有率逾 60%，累计经济效益近 900 亿元；相关技术成果已从轨道交通批量推广应用于新能源汽车、电力传输、风电光伏和海洋船舶等众多战略性新兴产业领域。

二、主持大功率半导体器件的研制及产业化

大功率器件是变流器技术的基础，为解决核心器件长期受限于人的难题，丁荣军从 2006 年开始主持高压晶闸管、IGBT 及 IGCT 三种器件的研究及产业化。目前已突破大功率半导体器件关键技术，全面掌握晶闸管、IGCT、IGBT、SiC 功率器件、功率组件全套技术，构建了集设计、制造、测试、应用于一体的完整产业平台；自主研发的 650 ～ 6500V 全系列 IGBT 芯片实现批量应用，打破了国际巨头对大功率晶闸管（智能电网用）、IGBT 芯片、SiC 功率器件的垄断，解决了 IGBT 模块导通损耗等"卡脖子"的技术难题，成功填补国内空白，为国家节约了至少上百亿元投资，为中国国防装备、轨道交通和新能源装备等民族工业实现自主、安全、可控的"中国芯"奠定了良好基础；主持建设的中国第一条 8 英寸 IGBT 芯片专业化生产线与配套封装线具备年产 12 万片 IGBT 晶圆、50 万只高压 IGBT 模块的能力，达国际先进水平。

三、探索前沿技术，推动行业进步与发展

为持续巩固核心技术的领跑地位，瞄准未来轨道交通技术发展趋势，2003 年丁荣军率先在国内组织启动了轨道交通领域的永磁同步牵引系统研究，经过团队十多年的技术攻关，目前已成功研制并获得了批量应用，各项性能稳定，综合节能达 30%，填补了我国自主研发城市轨道交通永磁牵引系统列车的空白，为推动产业发展，建设节能、绿色、低碳的生态宜居城市发挥了积极作用。

与此同时，他承担了中国制造 2025、工业强基等国家级战略咨询研究项目，带领团队积极开展基础性、前瞻性的科技创新，并在电力电子变压器、碳化硅器件、下一代以太网、能源互联网、智能驾驶、低真空管道超高速磁悬浮铁路等领域不断取得重大突破，构建了基于新能源、新材料和智能化技术的战略领先优势，为行业的技术进步和产业发展出谋献策。

四、坚持技术 + 机制双创新，大力推动科技成果产业化

在主持公司十年经营工作期间，他坚持技术研发与成果产业化紧密结合、企业规模与经营效益紧密结合，株洲所科技成果 85% 以上实现了产业化；持续强化机制变革与科技创新，建立与市场紧密联系的科研体制并推行同心多元化发展战略，形成了以电气传动与自动化、高分子复合材料、新能源装备、电力电子器件为主的四大产业板块。产品以铁路电气牵引系统为基础，辐射延伸至城市轨道交通、轨道工程机械、电动汽车、风力发电、光伏发电、乘用车电控、智轨列车、工业传动、船舶海工等多元化市场，短短十年，企业销售规模实现了从38亿到330亿的大步跨越，取得了显著的经济效益和社会效益，成功走出一条"以产业养科技、以科技促产业"的良性循环道路，为重点科研院所科技体制改革与科技成果产业化树立了旗帜和标杆。

Awardee of Communication and Transportation Technology Prize，Ding Rongjun

Ding Rongjun was born inYixing City of Jiangsu Province in November 1961. He is a member of the Communist Party of China，member of Hunan provincial Party committee，dean of College of Mechanical and Vehicle Engineering of Hunan University，academician of Chinese Academy of Engineering，was elected as representative of the Eighteenth and the Nineteenth National Congress of the Communist Party of China. For more than 30 years，Ding Rongjun has devoted himself to the research and application of electric traction and control of rail transit and high-power semiconductor devices. A number of his technologies have filled the "domestic gap" and reached the "industry-leading level" and even the "world level"，which makes great contributions to the leap of China's railway from ordinary load and normal speed to heavy load and high speed，as well as the development of high-power semiconductor technology and industry，and create significant social and economic benefits.

The traction converter and control and train control network led and developed by him have been widely used in high-speed transits，electric locomotives and urban rail vehicles，which makes an important contribution to the China's railway leaping to the era of high-speed and heavy load and realizing the dream of "globalization of China's high speed railway". In more than 30 years，Ding Rongjun presided over and participated in more than 30 national，provincial and ministerial major scientific research projects，winning two second prizes in National Prize for Progress in Science and Technology（ranking first），one second prize in State Technological Invention Award（ranking second），three special awards（with one award ranking first），seven first prizes（with four prizes ranking first），and six second prizes（with four prizes ranking first）in provincial and ministerial prize. He had 27 authorized patents（24 invention patents）such as *A Test Circuit for a Converter* and *A Synchronous Modulation Method Based on space Vector*，published 37 academic papers in journals such as the *Electric Drive for Locomotives* and *China Railway Science*，led the team to formulate nine international standards，more than 100 national and industrial standards，and won several honorary titles such as Zhantianyou Railway Science and Technology Achievement Award，Mao Yisheng Science and Technology Award，National Candidate of New Century Talents Project and National Model Worker.

冶金材料技术奖获得者

张治民

张治民，1956 年 6 月出生于山西省芮城县。1982 年毕业于哈尔滨工业大学锻压设备及工艺专业。1992—1994 年在日本横滨国立大学访学。回国至今在中北大学工作，先后从事科技产业、学科建设等工作，现为中北大学材料科学与工程学院教授。"973"技术首席、国防科技创新团队带头人、国务院特贴专家、全国优秀教师、第八届"中国兵工学会科学技术特等奖"获得者。

一直从事材料加工新技术及产业化研究，在轻量化构件精密塑性成形基础研究及工程化应用方面作出了一系列开创性工作。

一、高强铝合金逐次控制变形理论及技术

超重已成为制约高端装备发展的瓶颈。高强铝合金是轻量化的重要用材，但由于其塑性差、疲劳寿命低，应力集中敏感性大、承载能力差，流动性差、大型复杂构件成形缺陷多，无法制造出满足高冲击、大后坐力、高转速服役要求的构件。

针对上述问题，张治民研究变形温度、次数及道次变形量等参数对合金组织性能的影响及强韧化机理，提出了高强铝合金逐次控制变形、晶粒持续细化和纤维组织定向分布控制理论，发明了扩收复合挤压、分流导流开发成形、多向主动加载等金属流动调控技术，率先突破高强铝合金大型复杂构件整体塑性成形及工程化关键技术，提高了构件塑性和承载能力（伸长率由 7% 提高到 13%、承载能力提高近 1 倍），开创了高强铝合金在高冲击、抗疲劳构件上应用的先例，解决了战车、自行火炮、迫击炮、某导弹等装备超重无法定型的难题，结束了钢质轮毂、轮辋、座钣的历史，为装备轻量化开辟了新途径。先后研制 60 余种高强铝合金构件，保障了装备的批产，获"93 阅兵"装备保障突出贡献奖。

二、镁合金构件形性控制成形理论及技术

新一代弹箭武器要求有更高的速度、更远的射程、更大的威力，迫切需要减少无效重量，而采用高强耐热镁合金材料和大型薄壁带筋结构是装备轻量化的有效途径。Mg-Gd-Y-Zn-Zr 合金性能高，当前国内外研究仅限于试验样件和小构件，塑性成形的大构件未见应用，主要难点在于：①高合金化的铸棒规格越大，偏析越严重，塑性变形越难，无法获得大型锻坯；②大变形导致强烈的各向异性，变形不均匀造成力学性能差异大；③尚无整体成形带内环筋构件的技术及设备。

围绕上述难题，提出了从铸锭开坯到构件成形全流程连续累积变形组织、性能及精度一体化调控理论，定义了旋转挤压新概念，发明了大规格镁合金铸棒开坯方法和旋转挤压成套技术及装备；实现了高径比大于 5（极限 2.5）的均匀镦粗变形，成形的大锥型内环筋变壁厚壳体，抗拉强度由 180MPa 提高到 410MPa 以上，伸长率由 1% 提高到 7%，各向异性系数达 0.98；解决了镁合金无法作为承力构件应用的技术难题。该技术应用于某型导弹减重 20%～30%，有效提高了战技指标。该技术填补了镁合金高性能大型复杂构件塑性成形的空白，先后在导弹、鱼雷、坦克、卫星、登月车和车辆等装备关键重件上获得应用。

三、温挤成形理论及技术

发现高强度钢在 650～880℃ 具有良好的塑性，在该区域内形变诱导铁素体，不仅使晶粒超细化、流变应力大幅度下降，这种超细化的效果在随后的热处理中保留下来，并且可大幅提高产品性能和精度，首次建立了"项链式""糖葫芦状"动态再结晶细化机制模型和材料温变形模型，成为温成形技术的理论基础。

提出了高强钢温成形动态再结晶细化机制，建立了流变力学模型，发明了以温成形为核心的特种润滑、辊挤和复合挤压等技术群，降低成形力 30% 以上，构件性能提高10% 以上，材料利用率提高 1～2 倍，能耗减少 50%，模具寿命提高 1～3 倍；建立大口径弹体、引信体等生产线 7 条，解决了传统生产毛坯傻大黑粗、环境脏乱差的问题，为节能减排、提高材料利用率作出贡献。

组建了"国家级国防科技工业复杂构件挤压创新中心""镁基材料深加工教育部工程研究中心""镁合金关键技术及工艺国家地方联合工程研究中心""国家高性能铝镁合金构件成形与测试平台"，自主开发了国内外首台旋转挤压实验平台和旋转挤压成形设备及多向数控加载成形机。建成了国内一流铝镁合金复杂构件成形、产品开发与试制创新平台，配套各种产品 3 万件（套），产值 2.1 亿元，多个产品已成为重点型号采购的唯一来源。

作为带头人，创建了"山西省高校优秀创新团队""国防科技精密塑性成形创新团队""研究生优秀导师团队"。先后承担完成国家"863""973"、国家重点基金等项目；作为第一完成人，获国家、省部级科技奖 17 项，其中国家科技进步奖二等奖 1 项、国防科技进步奖一等奖 1 项、省发明一等奖 2 项、省部级二等奖 10 项；授权国家发明专利 65 项、

美国发明专利 2 项，制定 WJ 行业标准 2 项；SCI 收录论文 61 篇，EI 收录论文 116 篇。

Awardee of Metallurgy and Materials Technology Prize, Zhang Zhimin

Zhang Zhimin was born in Ruicheng County of Shanxi Province in June 1956. He got his doctoral degree from Harbin Institute of Technology in 1982. Now Zhimin Zhang is a full professor at the School of Materials Science and Engineering in North University of China. Prof. Zhang is the "973" project chief scientist and wins the special prize of the Science and Technology of China Ordnance Society.

In the past 38 years, Prof. Zhang has been engaged in the research of new technology and industrialization of complex components forming of aluminum and magnesium alloys. He creatively proposed the theory and technology based on the core of warm forming, including oriented distribution of fiber structure, continuous grain refinement, uniform performance control of large complex components and composite extrusion forming, which greatly improved components performance and material utilization.

(1) Prof. Zhang created a precedent for the application of high-strength aluminum alloys on components working under large impact loads and high fatigue life, and solved the problem that the overweight equipment cannot be finalized.

(2) Prof. Zhang invented the new forming technology and equipment of large complex magnesium alloys components, solved the technical problems of low performance and inability formation, and broke through the bottleneck that the application of magnesium alloys on the next generation lightweight equipment.

(3) Prof. Zhang invented the technologies of special lubrication, roll extrusion and composite extrusion based on the core of warm forming, which contributes to saving energy and reducing emission and improving material utilization.

Prof. Zhang developed the multi-directional computerized numerical control (CNC) forming hydraulic press and the multi-directional loading rotary extrusion with independent intellectual property rights. These supported the unit construction of the demonstrated application and production of the domestic forming equipment for the lightweight rotating body components of the launch vehicle. Based on these, the collaborative innovation platform for intelligent extrusion forming of large-scale components with international leading level was formed.

Prof. Zhang won Second Prize of National Scientific and Technological Progress Award and First Prize of National Defense Scientific and Technological Progress Award, he also won the First Prize of Scientific and Technological Invention of Shanxi Province two times. Prof. Zhang published about two hundred SCI and EI cited papers, and is authorized 68 Chinese and 2 American invention patents. He also set 2 WJ standards.

冶金材料技术奖获得者

邹 志 刚

　　邹志刚，1955年3月出生于天津市。1982年、1986年分别获天津大学学士、硕士学位；1996年于日本东京大学获理学博士学位。南京大学教授，长江学者特聘教授，中国科学院院士，世界科学院院士。中国光化学及光催化专业委员会主任委员，中国功能材料学会理事长，中国氢能源及燃料电池产业创新战略联盟战略指导委员会委员，中国空间站科学技术实验科学委员会和太空探索实验科学委员会共同主席，军委高层次科技创新人才带教导师。发表SCI论文600余篇，他引20000余次，连续5年入选爱思唯尔材料科学高被引学者；获中国发明专利80余项、美国发明专利1项、日本发明专利2项。主持了国家"十一五""十二五"期间国家重大基础科学研究计划，是两届"973"项目首席科学家。2012年和2016年分别获江苏省科学技术奖一等奖，2014年获国家自然科学奖二等奖。

　　长期从事新能源材料及相关研究，在新一代光催化材料等能源与环境材料的设计理论、核心制备技术和应用、新能源器件与系统的产业化等方面取得了系统性、原创性的成果。推动了新型太阳能电池、可再生能源制氢与氢燃料电池、太阳能环境净化与资源化利用等有关创新成果的产业化，相关产品获第46届日内瓦国际发明展金奖及阿卜杜拉·阿齐兹国王大学特别奖各1项。

一、发展了新一代高效可见光响应光催化材料

　　李克强总理在2019年《政府工作报告》中明确指出"推动加氢设施建设"，将氢能利用与发展列为国家战略。邹志刚针对氢能绿色制造的国际难题，首创可见光响应光催化水分解产氢材料，将太阳能可利用范围从4%提升至47%，实现国际最高效率，率先实现高效光催化海水制氢，开启了太阳能氢能转换新时代；形成太阳能制氢和氢能高效利用系列创新成果及产业化，7项发明专利获产业化转化，技术转让费达1.6亿元。

二、率先将光催化材料用于 CO_2 转换合成碳氢燃料，发展了人工光合成技术

减少碳排放已成为国际共识，我国节能减排面临重大压力，针对这一国际国内重大需求，邹志刚率先利用光催化将 CO_2 转化成碳氢燃料和氧气，开拓了获取非化石燃料的碳中和新途径，为治理和利用 CO_2 提供了新思路和新技术；这一技术已在密闭空间生命保障、载人深空探索和地外生存中得到应用并形成核心技术，为我国坚持科技兴军、建设航天强国提供科技支撑。

三、发现光催化协同降解新机理，推动了光催化材料迈向实际应用

针对巨毒、量大、其他环境净化技术无法处理的多环芳烃等污染物难降解的关键技术问题，从分子水平上揭示光催化降解多环芳烃的反应机理和途径，首次发现不同污染物间的协同降解效应。设计制造具有自主知识产权、日处理量达 20 吨的光催化污水处理设备。针对军用装备密闭空间大气污染严重、核生化特种污染难消除等难点，将光催化技术应用于化学毒剂消除、特种污水治理及特种化学土壤污染修复中，获军方高度好评。

Awardee of Metallurgy and Materials Technology Prize, Zou Zhigang

Zou Zhigang was born in Tianjin City in March 1955. He got Ph.D of the University of Tokyo, Japan in 1996, He is presently the professor of Physics in Nanjing University, the "Yangtze river scholar" distinguished professor, the Academician of Chinese Academy of Sciences, and the Academician of the World Academy of Sciences. He is also the Chair of Chinese Photochemistry and Photocatalysis Professional Committee, the director of the Functional Materials Society of China, the member of Strategic Steering Committee of the China Hydrogen Alliance, the co-chairman of the Science and Technology Experimental Committee and the Space Exploration Experimental Science Committee of China Space Station, the Instructor of the Military Commission's High-level Scientific and Technological Innovative Talents. Prof. Zhigang Zou have long-term devoted himself in the related research field of new energy materials, where he has made systematic and original contributions to the theory development, material preparation, and applications of energy and environmental materials and the new-generation photocatalytic materials, and the industrialization of new energy devices and systems. He published more than 600 SCI articles, cited without self-citation by more than 20000 times. As one of the academic leaders with international influence, he has been continuously elected as the highly cited scholar of material science by Elsevier for 5 years. He achieved more than 80 Chinese, 1 US, and 2 Japanese Patents of Invention. He led the national major basic science research program on high efficiency conversion of hydrogen energy during the periods of the Eleventh and the Twelfth Five Year Plans as the Chief Scientist of the "973"

Project twice. He won the First Prize of Jiangsu Provincial Science and Technology in 2012 and 2016, and the Second Prize of National Natural Science in 2014. He promoted the industrialization of the related innovations on new-generation solar cells, hydrogen produced by renewable energy resources, hydrogen fuel cells, solar energy derived environmental purification and resource utilization, etc. And correspondingly, he won the Gold Award and the King Abdulaziz University Special Award of the 46th Geneva International Invention Exhibition.

1. Developing the new-generation high-efficiency visible light responsive photocatalytic materials

Prof. Zou created visible-light responsive photocatalytic materials, and expand the usable solar energy for photocatalysis from 4% to 47%. He achieved the highest photocatalytic efficiency of water splitting in the world, and took the lead in realizing photocatalytically splitting seawater to produce hydrogen, which opened a new era of solar-to-hydrogen energy conversion. He has also achieved a series of innovative and industrial developments in the fields of visible-light responsive photocatalytic materials, solar energy derived hydrogen production, and high-efficiency hydrogen applications. His 7 innovative patents were successfully industrially transferred, with the technological transferring fee of 160 million RMBs.

2. Taking the lead in CO_2 conversion to synthesize hydrocarbon fuel by photocatalytic materials, developing the artificial photosynthetic technology

Prof Zou pioneered the research of converting CO_2 to hydrocarbon fuels and oxygen by photocatalysis. This research opens up the new avenue of carbon neutralization, offers new technology for harnessing and utilizing CO_2. This technology has been applied for the life support in confined space, deep space exploration and extraterrestrial survival as one of the core technology. It provides scientific and technological support for China's science and technology for military development and a strong space power.

3. Discovering a new mechanism of photocatalytic synergistic degradation, and developing high-efficiency photocatalytic material system for wide applications

Prof. Zou revealed the reaction mechanism and pathway of photocatalytic degradation of polycyclic aromatic hydrocarbons at the molecular level, and for the first time discovered the synergistic degradation effect between different pollutants. He thus designed the photocatalytic sewage treatment equipment with 20-ton daily capacity, which he owns the proprietary intellectual property rights. He also applied photocatalytic technology in the elimination of chemical agents, special sewage treatment, and remediation of special chemical soil pollutions for the army, which were highly praised by the army.

化学工程技术奖获得者

郑 裕 国

郑裕国，1961年11月出生于浙江省象山县。1983年毕业于浙江工学院（现浙江工业大学）并留校任教，先后任浙江工业大学生物与环境工程学院副院长、浙江工业大学生物工程学院院长。兼任手性生物制造国家地方联合工程研究中心主任，国家化学原料药合成工程技术研究中心副主任，教育部高等学校生物技术、生物工程类专业教学指导委员会副主任，生物转化与生物净化教育部工程研究中心主任和浙江省生物有机合成技术研究重点实验室主任等职。中国工程院院士。以第一完成人获国家技术发明奖二等奖2项，国家科技进步奖二等奖1项，省部级科学技术奖一等奖6项、二等奖1项，中国专利优秀奖1项。主持开发的产业化技术建成工业化生产装置10余套，经济和社会效益显著。

主要从事生物化工科研、工程技术开发和教学工作，研发成功系列医药及农药化学品绿色、高效生物合成方法与关键技术；建立了以生物技术为核心，融合有机合成与化学工程原理和方法的生物有机合成技术新体系，在假糖、酮糖类化合物生物合成和手性生物催化等领域取得独创性成果，为我国生物化工行业科技进步和产业发展作出了重要贡献。

一、发明高纯度井冈霉素高产新工艺，首创井冈霉醇胺生物催化水解、裂解合成新技术，实现了假糖类农药最大品种的绿色化和高值化

井冈霉素为氨基环醇假三糖化合物，是我国自主发明的首个生物农药，年水稻纹枯病防治面积达2亿亩次。井冈霉素发酵液结构类似物多，有效组分A效价低，投产以来一直以粗制品供应市场，满足了当时农药工业的需求。井冈霉素A经水解、裂解、水合后的产物井冈霉醇胺是新一代糖苷酶抑制剂药物的关键中间体。随着农药绿色化及井冈霉素高值化的巨大市场需求，高纯度井冈霉素和高附加值下游产品生产技术亟须突破。

郑裕国主持开发成功高纯度井冈霉素发酵过程调控与组分控制技术，百吨级发酵罐井冈霉素 A 发酵效价从 10000μg/ml 提高到 30000μg/ml 以上，原料成本下降近 70%，井冈霉素成为时空产率最高、生产成本最低的抗生素品种；井冈霉素 A 纯度从 10% 以下提高到 90% 以上，开发成功高纯度粉剂等系列规格的高品质制品。

创建井冈霉素裂解菌高通量筛选模型，发明了糖苷酶、葡萄糖 3- 脱氢酶和 C-N 裂解酶定向、同步催化新工艺，裂解产物井冈霉烯胺浓度高达 2000μg/ml 以上；发明分子量相近的井冈霉素裂解产物分离新方法，井冈霉烯胺收率提高 2 倍以上；优化井冈霉烯胺酰化、卤化、脱卤和水解工艺，开发成功井冈霉醇胺产业化技术。

建成国内外产量最大的高纯度井冈霉素和井冈霉醇胺生产线，高纯度井冈霉素国内外市场占有率达 80% 以上。与原粗制品相比，高纯度井冈霉素的问世减少农药用量 83% 以上，减量增效成效显著。相关成果获 2008 年国家技术发明奖二等奖。

二、发明阿卡波糖产生菌选育、组分代谢调控及分离纯化新技术，实现糖苷酶抑制剂类降糖药最大品种生产技术的重大突破

阿卡波糖为氨基环醇假四糖化合物，是全球最大的糖苷酶抑制剂类糖尿病治疗药物，也是我国口服降糖药的最大品种。阿卡波糖生物合成途径复杂、发酵效价低、杂质组分多，其生产技术长期被国际巨头拜耳公司垄断。针对阿卡波糖发酵高糖、高耗氧和高黏度等特性，他发明了阿卡波糖产生菌高通量筛选技术，选育获得具有高渗透压、高基质浓度耐受能力等独特生物学性状的高产游动放线菌；揭示了糖苷转移酶、阿卡维基转移酶等关键酶催化的阿卡波糖合成途径和小分子物质介导的合成促进机制，创建了连续变速补料发酵新技术，实现了阿卡波糖的高强度生物合成。阿卡波糖发酵效价提高 4 倍以上，主要基质和动力消耗分别下降 81.4% 和 65.4%。

发现了游动放线菌胞外糖苷转移酶催化形成结构类似杂质组分的分子机制，开发了低温预处理-两步层析阿卡波糖分离纯化新技术，阻断放罐后杂质组分形成，大幅降低了杂质组分含量，并建成国内最大的年产 50 吨阿卡波糖生产线；制定国际上杂质组分控制最严格的阿卡波糖原料药标准并颁布实施。相关成果获 2014 年国家科技进步奖二等奖。

三、发明系列生物催化剂筛选、改造和工业应用新技术，创建多个大品种医药、农药化学品化学-酶法合成新工艺，实现大品种原料药的绿色过程替代

生物催化是获得手性化合物最具前景的方法之一。针对传统生物催化工艺开发周期长、成本高、规模化应用难等瓶颈，提出了融合有机逆合成分析与酶分子设计的手性化学品路线重构新方法，实现化学-酶法高效、绿色合成。

手性二甲基环丙烷骨架是重要的生物活性分子结构单元。由于环丙烷骨架刚性的平面结构和特殊的键角，其衍生物的手性合成一直是手性技术的难点之一。他提出了有机腈生物催化合成含手性二甲基环丙烷骨架衍生物的新方法，发明抗重症感染一线药物亚胺培南/西司他丁钠关键手性中间体（S）-2，2- 二甲基环丙甲酰胺腈水合酶/酰胺酶两步酶法新工艺；发明普适性立体选择性酰胺酶高通量筛选技术，获得了对目标底物高立体选择性的新酰胺酶。关键手性中间体合成工序由 8 步缩短至 2 步，收率提高 7 倍以上。从源头上革除氯化亚砜、氯仿和吡啶等有机溶剂的使用，废水减排 2/3 以上。

领导团队开发成功亚胺培南酯常压氢化、西司他丁水解钠盐结晶纯化和贵金属催化剂回用等系列新技术，无缝对接手性生物催化工艺，首创了亚胺培南/西司他丁钠化学-酶法合成新工艺。该技术在海正药业建成我国第一套腈转化酶生产手性化学品的工业化装置和国内外第一条亚胺培南/西司他丁钠化学-酶法合成生产线，亚胺培南/西司他丁钠原料药出口多个国家和地区，被业内专家评价为"手性生物催化与化学合成结合在我国制药工程领域成功应用的范例"。相关成果获 2010 年国家技术发明奖二等奖。

双手性二醇是高端医药、农药和材料的重要手性砌块和前体。双手性羟基立体选择性构筑难度极高，是有机合成最富挑战的课题之一。郑裕国发明了氧化还原酶同步、分步不对称氢化构筑手性羟基新工艺，彻底革除易燃易爆和深冷等苛刻生产工艺，产物对映体和非对映体过量值均大于 99%。该技术推广应用于心脑血管疾病防治第三代他汀双手性侧链 β，δ-二羟基己酸酯的工业生产，已建成年产 200 吨双手性二醇侧链和 60 吨阿托伐他汀钙生产线，出口市场占有率 60% 以上。相关成果获 2015 年浙江省科学技术进步奖一等奖。

Awardee of Chemical Engineering Technology Prize, Zheng Yuguo

Zheng Yuguo, born in Xiangshan County of Zhejiang Province in November 1961, is the Academician of Chinese Academy of Engineering, a member of the 13th National Committee of the Chinese People's Political Consultative Conference and dean of the College of Biotechnology and Bioengineering, Zhejiang University of Technology.

Prof. Zheng has been engaged in biochemical research and teaching for more than 30 years. He has successfully developed a series of biosynthetic technologies for pharmaceutical and pesticide chemicals, making original achievements in pseudo-sugars and keto-saccharides production, as well as industrial biocatalysis. Prof. Zheng has won 2 Second Prizes of National Technology Invention Awards, 1 Second Prize of National Science and Technology Progress Awards, 6 First Prizes of Science and Technology Awards from Province and Ministry, and 1 prize of Chinese Patent Excellence Award.

（1）Validamycin is the first industrialized biological pesticide in China. With the increasing market demand for green and high-value added pesticides, efficient production of high-purity validamycin and its down-stream products is of great significance. Prof. Zheng constructed new route for validamycin production with high-purity and pioneered technologies regarding to biocatalytic hydrolysis and pyrolysis of validamycin to produce valiolamine, the key intermediate for the new generation of glycosidase inhibitor. The largest production line of high-purity validamycin was established. The product occupied over 80% of the international and domestic market, the use of which reduced pesticide dosage by more than 83%.

(2) Acarbose is used as the world's largest glycosidase inhibitor for diabetes treatment. To solve the bottlenecks including complex synthetic route, low fermentation titer and high impurity content of acarbose production, Prof. Zheng has invented new technologies regarding acarbose-producing strain breeding, metabolism regulation and separation and purification, achieving a major technology breakthrough in acarbose production. A manufacturing line of 50 tons per year of acarbose was established and the international acarbose API standard with most strict impurity regulation was laid out.

(3) Aiming at the bottlenecks such as long development time, high cost and difficulties in large-scale application of traditional biocatalytic process, Prof. Zheng proposed new methods for synthesis of chiral chemicals by integrating retrosynthesis approach and molecular design of enzymes. New chemo-enzymatic process for pharmaceutical and pesticide chemicals such as key chiral intermediates of the first-line anti-severe infection drug and the cholesterol-lowering drugs were set up, bringing huge economic and social benefits.

资源环保技术奖获得者

贺 克 斌

贺克斌，1962 年 8 月出生于四川省成都市。1990 年毕业于清华大学环境工程系，获工学博士学位。1993 年、1997 年和 1998 年分别在丹麦技术大学、美国哈佛大学和英国利兹大学做访问学者和访问教授。1996 年至今历任清华大学环境学院教授、清华大学研究生院常务副院长、清华大学环境学院院长。现任国家生态环境保护专家委员会副主任，中国环境科学学会副理事长，全国环境科学与工程教学指导委员会主任，全球排放研究计划中国工作委员会主席。国家自然科学基金委杰出青年基金获得者和"多介质复合污染与控制化学"创新群体带头人，教育部长江学者特聘教授和"区域复合大气污染与控制"创新团队带头人。获国家自然科学奖二等奖 1 项、国家科技进步奖二等奖 3 项；获2014 年美国国家科学院院刊"科扎雷利奖"和 2018 年联合国环境署"气候与清洁空气奖"团队奖。在 Nature、Science Advances、PNAS 等期刊发表 SCI 论文 300 多篇，SCI 引用 13700 多次，23 篇进入 ESI "高引用论文"；出版专著 6 部；授权专利和软著权 16 项。2014—2018 年入选爱斯唯尔"中国高被引学者"，2018 年入选科睿唯安"全球高被引科学家"。2015 年当选中国工程院院士。

长期致力于大气复合污染与控制研究，以高分辨率排放清单技术-复合污染来源识别的多维溯源技术-多污染物协同控制的系统分析技术为核心，推动区域空气质量动态调控新技术系统的发展与应用。

一、主持研发大气污染源高分辨率清单关键技术

自主设计在线排放测试系统，实现由时段平均向瞬态排放测试的技术跃升以及复杂工况与颗粒物排放关键理化参数的同步准确测定。开发出包括空间、时间和化学物种分配等功能的高分辨率排放源模式，将源清单时空分辨率和化学物种辨识精度提高一个数量级；提出合成源谱新方法，建立多模式机制化学物种排放的统一算法，将可解析的化

学物种从原来的十几种提高到 500 多种。自主设计并建立在线动态排放清单计算、数据同化与推送技术平台，实现了多年度、不同空间尺度、多化学组分的排放清单集成计算处理及与大气化学模式之间的无缝链接。开发了全国和重点区域 1990—2017 年高分辨率排放清单数据产品，包括 700 多种排放源、10 种污染物和 500 多种 VOCs，内层嵌套时空分辨率分别达到 1h 和 1km，解决了中国区域排放清单的模式适用性问题。成果被国际重大研究计划排放清单首席科学家 David G. Streets 等评价为"世界一流的工作"，四次入选"中国百篇最具影响力国际论文"，成果获 2015 年国家科技进步奖二等奖。

二、开发了基于观测和模型的多维溯源方法

自主设计 $PM_{2.5}$ 长期连续综合观测平台，突破半挥发有机 / 无机共存体系采样偏差消除和二次有机颗粒物定量表征等技术难点；经 1998 年连续 15 年观测，发现我国典型地区二次无机颗粒物在 $PM_{2.5}$ 中的比例逐年增加，重污染过程中二次无机 / 有机成分比例与 $PM_{2.5}$ 浓度同步快速增长，二次颗粒物的前体物已成为 $PM_{2.5}$ 的主要来源；上述发现成为我国将 $PM_{2.5}$ 纳入新的《环境空气质量标准》的重要科学依据。经长期观测发现中纬度地区 $PM_{2.5}$ 质量浓度变化呈周期性规律，提出 $PM_{2.5}$ "锯齿形污染过程"新概念，建立了基于积分面积比的定量识别区域来源的新方法；基于形貌和能谱微观特征，建立单颗粒物理化特征综合解析与来源识别方法。建立以示踪物种相对丰度为指标的生物质燃烧颗粒物"指纹库"，开发了生物质燃烧颗粒物来源识别新方法。综合运用外场观测、模型模拟和理论计算，发现潮解气溶胶表面非均相化学反应是导致华北冬季重污染快速形成的重要原因，二氧化氮成为硫酸盐快速增长中最重要的氧化剂。在三维大气化学模型中加入实验中筛选的新的非均相化学反应机制，明显改善了模型对重污染快速形成中二次无机成分的模拟能力。基于高分辨率排放清单，结合模型源追踪方法，开发出区域高分辨率来源识别新技术，可定量 10 多种主要行业的污染源和关键污染物在不同时空定位下对重污染过程中一次颗粒物及二次组分的贡献，全面提升了复合污染溯源精细程度。成果被国际同行评价为"原创性"工作，1995 年诺贝尔化学奖得主 Molina 教授将其作为特大城市空气质量研究的代表性工作多次引用和重点介绍；成果获 2009 年国家自然科学奖二等奖和 2011 年国家科技进步奖二等奖。

三、发展区域空气质量动态调控新技术系统

集成优控污染源筛选技术、控制方案设计与优化技术以及减排效果定量评估技术等，构建多污染物协同控制系统分析技术。突破了耦合生产端污染物排放信息的投入产出模型技术，实现了对跨区域贸易中隐含污染水平的定量分析；通过耦合动态排放清单模型、投入产出模型、大气化学模型、卫星反演模型和健康效应模型，发展了消费端大气污染核算及健康影响分析方法，定量了贸易中隐含的污染流动以及各种终端消费类型对大气污染和健康损失的贡献。推动了区域空气质量动态调控新技术系统的发展。成果获 2010

年国家科技进步奖二等奖和 2014 年美国国家科学院院刊 "科扎雷利奖",并入选 2017 年中国重大科学、技术和工程进展。

成果应用于国家制定和实施《大气污染防治行动计划（2013—2017）》《蓝天保卫战三年行动计划（2018—2020）》以及数十个省市制定地方实施方案,并应用于北京奥运、杭州 G20 等近 20 次重大活动空气质量保障。主持设计了我国排放清单编制技术指南体系,由环保部发布 8 项技术文件并应用于全国数百个城市。清单数据产品在国家空气质量集群预报系统上实现业务化应用,并应用于国家和地方环境气象业务预报,被国内外 300 多家研究机构和 TF-HTAP、MICS-Asia 等大型国际研究计划采用。

Awardee of Resources and Environmental Technology Prize, He Kebin

He Kebin was born in Chengdu City of Sichuan Province in August 1962. He received his BS（1985）, MS（1987）and PhD degrees（1990）in Environmental Engineering at Tsinghua University. He joined the Department of Environmental Science and Engineering at Tsinghua University as a lecture in 1990 and was then promoted to associate professor in 1992 and full professor in 1996. He worked as a visiting scholar at Technical University of Denmark（1993）, and the visiting professors at University of Leeds（1998）and Harvard University（2001）. He also served as the Executive Vice Dean of Graduate School of Tsinghua University（2007—2013）. In 2015, he was elected as Member of Chinese Academy of Engineering. Currently, He is Cheung Kong Professor of Environmental Engineering and the Dean of School of Environment at Tsinghua University. Prof. He has been conducting research on air pollution control for over 30 years, and made significant achievements that have been implemented in national action plan on acid rain and $PM_{2.5}$ pollution control, including the development of an online platform of Multi-resolution Emission Inventory for China（MEIC）, the establishment of a new approach for source apportionment of integrating emission, observation and simulation, and the development of a dynamic assessment model for air pollution control solutions. He has authored more than 300 peer review papers which have received 13000 citations, with an H-index of 60.

Prof. He is playing an important role in the community of environmental science and engineering. He is the recipient of the National Science Fund for Distinguished Young Scholar, and serves as Chairman of National Teaching Steering Committee on Environmental Science and Engineering, Vice chairman of National Expert Committee for Ecology and Environmental Protection, and Vice president of Chinese Society for Environmental Science. He launched a research group for source identification and controlling of complex air pollution, which was selected as the Creative Group of National Natural Science Foundation of China and entitled as the Creative

Group of Ministry of Education. He was selected as Elsevier Most Cited Chinese Researchers (2014—2018) and Clarivate Global Highly Cited Researchers in 2018.

He has won a series of awards at home and abroad, including 2nd-class State Natural Science Award (2009), 2nd-class National Awards for Science and Technology Progress (2010, 2011, 2015), 1st-class National Award for Graduate Education (2018), and second prize of National Teaching Achievement Award (2018) . He has received ICCT Funding Member Award from the International Council on Clean Transportation in 2012, Cozzarelli Prize from the Proceedings of National Academy of Science (PNAS) in 2014, and Climate and Clean Air Award for Transformative Policy from Climate & Clean Air Coalition under UNEP in 2018. His work published in Nature was selected as one of the top advances of science, technology and engineering from China in 2017.

资源环保技术奖获得者

李 家 彪

李家彪，1961年4月出生于浙江省杭州市。1989年同济大学硕士毕业，2001年获中国科学院海洋研究所博士学位。1989年至今在国家海洋局第二海洋研究所（2018年更名为自然资源部第二海洋研究所）工作，历任副所长、所长；2019年8月兼任浙江省海洋科学院首任院长。1993—1994年在法国海洋开发研究院进行访问研究。先后担任"973"项目、国家自然科学基金重大项目以及国家海洋重大专项首席科学家。兼任国家自然科学基金委海洋科学学科评审组组长，中国海洋学会副理事长，上海交通大学、浙江大学、北京大学教授，国际洋中脊科学组织联合主席，国际标准化组织海洋技术分委会创始主席。获国家科技进步奖二等奖2次、省部特等奖3次、一等奖8次；出版专著5部、图集1部、中英文论文集6部；发表论文173篇；授权国际、国内发明专利9项，主持国家标准11项。2015年当选中国工程院院士。

长期从事海底科学与探测工程研究，拓展了海底科学与海洋权益交叉融合的新领域，在我国大陆架划界和大洋硫化物圈矿中作出了开创性贡献。

一、开创我国大陆架划界科技新领域，推动国际大陆架划界实践与理论发展

20世纪90年代末，200海里以外大陆架划界（简称大陆架划界）成为国际海洋权益的竞争热点。作为我国大陆架划界工程的首席科学家，李家彪系统开展了划界地质理论和技术方法研究，创建了涵盖全球主要类型的大陆架划界地质模型，甄别法律条款的地质适用条件，奠定了大陆架划界地质学理论基础，有效解决了国际上初始扩张弧后盆地和大洋岛屿国家划界的理论依据和技术难题。主持完成我国首份东海大陆架划界案提交联合国，代表中国赴联合国完成技术陈述和答辩，成为"初始扩张弧后盆地划界的国际范例"，强化了我国作为宽大陆架国家的海洋权益主张。此后，该划界技术体系形成自主知识产权并被广泛应用于全球各国提交划界案的科学性评估，有关意见和建议在联合国划界案审议过程中得到大陆架界限委员会的关注和采纳。援助尼日利亚等非洲四国开展大陆架界限研究，推动塞舌尔大陆架划界案申请成功，成为"一带一路"海洋科技外交的新亮点。创立了大陆架划界领域国际高峰论坛——大陆架和区域制度的科学与法律问题国际研讨会，开展划界理论与实践的跨界对话，成为国际上最有影响力的海洋划界学术平台。

二、实现我国大洋硫化物找矿重大突破，成为该矿种全球第一个先驱投资国

21世纪初，国际海底管理局启动硫化物资源勘探规章制订进程，新一轮蓝色圈地运动正式拉开序幕。作为我国国际海底区域硫化物资源项目首席科学家，2005年，李家彪组织开展我国全球洋中脊大规模科考，持续十余年的探索创新使我国从起步、发展迅速进入国际先进行列。在全球洋中脊发现大量热液硫化物，约占全球发现的10%。2013年竞选担任全球领导洋中脊科学研究的国际组织——国际大洋中脊科学组织联合主席，是该组织第一位中国学者。首次在西南印度洋中脊实施海底OBS三维地震探测，获得了深部活动岩浆房和基底拆离断层存在的关键证据，发现了超级岩浆增生和深部热液通道与硫化物形成和分布的关系，建立了区域成矿模型，提出了有利成矿区段，向联合国提交了国际上首份硫化物矿区申请，代表中国完成矿区申请技术答辩，得到国际海底管理局的认可和核准，成功获得西南印度洋10000平方千米矿区，使我国成为该矿种全球第一个先驱投资国。

李家彪推动建设了长期稳定的业务化创新团队，先后担任中国大洋勘测技术与深海科学研究开发基地、国家海洋局专属经济区与大陆架研究中心的首任主任。"大陆架划界技术创新团队"入选2017年科技部创新人才推进计划重点领域创新团队，团队核心成员2019年成功当选新一届联合国大陆架界限委员会委员，为我国维护海洋权益、提升国际话语权和科技竞争力发挥了重要作用。

Awardee of Resources and Environmental Technology Prize, Li Jiabiao

Li Jiabiao was born in Hangzhou City of Zhejiang Province in April 1961. He is the director-general of Second Institute of Oceanography, Ministry of Natural Resources (SIO/MNR), co-chair of InterRidge (2013—2015) and founding chairman of ISO/TC8/SC13 Marine Technology. He graduated from Tongji University with a master's degree in 1989 and started his marine science career in Second Institute of Oceanography, State Oceanic Administration (SIO/SOA). He studied in French Academy of Marine Research and Development (IFREMER) from 1993 to 1994, and received a PhD from Institute of Oceanology, Chinese Academy of Sciences in 2001. He served as deputy director of SIO/SOA from July 2002 to December 2013. He became director-general of SIO/SOA (renamed by SIO/MNR in 2018) in December 2013, and the first president of Zhejiang Academy of Marine Sciences since August 2019.

He has been engaged in the research of submarine geosciences and seabed exploration engineering, and made pioneering contributions to the outer limits of continental shelf beyond 200 nautical miles and exploration of mid−ocean ridge sulphide resources of China. He created a set of geological models for the delineating outer limits of continental shelf covering main types of the world, which especially give an effective solution to the cases for the back−arc basins and oceanic islands. He technically leaded the submission by the People's Republic of China concerning the outer limits of the continental shelf beyond 200 nautical miles in part of the East China Sea, and opened the joint researches on the extended continental shelves of Nigeria, Mozambique and Seychelles etc. He pushed forward the global expeditions on mid−ocean ridge hydrothermal vents and sulphides of China, and leaded a first 3D OBS array experiment on the seafloor at 49.5° E of Southwest Indian ridge. In such a place, he found a super−magmatic accretion of ultraslow spreading ridge, deep hydrothermal channels of large−scale detachment faults, and then established a regional metallogenic model. He made contribution to the application for approval of a plan of work for exploration for polymetallic sulphides by China in the Southwest Indian Ocean as a team leader, which became first application for polymetallic sulphides approved by International Seabed Authority.

He has successively been the chief scientist of the National Key Basic Research Development Program of China (973 Programs), major program of the National Natural Science Foundation of China (NSFC) and national programs for the outer limits of continental shelf and deep−sea sulphide resources. He was a head of the Marine Science Evaluation Group of NSFC (2017, 2018), vice president of Chinese Society for Oceanography. He was elected academician of the Chinese Academy of Engineering in 2015.

资源环保技术奖获得者

王 浩

　　王浩，1953 年 8 月出生于北京市。1978 年进入清华大学水利工程系学习，先后获得学士、硕士学位；1987—1991 年在清华大学经济管理学院就读系统工程专业在职博士生。1985 年进入中国水利水电科学研究院水资源研究所工作至今。2001—2013 年担任中国水利水电科学研究院水资源研究所所长。现任流域水循环模拟与调控国家重点实验室主任，中国水利水电科学研究院水资源所名誉所长；兼任中国可持续发展研究会理事长、中国水资源战略研究会常务副理事长、全球水伙伴（中国）副主席等职。2005 年当选中国工程院院士。

　　长期从事水文水资源研究，取得了系列原创性成果，整体推动了现代水资源科技发展，有力支撑了近 30 年来我国治水实践。

一、原创提出了"自然-人工"二元水循环理论与模拟方法，为变化环境下水资源演变的认知提供了科学范式与工具，引领了国际水文与水资源科学研究

　　针对强烈人类活动对我国流域水循环过程的影响，将人类活动和自然作用并列作为流域水循环的双重驱动力，提出了"自然-人工"二元水循环基础理论，构建了流域二元水循环分布式模拟模型；提出了基于大气水汽通量解析的全口径、层次化水资源动态评价方法，系统揭示了全国及黄河、海河等流域的水资源演变规律。上述成果在国内外产生重大影响，2010 年担任 EGU 年会水文分会中"流域二元水循环与城市水文模拟"分会场主席并做主旨发言。上述理论于 1997 年正式提出，较之国际水文学会新十年（2013—2022 年）主题 Panta Rhei—Everything Flows：Change in hydrology and society 整整早了 15 年。

二、创立发展具有中国特色的水资源合理配置理论与方法，支撑了近 30 年来我国流域和区域水资源规划实践

"八五"期间，将水资源系统和宏观经济系统有机结合，创建了基于宏观经济的水资源合理配置理论，提出了水资源优化配置的多层次、多目标决策支持方法，提出了华北地区水资源优化配置方案，并得到实践的长期应用检验，成效引起国内外强烈反响和广泛认同。

"九五"期间，根据西北地区水资源和生态环境状况，创建面向生态的水资源合理配置理论方法，提出了西北地区水资源配置方案，为西部大开发战略的实施提供了有力支撑。成果全面应用于西北水资源和社会经济发展规划、塔里木河和黑河流域规划、中哈国际河流谈判等重大生产实践。

"十五"期间，建立了生态需水类型划分基本准则，提出了多参数河流生态需水理论和计算方法，初步形成了符合我国实际的生态需水理论方法体系；将土壤水资源纳入合理配置范畴，发展提出了广义水资源合理配置理论方法。

"十一五"以来，提出了水资源量-效-质一体化评价方法，实现了水资源数量、质量、效用的统一度量，并据此建立了量-质-效一体化配置理论与方法。

三、创新研发复杂水资源系统规划与调度关键技术，全面应用于全国水资源综合规划以及南水北调工程、黑河流域等规划和运行管理实践

建立了我国水资源综合规划的整体技术框架，全程参与了第一次《全国水资源综合规划》技术大纲和技术细则的起草和编制；创建了跨流域调水工程水资源规划理论与方法，科学确立了南水北调工程的调水规模，并获国务院批准。上述理论方法已成为跨流域调水工程规划的通用方法，在多项重大调水工程中得到应用。

主持研发了南水北调中、东线水量与水质、常规与应急调度与运行决策支持系统，实现"数值模拟—评价诊断—实时预测—追踪溯源—水量调度—自动控制"六大环节联动调控。成果已经在南水北调中、东线调度工作中业务化运行，对南水北调中、东线水资源高效科学调度提供了关键技术保障。

四、为节水型社会建设、最严格水资源管理和水生态文明建设等国家重大水公共政策制定与实施提供核心科技支撑

构建了节水型社会建设基础理论体系，研发了总量控制与定额管理相结合的节水型社会建设成套关键技术，相关成果应用于 31 个省级行政区 100 个国家级试点和 200 多个省级试点。

提出的水资源量-质-效一体化调控理论与方法成为国家提出实行最严格水资源管理制度的重要科学依据，并全面支撑了最严格水资源管理制度实施面临的指标分解、评价、

复核、考核等核心技术工作。

参与国家推行水生态文明建设工作的顶层设计，带领团队编制了全国第一个和40%的国家水生态文明试点城市方案，全部作为顶层设计予以实施；组织编制完成《全国水生态文明市（县）评价标准》，成为国家水生态文明建设评价依据。

提出了面向可持续发展的全成本水价构成理论，开发了水价的会计学计算方法和核算均衡模型，为我国水价制定与改革提供了理论依据和实施方法，并应用于深圳对香港供水、珠海对澳门供水的水价调整和全国城市水价制定工作中。

五、积极推广中国水资源管理技术与经验，为水资源科学知识传播作出杰出贡献

从20世纪80年代后期至今，先后主持完成10多项国际合作项目，积极推广中国水资源管理技术与经验，多次应邀参加世界水论坛、欧洲地球科学联盟学术年会等重大国际会议。先后为75个国家的代表做中国水资源管理专题技术讲座。主持编写了首部面向中小学生的《水知识教育读本》，编写了《水文学方法》丛书和《水资源学》等系列专著，担任第一部全面反映中国水资源的大型纪录片《水问》的首席技术顾问。

近五年，面向新时期国家治水实践需求及其关键科学问题，先后创建了梯级水库群全生命周期风险动态识别与防控、太阳能光伏提水修复草场和农田、江河水量调度、城市水量与水质调控等理论与技术，均已得到实践检验和大范围推广应用，为国家水安全保障作出了重要贡献。

迄今已培养博士后30余名、博士生110余名、硕士生80余人，为国家输送了大量高层次水利科技人才。其中，10余人次获国家杰出青年基金和中国青年科技奖，入选国家"万人计划"科技领军人才。

Awardee of Resources and Environmental Technology Prize, Wang Hao

Wang Hao was born in Beijing City in August 1953. He is currently a chief at the State Key Laboratory of Water Cycle Simulation and Regulation, and the honorary director of the Department of Water Resources, China Institute of Water Resources and Hydropower Research. He is also the president of China Sustainable Development Research Association, executive vice president of China Water Resources Strategy Research Association, vice president of Global Water Partnership (China), and former vice chairman of China Society of Natural Resources. He was born in Beijing on August 13th, 1953. He earned his bachelor's and master's degrees from Tsinghua University during 1978 to 1985, doctorate in Systems Engineering from Tsinghua University in 1991. Dr. WANG has been working in the Department of Water Resources, China Institute of

Water Resources and Hydropower Research since 1985. He has worked as the Ding of Department of Water Resources from 2001 to 2013, China Institute of Water Resources and Hydropower Research. In 2005, he was elected as an academician of the Chinese Academy of Engineering.

Dr. Wang is actively engaged in professional water associations and dedicated himself to the research of hydrology and water resources for years. A series of original innovation he has proposed is widely recognized by domestic and foreign counterparts. These achievements have initially promoted the rapid development and utilization of water resources and strongly supported the practice of water regulation in China in the past 30 years.

(1) The "natural-social" dualistic water-cycle theory and simulation method, which can provide scientific paradigms and tools for a better understanding of water resources under the changing environment.

(2) The theory and method of rational allocation of water resources were also established and developed with Chinese characteristics, which has been widely practiced for a significant reform in water resources planning both in basin and regional scale in China during the last 30 year.

(3) While, applying to the national integrated planning of water resources, the key technologies for planning and scheduling complex water resources systems have been innovatively developed by Hao WANG., e.g., the South-North Water Diversion Project and the Heihe River Basin Project.

(4) Dr. WANG provides technological and scientific knowledge for underpinning the planning and implementation of major national water policy, e.g. the construction of water-saving society, the most stringent water resources management, and the construction of water ecological civilization.

(5) The techniques and experiences of water resources management in China have been drastically popularized by Dr. WANG. As a proponents of integrated water resources management, he has made a remarkable contribution in the dissemination of water resources research.

工程建设技术奖获得者

雷 增 光

雷增光，1961 年 4 月出生于陕西省渭南市。1986 年获清华大学工程物理系硕士学位，2006 年获清华大学工程物理系博士学位。1986 年 5 月—2002 年 4 月任核工业四〇五厂技术干部、车间副主任、厂长助理、副厂长、总工程师、常务副厂长；2002 年 4 月—2010 年 5 月任核工业理化工程研究院院长；2010 年 5 月至今任中国核工业集团有限公司总工程师。先后担任中国科学技术协会第九届全国委员会常务委员、中国核学会副理事长、国家国防科技工业局科学技术委员会委员、中国核能行业协会第二届专家委员会副主任、清华大学工程物理系兼职教授。先后获国家科技进步奖二等奖 3 项、省部级科技奖 19 项；发表论文和研究报告多篇，策划并参与编写出版专著《气体专用设备设计指南》。2004 年入选"新世纪百千万人才工程国家级人选"，2012 年获得"第三届国防科技工业杰出人才奖"，2014 年获得第五届"全国杰出专业技术人才"荣誉称号。

长期从事铀浓缩技术研发和工程创新，主持和参与了我国铀浓缩专用设备研制和工业化应用各环节的工作，为突破设备研制、批量制造和工厂设计运行等关键技术作出了突出贡献。

一、首座铀浓缩离心工程技术创新

我国首座铀浓缩离心工程主工艺系统从国外引进，供取料及辅助系统由中方自主设计建造。作为工程建设副总指挥和运行管理总工程师，雷增光在级联方案和供取料工艺优化、检测控制系统自主化等方面取得了多项创新成果。主持建立了多层架柔性级联运行方案计算方法和优化方法，实现了多种丰度产品的生产，效率明显优于外方提供的方案，为国产离心级联的设计奠定了基础。提出用"容器净化法取代扩散净化级联供料"和"用加压取料法收取级联精料"、用"外冷外热式冷升器代替内冷内热式冷升器"等工艺方案，并主持试验验证和实施，供取料能力提高 5 倍，达到同类技术国际先进水平。

主持对外方检测控制系统、专用仪表国产化，建立了基于通用软件平台的控制系统，解决了原系统故障率高且备用件缺乏的问题，为国产铀浓缩工程控制系统提供了设计经验和专用仪表。

首座铀浓缩离心工程建设中的技术创新推动工程比计划提前 300 多天建成投产，至今已安全稳定运行 20 余年（超设计寿命），并仍保持 90% 以上的生产能力。

二、第一代铀浓缩专用设备工业化应用研究

在单机研制成功基础上，2002 年起作为项目第一负责人负责组织第一代铀浓缩专用设备工业化应用研究，主要解决专用设备的可靠性、经济性和一致性问题。在可靠性研究方面，提出"个、十、百、千、万"的可靠性考核思路，组织建立可靠性试验考核体系，主持设计并建立了从材料、零部件到整机共 180 余套可靠性及加速寿命试验装置和系统，通过试验研究提出了上百项工艺优化改进方案，极大地提高了设备的可靠性，使预期寿命大幅提高，优于设计指标。

主持开展一致性和经济性研究，提出了设计参数和加工工艺综合优化的思路，研制成功 50 余台套专用加工和检测设备，加工和检测效率提高了数倍，使第一代专用设备的一致性和经济性得到明显提高，并为专用设备制造厂建设奠定了基础。通过千台规模考核鉴定试验，实现了设备专用材料、设计、生产工艺定型。

组织开展第一代专用设备制造厂建设，制定了生产线流程方案、原材料、外协件的批量检测方法，解决了一系列小批量试制时从未遇到的技术和管理问题。提出以提高自动化生产水平为手段促进产品一致性和经济性提高的思路，取得了良好效果，制造厂提前半年建成投产。第一代专用设备于 2007 年中试成功投运，2010 年商用示范工厂建设完成，2012 年顺利通过国家验收。铀浓缩专用设备研制成功是我国核工业继两弹一艇、秦山核电站之后取得的又一重大自主创新成果，是我国核科技工业的重大跨越。

三、第二代铀浓缩专用设备研制和工业化应用研究

我国铀浓缩技术坚持"研制一代、生产一代、预研一代"的发展路线，为进一步提高技术性能和经济性，2004 年开始了第二代铀浓缩专用设备研制。雷增光作为项目第一负责人、总设计师，主持确定了在第一代专用设备基础上以提高转子线速度为主、增加长度为辅的总体技术路线，主持确定了新的转子设计方案，使设备能力大幅提高，并保持两代设备外部接口一致，满足直接替换的技术要求。

针对第二代专用设备的技术特点，主持开展了强旋转、更高马赫数流场中分离部件对流场、温度场、分离性能等的影响规律研究，组织建立了完善的物理分离性能试验手段，提出三维流场数值模拟与试验修正结合的方法，攻克超高马赫数流场分析难题，使物理性能研制周期缩短一半以上。主持建立了第二代专用设备零部件及整机可靠性和寿命考核试验台，提出基于性能退化的可靠性设计方法，掌握了专用设备的可靠性试验、寿命验证试验技术，提高了设备的固有可靠性。组织攻克了大尺寸薄壁件加工变形、异形零件加工等难题，研制了多种专用加工、装配和检测设备，完成了从研制到批量生产的技术转化。研究提出把第二代专用设备中试考核试验安装到第一代商用工厂中的思路，并解决了机型混装的关键技术问题，缩短了研发时间，节约了数亿元投资。第二代专用设备于 2012 年在分离工厂正式投入运行考核，性能和可靠性指标均达到设计要求。2018年，我国第二代铀浓缩专用设备示范工程全面建成，标志着专用设备具备大规模商用条件，技术水平、经济性得到了进一步提升，达到国际先进水平。第二代专用设备的研制和工业化进一步提高了我国在国际铀浓缩领域的地位和竞争力，是中国核能发展燃料供应的重要保障，对提升我国核电竞争力至关重要。

Awardee of Engineering and Construction Technology Prize, Lei Zengguang

Lei Zengguang was born in Weinan City of Shaanxi Province in April 1961. He graduated from Tsinghua University and obtained a master's and a doctor's degrees in Engineering Physics in 1986 and 2006, respectively. From May 1986 to April 2002, he worked for Shaanxi Uranium Enrichment Co., Ltd as chief engineer and deputy general manager. He served as president of the Institute of Physical and Chemical Engineering (IPCE) from April 2002 to May 2010, and as chief engineer of China National Nuclear Corporation (CNNC) from May 2010. He has successively acted as the member of the Ninth National Committee of the China Association of Science and Technology, the Vice-Chairman of the Chinese Nuclear Society, the member of the Science and Technology Committee of the State Administration of Science, Technology and Industry for National Defense, the Vice-Chairman of the Second Expert Committee of the China Nuclear Energy Association, and a part-time professor of the Department of Engineering Physics of Tsinghua University.

After graduating from Tsinghua University in 1986, Mr. Lei has been engaged in research and development of uranium enrichment technology and technical innovation. He has led and participated in the development and industrial application of China's special equipment for uranium enrichment.

He is the academic leader in the field of uranium enrichment technology. Mr. Lei has led and participated in the construction and operation of China's first centrifugal uranium enrichment project, the industrial research and manufacturing plant construction of the first generation of uranium enrichment equipment, and the development of the second generation of special equipment for uranium enrichment. He has made outstanding contributions to breakthroughs in the key technologies of special equipment development, batch production and plant construction and operation. The special equipment for uranium enrichment represents another significant technological leap in China's nuclear industry, following "A-bomb, H-bomb and nuclear-powered submarine" and Qinshan nuclear power plant. Since 2010, Mr. Lei has assumed the position of the chief engineer of CNNC. He has taken charge of the formulation of the CNNC's strategic plan for scientific and technological development and the top-design of "Longteng Science and Technology Innovation Project", organized and implemented scientific and technological innovation, and made many major achievements. Mr. Lei has won 3 second prizes of National Science and Technology Progress Award. In 2004, he was selected as a national candidate for the Millions of Talents Project in the New Century. In 2012, he won the Third Outstanding Talents Award of Science, Technology and Industry for National Defense. In 2014, he was awarded honor of the Fifth National Outstanding Professional Personnel.

工程建设技术奖获得者

吴希明

吴希明，1964年9月出生于福建省邵武市。博士生导师，研究员。1984年本科毕业于南京航空航天大学。1984—2013年在中国航空工业602所（中国直升机设计研究所）从事直升机研发工作，先后担任设计员、副/正组长、副/正主任、副总师和总设计师；2014年至今任中国航空工业集团有限公司科技委副主任、中国航空研究院副院长和航空工业直升机公司总设计师。

作为我国直升机技术领域的领军人物、中航工业直升机设计首席专家，长期从事直升机总体设计和直升机技术预先研究工作，成功主持多个国家重点直升机型号研制工作、国家"863"计划项目研究等科研项目。先后担任直八、直九、直十一等直升机型号副总设计师，现任直十、直十九武装直升机和重型直升机等三型国家重大工程型号总设计师。曾荣获国家科技进步奖一等奖1项，国防科技进步特等、一、二、三等奖7项；中共中央、国务院、中央军委"高技术武器装备发展建设重大贡献奖"金奖和"国防科技工业杰出人才奖"，国防科工委和航空工业一、二、三等功8次，航空工业"航空报国金奖"6次；"全国劳动模范""全国优秀科技工作者"、全国"十大杰出青年"和"年度科技创新人物""国防科技工业有突出贡献中青年专家"、首批"新世纪百千万人才工程"国家级人选等多项荣誉。

一、主持自主研制了我国首型、全国产化的专用武装直升机直十，我军方评价"对实现我军跨越式发展产生重大影响"

主持突破了总体设计参数/气动布局和结构/系统构型多学科综合优化设计、机弹相容设计、生存力综合优化设计等关键技术，在国内首次制定了独特的高机敏性、高生存力直升机总体方案，使直十主要作战性能达到世界先进水平。

主持突破了旋翼系统气动布局设计技术，首次在我国实现了球柔性旋翼自主研制，其性能、噪声、维护性达到世界先进水平。

制定了全机抗坠毁优化匹配体系、模型和方法，主持研制了关键构件和系统，在我国首次实现直升机全机耐坠毁研制并达到世界先进水平。

二、主持实现研发能力的跨越式提升，助推了产业井喷式发展

作为行业总师，主持建立了我国先进直升机完整的数字化自主设计、验证技术体系和先进的试验验证手段，使我国直升机实现了完全自主研发的历史性跨越，支撑了现有近 50 型直升机的自主研发，助推了我国直升机产业井喷式发展。

主持建立了支撑我国各型先进直升机型号研发的完整设计理论、方法、数据库、工具，主持研制了旋翼塔等先进、体系化的试验与验证手段。

主持发展了气动布局、飞行力学、旋翼气动等的设计分析方法，实现了运动、变形、载荷高度耦合旋翼系统疲劳验证等试验技术的突破，建立了多元飞行参数及关键部位载荷、振动实时遥测监控等飞行试验方法。

三、策划技术发展，主持重型直升机论证和关键技术攻关，引领直升机创新

提出了彰显高原能力的我国独特型号发展安排，主持制定了直升机创新超越的发展重点和关键技术，指导我国直升机行业的整体推进和有序发展。

制定了世界上独有的高原重型直升机总体方案，主持攻克了大型球柔性钛合金桨毂等关键技术，填补了重型直升机的空白。

主持揭示了共轴刚性旋翼流场机理，构建了其气动特性分析体系和试验技术，为我国下一代直升机装备发展奠定了基础。

Awardee of Engineering and Construction Technology Prize, Wu Ximing

Wu Ximing was born in Shaowu City of Fujian Province in September 1964. In 1984, he graduated from Nanjing University of Aeronautics and Astronautics, is doctoral tutor, professor, worked in helicopter research and development at China Helicopter Design and Research Institute from 1984 to 2013, as a designer, team leader, department director, deputy chief and chief designer of institute. Since 2014, he is Deputy Director of the Science and Technology Commission, Aviation Industry Corporation of China, Ltd., Vice President of the Chinese Aeronautical Establishment and Chief Designer of China Helicopter Corporation.

He is China Helicopter Chief Expert, long-term engaged in the overall design of helicopter and helicopter technology research, successfully presided several helicopters development, the national "863" project research and other scientific research projects.

As a leader in the field of helicopter technology in China, he has presided over the research work on key technologies of helicopters for a long time, and was deputy chief designer of helicopters such as Z8, Z9 and Z11, is chief designer of Z10、Z19 attack helicopters and heavy helicopter, he hosted the independent development of China's first and full domestic made attack helicopter Z10, host to achieve the development capacity of the leap-forward promotion, to promote the development of the china helicopter industry, and plan the development of China helicopter technology, preside over heavy helicopter design and key helicopter technology researches.

Wu Ximing has won the first prize of "national award for science and technology progress" once, award for "national defense science and technology progress" seven times, Aviation industry "aviation gold medal" six times, "National Model Labor", "National Excellent Science and Technology Workers", the national "Top Ten Outstanding Young People", national "Science and Technology Innovation Person of the Year", "National Defense Science and Technology Industry outstanding expert", and many other honors.

Published monographs "Helicopter Dynamics Engineering Design" and "Tilt-Rotor Flight Control", published a number of academic papers, such as "Aerodynamic Problems and Research Progress of Rigid Coaxial Rotor". As the chief designer of helicopter in the aviation industry, through the organization of helicopter development and technical research, he established an experienced, skilled engineering personnel team and trained several helicopter chief designers.

工程建设技术奖获得者

朱 坤

朱坤，1966 年 2 月出生于湖南省。1988 年、1991 年分别于北京航空航天大学获学士、硕士学位。1991—2009 年历任航天科工三院三部工程师、高级工程师、研究员，2009 年至今历任航天科工三院科技委常委、副主任。现任复杂系统控制与智能协同技术重点实验室首席科学家。获国家新世纪"百千万"人才、国防工业"511 人才工程"技术带头人、国防科技有突出贡献中青年专家、航天基金奖特别奖、航空航天月桂奖等。

长期从事我国反舰导弹技术研究，针对导弹水下发射这一世界性难题，持续研究 20 多年，攻克我国第一代潜射反舰导弹技术瓶颈，为填补我军装备空白作出重要贡献；主持研制成功国际领先水平的新一代反舰导弹。先后获得国家科技进步特等奖和一等奖、二等奖各 1 项，省部级奖励 8 项，在反舰导弹技术开创性研究及应用方面取得了突出成就。

（1）全程参加第一代潜舰导弹研制，攻克跨介质攻击和出水姿态控制等难题，为我国掌握潜舰导弹技术作出了重要贡献，获国家科技进步奖一等奖。

（2）提出某新型中程反舰导弹方案，奠定中程反舰导弹射程成倍提升和系列化发展基础。大力提倡一体化优化设计方法，攻克多部件共用、总体 / 结构一体化难题，使导弹作战能力大幅提升。基于该方案的导弹族构成我国"近海防御"的中坚力量。

（3）作为主要技术负责人，主持导弹水下有动力发射技术攻关，建立了一整套导弹水下有动力发射及试验验证方法，提出双介质能量优化控制等技术，攻克了导弹水下点火、水下高速运动空泡抑制、跨介质控制等难题，实现大深度、高海况水下发射，使我国成为世界上第四个掌握该技术的国家，获国家科技进步奖二等奖。

（4）提出新一代反舰导弹方案，主持预研、研制、装备和系列化发展，成为海军主战装备。提出总体技术方案，突破新型发射方式、一体化设计、超低空掠海飞行、目标选择与精确打击、高效毁伤、电子对抗等技术，主要技术指标大幅提高，使我国反舰导弹技术水平实现跨越式提升，批量装备我海军，大大提高了我海军远海防卫作战能力。

获 2017 年国家科技进步奖特等奖。

（5）主持国家某科技工程重大专项飞行器研制工作，多项技术取得重大突破，达到世界前沿，推动了我国该技术领域发展进程。

Awardee of Engineering and Construction Technology Prize, Zhu Kun

Zhu Kun was born in Hunan Province in February 1966. He graduated in 1988 with a bachelor degree and went on studying for a master degree in 1991 at Beihang University. From 1991 to 2009, he severed as an engineer, senior engineer and professor of Beijing Electro-mechanical Engineering Institute of the Third Academy of CASIC. Since 2009, he has been appointed as a member of science and technology commission and deputy director general of the Third Academy of CASIC and has been working on the anti-ship missile research technology. Now, he has been served as the chief designer for seven types of missiles and the chief scientist of the key lab of complex systems & intelligent collaboration technology.

Professor Zhu Kun has been researching on China's anti-ship missile technology for a long time and has focused on the worldwide problem of underwater missile launch for more than 20 years. He has made a great contribution on the first generation submarine-launched anti-ship missile technology, which has broken the bottleneck and filled the blank of our military equipment. Under his leadership, a new generation of internationally advanced anti-ship missile has been successfully developed. He has won the special prize, 1st Prize and 2nd prize of the State Science and Technology Progress Awards, and 8 provincial/ministerial level awards for his outstanding achievements on the pioneering research and application of anti-ship missile technology.

（1）He fully participates in the development of the first generation of submarine-to-ship missile, and overcomes key technical problems such as cross-medium attack and exit-water attitude control. He has won the 1st Prize of the State Science and Technology Progress Awards for his outstanding contributions to submarine-to-ship missile technology.

（2）He proposes a scheme of new medium range anti-ship missile and lays the foundation of the multiplying increase in range and serialization development of the medium range anti-ship missile. He strongly advocates integrated optimized design method and solves the difficulty problems on multi-component sharing, overall structural integration which have been greatly improved the missile's combat ability. The missile family based on the scheme is the backbone of China's coastal defense.

（3）As the main charger of the technology, he led his research team focusing on missile underwater propelled launch and established a whole set of demonstration method for missile underwater propelled launch and test. He presented techniques such as double medium energy optimization control method and overcame the technical problems such as underwater ignition, underwater cavity bubble suppression in high speed movement, cross-medium control which realized underwater launch in a deep, and high sea state. The achievement makes China the fourth country in the world to master this technology. He also won the 2nd Prize of the State Science and Technology Progress Awards for this contribution.

（4）He put forward a new generation of anti-ship missile scheme, in which, he led the pre-research, and research works on the equipment and serialized development. He also presented general technology scheme and increased the technical specifications of some technologies such as new launch mode, integration design, and sea-skimming flight in ultra low altitude, target selection and precise strike, high-efficiency damage, electronic countermeasures. The technical level of China's anti-ship missile has achieved a leap forward promotion. With the batch of equipment, China's naval offshore defense ability has been greatly promoted. He won the Special Prize of the State Science and Technology Progress Award in the year of 2017.

（5）He holds a national major scientific project on special aircraft research. With his efforts, breakthroughs are made on several technologies and have reached the forehead of the world.

He has won 8 provincial/ministerial level awards, and won the title of New Century Talents Project of China, 511 Talents Engineering Technology In National Defense Industry, Young and Middle-Aged Experts with Outstanding Contributions to National Defense Science and Technology, special prize of China space foundation, Aerospace Laureate Awards and other awards.

何梁何利基金科学与技术创新奖获得者传略

PROFILES OF THE AWARDEES OF PRIZE FOR
SCIENTIFIC AND TECHNOLOGICAL INNOVATION OF
HO LEUNG HO LEE FOUNDATION

青年创新奖获得者

樊 春 海

樊春海，1974年3月出生于江苏省张家港市。1996年毕业于南京大学生物化学系，2000年获南京大学理学博士学位，2001—2003年在加州大学圣巴巴拉分校从事博士后研究。2004年1月回国任中国科学院上海应用物理研究所研究员；2018年4月至今任上海交通大学化学化工学院王宽诚讲席教授。获2016年国家自然科学奖二等奖，2019年度美国化学会"测量科学进展讲座奖"。2007年获国家杰出青年基金，2012—2016年任科技部重大科学研究计划首席科学家。兼任 *ACS Applied Materials & Interfaces* 副主编、*Chem Plus Chem* 编委会共同主席。入选美国科学促进会、国际电化学学会和英国皇家化学会会士，并连续五年入选"全球高被引科学家"。

主要从事分析化学研究，在生物大分子限域识别和核酸传感、成像分析等方面开展了深入和系统的工作。针对界面限域环境下生物分子识别的复杂性挑战，提出框架核酸概念并引入分析化学领域，建立了"先组装、后检测"的框架核酸传感与成像新方法，突破了界面限域组装与识别难题，对促进生物分析的发展作出了贡献。

提出"框架核酸"概念并发展了界面有序化构筑新思想，突破了生物界面限域环境下组装与识别的瓶颈；开拓框架核酸电化学传感分析新方法，发展出复杂生物体系中高信噪比检测的新技术；发现细胞膜微纳界面调控的新机制，建立了核酸分子活细胞原位实时成像新方法。相关工作为 *Science*、*Nature* 等期刊广泛引用和正面评价，如被 *Nat Nanotech* 2014综述列为生物传感"多尺度界面工程"的两个方向之一；诺贝尔奖得主 Novoselov 在 *Science* 2014展望论文中重点介绍等。研制成多种高性能的电化学生物传感器件，并制定了二类相应的标准物质。相关应用成果获得广泛好评，电化学DNA传感器工作被列入 IUPAC 技术报告，被 *Nat Mater* 社论评论为框架核酸实现生物传感检测的范例。

迄今以通讯作者发表SCI论文237篇，包括 *Nature* 1篇、*Nature* 子刊15篇、*Sci Adv*

1 篇、*JACS* 15 篇、*Angew Chem* 25 篇、*AM* 21 篇、*Chem Rev* 2 篇、*Acc Chem Res* 4 篇、*Chem Soc Rev* 4 篇、*Nat Chem* 和 *Nat Biomed Eng* 观点评述各 1 篇，SCI 他引 30000 余次；获授权中国发明专利 16 件、美国专利 2 件。

Awardee of Youth Innovation Prize，Fan Chunhai

Fan Chunhai was born in Zhangjiagang City of Jiangsu Province in March 1974. He works in the areas of nucleic acids analysis. He proposed the concept of framework nucleic acids（FNAs）, and developed a novel strategy for ordered construction of biosensing interfaces，which represents an important advance in interfacial biomolecular recognition，nucleic acids sensing and live-cell imaging. He published 237 papers including in Nature and Nature journals，with over 30000 citations and H-index of 92. He was awarded the National Natural Science Prize（2nd class, 2016）, and the ACS Advances in Measurement Science Lectureship Award（2019）. He received the Distinguished Researchers of NSFC in 2007, Principle Scientist of 973 in 2012. He is an elected fellow of AAAS, ISE and RSC, and he is recognized as Highly Cited Researchers over the last 5 years.

青年创新奖获得者

何 元 智

何元智，女，1974 年 8 月出生于四川省自贡市。2001 年毕业于解放军理工大学通信与信息系统专业，获工学博士学位。2001 年毕业后在解放军某研究所工作，现为军事科学院系统工程研究院研究员。国家高新工程型号总师，国家创新人才推进计划中青年科技创新领军人才，卫星通信领域主要学术带头人，卓越青年基金获得者，军事科学院首席专家，博士生导师。先后兼任国家高技术发展计划专家组专家、国家重点基础研究发展计划专家组专家、中国电子学会和中国通信学会卫星专委会委员、中国卫星通信广播电视用户协会常务理事、北京通信学会副理事长。作为负责人，承担了国家高新工程重点型号项目、国家人民防空重大工程建设项目、国防科技卓越青年基金等，获国家科技进步奖一等奖 1 项、二等奖 1 项，省部级科技进步奖一等奖 7 项，授权发明专利 23 项。获中国科协"求是"杰出青年奖、国务院政府特殊津贴，被评为全国三八红旗手、巾帼建功先进个人，因科技创新突出贡献多次立功嘉奖。

主要从事卫星通信领域科研工作，在卫星通信网络理论方法研究、体制设计和技术攻关方面取得多项重大创新性成果。

一、空间频轨分析方法

针对空间卫星通信频率轨位资源严重受限的瓶颈问题，提出并设计了多域关联的空间频轨分析方法，建立了密集频轨条件下拓频保轨技术体系，增强了空间频率轨位资源战略储备能力，为国家空间通信系统建设与发展奠定了基础。

二、分布式星群网络理论

提出以小占位、分布式、可重构为特征的分布式星群网络基本概念、构型方法、群内 / 群间组网体制和自愈算法，建立近距、广角、大动态条件下的分布式星群组网机理与实现方法，在星群自适应捷变重构机制、星群分布式协同传输去相关等方面取得重大突破，成果应用于多项国家重大科研计划项目。

三、多波束卫星组网方法

构造多维联合寻址协同控制模型，提出密集和移动波束环境下多级混合链路和功率控制方法，设计了适合卫星信道长时延及误码特性的星地传输体制和路由交换协议，支持基于虚拟逻辑平面的网络参数自动获取和波形灵活重构，解决了广域复杂环境下大容量移动用户随遇接入、动中组网的国际性难题。

四、自适应卫星广播技术

攻克大动态信道条件下自适应卫星广播技术，设计了面向任务的广播信息分类结构和表示规则，建立了广播帧与信道条件的精细匹配模型，实现了大范围分布式多源异构信息的统一汇聚和高效分发，解决了暴雨、大雪、干扰等极恶劣环境下小口径用户对广播信息可靠接收的国际性难题。

主持研制了我国新一代宽带卫星通信系统和我国第一代静止轨道卫星移动通信系统，成果在全国范围成建制配发并广泛应用，为推动我国卫星通信技术水平的跨越式发展作出了贡献。

Awardee of Youth Innovation Prize, He Yuanzhi

He Yuanzhi, female, was born in Zigong City of Sichuan Province in August 1974. She is the Chief Expert in the Academy of Military Sciences. She is the recipient of National Defense Outstanding Young-Scientist Award in 2018; the First Prize of National Science and Technology Progress Award (the leading PI) in 2018; the Second Prize of National Science and Technology Progress Award in 2011; the First Prize of Ministry-level Science and Technology Progress Award seven times; "Qiu Shi" Award, China Association for Science and Technology in 2018; Special Government Allowance of the State Council in 2016; National Women Pacesetter Award in 2019. Dr. He served as the Panelist of National High-Tech R&D Program (863 Project), Ministry of Science and Technology of China.

Dr. He is interested in the networking theories, methods and technologies in satellite communication.

（1）In order to solve the problem of limited orbital and frequency resources of satellite communication, a space frequency and orbit analysis algorithm is proposed, which enhances the strategic reserve capacity of national space frequency orbit resource and fixes a foundation for constructing and developing of national space communication system.

（2）The basic concept, configuration method, and networking regime of distributed satellite cluster Network, have been proposed. Major breakthroughs have been made in technology according to distributed cooperative transmission, adaptive network reconstruction, and so on, which have been used in several national great science and technology projects.

（3）For dynamic networking in multi-beam satellite communication system, a cross layer collaboration control model has been constructed to multilevel link controlling and hybrid power controlling. With this method, it could be realized for mobile users with large capacity to flexibly networking in wide area and complex environment.

（4）She proposed a method to realize self-adapting information broadcasting in the dynamic change satellite channels, and build the exact models to match the broadcasting frames and different channels. Based on the above, it could be realized for small aperture users to receive satellite broadcasting information reliably in severe transmission channels.

（5）Be the technology PI, she was responsible for developing the new generation wild-band satellite communication system and the first generation satellite mobile communication system, which have been wildly used in China.

青年创新奖获得者

黄 和

黄和，1974年11月出生于四川省雅安市。南京工业大学药学院教授，南京师范大学食品与制药工程学院院长、教授（聘任）。1997年本科毕业于浙江大学化学工程系生物化工专业，2002年博士毕业于美国普渡大学化工系化学工程专业。2004年起就职于南京工业大学，先后任南京工业大学科学技术研究部常务副部长、处长，江苏省工业生物技术创新中心主任，南京工业大学药学院院长，南京师范大学食品与制药工程学院院长。2012年获国家杰出青年科学基金项目资助，2013年入选教育部长江学者奖励计划特聘教授，2014年入选首批国家"万人计划"科技创新领军人才，是"十二五"特种生物资源开发利用关键技术主题项目首席专家、"十三五"国家重点研发计划"食品安全关键技术研发"重点专项指南编制组副组长。

长期从事微生物资源开发及利用方面的研究工作。作为第一完成人，获国家技术发明奖二等奖2项、省部级技术发明奖一等奖4项，获闵恩泽能源化工杰出贡献奖；授权发明专利72项；在 *Biotechnology Advances*、*ACS Catalysis* 等本领域权威期刊上发表SCI论文300余篇，论文被SCI他引4000余次，2014—2018年连续五年入选Elsevier化学工程领域中国高被引学者榜单。

一、突破富马酸、苹果酸等酸味剂生物制备关键技术，大幅提升我国酸味剂生物制造水平，满足了食品、医药行业重大需求

富马酸和L-苹果酸是重要的酸味剂，由于传统石化法生产路线存在安全隐患，因此亟待用生物法替代传统石化法。但是，过去生物法生产富马酸产量低、成本高，并且L-苹果酸的主要生产菌黄曲霉会产生I类致癌物黄曲霉素，所以生物法一直没有大的突破。针对上述问题，黄和开展了发酵-酶法制备富马酸和L-苹果酸的研究，实现了生物基富马酸和L-苹果酸的耦联生产。

1. 突破发酵法制备富马酸的关键技术

富马酸的生产菌株米根霉（*Rhizopus oryzae*）是一种丝状真菌，遗传背景不清晰，选育难度大。针对这一问题，通过系统研究米根霉的物质能量代谢特性，开发高通量筛选方法，获得了高性能菌株，突破了廉价淀粉质原料利用的技术瓶颈。针对丝状真菌在发酵过程中易附壁、缠绕、结块等问题，通过解析米根霉生长与代谢的生物学机制，开发了基于形态发育动力学的表型控制策略，实现了规模化生产中菌体形态的稳定控制。通过对米根霉呼吸特性的研究，发现抗氰呼吸途径，开发分阶段溶氧调控工艺，实现了产物的定向积累。

2. 实现L-苹果酸的发酵-酶法耦联生产

在发酵法制备富马酸的基础上，建立发酵母液原位循环分离富马酸的工艺路线，开发发酵-酶法耦联生产L-苹果酸的成套技术，较传统工艺能耗降低60%、成本降低40%。以淀粉为原料生产的全生物法苹果酸产品质量标准得以大幅提升，产品通过天然度认证。研究成果在酸味剂行业的龙头企业安徽雪郎生物科技股份有限公司（原南京国海生物工程有限公司）进行推广，实现了生物基富马酸和L-苹果酸的批量生产。该项成果获2012年教育部技术发明奖一等奖（排名第一）和2013年国家技术发明奖二等奖（排名第一）。

二、攻克不饱和脂肪酸代谢定向调控技术，开发了生物法生产二十二碳六烯酸（DHA）等脂肪酸产品

DHA是一种重要的ω-3长链多不饱和脂肪酸，发酵生产藻种长期受美国马泰克（Martek）公司专利保护。为打破马泰克以隐甲藻（*Crypthecodinium cohnii*）为核心的微藻DHA专利技术垄断，黄和开展了新藻种来源DHA油脂制备和产业化研究，建立了具有自主知识产权的工业化成套新技术。

1. 攻克微藻高密度发酵与脂肪酸定向调控关键技术

自主筛选了DHA生产新藻种——裂殖壶菌（*Schizochytrium* sp.），通过优化代谢途径和氧化损伤修复定向提高菌种的产油能力，开发基于细胞生理和多维组学的代谢过程精准调控技术，自主设计适合不饱和脂肪酸发酵的生物反应器，完成了高密度发酵的逐级放大。相关技术在江苏天凯和武汉嘉必优等油脂企业应用，80吨罐发酵周期从7天缩短为4天，生物量达200 g/L，DHA含量超过55%，指标国际领先。同时，联合国内企业共同推动裂殖壶菌新资源食品的认证，促进了产业健康发展。

2. 开发绿色高效的不饱和脂肪酸油脂提炼工艺

不饱和脂肪酸油脂加工过程复杂且易氧化，影响产品成本和品质。黄和开发了基于酶法的无溶剂油脂提炼技术及配套装备，避免使用易燃易爆溶剂，提高了生产安全性，并且提取效率提高了10倍、综合成本降低80%，实现了DHA油脂的连续高效生产，产品质量指标超过美国马泰克同类产品。DHA油脂的国内市场占有率超过80%，获2017年教育部技术发明奖一等奖（排名第一）和2018年国家技术发明奖二等奖（排名第一）。

三、针对我国地域特色，致力于特殊微生物资源的挖掘和开发工作，着重解决发酵产业"卡脖子"问题

我国地域辽阔，多样的生态环境中蕴藏着丰富的、拥有特殊功能或特殊代谢产物的微生物资源，但我国对微生物资源的挖掘和保护起步晚、基础薄弱，菌种多依赖于国外保藏中心，高附加值新产品研发和产业化往往受制于人。

为充分挖掘具有我国地域特色的微生物资源，将其转化为发酵产业的发展优势，黄和牵头组建了江苏省工业生物技术创新中心，十余年来坚持从海洋、雪原、盐碱地等特殊环境中采集菌种，系统开展微生物资源挖掘和利用方面的研究工作。开发利用多维组学技术分类挖掘，建立了 2000 多株带有独特表型及特殊功能基因的工业微生物资源库。在此基础上，解析重要化合物的高效合成途径，优化微生物代谢过程，突破工程应用关键技术，先后与多家企业开展产学研合作，完成了纽莫康定 B_0（新一代抗真菌药物前体）、维生素 K2（新型骨钙强化剂）、海藻糖（新型功能糖）等多种重要产品的中试或产业化推广，研究成果获比尔及梅琳达·盖茨基金会 Grand Challenges 2015-Young Scientists。

Awardee of Youth Innovation Prize，Huang He

Huang He was born in Ya'an City of Sichuan Province in November 1974. He is currently a professor in Nanjing Tech University and Nanjing Normal University. He received his bachelor's degree for biochemical engineering from Zhejiang University in 1997, and Ph.D in chemical engineering from Purdue University in the United States in 2002. Prof. Huang joined Nanjing Tech University in 2004. He served as executive deputy director in Department of Science and Technology Research of Nanjing Tech University, director of Jiangsu Industrial Biotechnology Innovation Center, dean of School of Pharmacy in Nanjing Tech University and dean of School of Food Science and Pharmaceutical Engineering in Nanjing Normal University, etc.

He focuses on industrial microbial technology development and bio-based chemicals production. He has authored over 300 research SCI papers, including prestigious journals such as *Biotechnology Advances* and *ACS Catalysis* and holds 72 patents. Prof. Huang's publications were cited by SCI for more than 4,000 times and he was consecutively selected as Chinese Most Cited Researchers from 2014 to 2018 in chemical engineering research field by Elsevier. His major contributions are as below：① Made breakthrough on technologies of bio-production of fumaric acid and malic acid, which greatly improved the bio-manufacturing level of acidifiers to meet the major needs of the food and pharmaceutical industries in China；② Developed a new algae（*Schizochytrium* sp.）to produce unsaturated fatty acid products such as docosahexaenoic acid（DHA），which broke overseas technical monopoly, and built up a new set of industrialized innovative technologies with independent intellectual property rights; ③ Established a special microbial resource bank with regional characteristics, collecting microbial resources from areas such as ocean, snowfield and saline-alkali land in China, focusing on source innovation and solving the problem of cutthroat technology in the fermentation industry.

Based on his contributions and achievements mentioned above, Prof. Huang, as the first accomplisher, has won the second-class awards of State Technological Invention Award twice (2013 and 2018), the first-class awards of Technological Invention by Ministry of Education (twice, 2012 and 2017), etc. He is also the winner of The National Science Fund for Distinguished Young Scholars (2012), Chang Jiang Scholars Program (2013), Ten-thousand Talents Program (2014) and Grand Challenges 2015-Young Scientists selected by Bill & Melinda Gates Foundation. In the mean time, Prof. Huang is the chief scientist of key technology projects for the development and utilization of special biological resources in the 12th Five-Year Plan and deputy leader of the 13th Five-Year national key R&D program "Food safety key technology research and development".

青年创新奖获得者

陆 宴 辉

陆宴辉，1980年2月出生于江苏省海门市。2008年6月毕业于中国农业科学院研究生院，获农学博士学位。2008年7月至今在中国农业科学院植物保护研究所工作；2012年3月起先后任植物病虫害生物学国家重点实验室副主任、常务副主任；2019年3月起任中国农业科学院植物保护研究所副所长。2013年4月起在新疆农业科学院进行挂职，2017年5月起任院长助理。获第13届"中国青年科技奖"、首届"中国优秀青年科技人才奖"、国务院政府特殊津贴以及第22届"中国青年五四奖章"。

主要从事棉花害虫生物学与防控技术研究，长期扎根新疆和华北棉区，在棉花害虫发生机制与防控技术研究领域取得了重要进展。

一、转 Bt 基因棉花害虫地位演替机制

1997年，我国开始商业化种植转 Bt 基因抗虫棉花（简称"Bt 棉花"）。Bt 棉花的大面积种植有效控制了靶标害虫棉铃虫的发生危害，棉田化学杀虫剂使用量随之大幅度减少。上述变化可能会引起棉田非靶标害虫种群地位发生演替。

陆宴辉全面分析了华北地区 Bt 棉花大面积种植后非靶标害虫盲蝽在棉花等多种寄主作物上的种群发生趋势，并深入解析了其地位演替的生态学机制。模拟研究表明，与常规棉花相比，Bt 棉花本身对盲蝽种群发生没有明显影响；而常规棉田防治棉铃虫使用的广谱性化学杀虫剂能有效控制盲蝽种群发生，起到兼治作用。区域性监测发现棉田盲蝽的发生数量随着 Bt 棉花种植比率的提高而不断上升，而且盲蝽种群数量与棉铃虫化学防治次数之间呈显著负相关。这说明 Bt 棉花种植后防治棉铃虫化学杀虫剂使用的减少直接导致棉田盲蝽种群上升、为害加重；同时 Bt 棉田盲蝽种群暴发波及同一生态系统中枣、苹果、梨、桃、葡萄等其他寄主作物，呈现出多作物、区域性灾变趋势。

基于棉花害虫与天敌种群发生的区域性监测，系统分析了华北地区 Bt 棉田广谱捕食

性天敌（包括瓢虫、草蛉和蜘蛛）及其主要捕食对象——棉蚜伏蚜的种群演化规律，并阐述了相应的生态学机制。研究表明，随着 Bt 棉花的大面积种植以及棉田化学杀虫剂的减少使用，棉田捕食性天敌的种群快速上升，从而有效抑制了伏蚜的种群发生；同时，棉田捕食性天敌种群数量的增加促进了大豆、花生、玉米等邻近作物田中天敌种群的建立和扩增，显著提升了整个农业生态系统中的生物防治功能。

最新研究发现，盲蝽不仅具有植食性，还兼具肉食性，对棉蚜具有较强的捕食作用。同时，盲蝽取食为害棉花叶片，能抑制同一棉株上棉蚜的种群增长，构成明显的种间竞争关系。综合捕食和竞争两方面因素，盲蝽发生能显著降低棉蚜种群增长，对棉蚜产生明显的控制作用。长期监测数据分析表明，盲蝽发生数量的增加明显促进了 Bt 棉田捕食性天敌对棉蚜种群的生物控制功能；同时，盲蝽还能捕食棉铃虫卵和初孵幼虫、叶螨、粉虱等多种害虫。因此，当盲蝽密度超过经济阈值时，应作为作物害虫进行防治；当发生密度低于经济阈值时，可作为有益天敌予以利用。

综上所述，Bt 棉花对棉田害虫发生与防治产生了深远影响。Bt 棉花的种植控制了棉铃虫种群发生，使用于棉铃虫防治的杀虫剂使用量大幅下降，进而导致自然天敌对蚜虫的种群控制作用明显提高。盲蝽随着棉田杀虫剂的减少使用而发生加重，由于其杂食性进一步增强了自然天敌对蚜虫的生物控制功能。研究结果先后在 *Nature*、*Science*、*PNAS* 等期刊上发表，一项研究入选 2012 年度"中国科学十大进展"。这一系列工作成为了国际上转基因作物环境安全领域最具代表性的研究之一，全面澄清了关于转基因棉花环境安全问题的争议和误解，有力推动了转基因生物安全学学科的创新与发展，也为我国转基因棉田非靶标害虫治理对策的制定提供了科学依据。

二、棉花害虫绿色防控技术

系统研究了华北棉区盲蝽主要种类的地理分布与种群发生规律，深入探讨了温度、湿度等环境因素以及寄主、天敌等生物因子对盲蝽发生消长的影响作用，进而制订盲蝽调查测报技术标准 4 项，预测准确率达 90% 以上。系统评估了盲蝽对 200 多种植物的选择偏好性，阐明了盲蝽季节性寄主转换规律以及盲蝽与寄主植物之间的化学通讯机制。在此基础上，提出了适用于果棉混作、粮棉混作、牧棉混作等不同种植模式的盲蝽区域性种群治理对策，研发了诱集植物、食诱剂、驱避剂等多项盲蝽绿色防控技术，集成了盲蝽绿色防控技术体系并制订农业行业标准 4 项。上述技术规程在棉花以及同一种植区域内果树、茶树、苜蓿等多种作物上进行了示范推广，防控效果超过 90%，化学杀虫剂用量较常规减少 30% 以上，显著提高了我国盲蝽种群绿色防控和可持续治理的水平。

在新疆棉区，在喀什、阿克苏、库尔勒以及昌吉、石河子和博乐建立了 6 个试验点，系统研究了新疆棉花害虫发生规律与灾变机制，发现自然天敌控害能力弱是导致棉蚜等害虫暴发成灾的主要原因，从而提出了以有益天敌保育及其控害功能提升为主的棉花害虫绿色防控对策。研发了食诱剂应用、功能植物保护与利用、天敌饲养与释放等绿色防控新技术，集成优化了新疆棉花害虫绿色防控技术规程，测报准确率与防治效果均达90% 以上，化学杀虫剂使用量较常规降低 25% ～ 40%。同时，积极推进棉花害虫绿色防控技术的推广普及，被新疆维吾尔自治区农业厅聘为"农业有害生物首席咨询专家"。

上述两方面工作显著促进了我国棉花害虫绿色防控水平的提高，为我国棉花产业提质增效以及棉区生态环境安全提供了有力的科技支撑。先后发表研究论文 100 多篇（SCI收录 50 余篇），编写著作 5 本；授权国家发明专利 22 项；制订农业行业标准 10 项；参与获得国家科技进步奖二等奖 1 项、省部级一等奖 2 项，有效促进了我国农业害虫综合防治学科的发展与进步。

Awardee of Youth Innovation Prize，Lu Yanhui

Lu Yanhui was born in Haimen City of Jiangsu Province in February 1980. He graduated and obtained his doctoral degree in agriculture from the Chinese Academy of Agricultural Sciences（CAAS）in June 2008. He has since been employed at the Institute of Plant Protection（IPP），CAAS，where he was promoted as Deputy Director and Executive Deputy Director of State Key Laboratory for Biology of Plant Diseases and Insect Pests in March 2012 and subsequently assumed the position of Deputy Director of IPP in March 2019. He equally temporarily serves in the Xinjiang Academy of Agricultural Sciences（XAAS），where he now holds the post of Assistant Dean. He was awarded with the 13th Science & Technology Award for Chinese Youth，the 1st China Outstanding Youth Science & Technology Talent Award and enjoys State Council Special Allowance. He was also the winner of the 22nd China May 4th Youth Medal.

Dr. Lu is actively engaged in applied ecological research of cotton pests and the associated development of sustainable and 'green' pest management technologies. He spends most of his time conducting and coordinating both field and laboratory experiments in cotton cropping regions of North China and Xinjiang. He has made large strides in understanding the determinants of insect pest population build-up in Bt cotton cropping system，and has illuminated multiple aspects of the biology，ecology and in-field manipulation of both pests and beneficial insects in China's cotton crop.

1. Status evolution of insect pests in Bt cotton

In 1997，Bt cotton was released for commercial use in China against the cotton bollworm，*Helicoverpa armigera*，and has since been adopted by vast numbers of Chinese cotton growers（i.e.，presently 100% adoption in northern China）. Genetically engineered crops that express Bt δ-endotoxins（Cry proteins）can effectively control a range of arthropod pests，restore or enhance crop yield，lower insecticide use，and ultimately improve farmer income and welfare. The wide adoption of Bt cotton effectively suppressed China's cotton bollworm population, but the associated reduction in chemical insecticide use equally induced an ecological niche succession for various non-target pests.

2. Green prevention and control techniques of cotton pests

In cotton-growing regions of northern China, Dr. Yanhui Lu and his team have systematically investigated the geographical distribution and population dynamics of several key mirid bugs. They equally examined the relative impact of abiotic factors (e.g. temperature, humidity) and biotic factors (e.g. host plants, natural enemies) in shaping those dynamics, leading to the development of 4 technical standards for mirid bug population forecasting and 'early warning' with >90% accuracy rates. Additionally, systematic field studies have uncovered host plant preferences of different species of mirid bugs (i.e., *Apolygus lucorum*, *Adelphocoris suturalis*, *Ad. fasiaticollis*, *Ad. lineolatus*) and generated critical insights into their biology, ecology and host plant selection. More specifically, the work of Dr. Lu and his team has documented chemical communication mechanisms that guided seasonal host plant selection of mirid bugs, ultimately enabling the development of area-wide management strategies for these pests. These 'green prevention & control' techniques comprised the use of attractant plants, food attractants and repellents, and have been extensively used in diverse set of cotton agro-landscapes. Integrated 'green prevention & control' techniques and industrial standards have been validated, adapted and widely-adopted in China's cotton fields, fruit orchards, tea plantations, alfalfa and other crops. Their on-farm use has led to a 90% suppression of pest populations, lowered synthetic insecticide use by 30% and has fast become a core component of 'green prevention & control' approaches for mirid bugs in China.

青年创新奖获得者

刘　真

刘真，1988年11月出生于山东省青州市。2006—2010年就读于山东师范大学生命科学学院，获理学学士学位；2017年毕业于中国科学院脑科学与智能技术卓越创新中心/神经科学研究所，获神经生物学博士学位；2017—2018年留所继续开展博士后研究。2018年9月任中国科学院脑科学与智能技术卓越创新中心/神经科学研究所灵长类生殖工程课题组组长，博士生导师，研究员。获得"万人计划"青年拔尖人才、中科院创新交叉团队负责人、博士后创新人才计划、中国科学院院长特别奖、上海市青年科技英才扬帆计划等奖励和资助。

主要从事非人灵长类胚胎、生殖及干细胞领域的研究，在非人灵长类遗传修饰技术研发及模型构建方面做了多项重要工作。

一、体细胞克隆猴技术的建立及应用

体细胞克隆技术被认为是构建非人灵长类遗传修饰模型的理想方法，利用该技术可短期内批量获得遗传背景一致且无嵌合体现象的遗传修饰动物模型。体细胞克隆猴的研究从2002年就开始陆续有报道，其间有来自美国、日本、德国、新加坡、韩国、中国等多个研究机构对该研究发起攻关，但均未成功。刘真作为克隆猴团队核心成员，自2012年开始对体细胞克隆猴这一领域难题进行研究，经过多年积累尝试，通过克隆技术流程等改进优化和表观遗传调控因子的合理利用，最终成功建立了体细胞克隆猴技术，得到2只健康存活的克隆猴"中中"和"华华"。在此基础上，进一步利用建立的体细胞克隆猴技术获得了5只遗传背景一致的BMAL1基因敲除克隆猴模型，首次证明该技术可用于批量构建遗传背景一致且无嵌合体现象的疾病克隆猴模型。Cell杂志主编Emilie Marcus称赞体细胞克隆猴的工作为"生物技术领域近20年来的里程碑事件"。2012年诺贝尔奖得主约翰·格登在同期Cell杂志发表评论"一个可定制卵母细胞的时代开启了"。体细胞克隆猴的工作于 2018 年作为封面文章发表于 *Cell* 杂志，并获评 2018 年度"中国科学十大进展"、2018 年度"中国生命科学十大进展"和 2018 年度"CCTV 科技创新团队奖"，研究集体被评为 2018 年度"中国科学院年度团队"，研究成果入选"*Cell* 2018 年最佳八篇文章"和"*Nature* 2018 重大科学事件"。

二、MECP2 自闭症转基因猴模型构建

基因编辑技术问世之前，胚胎病毒感染转基因是唯一可用于遗传修饰猴模型构建的方法。此方法可以用于构建特定基因过表达的转基因猴模型。MECP2 基因是一个自闭症相关基因，患者中该基因的过表达和缺失都会导致自闭症谱系障碍的发生。通过转基因过表达构建的 MECP2 转基因小鼠无法模拟患者中的疾病表型，经与其他课题组合作，刘真构建了具有多种类似人自闭症表型的 MECP2 过表达转基因猴，且发现 MECP2 转基因及类似自闭症表型可以通过生殖细胞传递到子代猴，为自闭症的发病机制研究和干预手段研究提供了更加高等的理想动物模型。该工作于 2016 年发表于 *Nature* 杂志，并获评 2016 年度"中国科学十大进展"、2016 年度"中国生命科学十大进展"。

三、精巢异种移植介导的食蟹猴繁殖加速技术

小鼠的性成熟时间约 2 个月，而常用的非人灵长类动物恒河猴和食蟹猴的性成熟时间为 4～5 年。非人灵长类漫长的性成熟时间是限制其广泛应用的重要因素。针对此问题，刘真及团队开发了基于精巢异种移植的食蟹猴繁殖加速技术。通过将 1 岁的食蟹猴的单侧精巢组织块移植到去势裸鼠的背部，于 10 个月后成功得到了有活力的精子并利用获得的精子得到了健康存活的食蟹猴后代。该技术显著缩短了食蟹猴的传代周期（从 5 年缩短到 2.5 年）。繁殖加速技术在传代方面的优势以及体细胞核移植技术在模型构建方面的优势的综合利用，将进一步推动非人灵长类遗传修饰模型在生命科学领域的广泛应用。

Awardee of Youth Innovation Prize，Liu Zhen

Liu Zhen was born in Qingzhou City of Shandong Province in November 1988. He graduated from the Center for Excellence in Brain Science and Intelligent Technology/Institute of Neuroscience（CEBSIT/ION），Chinese Academy of Sciences with a doctorate in neurobiology in 2017. From 2017 to 2018，he continued his post-doctoral research in CEBSIT/ION. From September 2018，he was employed as a Principle Investigator of Laboratory of Primate Reproductive Engineering in CEBSIT/ION. He is experienced in primate embryo development，stem cell and reproduction，and make a series important works in monkey gene-manipulation technology development and model generation.

1. Establishment and application of monkey somatic cell nuclear transfer (SCNT) technology

Somatic cell nuclear transfer has been considered as an ideal method in generating gene-modified monkey models. Zhen Liu and colleagues succeeded in obtaining the first clone monkeys "Zhongzhong" and "Huahua" by SCNT through optimizing the SCNT protocol and using epigenetic regulators. Then he and colleagues generated the first group of gene-modified monkey model with identical genetic background by established SCNT technology. The monkey clone work was published in CELL as a cover article in 2018.

2. MECP2 transgenic monkey model with autism like behaviors

MECP2 is an autism related gene and people showed autism behavior when MECP2 overexpression or mutation. Using lentivirus infection method, Zhen Liu and colleagues generated MECP2 transgenic monkey models showed autism like behaviors and proved that the MECP2 transgene and autism like behaviors could be passaged to next generation. This work was published in Nature in 2016.

3. Monkey passage acceleration by testicular xenografting

Long duration for monkey sexual maturation and passage limit the wide application of gene-modified monkey models. Zhen Liu and colleagues developed the testicular xenografting method and succeeded in shorting the passage time from 5 years to 2.5 years. This work was published in Cell Research in 2016.

青年创新奖获得者

孙　剑

　　孙剑，1976年10月出生于陕西省西安市。1997年在西安交通大学自动控制专业获得学士学位；2000年、2003年在西安交通大学人工智能与机器人研究所分别获得硕士、博士学位。毕业后加入微软亚洲研究院，任至首席研究员；2015—2016年在微软美国研究院任合伙人级研究主管；2016年7月起任旷视科技首席科学家、旷视研究院院长；2016年起任西安交通大学兼职教授；2019年起兼任西安交通大学人工智能学院院长。

　　主要研究方向是计算机视觉、深度学习、计算机图形学，在上述三个领域的基础研究和应用技术方面作出了一系列开创性工作。发表科学论文100余篇，谷歌学术引用总数超过89000次，高引论文（引用超1000次）12篇。在2009年和2016年两次获得了计算机视觉年会CVPR最佳论文奖。2014—2020年任CVPR国际会议领域主席。

　　其代表工作之一是2015年的"深度残差网络ResNets"，通过引入残差学习的思想来学习神经网络中层与层之间的变化关系，提出了一个深度残差学习的框架，成功克服了深度神经网络训练难的世界级难题。该残差学习框架首次成功训练出深达152层甚至上千层的深度神经网络，并在2015年ImageNet图像识别任务中获得三项冠军，第一次超过了人类的性能，是计算机视觉和深度学习领域的重大突破。目前，该方法已成为计算机视觉和深度学习的最主流方法之一。该成果获得了2016年计算机视觉年会CVPR最佳论文奖，谷歌学术引用27785次，是近五年在深度学习和计算机视觉领域被引用数最高的论文之一，并已被广泛应用于工业界，包括2016年微软对话语音识别、2016年谷歌神经翻译和2017年DeepMind的AlphaGo Zero（基于一个80层的ResNet）等系统中。

　　领导研究了快速交互式图像分割、高精度前景抠图、图像补全、快速图像滤波、暗通道去雾等技术，并被广泛应用在计算机视觉和图形学领域的基础研究和业界产品中。其中，暗通道去雾技术获得2009年计算机视觉年会CVPR最佳论文奖，这也是亚洲人首次获得该奖项。因为在计算机视觉与计算机图形学的跨领域研究，孙剑被 *MIT Technology*

Review 评选为 2011 年"全球 35 岁以下杰出青年创新者"。

在基础研究的产品化方面积累了许多成功经验。在微软工作期间，将多项基础研究转化为核心产品（Windows、Office、Azure、Bing 等）的重要功能，因其杰出贡献而任至微软合伙人。目前，由其领导的旷视科技研究院团队在 2017/2018 连续获得 COCO 世界图像理解大赛冠军，并推出了目前业界广泛使用的移动端高效神经网络 ShuffleNet；同时在计算机视觉基础研究和云服务、移动端、芯片等应用方面开展了广泛的研发实践。

此外，因其在视觉场景理解的模式表征与计算及方法方面的研究成果，孙剑曾荣获 2015 年教育部自然科学奖一等奖和 2016 年国家自然科学奖二等奖。

Awardee of Young Innovation Prize，Sun Jian

Sun Jian was born in Xi'an City of Shaanxi Province in October 1976. Dr. Sun received his B.S., M.S., and Ph.D. degree from Xian Jiaotong University in 1997, 2000 and 2003, respectively. Immediately following his studies, Dr. Sun joined Microsoft Research Asia as an Associate Researcher, and was subsequently promoted to Principal Research Manager. He later relocated to Microsoft Research in Redmond, US, where he held the position of Partner Research Manager from 2015 to 2016. Dr. Sun joined Megvii Technology as Chief Scientist in July, 2016 where he also serves as Managing Director of its research arm Megvii Research. Dr. Sun has been an Adjunct Professor at Xi'an Jiaotong University since 2016, as well as Dean of the College of Artificial Intelligence at Xi'an Jiaotong University since 2019.

Dr. Sun's main research areas are computer vision, deep learning and computer graphics and he has made ground-breaking achievements in fundamental research and technological applications in these three domains. Dr. Sun has published more than 100 scientific papers, which have been cited over 89,000 times on Google Scholar, including 12 highly-cited papers (papers with more than 1,000 citations) in total. Dr. Sun was the recipient of Best Paper Award at the Conference on Computer Vision and Pattern Recognition (CVPR) in 2009 and 2016.

One research project illustrative of Dr. Sun's work is "ResNets (Deep Residential Networks)", which was started in 2015. By introducing the concept of residual learning to study the relationship between layers in the neural network, he proposed a framework for deep residual learning, successfully solving the problem of training deep neural networks that was once considered a global challenge. His structure successfully trained deep neural networks of 152 layers, and even thousands of layers, for the first time. This research breakthrough won three top prizes at the 2015 ImageNet Computer Recognition Challenge, surpassing human performance for the first time and is considered to be a key breakthrough in the field of visual and deep learning. Currently, his vision and methodology is a mainstay in the field of computer vision and deep learning. Dr. Sun's accomplishment earned him the CVPR Best Paper Award in 2016, which has achieved over 27, 785 Google Scholar citations, making it one of the most cited papers in deep learning and computer vision over the past five years. Additionally, it has been widely implemented within the industry such as Microsoft Conversational Speech Recognition System in 2016, and the AlphaGo Zero of DeepMind (based on a 80-layer ResNet) in 2017.

Dr. Sun was designated as one of "35 Innovators Under 35" by MIT Technology Review in 2011 for his cross-disciplinary research in computer vision and computer graphics. His research results in rapid interactive image segmentation, high-precision foreground cuts, image completion, fast-guided image filtering, dark-channel image defogging have been widely implemented in fundamental computer vision and graphics research and applied in numerous related products. Dr. Sun won the CVPR Best Paper Award in 2009 for his work on dark-channel image defogging, making him the first Asian to win the title.

Dr. Sun also has considerable pedigree for developing fundamental research into real-world products. During his tenure at Microsoft, several of his research accomplishments were adapted to become key functions of the company's core products, such as Windows, Office, Azure, and Bing. Dr. Sun was also promoted to the position of Partner Research Manager in Microsoft Research in recognition of his many outstanding contributions. Currently, Dr. Sun leads Megvii Research, where his team bagged Competition Winner Award s at the COCO Detection Challenge in 2017 (COCO and Places Challenges), as well as in 2018 (COCO and Mapillary Challenges). Dr. Sun and his team also developed ShuffleNet, an extremely efficient convolutional neutral network for mobile devices. Dr. Sun and the Megvii Research he leads are now engaged in extensive R&D activities for the fundamental research of computer vision, as well as for applications such as cloud services, mobile devices and chips.

The Ministry of Education of China endowed Dr. Sun with Top Prize in its 2015 Natural Science Awards for his research into model representation and computing & methodology in visual scene understanding. He also scooped Second Prize at the 2016 National Natural Science Awards for the same research. Currently, he is Principal of the "Next Generation Theories, Methodologies and Key Technologies on Deep Learning" project, which falls under the key state R&D program "Key Scientific Issues of Transformative Technology". Dr. Sun is now Area Chair of CVPR (2014-2020).

青年创新奖获得者

王 书 肖

王书肖，女，1974年6月出生于河北省藁城县。2001年毕业于清华大学环境工程系，获工学博士学位；2001—2003年在哈佛大学环境中心进行博士后研究工作。2003年12月回国至今在清华大学环境学院工作，2010年10月—2017年5月任大气污染与控制研究所所长，现任国家环境保护大气复合污染与控制重点实验室主任和国家创新人才推进计划重点领域创新团队负责人。先后入选教育部长江学者特聘教授、国家"万人计划"领军人才、国家环境保护专业技术领军人才、北京市有突出贡献人才，并获得国家自然科学基金委杰出青年科学基金资助。兼任 *Journal of Environmental Management* 副主编、*Environmental Science & Technology Letters* 和 *Journal of Environmental Sciences* 编委、UNEP 大气汞 BAT/BEP 导则专家组燃煤组主席、国家大气污染防治攻关联合中心研究室首席专家、环境损害鉴定评估专家委员会环境空气组组长、挥发性有机物污染防治专业委员会副主任委员、中国环境科学学会臭氧污染控制专业委员会常务委员等。

主要从事大气污染防治研究，在高分辨率动态源排放清单技术、二次颗粒物形成机制和数值模拟以及多污染物协同防控系统分析技术等方面做了一系列开创性研究工作。

一、高分辨率动态源排放清单技术

针对大气污染物排放的定量表征这一国际研究热点和难点问题，系统测试电厂、工业和民用炉灶的挥发性有机物（VOCs）化学成分谱、颗粒物粒径分布和化学成分谱，建立了针对不同燃料、工艺设备和烟气净化设施的大气污染物排放因子库，使我国排放因子的本土化率提高到70%、数据质量达到B级以上，并将涵盖的VOCs物种从40大类增加到115类，有效增补了传统源谱低估的二次气溶胶生成潜势。

开发了社会经济发展、工艺技术更替、排放特征变化间的动态耦合模型，建立了基于工艺过程的工业点源排放清单、基于大样本燃料使用调研和居民分布的面源排放清单、基于气象条件和土壤性质的动态农业氨排放清单，发展了基于模型和观测数据的排放清单校验方法，主要污染物排放量不确定性降低 50% ～ 70%，源清单时空分辨率提高一个数量级，满足了空气质量模拟和区域及城市大气污染防治的迫切需要。

集成能源利用、技术演进和污染控制，建立了控制情景与排放预测的动态源清单技术方法，实现了排放预测从行业到工艺技术的提升。作为核心成员，参与构建了中国多尺度排放清单模型（MEIC）。所建立的排放清单为国家硫氮总量控制、国家大气环境保护战略和大气复合污染来源识别提供了重要科学依据，并被国内外数十家研究机构和"半球空气污染传输研究计划"、GAINS-Asia 等多项大型国际研究计划采用。

二、二次颗粒物形成机制和来源解析

三维化学转化与物理传输模型是研究污染物的大气化学行为和大气化学机制的重要工具。但是，现有的主流模型对 PM$_{2.5}$ 的二次组分显著低估。

针对二次有机气溶胶（SOA）模拟低估的问题，王书肖团队综合外场观测和烟雾箱实验，加入了中等挥发性和半挥发性有机物（I/SVOC）等前体物，并考虑了挥发性和氧化态对反应路径的影响，建立了二维挥发性区间模型（2D-VBS），采用三层 2D-VBS 分别模拟人为源 SOA 的老化过程、自然源 SOA 的老化过程以及一次有机颗粒物和前体物氧化生成 SOA 的过程，提出了用于三维网格模拟的化学机制和相应的参数化方案。将 2D-VBS 模型植入三维化学转化与物理传输数值模型中，开发了 WRF/CMAQ/2D-VBS 空气质量模拟系统，与观测值的比较表明，该系统显著改善了对 SOA 的模拟效果，并实现了有机颗粒老化程度的模拟，进而揭示了一次颗粒物及中等和半挥发性有机物对重污染期间大气 PM$_{2.5}$ 的重要贡献。

针对中国硫酸盐模拟普遍偏低的问题，改善了矿物质颗粒物排放的估算，通过引入二氧化硫在矿物质颗粒物表面的非均相反应，改善了当前空气质量模型对于二次无机气溶胶的模拟效果。研究发现，矿物质颗粒物的促进作用使得四川盆地和华北平原的硫酸盐年均浓度显著提高，这一作用在污染最严重的冬季影响最大，对重污染过程中硫酸盐浓度的贡献率高达 37%。

发展了基于立体观测、源追踪模型和受体模型的大气 PM$_{2.5}$ 综合源解析技术，实现了二次颗粒物的精准溯源，解析了区域传输与本地不同排放源对京津冀地区大气 PM$_{2.5}$ 的贡献，推动京津冀及周边地区实施大气污染联防联控。

三、多污染物协同防治系统分析技术

多种前体物排放与二次污染物之间存在很强的非线性关系，是传统敏感性分析方法无法解决的国际难题。针对这一问题，王书肖带领团队将拉丁立方体及哈默斯利序列多维采样与三维大气化学模式结合，突破多污染物、多部门、多区域分类减排与环境效应的非线性响应模拟技术，实现了对控制措施实施效果的实时定量分析。

作为国家大气污染防治攻关联合中心研究室首席专家，利用大数据和系统分析技术，领导研发了基于费效评估的区域空气质量调控技术与决策支持平台，通过由空气质量目标到多污染物减排量的映射，结合大气污染减排成本分析，确定实现多种空气质量目标的各种污染物减排量，形成了基于环境效益的多污染物非线性区域空气质量调控方法学和技术体系，实现了贯穿"经济-能源-排放-环境-影响"的大气污染防治科学综合决策，提出北京及周边地区分区域、分阶段细颗粒物防治目标、策略和技术途径。

成果广泛应用于国家和数十个省市的"大气十条"和"蓝天保卫战三年行动计划"的制定和实施，促进我国 PM$_{2.5}$ 污染治理取得显著成效。作为领衔专家之一，在 APEC 和"九三阅兵"等北京市多次重大活动空气质量保障中发挥了核心技术支撑作用，确保了重大活动空气质量保障全部达标。作为北京市突发事件应急委员会专家，及时对污染过程进行研判和评估，为首都空气质量改善作出了重要贡献。

Awardee of Youth Innovation Prize，Wang Shuxiao

Wang Shuxiao, female, born in Gaocheng County of Hebei Province in June 1974, obtained the PhD from the School of Environment of Tsinghua University in 2001, and conducted post-doctoral research at Harvard University Center for the Environment during 2001—2003. She has returned to China and worked as a professor in Tsinghua University since December 2003. She served as Director of the Institute of Air Pollution and Control from October 2010 to May 2017. Currently she is the director of State Environmental Protection Key Laboratory of Sources and Control of Air Pollution Complex and leader of the Innovation Team in Key Areas under the Innovative Talents Promotion Program. Prof. Wang was awarded as Cheung Kong Scholar Professor, 10, 000 Talents Program, Leading Talents of Environmental Protection Technologies, and Outstanding Talents of Science, Technology and Management in Beijing. She is the recipient of the National Science Fund for Distinguished Young Scholar. She is also the Associate Editor of Journal of Environmental Management, Editorial Board Member of Environmental Science & Technology Letters and Journal of Environmental Sciences, member of the UNEP Expert Group on BAT/BEP Guidance for Mercury Emission Control, etc.

Wang Shuxiao's research interests focus on air pollution control. She has made impressive contributions in the high-resolution emission inventory of air pollutants, secondary particle formation mechanism and numerical simulation, and systematic analysis of joint multiple-pollutant control. Prof. Wang has measured the emissions of PM$_{2.5}$ and VOCs from stationary combustion sources, developed a unit-based high-resolution emission inventory and forecast model, and proposed an observation-based emission validation method. She has established the two-dimensional volatility basis set (2D-VBS) in simulating the aging of SOA and identified the important contribution of semi-and intermediate-volatile organic compounds to SOA. Her academic contribution also includes the non-linear response surface modelling technique (RSM) of $PM_{2.5}$ and ozone pollution to primary emissions. She has led the development of Air Benefit and Cost and Attainment Assessment System (ABaCAS), which has provided key technical support to the regional air pollution control in China.

Prof. Wang's research has been widely adopted in the formulation and implementation of the Action Plan for Air Pollution Prevention and Control and has contributed to China's remarkable achievements in $PM_{2.5}$ pollution control. Prof. Wang serves as the leading expert of air pollution control in Beijing, and provides systematic process analysis for each pollution episodes as well as the long-term air pollution control strategy.

She has won a series of awards, including 2nd-class National Awards for Science and Technology Progress (2010, 2011, 2015), China Youth Science and Technology Award, and Best Paper Award of Journal of Environmental Sciences.

青年创新奖获得者

肖 飞

　　肖飞，1977年10月出生于湖北省武汉市，工学博士。2002年至今在海军工程大学军用电气与技术研究所工作，历任助教、讲师、副教授、教授，于2017年10月起担任所长。国家自然科学基金委"电力系统电磁兼容"创新研究群体的骨干成员。第七届教育部科技委能源与交通学部委员，中国造船工程学会第八届轮机学术委员会船电技术分会副主任委员，中国电源学会理事，《电源学报》编委。

　　从事科研工作以来，先后主持国家、国防各类重大重点项目30余项，发表学术论文100余篇，获授权发明专利20项。获得国家科技进步奖一等奖2项、国家科技进步奖二等奖1项、国家创新团队奖1项、军队科技进步一等奖4项、第十九届全国发明展览会金奖、首届"全国创新争先奖牌"、第十七届中国科协"求是"杰出青年实用工程奖、中国"五四青年奖章"、中国青年科技奖；荣立一等功1次、二等功3次。被评为全国优秀科技工作者，入选国家科技部"万人计划"、国家百千万人才工程。

一、研制成功多型潜艇急需的供发电系统，解决了我国独立供电系统的瓶颈难题

　　（1）针对我国潜艇在有限空间内同时为全艇交流供电和直流推进供电的重大技术难题，在国际上首创发明并研制成功交直流电力集成双绕组发电机，成功实现了由一台双绕组发电机同时实现交流和直流两台发电机的功能，显著提高了安全裕度、发供电系统功率密度和可靠性，实现了潜艇总体优化布置和减振降噪。根据双绕组发电机的数学模型，建立了交直流系统性能分析方法，实现了电机交直流输出性能准确分析；根据双绕组发电机交流电压稳定、直流电压浮动的原则，设计了包括电压调节器、相复励系统在内的无刷励磁调节系统，为电机安全、可靠运行提供保证。

　　（2）针对现役潜艇发电系统机组体积大、效率低、基频低且难以抑制的问题，在国际上率先提出了基于异步原理、可与汽轮机直联的高速感应发电机系统方案。针对

传统感应发电机励磁控制复杂问题，创造性地将级联拓扑结构的电力电子励磁技术引入高速感应发电机系统，实现了发电机输出电压稳定和连续调节；同时提出一种新算法，克服了传统移相均压算法导致均压与输出供电品质相制约的技术难题。该成果经鉴定属原理和方法创新，达到国际领先水平，解决了新型潜艇高速感应发电机研制的急需。

二、在大容量电能变换系统领域，从基础理论研究到关键技术攻关、装备和产品研制，为我军全面实现舰船动力从传统方式向综合电力方式的革命提供了重要支撑

（1）主持完成舰船综合电力系统直流区域变配电分系统研制，为舰船综合电力系统提供了重要支撑。变配电分系统是舰船电力系统的"动脉"，对主供电线路中的电力进行变换、配置与传输，是影响舰船电力系统整体性能的核心装备。传统舰船变配电分系统采用干馈式辐射状网络结构，存在生命力低、重量大、成本高、灵活性差的缺陷。肖飞项目组在国内首次提出直流区域配电系统的概念，对直流区域配电系统的网络结构、保护方法、稳定性理论等关键技术进行深入研究，研制出一种具有高度开放式拓扑结构的兆瓦级直流区域变配电分系统。研制成功的样机各项电气性能指标显著优于国外同类系统，其体积功率密度提高了37.8%、重量功率密度提高了79.7%、系统效率提高1.6%。成果被应用于我国新型护卫舰，并推广用于南沙岛礁风光储一体式发电站，目前已在美济礁和赤瓜礁建成两套一体化电站。2015年7月—2019年2月，累计发电量217万度，节约燃油消耗约532吨，减少CO_2排放约1628吨。

（2）瞄准我军舰船电力推进需求，主持研制了从几兆瓦到几十兆瓦级包含感应、永磁两大类推进电机的驱动系统，为推动综合电力技术的工程应用发挥了重大作用。研制成功的1.8MW永磁推进系统各项性能指标均明显优于国内外同类装置，其中振动噪声较国外同类装置在各频点降低了10～30dB，在海军组织的首次实物竞优中以明显优势胜出，目前已列装我国最新水声监听船，运行情况良好；研制成功的数十兆瓦级变频调速装置与英美海军唯一采用的同等级推进模块相比，体积功率密度提高了24.4%、重量功率密度提高了20.9%、效率提高了0.1%，成果被应用于我国新型护卫舰。

三、主持多型大容量电能变换系统研制，推动舰船综合电力技术向陆用、民用领域转化

（1）相对于西方军事强国，我国在电传动军用车辆领域的研究起步较晚，现有的电传动功率较小，不能满足大型主战车辆的使用需求。肖飞瞄准该问题，带领项目组持续攻关，实现极端恶劣环境下持续可靠工作（环境温度 ≥ 85℃）及转矩精确控制（转矩精度 ≤ 2%）。研制成功的坦克推进变频器即将应用于第四代坦克战车。

（2）目前的列车牵引系统主要是异步牵引系统，相比之下，永磁牵引系统效率更高、功率密度更高、转矩响应能力更强，代表了轨道牵引未来的发展方向。肖飞主持研制轨道交通车辆永磁同步牵引系统，突破了在超低开关频率工况下电流谐波优化技术及方波弱磁控制技术，研制成功的地铁永磁同步牵引系统已应用于北京地铁9号线。

（3）在我国，单机容量2MW级的风力发电机组配套的全功率变流器几乎被国外产品所垄断，严重制约了风电产业的发展。为此，肖飞提出了一套完整的兆瓦级、两电平-背靠背风力发电变流器的优化设计与控制方法，于2008年在国内首次研制成功2兆瓦级直驱式风力发电用电力电子变流器系统，打破了该领域被国外产品垄断的局面。该2MW级大功率风电变流器的成功研制迫使国外公司同类产品价格从2008年的230万元/套下降到目前的60万元/套，每年为国家节约采购经费约10亿元。

Awardee of Youth Innovation Prize, Xiao Fei

Xiao Fei, born in Wuhan City of Hubei Province in October 1977, is now a professor and doctoral tutor at Naval University of Engineering.

Prof. Xiao has been long engaged in the research on the vessel integrated power system (IPS). The IPS integrating the mechanical propulsion system and the power generation system independent of each other in the form of electric energy can greatly improve the ship maneuverability, noise isolation and adaptability. This is honorably called "the third revolution" in the field of marine power. In this field, Prof. Xiao has achieved a series of innovative research results which are in the lead internationally. The achievements he has made are as the following aspects.

Prof. Xiao, a leading researcher, has successfully developed many types of power supply systems which submarines urgently need and solved the tough problems with the independent power supply system of our own.

He is the first to propose the concept of DC zonal power distribution system in China. He has developed a megawatt DC-zonal electrical distribution system with the high-level open type topology. It has provided an important support for researching and developing the vessel IPS.

He took charge of the tasks of developing the driving systems of induction and permanent magnet motors ranging from several MW to tens of MW and make effort to promote their use. He has played a major role in the application of integrated power technology to engineering.

Since he began his scientific research, he has made great achievements and won a lot of awards, which include: taking charge of more than 30 national key projects and major defense projects, publishing over 100 academic papers, owning 20 granted patents, winning an Innovation Team Award of State Scientific and Technological Progress (SSTP)(ranking second), two first-class awards (ranking second respectively) and a second-class award (ranking second) of SSTP and the National Excellent Innovation Award (ranking second), being given the title of National

Excellent Science and Technology Worker and selected as one of the members of China's "Million Plan" and "Billions of talents project", getting the Outstanding Youth Practical Engineering Award of the 17th Chinese Association of Science and Technology and China's Youth Science and Technology Award, being awarded China's "May 4th Youth Medal", and enjoying the special government allowance from the State Council.

产业创新奖获得者

常 兆 华

　　常兆华，1963年7月出生于山东省淄博市。1992年毕业于纽约州立大学宾汉姆顿分校，获生物科学博士学位。1990—1995年在美国医疗器械公司 Cryomedical Sciences Inc 工作，先后担任高级工程师、首席科学家、研发部主任兼工程部副总裁等职；1996—1997年在美国 Endocare Inc 工作，担任研发副总裁；1998年回国创建上海微创医疗器械（集团）有限公司（简称微创®）。现代微创医疗器械及技术教育部工程中心创建者、主任，上海理工大学教授。

　　从事生物医学工程研究并开展企业创新管理，在国产介植入医疗器械领域的技术研究和产业化开拓等方面作出了一系列开创性工作。

一、创建"创新反应炉"及"线-站"式创新体系

　　创建一套行之有效的技术创新与产业化融合的管理模式，首创以"创新反应炉"为核心和"线-站"为特征的流水线创新体系，促使科技成果转化小概率事件变成大概率。在创新模式下取得多项原创性成果，孵化近30家高科技医疗企业；开发出心脏支架、人工心脏瓣膜、大动脉覆膜支架、颅内支架、肿瘤冷冻消融设备、人工关节、心脏起搏器等上百种高端医疗器械，几乎覆盖欧美介植入器材主要产品线，改写了我国该领域依赖进口的历史；平均每8秒就有一个微创®产品用于救助一条生命。微创®累计申请国内外专利3766件，已授权2134件，涵盖全球28个国家（地区），产业化成果填补10多项国家空白，累计为国家节约数百亿元医保资源。

二、开创介植入医疗器械国产化进程并取得多项原创性重大成果

　　微创介入技术是一种通过体表小切口将器材送到体内病灶进行医治的高科技手术方法，有创伤小、手术简单和术后恢复快等优点。与欧美90%普及率相比，我国早期只有

几家医院开展此手术。欧美对介植入性器材的绝对垄断使其得以将产品以数倍于本国价格向中国兜售，在一定程度上造成我国微创介入临床治疗的超低普及率。

常兆华带领技术团队在进行前瞻性布局的同时，对多项高精尖产品进行高强度技术攻关，经过 20 年不懈努力，取得多项原创性成果。

1. 心脏支架

带领团队研制出国内第一个心脏药物支架，攻克激光雕刻、药物载体和涂层制备及输送系统设计和生产工艺等关键技术，成为继美国两款产品之后全球第三款同类产品；以第一完成人获得 2006 年国家科技进步奖二等奖。开创性提出"靶向"概念并率领团队埋头攻关 10 年，于 2014 年将首个冠脉雷帕霉素药物靶向洗脱支架系统（简称 Firehawk®）推向市场。2018 年，一项按欧美规范及最苛刻全人群患者选择方式，由欧美医生在欧洲 10 国独立进行的大型临床试验成果在《柳叶刀》刊登，证实 Firehawk® 以仅需 1/3 通常药剂量获得欧美金标准支架同等甚至更佳疗效且更安全和实惠（大幅缩短术后服药时间，可为患者节省近万元医药费）；Firehawk® 解决了再狭窄和晚期血栓难以兼顾的矛盾，被欧美医学界评价为中国医疗器械产业短短 20 年历史中取得的一个伟大里程碑，中国成为全球心脏支架技术引领者；这也是《柳叶刀》创刊近 200 百年来首次出现中国医械身影，被媒体评为"2018 年中国十大科技新闻事件"。Firehawk® 在头发丝般金属网架上浓缩了激光微雕、航天级目标智能捕捉定位以及超微凹槽空间内 3D 打印自动化填充等多项尖端技术，这些已在娴熟应用的技术至今仍被欧美工程师认为是不可能突破的"技术魔咒"。Firehawk® 已在全球 36 个国家使用，植入成功率超过 99.995%，以器械失效为主因的手术死亡率低于 3PPM，为解决全球性心脏病难题提供了信得过的中国方案。

2. 大血管覆膜支架

主导开发国内第一个大动脉覆膜支架系统（一种对主动脉瘤进行腔内隔绝治疗的介入器械，简称 Aegis®）并实现了产品系列化和关键原材料国产化，取代了 20 多万元的单价进口产品，累计将 8 万名危重患者从死亡线上拉回来。推出全球独创术中支架系统（简称 CRONUS®）用于治疗极其凶险的主动脉夹层动脉瘤，使传统手术必须进行的两次开胸简化为一次手术完成全部治疗，术中死亡率从 50% 以上降低到 5% 以下。突破超薄覆膜人造血管制造技术，使我国成为全球第二个掌握该制造工艺的国家。以第一完成人获 2017 年国家科技进步奖二等奖。

3. 颅内支架和肿瘤冷冻消融系统

主导开发国内首个颅内动脉支架（简称 APOLLO）和全球首个颅内覆膜支架（简称 WILLIS®），其中，WILLIS® 是全球首个获准上市的用于治疗颅内动脉瘤的覆膜支架产品，被国际权威神经介入治疗学家认定为全世界 2007 年血管内治疗颅内动脉瘤的进展之一。两款支架技术已推广至 1000 多家临床研究中心，完成颅内介入手术 54000 多台，大幅提高了缺血并脑卒中病例治疗率，每年上万名患者受益；国产化的脑动脉瘤临床治疗产品使进口栓塞治疗产品价格降低 50%。

发明低压气体恶性肿瘤冷冻消融系统，兼具零下 180℃超低温消融及微创特点，使肝癌和肺癌等肿瘤患者在不开刀情况下完成治疗，创造性地将制冷源转化为普通工业气瓶，使冷冻消融这一绿色肿瘤治疗方式向偏远地区普及成为可能，该技术代表了世界肿瘤治疗的先进水平和发展方向。

作为上海理工大学教授，于 2006 年创建上海市地方院校第一个教育部工程中心；于 2005 年和 2010 年作为学科带头人设立生物医学工程一级硕士点和博士点，培养博士研究生 9 名、硕士生 10 余名、专技人才百余名。先后主持国家发改委重大专项、"863" 重大科技攻关、上海市重大产业化等 28 项省部级以上重大专项，以第一完成人获国家科技进步奖二等奖 3 项、上海市科技进步奖一等奖 2 项；以第二完成人获上海市科技进步奖二等奖 1 项。获国内外发明专利 49 项（国际专利 26 项），发表学术论文 50 余篇。

作为第十一、十二、十三届全国政协委员，提交数十篇与促进医疗行业发展相关的政协提案，积极参与国家医疗行业监管法律法规的修订和完善。联合上海交通大学、海军军医大等成立"微创介入与植入医疗器械产业技术创新战略联盟"；与东方医院共同发起成立"中国介入呼吸病学创新产业联盟"并担任名誉主席，推进产学研医资多种创新资源整合。入选为"纪念改革开放 40 年 40 名医药产业风云人物"。

Awardee of Industrial Innovation Prize，Chang Zhaohua

Chang Zhaohua was born in Zibo City of Shandong Province in July 1963. He is Chairman and Chief Executive Officer of Shanghai MicroPort Medical（Group）Co., Ltd.（"MicroPort®"）. He is also the founder and head of the Engineering Research Center for Modern Minimally Invasive Medical Devices & Technology under the Ministry of Education. He currently serves as a professor at School of Medical Instrument, University of Shanghai for Science and Technology.

Dr. Chang is committed to the technical research and industrialization of Chinese-made interventional and implantable medical devices. For product development and company management, he has established the innovation system, which has incubated nearly 30 high-tech medical device enterprises and developed hundreds of high-end medical devices. MicroPort® has contributed to filling the void of products in more than a dozen segments of the domestic medical device industry and ended the monopoly of imported products in the domestic market. Every eight seconds, one of the MicroPort® devices is used to save a life.

Approximately 5 million coronary stents produced by MicroPort® have been used to treat over 3.5 million patients worldwide. In 2018, the results of the large-sale European trial of the Firehawk® coronary stent, which had been independently developed by MicroPort®, were published in the world leading medical journal the Lancet. The Lancet declared that Firehawk® had solved a major medical issue that had challenged interventional cardiologists in the past decade.

The breakthrough showed that the innovative achievement of MicroPort® has won international recognition.

Dr. Chang has led a team to develop the first aortic stent-graft system in China, which resulted in a full product range and the domestic production of key raw materials. The aortic stent-graft system has replaced the imported products worth more than 200, 000 yuan each and saved a total of 80, 000 patients in a critical condition.

Under the leadership of Dr. Chang, China's the first intracranial stent for the treatment of ischemic cerebrovascular disease has been developed. The technology has been adopted at more than 1000 clinical centers, greatly improving the treatment rate of ischemic stroke cases and benefiting tens of thousands of patients each year.

Dr. Chang has invented the argon-helium cryoablation system, which is expected to alleviate the pains of hundreds of thousands of patients with advanced liver cancer, lung cancer and other types of cancer each year and effectively prolong their lives.

Dr. Chang has trained more than 100 professionals in medical device industry and led over 28 national and local projects of scientific researches and industrialization. Furthermore, he has actively cooperated with universities and hospitals to establish industrial leagues, and advanced the integration of various resources from the industry, universities, research institutes, hospitals and capital markets, which are required for innovation.

产业创新奖获得者

李 青

李青，女，1965年3月出生于河北省深泽县。正高级工程师，河北工学院学士，北京交通大学和清华大学硕士。东旭集团有限公司总裁兼总工程师，平板显示玻璃技术和装备国家工程实验室主任，武汉理工大学兼职教授，中国硅酸盐学会电子玻璃分会理事长。

作为电子玻璃工程技术领域的领军者，主要从事光电显示玻璃技术和装备的自主研发与创新工作，在光电显示用玻璃基板技术、触控屏玻璃技术及其装备开发等方面作出了一系列开创性研究及产业化推广工作。承担国家、省、市重大科技专项20余项。主持攻克了玻璃基板高均匀、超净面、强理化性能三大世界性难题，建成国内首条具有完全自主知识产权的玻璃基板生产线并推广至20余条产线，实现了产业化和规模化，国内市场占有率第一。国产化撬动进口玻璃大幅降价，为下游节约成本超2000亿元，不仅打破了国外垄断、填补了国内空白，还引领了产业转型升级，推动了我国光电显示产业健康安全发展，为我国显示产业规模位居世界第一作出了重大贡献。

李青牵头制定国标5项、编写专著2部；获发明专利38件、软著12项；发表论文46篇。作为第一完成人，获国家科技进步奖一等奖1项、省部级科技进步奖一等奖3项。

一、玻璃液处理技术研究

针对光电显示器对玻璃基板高光学均匀性的要求，建立了气泡吸收与搅拌均化综合效果评价模型，发明具有澄清、冷却、搅拌、均化与供料功能的"五仓型"铂金通道设备及智能集成控制系统。其中，冷却仓吸收了黏稠玻璃液中的微气泡，搅拌仓消除了细条纹，均化仓精确控温消除了粗条纹。

利用冷却仓与搅拌仓联动物理模拟，建立微气泡吸收A与成分均化H的综合效果评价模型Z，分析下倾角α对Z值的影响规律，发现α取值在8°～10°时，冷却仓结构最优，微气泡吸收最全；通过构建不同搅拌叶片仿真，建立双重搅拌增强均化模型，发现细条纹在黏稠玻璃液中得以消除的搅拌叶片关键结构，发明了大小叶片交错型搅拌器，利用叶片旋转线速度差对玻璃液拉伸、扭转、剪切，使条纹达到 00 最高级；制定非等梯度降温工艺，开发温度智能跟踪与快速调控的 DCS 系统实时控制，使得玻璃液在 1430～1150℃降温区域内，均质仓内截面温差 <1℃，有效消除了粗条纹。

基于上述创新研发了特种铂金制备、通道微环境控制、自适应膨胀保温等新技术，并发明了铂金通道技术与装备，制备出光学 H1 级高均匀玻璃。该成果被鉴定为国际领先，相关专利"铂金通道中玻璃液的处理方法"获 2015 年中国专利金奖。

二、玻璃基板加工技术研究

针对玻璃基板的无损洁净加工难题，开发了双光束散射表面颗粒检查技术，管控颗粒发生源，建立高频渗透切割工艺参数模型，开发"柔性"掰断和"水吸法"研磨技术，实现玻璃基板超净面加工。

玻璃内部缺陷极易误检为表面颗粒，发明了 $1～10\mu m$ 微颗粒双光束检查技术，利用两列线性光源低角度暗场照射、优化检查软件，实现了精准检测，发现了 80% 的微颗粒源自切割和研磨；针对切割中的颗粒污染，攻克复合型钻石刀轮低渗透切割技术，获得最佳渗透深度为板厚的 1/10～1/7 最优参数，实现了柔性切割与掰断；针对研磨粉游离扩散造成的次生微颗粒污染难题，开发了水吸法研磨技术，使含颗粒的研磨废水与玻璃基板表面有效分离，微颗粒数量大幅下降；通过准确判定玻璃基板微颗粒来源，应用低渗透切割技术与水吸式研磨技术，实现了将玻璃基板上的微颗粒控制在每平方米 30 个以下，优于国际同行业水平。

基于上述创新成果转化的玻璃基板自动加工生产线被科技部认定为国家战略性创新产品。

三、玻璃液黏温特性研究

通过研究以 SiO_2、Al_2O_3、B_2O_3 及碱土金属氧化物 RO（RO=Mg、Ca、Sr、Ba）等为原料的化学组成，发现 B_2O_3 配位数变化的因子在高温时对 SiO_2、Al_2O_3 熔解有助熔作用，在低温时对 SiO_4 有混熔及修补被破坏的网格节点作用；增加 BO_3 含量的同时大幅增加 Al_2O_3 的含量，可增强玻璃网络结构，再调控氧与铝、硼、硅摩尔比，可使网络结构桥氧联接达 96% 以上，结构致密。通过研究 Al_2O_3 与 RO 的配比关系，发现摩尔比只有满足 $Al_2O_3/RO>1.0$ 时，才具有更高的抗析晶效果，使力学性能、热稳定性能更强；当 Al_2O_3/SiO_2 摩尔比 n 逐渐增大后，发现玻璃网络中非桥氧减少，导致退火点（Ta）和应变点（Tst）不断升高，且高温下的熔化温度（Tm）和成型温度（Tf）呈现下降趋势。

基于以上研究开发了一种 TFT-LCD 高耐热温度、高耐腐蚀性、低膨胀系数玻璃料方，制定了与之匹配的熔制、均化、成形的黏度与温度工艺曲线，解决了 TFT-LCD 玻璃高温熔化、成形难题。

四、液态玻璃薄化拉伸工艺研究

通过研究超薄玻璃基板生产时所必需的压差匹配参数，发现窑炉、铂金通道、成形等工序环境压力相互制约关系，并以标准静压箱为参考基准，自动控制各区域环境压力与标准静压值的差值，建立玻璃基板薄化生产环境。

为解决超薄玻璃基板生产板面会出现收缩不一致、厚薄不均匀难题，研发超薄玻璃基板生产关键核心设备拉边机，在成形时促使玻璃板拉宽、变薄，并使其厚度均匀化。研究牵引辊线速度与拉边轮转速，再结合在线称重与测厚技术，实现不同厚度玻璃基板生产。

Awardee of Industrial Innovation Prize, Li Qing

Li Qing, female, was born in Shenze County of Hebei Province in March 1965. Ms. Li, a senior engineer, achieved a bachelor degree at Hebei Institute of Technology, a master degree at Beijing Jiaotong University and a master degree at Tsinghua University. Ms. Li currently serves as President and General Engineer of Tunghsu Group Co., Ltd., Director of National Engineering Laboratory of Flat Panel Display Glass Technology and Equipment, and an adjunct Professor at Wuhan University of Technology. She also serves as Chairman of Electronic Glass Branch of China Silicate Society. She used to be Vice-Chairman of the 10th Committee of Hebei Province Federation of Returned Overseas Chinese, and a representative of the 13th Hebei Provincial People's Congress.

As a leader in the field of electronic glass engineering technology, Ms. Li is mainly engaged in the independent research and development and innovation of optoelectronic display glass technology and equipment. Ms. Li undertook a series of groundbreaking research and industrialization promotion on glass substrate technology for optoelectronic display, touch screen glass technology and equipment development. She carried out over 20 major science and technology projects at the national, provincial or municipal levels. After leading to solve three world-wide problems regarding high uniformity, ultra-clean surface and strong physical and chemical properties of glass substrates, she established the first glass substrate production line in China with fully independent intellectual property rights, and then extended to over 20 production lines, which achieved industrialization and full-scale and ranked the first in terms of domestic market share. The localization process facilitated a significant decrease in the price of imported glass, which helped the downstream companies save over RMB200 billion. Accordingly, the monopoly of foreign technology was broken and the domestic gap in this area was filled. This led the industrial transformation and upgrading, promoted the healthy and safe development of China's optoelectronic display industry, and made a significant contribution to the scale of China's display industry which has ranked the first in the world.

产业创新奖获得者

任 发 政

任发政，1962 年 8 月出生于辽宁省营口市。1987 年毕业于北京农业大学动物科学技术学院，后留校任教；2002 年 12 月起任中国农业大学食品科学与营养工程学院教授；2004 年负责组建教育部北京市省部共建功能乳品实验室；2012 年起担任食品质量与安全北京实验室副主任；2015 年起担任北京食品营养与健康高精尖中心副主任；2018 年起担任中国农业大学益生菌研究中心主任。现任国际乳品联合会中国国家委员会执行主席、中国乳制品工业协会副理事长、中国奶业协会副会长、中国畜产品加工研究会副会长及中国高科技产业化研究会特聘副理事长。获国家科学技术进步奖二等奖 2 项、省部级科技奖励 12 项；以第一及通讯作者发表 SCI/EI 论文 150 篇，获授权发明专利 65 项；培养博士、硕士研究生 130 名，博士后 19 名。

长期从事乳品精深加工理论与技术研究，在牦牛乳特征解析与高值化加工利用、奶酪品质提升与工业化制造、自主知识产权益生菌国产化等方面取得了系列创新成果，对乳品工业产业升级与技术进步发挥了重要作用。

一、牦牛乳特征解析与高值化加工

全球 90% 的牦牛生活在我国青藏高原，牦牛乳是牧民赖以生存的宝贵资源和增收的重要途径，占其全部经济来源的 60% 以上。但由于牦牛是天然放养，缺乏鲜乳收购标准与技术体系，工业化加工比例低。任发政带领团队深入高海拔牧场，跟踪研究牦牛泌乳规律，解析牦牛乳脂肪酸、脂肪球膜脂质等组分构成特征，阐释了牦牛乳与荷斯坦牛乳酪蛋白胶束理化性质的差异，建立了牦牛乳泌乳数据库；依据牦牛泌乳特性，起草了牦牛生鲜乳收购、奶户管理等行业规范；协助企业制定牦牛乳收购管理体系，开发了牦牛酸乳等乳制品，对推进鲜牦牛乳加工发挥了重要作用。

"曲拉"是牧区主要牦牛乳制品，是生产干酪素的重要原料，也是牧民收入的主要来源，但是传统"曲拉"加工工艺粗放、色泽及溶解性差、价格低。任发政带领团队深入分析"曲拉"传统生产工艺弊病，明确了乳糖残留量是"曲拉"色泽劣变的关键控制因素，解析了"曲拉"乳化性降低的根源；采用梯度控温清洗、梯度 pH 分级溶解等技术，获得了高溶解性和乳化性的"曲拉"干酪素，显著提高了牦牛乳附加值，促进了牦牛乳产业升级，成果获 2010 年度国家科学技术进步奖二等奖。

二、奶酪品质提升与工业化制造

奶酪（即干酪）是奶业发达国家的主要乳制品，但是我国奶酪加工的凝乳、熔化与成熟等基础研究缺乏，加工技术相对落后，产品也严重依赖进口。

任发政带领团队采用低温酸化与皱胃酶分段凝乳方式，将诱导酪蛋白胶束结构变化与聚集重排分开，构建了酸与酶共促乳蛋白凝胶模型，完善了奶酪酸酶共促凝乳形成机制；明确了奶酪制作关键工艺对马苏里拉奶酪熔化品质的影响规律，研发了钠钙置换技术，实现了对奶酪组分及微观结构的有效调控，突破了奶酪熔化性差的技术难题；研发了辅助发酵剂热激定向修饰技术，抑制了辅助发酵剂菌株产酸能力，改变了细胞膜通透性，加速了切达奶酪的快速成熟，降低了生产成本；筛选出高产氨基转移酶和酯酶等附属发酵剂菌株，有效富集了奶酪坚果等特征风味。相关创新技术有力推进了奶酪国产化进程，获 2013 年度国家科学技术进步奖二等奖。

三、益生菌稳态化技术突破与国产化

发酵乳是我国增长最快的乳制品，也是益生菌的重要载体。由于我国缺乏高活性自主知识产权菌株稳态化生产技术，益生菌相关产品长期被国外垄断。

任发政带领团队从云南、西藏及广西等地分离筛选优良乳酸菌菌株，建立了菌株资源库，完成了动物双歧杆菌 A6 及副干酪乳杆菌 L9 等功能菌株的全基因组测序分析，为解析菌株功能机制奠定了坚实基础；阐释了长双歧杆菌 BBMN68 延缓衰老等功能机制，为功能菌株应用奠定了理论依据；创新了乳酸菌高密度培养与冻干保护技术，突破了自主知识产权益生菌株高密度发酵与活性保持技术瓶颈，使双歧杆菌冻干粉的活菌数达到国际先进水平；建立了符合 GMP 标准的益生菌生产技术转化平台，实现了自主知识产权菌株的工业化生产，打破了国外垄断，成果获 2014 年河北省科技进步奖一等奖。

Awardee of Industrial Innovation Prize，Ren Fazheng

Ren Fazheng was born in Yingkou City of Liaoning Province in August 1962. After graduation from Animal Science and Technology Department at Beijing Agricultural University in July 1987, he started working as an assistant professor there. Starting from December 2002, he worked as a professor in College of Food Science and Nutritional Engineering at China Agricultural University. Professor Ren has been in charge of the Key Laboratory of Functional Dairy, Co-constructed by Ministry of Education and Beijing Government since 2004. Since 2018, he has been the director of the Probiotics Research Center of China Agricultural University. Currently he is the executive president of Chinese National Committee of the International Dairy Federation, the vice president of China Dairy Industry Association and Dairy Association of China.

Professor Ren has been dedicated to studying the theory and technology of deep processing of dairy products. He has made a series of innovative achievements in key technologies of dairy industry, especially in the analysis and high-value utilization of yak milk, the improvement of cheese quality and the industrialization of probiotics with independent intellectual property rights. He was awarded 2 Second Prizes of National Scientific and Technology (ranked the first) and 12 Ministerial and Provincial-Level Science and Technology Awards. He has published 150 SCI/EI papers (first or corresponding author) and obtained 65 patents so far.

Professor Ren loves the motherland and dedicates to dairy research. He devotes himself to the construction of dairy science technology platform and talent cultivation. In 2004, he set up the open research platform of key and common technologies for the dairy industry. He collaborated with Yili, Mengniu and Sanyuan groups to establish postdoctoral workstations. In addition, he has mentored 15 young faculty members, 19 postdoctoral associates and 130 graduate students so far. As the chief expert of China Dairy Industry Association and the special expert of National Development and Innovation Committee, he drafted the China's dairy industry policy (2009), which played an important role in the industrial upgrading and technological progress of national dairy industry.

产业创新奖获得者

孙宝国

孙宝国，1961年1月出生于山东省招远市。1984年毕业于北京轻工业学院（现北京工商大学）化工系，后留校工作至今；2003年获清华大学化学工程博士学位。历任北京轻工业学院副院长，北京工商大学副校长、校长，兼任中国食品科学技术学会副理事长。2009年当选中国工程院院士。主持国家自然科学基金项目7项、国家"973""863"和国家科技支撑项目7项；作为第一完成人，获国家技术发明奖二等奖和国家科学技术进步奖二等奖4项；已出版学术著作11部，发表学术论文300余篇；获授权发明专利20余项。

作为香料和食品风味化学专家、我国含硫香料的开拓者、咸味香精的奠基人，长期从事食品风味化学研究，致力于通过改善食品香味、提升食品质量、保障食品安全以推动食品产业的发展。

一、潜心香料香精科技研发，打破国外技术封锁和产品垄断，提升中国肉味香精在国内外市场的竞争力

2-甲基-3-巯基呋喃（国外商品代号030）和甲基2-甲基-3-呋喃基二硫醚（国外商品代号719）是从海鲜和畜禽肉中发现的关键肉香味物质，是重要的肉味香料。美国国际香料公司在20世纪70年代以合成技术率先实现了商业化生产，中国进口价曾分别高达9万元/千克和14万元/千克，几乎与当时的黄金同价。为了打破国外垄断，摆脱依赖进口的尴尬局面，"030的合成"被国家列为"七五"重点科技攻关项目。孙宝国带领团队最终研发合成了以030和719为代表的100多种含硫香料，突破了制约我国含硫香料生产的一系列行业共性关键技术，奠定了我国3-呋喃硫化物系列和不对称二硫醚类食品香料制造的技术基础。产品质量达到世界领先水平，成本不到进口产品价格的1%，不仅满足了国内需要，还占据了大部分国际市场，使我国成为世界上两个能够生产此类高档香料的国家之一和含硫香料生产大国。上述成果分别于1999年和2005年获得国家科学技术进步奖二等奖和国家技术发明奖二等奖。

在对 600 多种含硫化合物分子结构和香味特征分析、归纳、总结的基础上，孙宝国提出了肉香味含硫化合物分子特征结构单元模型。将该模型用于肉香味新含硫香料的分子设计与合成，可有效避免合成的盲目性，提高遴选成功率。同时结合对以"蒸煮文化"为基础的中国烹饪技艺的领悟，凝练出"味料同源"的中国特色肉味香精制造新理念，研究成功了以畜禽肉、骨、脂肪为主要原料的肉味香精制造技术。该技术使中国肉味香精制造技术跃居世界领先水平，已成为我国肉味香精生产的主体技术，并于 2000 年获得国家科学技术进步奖二等奖。

二、关注食品安全科普，提升全民科学素质，承担科学家社会责任

2008 年中国奶制品污染事件震惊全国，此后屡见报道的食品安全事件造成了公众严重的心理恐慌。一些人误认为添加剂就是食品添加剂，"食品添加剂"成了非法添加物的替罪羊。作为这一领域的专家学者，孙宝国感到有责任为公众普及食品添加剂的科学知识，消除不必要的误会，并通过作报告、接受专访、出版科普书等多种形式进行食品添加剂的科普宣传。2010 年至今，已在内地和澳门特别行政区等地为政府部门、媒体和公众作食品添加剂科普讲座 200 多场。

2012 年，孙宝国主编了科普书《躲不开的食品添加剂》，填补了我国食品添加剂与食品安全领域科学真相与公众认知之间的信息真空，为保障我国食品工业的健康有序发展、倡导和维护正确的社会舆论导向起到了积极作用。该作品出版当年即获选"十二五"国家重点图书，2013 年获得了中国石油和化学工业联合会科技进步奖一等奖，并荣获了2016 年度国家科学技术进步奖二等奖。孙宝国还与食品伙伴网、食品添加剂和配料协会等专业网站联管联办科普栏目；并建立"躲不开的食品添加剂"微信公众号，使手机成为普及食品添加剂科学知识的口袋书。中国食品科学技术学会报告中指出，"在 2011 年中国公众关注的 12 个主要食品安全热点中，食品添加剂是主流，占到 12 个热点的 25%；而 2015 年中国公众关注的食品安全热点中，食品添加剂已降至 5% 以下。显示了以孙宝国院士为代表的科技界参与公众科普的力量与价值。"

三、开展白酒化学研究，推动白酒现代化、国际化发展

2011 年起，孙宝国开始进行中国传统白酒现代化工作，提出"健康白酒是中国白酒的发展方向""应结合香型创新、理念创新以及技术创新来推动中国白酒的国际化"的重要理念；同时提出了"白酒是中国的国酒"、白酒产品的发展方向是"风味、健康双导向"、白酒产业的发展方向是"生产现代化，市场国际化"等观点，得到产业界和国内外学术界的广泛认可。带领团队首次在白酒中发现了多肽、乳酸丙酯等物质，构建了含有 1000 多种物质的白酒风味物质色谱–质谱数据库，在大曲中率先筛选得到高产糠硫醇的酿酒酵母。在芝麻香型白酒特征风味物质的确证工作方面取得了一定成绩，推动了相关行业标准的修订。2018 年应邀在 *Journal of Agricultural and Food Chemistry* 上发表有关白酒的综述，标志着"Baijiu"一词得到了国际认可；修订版的白酒国家标准中也正式将"Baijiu"作为标准翻译。2019 年由其主编的《国酒》一书正式出版，书中用通俗的语言介绍白酒和黄酒的概念、工艺等，成为科普酒知识、进一步展现文化自信和民族自信的又一代表作，受到普遍关注和好评。

Awardee of Industrial Innovation Prize，Sun Baoguo

Sun Baoguo was born in Zhaoyuan City of Shandong Province in January 1961, graduated from Beijing Institute of Light Industry (predecessor of Beijing Technology and Business University (BTBU)) in 1984 and has worked in the University since then. In 2003, he received PhD degree from Tsinghua University. He served as Vice President of BILI and BTBU from 1997 to 2014. Since 2014, he became the President of BTBU. He also serves as Vice President of Chinese Institute of Food Science and Technology. He was elected as academician of China Academy of Engineering in 2009.

Sun Baoguo is an expert in food flavor and fragrance. He created a characteristic molecular structural unit model for sulfur-containing meat flavors and developed a series of manufacturing technologies for many important meat flavors. 2-methyl-3-mercapto furan (commodity code 030) and methyl-2-methyl-3-furyl disulfide (commodity code 719) are key meat flavor substances with import prices at 90,000 CNY/kg and 140,000 C/kg respectively, almost the same as gold at that time. Overcoming many difficulties and experiencing numerous failures, Prof. Sun finally synthesized more than 100 kinds of sulfur-containing spices represented by 030 and 719, broke the product monopoly and enhanced the competitiveness of Chinese meat flavor in domestic and foreign markets. Further, he developed the preparation concept for Chinese characteristic meat flavorings, 'the identical origin of aroma with raw material', and crucial techniques of preparing meat flavorings based on meat, bone and fat. These achievements were rewarded 1 Second Prize of National Technologic Invention and 2 Second Prize of National Scientific and Technologic Progress from State Council of China.

He has been devoted to the popularization of food safety, improving the scientific quality of the Chinese, and assuming the social responsibility of scientists. The book named *Inevitable Food Additives* scientifically interpreted the history, types, efficacy, use of food additives and their effects on our lives which plays a positive role in ensuring the healthy development of food industry in China and advocating and maintaining the correct orientation of public opinion. Thus he gained another Second Prizes of National Scientific and Technologic Progress Meanwhile, he has long worked on flavor chemistry of Baijiu and proposed the development strategy of Baijiu which emphasizes on the double guidance of health and flavor which embodies cultural confidence, and promotes the internationalization of Baijiu modernization.

产业创新奖获得者

孙 立 宁

孙立宁，1964年1月出生于黑龙江省鹤岗市。1993年毕业于哈尔滨工业大学机械系，获工学博士学位。1993年至今在哈尔滨工业大学工作；1998—2008年任哈尔滨工业大学机器人研究所所长；2007年起任机器人国家重点实验室副主任。先后荣获国家杰青、长江学者特聘教授、万人计划领军人才等称号，并担任中国微米纳米学会微纳机器人分会理事长、中国医疗器械行业协会医用机器人分会理事长、中国机电一体化技术应用协会副会长、中国自动化学会机器人委员会副主任、国家"863"计划微纳制造领域专家、MEMS重大专项总体组组长。主持"973""863"、国家自然科学基金、国防基金等项目20余项，在机器人机构、驱动与控制、作业机理与方法、系统集成等方面取得重要成果，并在神光Ⅲ等重大工程及微纳制造、生命科学及国防等领域得到成功应用。获国家发明／进步二等奖2项、省部级奖励8项；发表论文300余篇，出版专著5部；获发明专利80项。

长期从事微纳机器人前沿研究，先后建立了微纳米机器人与系统集成研究平台、高性能工业机器人及机电一体化装备研究平台、医疗微创手术机器人集成研究平台，实现了微纳技术装备产业化、工业机器人与自动化生产线产业化、微创外科手术机器人及家政服务机器人的示范应用。

一、微纳米机器人与系统集成研究

针对纳米精密定位中的大行程高分辨率定位、高速高精度定位、微定位技术，解决了其中的机构设计、压电陶瓷建模与驱动、微定位精密测量、压电陶瓷控制方法等关键技术难题，研制出6自由度宏微精密定位机构、高速高精度定位机构、纳米微驱动机构；提出了具有工程实用价值的压电陶瓷迟滞模型和归一化控制模型。在压电陶瓷的建模与控制等相关理论与技术上有明显创新，达到了国际先进水平。

针对微操作机器人关键技术，提出2种微操作结构，研制出组合式微夹持器、球基微操作器、基于 PVDF 微力传感器、缩放式主操纵手、基于小波变换的显微视觉系统、微操作虚拟现实系统，研究了 3 种微操作策略。在显微视觉、微操作策略等方面达到国际先进水平。

推动纳米微驱动技术实现产业化，相关产品已推广应用并替代进口产品。研制出 8 种微操作机器人并推广应用，研制的神光Ⅲ靶支撑和传感器支撑机器人应用于国家重大科学工程"神光Ⅲ原形装置"项目上；研制的激光陀螺精密调腔机器人应用于国防军工生产上；面向 MEMS 制造领域研制了 6 种微操作机器人，应用于型号研制、生产和科研中，填补了国内空白，在激光约束聚变、惯性器件制造、MEMS 制造、生物医学、光学精密工程、集成电路封装与测试、超精密加工等领域显示出广阔的应用前景，对提升我国精密 / 超精密作业机器人与机电一体化装备的自主创新能力和研发水平起到了重要的示范带动作用。

二、高性能工业机器人及机电一体化装备研究

在工业机器人技术研究方面，开发出了系列化工业机器人和多种危险环境作业机器人。工业机器人实现了产业化应用，处于国内领先水平；承担的 CAD/CAE 融合工业机器人设计平台项目为工业机器人正向优化设计打下了坚实基础；承担的多平台高节拍汽车柔性定位平台系统项目为多自由度工业机器人柔性生产线应用提供了应用基础，研制突出产品柔性和运行柔性，其特有的高速精准特性有助于与标准机器人配合实用，实现生产柔性化，大幅加快作业节拍，提高生产效率；开发了 20DOF 柔性定位平台。在工业机器人机构设计、控制器设计、力位柔顺控制方面取得了一系列研究成果。

在工业机器人及智能制造装备方面，组织开发出多种型号工业机器人及包装码垛生产线，开发出 6～500kg 载荷的系列化工业机器人以及装配、包装、喷涂、抛光、激光加工等生产线，实现了工业机器人与自动化生产线产业化，并取得显著的经济社会效益。

三、医疗微创手术机器人集成研究

结合我国具体的技术现状、医疗环境、社会需要和实验室技术条件，以影像引导高精度定位操作、微创手术机器人、眼科机器人、脊柱手术机器人、虚拟手术仿真系统、人体康复与服务机器人、数字化医疗装备等为研究重点，从生物医学的整体角度开展了医用机器人及其相关交叉学科的前沿基础理论与技术方法研究与开发。集中开展了新型医用手术机器人机构关键技术的研究与开发，包括专用型医用机械臂，基于力反馈交互主手设备及其他医用机械机构，医学图像 3D 建模和仿真，机器人智能控制及交互，增强现实与影像导航融合技术，呼吸跟踪技术，医用软组织仿真，生物力学建模，生肌电信号采集及处理等。建立了若干个机器人辅助外科手术系统、沉浸式手术仿真系统、基于增强现实的影像导航系统、康复与护理服务机器人系统等样机，并应用于动物实验或临床应用，产生了重大的社会效益，带动了一系列相关医疗领域高新技术应用的研究与开发。

在医疗特种机器人方面，开发了数字化机器人辅助骨科手术系统，获得黑龙江省科学技术奖二等奖，实现了工程化与示范应用；开发出微创外科手术机器人，基于生物信息控制的智能假肢、助行与康复训练机器人以及肠道诊疗机器人等医疗机器人系统和多种教育与家政服务机器人等产品，实现了应用示范。

此外，针对现代纳米医学、纳米药物、靶向给药癌症治疗基础理论与关键技术的研究，孙立宁团队探索多学科交叉前沿，提出一种融合纳米游动机器人和微纳操作机器人而形成的任务协同、功能共融的多尺度微纳米机器人创新体系结构；构建集测试、操纵功能于一体的微纳操作机器人，实现了跨尺度生物分子/细胞的精密操控、多维生物信息检测和多特征参数提取，为主动靶向纳米游动机器人的设计制备优化、运动控制、精准靶向给药提供了方法和平台支持。研究所取得的成果将为现代纳米医学提供关键理论与技术支撑，增强我国在生物医药与治疗领域的原创能力，加速我国靶向药物研发进程。同时，多尺度微纳米机器人新体系的构建拓宽了机器人技术在微纳尺度下的应用，其驱动、检测、控制方法将为纳米机器人的研究提供理论和技术支持。

Awardee of Industrial Innovation Prize, Sun Lining

Sun Lining was born in Hegang City of Heilongjiang Province in January 1964. In 1993, Prof. Sun received his Ph.D degree in Engineering from the Mechanical Engineering Department of Harbin Institute of Technology(HIT), and joined HIT after graduation.

He is a National Outstanding Youth Fund Winner, Changjiang Scholar Distinguished Professor by the Ministry of Education, and leading scientist of Ten-thousand Talents Program, and he also served as the chairman of Micro-Nano Robot Branch of Chinese Society of Micro-Nano Technology, a Subject Matter Expert of Robotic Technology in the Tenth Five-Year "863" Program of China, a main group leader of MEMS major projects in the Tenth Five-Year "863" Program of China, and an expert of Advanced Manufacturing Technology Expert Group in the 11th Five-Year "863" Program of China.

Prof. Sun has been engaged in the frontier research of micro-nano robots for more than 30 years presided over more than 20 projects such as National "973" Program, National "863" Program, National Natural Science Foundation, and National Defense Fund and achieved many breakthrough results in micro-nano operational robot and equipment, advanced robot and control, electromechanical integration equipment, etc., which has been successfully applied in major projects such as "Shenguang 3" and in many fields such as micro-nano manufacturing, life sciences and national defense.

He has received two National Science and Technology Award Grade II and three Provincial Science and Technology Prize Grade I and has more than 300 academic papers and 5 monographs being published and has more than 20 patents of invention being authorized.

Prof. Sun has built the micro-nano robot systems, the high-performance Industrial robots and mechatronics equipment, and the medical minimally invasive surgery robot integration research platform. Prof. Sun introduced the micro-nano robot technology into the military and civilian field of the laser confinement fusion and the Inertial device manufacturing. This technology has filled the gaps between domestic and international and achieved good economic and social benefits. In the industrial robots and the intelligent manufacturing equipment fields, Prof. Sun leading to building a series of industrial robots and packaging and palletizing the auto-production line. This technology is received many national awards and realized the industrialization of industrial robots and automated production lines. The output value is more than RMB 200 million. In the medical robot field, Prof. Sun leading to building a digital robotic-assisted orthopedic surgery system. This technology is received Science and Technology Award Second Prize of Heilongjiang Province. And this technology is also achieved practical application.

产业创新奖获得者

沈 政 昌

　　沈政昌，1960年5月出生于江苏省常熟市。2007年毕业于北京科技大学矿物加工工程系，获工学博士学位。现为北京矿冶科技集团有限公司教授级高级工程师、首席专家。

　　作为我国矿冶装备领域的学术带头人，一直工作在科研一线，致力于实现低品位、难处理矿产资源的大规模开发和高效利用，在浮选装备大型化、系列化和专用化领域成果卓著。历获国家科技进步奖二等奖2项、国家发明奖3项、中国专利优秀奖4项、部级科技成果奖26项。出版学术专著4部，发表论文100多篇。荣膺"全国杰出专业技术人才""杰出工程师奖"等荣誉称号，获国务院特殊津贴。

一、浮选机大型化从赶超先进到引领发展

　　全球优质矿产资源开发殆尽，选矿厂的矿石处理量越来越大。开发大型高效浮选技术装备、规模化利用低品位矿产资源成为必然选择，而这一领域长期被国外公司垄断。大型浮选机内为气液固三相流，流体动力学特征非常复杂，通过研究不同区域内的流场特征参数及其对矿化效果的影响，定义了"大型浮选机内浮选动力学分区"，提出了"提高大型浮选机运输区高度有利于粗粒矿物回收""加强预矿化作用可增加细粒矿物回收"的新观点，明确了提高大型浮选机分选指标的技术方向；提出了基于平均叶轮搅拌雷诺数相等、以几何相似及悬浮相似为核心的趋势外推浮选设备放大理论，为浮选机大型化提供了支撑。

　　创新开发了广域输出角后倾叶轮、叶轮腔内定向流空气分配器和泡沫快速输送技术等一批核心关键技术，研制成功了具有自主知识产权的40—320立方米系列大型浮选机，改变了我国长期使用20立方米以下浮选机的局面，推进了我国选矿厂的大型化和现代化进程，使中国成为与芬兰、美国并列的具有浮选机大型化能力的三大强国。其开发的大型浮选机服务于我国90%以上的大型选矿厂并出口到10多个国家，在国内外182座大型

矿山推广 2300 多台套，每年累计处理矿石近 6.5 亿吨，为我国乃至世界矿产资源的高效综合利用作出了显著贡献，奠定了我国大型浮选装备的国际领先地位。2018 年，成功开发出世界上最大规格的 680 立方米超大型智能高效浮选装备，使我国浮选装备大型化技术实现了从追赶到领跑的跨越。

二、宽粒级浮选推动难处理资源有效利用

目前，矿石中难选的粗、细粒矿物所占比例显著增加，而粗、细矿物颗粒的回收是矿物加工领域的共性难题，其所需的分选环境与常规粒级矿粒截然不同。沈政昌创造性地提出在同一体系内构建不同动力学分区的"差异化分选"理论，通过在浮选槽内构建不同动力学分区来满足不同粒级矿物浮选所需的水力学环境，并据此成功开发出宽粒级浮选装备，有效解决了宽粒级矿物回收难题。这一机型在我国最大的贵溪冶炼厂建立了铜炉渣资源化利用示范工程，实现了铜炉渣浮选法回收连续生产，填补了国内外炉渣浮选设备技术的空白。仅冶炼炉渣资源化利用就实现年处理铜炉渣 1200 万吨，占我国总量 70% 以上，成为铜冶炼企业建设的标准配置。

三、浮选机联合机组变革选矿厂配置设计

我国有大量中小选矿厂亟须技术升级，以摆脱经营困难，提高资源利用水平。沈政昌研发的充气式自吸浆浮选机可实现浮选机组的水平配置，简化工艺流程、节省基建投资、降低运行成本并改善分选指标。沈政昌提出了充气式自吸浆浮选机设计架构和理论模型，推导了基于关键结构和工艺参数的吸浆量计算公式，验证了这一机型的工程可行性；发明了具有两个独立工作区的叶轮，上叶片用于卷吸给矿或中矿，下叶片用于循环矿浆和分散空气，这一独特设计攻克了充气条件下无法自吸给矿和中矿的世界性难题。利用这一机型，在世界上首创了充气式浮选机联合机组配置技术，使不同浮选作业处于同一水平标高，推动了选矿厂设计和设备配置技术的变革，成为具有我国特色的浮选装备技术。我国 5000 吨／日以下规模选矿厂 85% 应用该技术。通过对 92 家典型选矿厂的统计，仅能耗一项每年可节电超过 1 亿度，社会经济效益十分显著。

四、系列专用浮选设备保障资源高效开发

我国对铜、铁、铝和石墨等大宗金属和非金属矿物的需求巨大，而我国矿产资源禀赋相对较差、矿物性质差异大，分选的难度大，近年来获取的国外矿权也大多如此。因此，提高矿产资源的高效开发和综合利用水平对我国来说尤显急迫。为此，沈政昌立足国情，针对不同矿物的特点开发了一系列专用浮选装备。

开发了适用于铁精矿"提铁降杂"的浮选装备技术，解决了矿浆比重大、易沉槽和泡沫黏、难输送的难题，并应用于鞍钢、酒钢、秘鲁铁矿和印度 JSL 等企业，保障了"精料入炉"。开发了适用于"选矿–拜耳法"的低铝硅比铝土矿浮选装备技术，解决了小充气

量下空气分散度差和泡沫回收效率低的难题，在中州铝业建成了我国第一条铝土矿选矿示范生产线并实现大规模推广应用。开发了盐类矿物浮选装备技术，攻克了卤水钾盐浮选中气体难分散、颗粒易结晶等工艺技术难题；建立了罗布泊钾盐浮选法示范工程，使之成为我国最大的硫酸钾生产基地。该技术已推广应用于青海钾盐、藏格钾盐和老挝开元钾盐等项目，显著促进了我国钾盐资源的规模开发。此外，还开发了大鳞片石墨矿专用浮选装备技术、低品位胶磷矿专用浮选装备技术和贵金属快速浮选装备技术等一系列专用装备，形成了中国特色的矿物加工装备技术，极大地促进了我国矿产资源的高效综合开发，保障了多种矿物的战略供给。

Awardee of Industrial Innovation Prize，Shen Zhengchang

Shen Zhengchang was born in Changshu City of Jiangsu Province in May 1960. He obtained the bachelor's and Ph.D's degree from the University of Science and Technology Beijing（USTB）in 1982 and 2007 respectively. He is now working as professor and Chief Expert at the BGRIMM Technology Group. Prof. Shen has devoted himself to the development of advanced mineral processing technology for 37 years. As the academic leader in the research area of mineral processing equipment，Prof. Shen made remarkable contributions to the scale-up design，systematization and specialization of froth flotation equipment. He was awarded "The 2nd-Class Prize Of The National Science-Technology Advancement twice"，"The National Invention Prize" three times and "The China Patent Excellence Award four times". Prof. Shen has also received 26 provincial and ministerial-level recognitions and honors for his achievement in science and technology. 4 academic monographs and more than 100 papers have been published by Prof. Shen. He was granted "The Special Allowance Of State Council" and named "The National Outstanding Professional".

Froth flotation is one of the most important mineral processing techniques. It is a highly versatile method to separate mineral particles from gangue particles based on their different surface characteristics. About 90% of the nonferrous and 50% of the ferrous minerals were addressed by flotation process worldwide. The natural resource endowment of China is relatively poor and it has been more and more difficult to extract valuables from ore deposits in recent years. Tomake the mineral processing more efficient and hence fulfill the country's demands of minerals，Shen Zhengchang has been dedicated to the research and development of new technology for decades and lots of mile-stone achievements have been obtained as rewards for his hard work. His contribution includes flotation equipment scale-up design，flotation technology for minerals with wide size distribution，combined flotation technology and specialization of flotation technology.

产业创新奖获得者

王 华 平

　　王华平，1965年7月出生于江苏省宜兴市。1989年毕业于中国纺织大学（今东华大学），获化学纤维专业硕士学位，同年留校工作；2001年获得东华大学材料学博士学位。先后担任东华大学材料科学与工程学院副院长、高性能纤维及制品教育部重点实验室（B）主任、东华大学研究院副院长、国家先进功能纤维创新中心主任。兼任产业用纺织品教育部工程研究中心副主任、中国纺织工程学会化纤专业委员会副主任、中国化学纤维工业协会常务理事、中国材料研究学会高分子材料与工程分会常务理事、纺织类专业教学指导委员会纤维材料分教学指导委员会主任等。作为主要技术负责人，积极参与"中国化纤工业十二五及十三五规划"等研究与制订；创建了中国化学纤维流行趋势研究与发布平台、国家先进功能纤维创新中心。获国家科技进步奖二等奖5项、省部级科技奖23项；发表SCI论文98篇；授权发明专利108项；培养博士生20名、硕士生50名。先后获全国优秀科技工作者、中国纺织学术大奖、改革开放40年纺织行业突出贡献人物等荣誉。

　　长期致力于纤维材料科学和工程研究，在聚酯纤维材料改性、加工及其资源综合利用基础理论、关键技术和应用开发方面作出了一系列开创性研究工作，其成果在恒力、新凤鸣、桐昆、百宏、大发、恒逸等企业广泛应用，推动了千万吨聚酯的技术创新与持续进步。

一、研发聚酯纤维舒适改性及微纳复合改性关键技术，提升聚酯纤维功能与附加值

1.聚酯纤维舒适改性关键技术

　　聚酯纤维是纤维产业的第一大品种，为了改善其舒适性，满足我国运动休闲面料行业的需求，王华平带领团队系统剖析面料导湿机理，创建纤维集合体的 Monte Carlo 模型，定量分析了润湿—芯吸—导湿协同效应，揭示了纤度、形状、表面特性等对面料吸湿导

湿的影响规律。提出了流场控制的高规整十字、组合异形等喷丝板设计新方法，提高了聚酯纤维异形度、规整性及后加工适应性；研究高剪切速率下异形纤维的成形机理及特征，开发了缓冷与强冷结合、先结晶后加弹等关键技术，解决了高异形度纤维截面形状的保持和控制难题；研制多组分共聚改性及纤维表面协同改性技术，开发高导湿、高仿棉、高保型等纤维，高导湿面料滴水扩散时间小于1秒。其中，"高导湿涤纶纤维及制品关键技术集成开发"获2007年国家科技进步奖二等奖（排名第一）。

2. 聚酯纤维微纳复合改性关键技术

微纳复合技术是实现纤维功能化的有效手段。为了开发高品质多功能纤维，必须保证微纳无机功能材料在高黏度聚合物基体中均匀分散。作为主要负责人，研发了微纳粉体表面包覆、原位修饰等专用技术，建立了纤维级高浓度母粒制备与评价体系，大大减少了加工过程中的二次团聚；建立了微纳复合纤维纺丝动力学模型，确定了功能纤维纺丝成形机理与特征，开发了非均相共混、高温高压纺丝等核心技术；研制了抗紫外、抗菌、凉感、发热等高效多功能纤维及制品，推动了纳米材料的产业化应用及功能纤维的技术进步。其中，"热塑性高聚物基纳米复合功能纤维成形技术及制品开发"获2006年国家科技进步奖二等奖（排名第二）。

二、研发精细化及柔性化纺丝成形关键技术，推进聚酯纤维熔体直纺工程技术升级

1. 聚酯精细化纺丝工程技术与高品质超细旦长丝制备

为了提升聚酯纤维工艺与品质管理效率和水平，创建了聚酯熔融纺丝工程模型，确定输送、纺丝等工艺参量对纤维性能指标与不匀率的影响规律，建立了熔体直纺聚酯FDY及DTY质量与工艺精细化控制体系。针对超细旦涤纶成形条件苛刻、品质难以控制的问题，研发聚酯微量多元醇与无机粉体组合改性技术，扩展了加工窗口及适应性；研发了亚微米过滤、自洽整流、张力自动补偿与控制等关键技术，显著提升熔体均质化、纺丝成形稳定化水平，生产效率达99.99%，大幅提升了产品品质。开发的高品质超细旦纤维直径小于7微米，铸就了全球熔体直纺超细旦纤维强国地位，成为我国纤维行业质量提升与跨越式发展的标志。其中，"高品质熔体直纺超细旦涤纶长丝关键技术开发"获2011年国家科技进步奖二等奖（排名第一）。

2. 聚酯纺丝高效柔性化工程技术及差别化产品开发

大容量熔体直纺流程长、交互影响大，共聚、共混等差别化技术开发及其协同控制困难。作为主要研究人员，研发了多元共聚、在线多点添加、动态混合等关键技术，实现一线多品种同步纺丝，制备了有色、超有光、亲水、深染等品种；开发双头双排多孔纺、多头纺、在线混纤等模块，结合异形、纺丝动力学改性技术，制备扁平、异收缩等产品；成功实现了熔体直纺高效柔性与低耗环保生产，聚酯和长丝能耗比国际一级标准降低37%与34%。其中，"超大容量高效柔性差别化聚酯长丝成套工程技术开发"获2013年国家科技进步奖二等奖（排名第四）。

三、研发再生循环与生物基聚酯纤维加工关键技术，提高聚酯纤维资源利用率

我国聚酯年产量大、总储量高、再生率低，大量聚酯废弃物被当作垃圾掩埋、焚烧，不仅资源浪费大，而且环境负担重。他带领团队系统研究废旧聚酯制品中化物料、混杂高聚物在再生过程中的作用机理，开发废旧聚酯纺织品高效前处理技术，突破了资源化及标准化瓶颈；研制再生聚酯调质、调黏、调色配色等关键技术，创建物理化学法聚酯再生技术体系；开发再生低熔点、再生多功能纤维，提升废旧聚酯的回收利用率与品质。创新构建的物理化学法再生聚酯中国方案可年回收废旧聚酯瓶片及纺织品 100 万吨，助力城市固废处理。其中，"废旧聚酯高效再生及纤维制备产业化集成技术"获 2018 年国家科技进步奖二等奖（排名第一）。

此外，针对生物基聚酯 PTT 聚合副反应多、聚合与纺丝加工稳定性差等难题，作为主要负责人，在研究 PTT 聚合特征的基础上构建高效短流程连续聚合工程技术体系；开发了高压挤出、低温冷却、超喂入卷绕的长丝高速纺丝技术和低回缩、高温低压卷曲的短纤维成形技术。结合共聚、共混、异形纺丝和多组分纺纱织造与同浴染色技术，开发了 30 多种 PTT 切片、纤维及面料，推动了 PTT 聚合、纺丝、织造及染整产业链的协同创新。

Awardee of Industrial Innovation Prize, Wang Huaping

Wang Huaping was born in Yixing City of Jiangsu Province in July 1965. He is leading talents in Science and Technology innovation in the Chinese fiber industry and has been dedicated to Fiber Science and Engineering research for a long time. He has achieved a series of innovative achievements in the basic theory, key technologies and application research of polyester fiber material modification, processing and comprehensive utilization of resources. He was rewarded National Sci-Tech Advance Award 5 times and Provincial and ministerial Prize 23 times. He owns 108 authorized National Invention Patents and has published 98 SCI papers. He was awarded the honorary title of China Textile Academic Award, National Excellent Science and Technology Worker, Outstanding Contribution to the Textile Industry in the 40 Years of Reform and Opening-up.

He has adhered to fiber technology innovation for a long time and achieved remarkable results. Researcher Wang Huaping focuses on the combination of original Innovation and Engineering application. He presided over the development of high-wet, ultra-fine denier polyester fiber preparation and fabric development key technology, breaking through the bottleneck of differentiated fiber quality and high value-added applications. He integrated the development of melt straight-spun polyester fiber high-efficiency and low-carbon flexible processing technology, which promotes the development of high-capacity polyester fiber preparation and application technology. He carried out research on key technologies for waste polyester fiber recycling, promoting the utilization of textile resources and the development of the recycling industry. He also tackled the key technologies of bio-based Polyester (PTT) industrialization development, established a new system for industrial chain application, and expanded new resources for polyester fiber. The results have been widely used in more than 30 companies such as Hengli, Xinfengming, Baihong, and Hengli, which have promoted technological innovation and continuous improvement of the production capacity of 10 million tons of polyester.

He focuses on talent training and base construction and makes outstanding contributions. Researcher Wang Huaping pays attention to team building, talent training and base building, actively promotes the State Key Laboratory of Fiber Materials Modification and National Key Discipline Construction of Materials Science. As a backbone, he participated in the "12th Five-Year Plan and the 13th Five-Year Plan for Chinese Chemical Fiber Industry". He founded the China Chemical Fiber Trend Research and Publishing Platform and the Advanced Functional Fiber National Manufacturing Innovation Center. He also promoted the construction of fiber standardization system, and actively promoted the green manufacturing and intelligent manufacturing capabilities of the chemical fiber industry.

产业创新奖获得者

朱 真 才

朱真才，1965年10月出生于安徽省怀宁县。2000年毕业于中国矿业大学机械设计系，获工学博士学位。1989—2001年在中国矿业大学科研所工作，任助工、工程师、高工。2001年8月—2003年7月在中南大学矿业工程博士后流动站进行博士后研究。2003年8月—2011年10月任中国矿业大学机电工程学院副院长、院长；2011年11月—2019年1月任中国矿业大学科学技术研究院院长；2019年2月起任江苏省矿山机电装备重点实验室主任；2019年8月起任江苏省矿山智能采掘装备协同创新中心主任。2006年10月—2007年9月在德国Wuppertal大学任客座教授。先后担任中国工程机械学会矿山机械分会秘书长、理事长，中国煤炭学会煤矿机电一体化专业委员会副主任委员，煤矿安全标准化技术委员会提升安全及设备分技术委员会副主任委员，第五届国家安全生产专家组成员。

长期从事矿山高效运输研究，在矿井提升与运输装备领域作出了一系列开创性研究工作。

一、矿井大吨位提升容器

研发了矿井大吨位提升容器（箕斗、罐笼），突破容器载重能力大、装载空间大、停车位置精准等关键技术，满足了年产千万吨矿井高效运输能力的需求。发明了窄长型薄壁箱形结构的大吨位箕斗，箕斗单次载重量由过去的20吨提高到50吨（世界最大吨位）；发明了局部刚性、整体柔性的大吨位罐笼，罐笼装载空间大（长、宽、高分别为8m、3.9m、11.7m），单次载重量由过去的20吨提高到60吨（世界最大吨位）。

近10年来，徐州煤矿安全设备制造有限公司采用该技术生产的大型提升容器在国内市场占有率达80%。成果获2015年国家技术发明奖二等奖。

二、提升机大功率传动与可靠制动技术

攻克了提升机大功率传动与可靠制动技术，突破传动滚筒衬垫高摩阻、制动闸瓦热稳定性、制动性能参数在线检测等难题，实现了大型提升机设计制造国产化。研发的传动滚筒衬垫摩擦因数由过去的 0.2 增大到 0.28，提高了 40%，替代了德国进口衬垫 K25；研制的无石棉闸瓦摩擦因数达 0.55～0.60，超过《煤矿安全规程》要求的闸瓦摩擦因数 0.30～0.35，提高了 70%；研发了制动器制动性能检测装置，实现对制动力矩、减速度、闸瓦间隙、空动时间与贴闸压力 5 个性能参数的在线检测。

近 10 年来，中信重工机械股份有限公司采用该技术生产的大型提升机在国内市场占有率达 90%。成果获 2010 年国家科技进步奖二等奖。

三、提升机立体式安全保护系统

系统建立了矿井提升冲击动力学理论，突破防过卷过放、防撞防坠、弹性承接等关键技术，在国内外首次构建了提升机立体式安全保护系统。研制出多盘摩擦缓冲器作为防过卷过放保护装置；研制出罐笼弹性承接装置替代原有摇台，提高装卸载效率达 30% 左右。

研究成果在全国 600 多台提升机上应用。成果获 2001 年国家技术发明奖二等奖。

四、矿山长距离大运力带式输送机

研制了矿山长距离大运力带式输送机，突破了低速大扭矩永磁电机直驱、沿线张力控制、空间转弯、安全保障等关键技术，实现了我国大型带式输送系统的跨越式发展。攻克了带式输送机大功率永磁电机直驱技术，最大额定功率 1600kW，节能 15%～30%；发明了可控制动托辊，实现了沿线动张力的分布式调节，使输送带沿线动张力峰值降低 80%；研制了自适应调节托辊组，确保了转弯段的稳定运行，转弯半径由 1000m 减小到 300m；发明了自动巡检装置及故障检测装置，实现了带式输送机的主动预警防控。

研究成果在全国 70 多个单位推广应用。成果通过 2019 年国家科技进步二等奖评审（已公示）。

Awardee of Industrial Innovation Prize，Zhu Zhencai

Zhu Zhencai，born in Huaining County of Anhui Province in October 1965，graduated from the mechanical design department of China University of Mining and Technology with a Doctor degree in Engineering in 2000，secretary-general and director-general of the mining machinery branch of China Construction Machinery Society，vice-chairman of the mechatronics committee of coal mines of China Coal Society, vice-chairman of the safety and equipment sub-technical committee of coal mine safety standardization technical committee, and member of the Fifth National Production Safety Expert Group.

1989—2001, assistant, engineer and senior engineer, Scientific Research Institute of China University of Mining and Technology.

2001.08—2003.07, postdoctoral research, Mining Engineering Postdoctoral Research Station of Zhongnan University.

2003.08—2011.10, tutor, associate professor, professor, vice dean and dean, School of Mechatronic Engineering of China University of Mining and Technology.

2006.10—2007.09, visiting professor, Wuppertal University, Germany.

2011.11—2019.01, dean, Institute of Science and Technology of China University of Mining and Technology.

2019.02—Now, director, Jiangsu Key Laboratory of Mine Mechanical and Electrical Equipment.

2019.08—Now, director, Jiangsu Collaborative Innovation Center of Intelligent Mining Equipment.

Professor Zhu has long been engaged in the mine transportation research and has made a series of pioneering research work in the field of mine hoisting and transportation equipment. His contribution includes large-tonnage hoisting conveyance of mine, high-power transmission and reliable braking technologies of hoist, omnidirectional safety protection system of hoist and belt conveyor with long distance and large capacity in mine.

区域创新奖获得者

多　吉

多吉，1953 年 9 月出生于西藏自治区加查县。1978 年 8 月毕业于成都地质学院区域地质及矿产普查专业。历任西藏地热队技术员、技术负责、副总工程师、总工程师，西藏地勘局总工程师、局长，西藏国土资源厅党组书记。2001 年 11 月当选中国工程院院士。2011 年 1 月—2016 年 1 月任西藏自治区人大常委会副主任兼自治区国土资源厅总工程师，2017 年 7 月起任西藏自治区人民政府参事。兼任西藏地质学会副理事长，国际地热学会会员，中国能源研究会常务副理事，中国科学院成都分院山地所客座教授、博士生导师，成都理工大学客座教授、博士生导师，西藏大学兼职教授，西藏自治区科学技术协会名誉主席。先后培养硕士、博士研究生及博士后 27 人，并以第一作者著有多部较高影响力的论文和专著。曾获全国地矿系统优秀科技工作者，西藏自治区先进工作者，西藏自治区"九五"期间全区科技工作先进工作者，李四光地质科技荣誉奖，中组部、中宣部、人事部、科技部"杰出专业技术人才"，中国科协周光召基金会地质科技奖；获全国"五一劳动奖章"、西藏自治区"全区优秀共产党员"、中组部"全国优秀共产党员"、全国 60 位最具影响的全国劳模、中宣部 2018 年度"最美科技工作者"等荣誉。

多吉从事地质研究工作 41 年，在地质环境、自然资源、基础地质等方面作出了卓越贡献，并进行了一系列开创性研究工作。

一、实现我国高温地热资源勘探和新能源开发重大突破

（1）主持羊八井地热田深部高温资源勘探工作，获得单井发电潜力超万千瓦级的高温地热井，填补了我国在该领域的研究空白。对中国最大的高温地热田羊八井的深部高温地热勘查突破发挥了至关重要的作用，在羊八井地下 1500 米深处钻出了截至目前我国温度最高、流量最大的可采地热井，结束了我国没有单井产量万千瓦级地热井的历史，成果获国土资源部储量奖二等奖、西藏自治区科技进步奖二等奖、地质矿产部找矿奖二

等奖和勘查三等奖。

（2）积极推动我国清洁能源开发利用，为全国地热资源勘查和开发作出了突出贡献；积极开展我国地热资源开发利用战略研究，为地热能资源开发利用提出发展战略思路，为国家地热能产业发展提供了重要依据，推动我国能源革命和消费升级，研究成果获 2017 年度国家能源战略研究成果二等奖。

二、创新提出地质研究理论

（1）与有关专家共同发现并主持评价了目前全球规模最大的新型热泉型铯硅华矿床，首次确立了铯矿床新类型，填补了该领域的空白，获得原地矿部科技进步奖二等奖和国家科技进步奖二等奖。

（2）发现距今 41 亿年锆石，是目前我国最古老也是全球获得的第二古老碎屑锆石年龄，为基础地质研究提供了重要科学依据。

三、建立国家资源基地

（1）20 世纪 90 年代，针对地热勘查资金萎缩的困境，及时提出转向固体矿产勘查工作方向，发现并评价多个大中型矿床，为地勘队伍的可持续发展打下了坚实基础。在担任西藏地勘局和国土资源厅总工程师期间，始终把为国家和自治区找矿、找好矿、找大矿作为工作重心，相较"十五""十一五""十二五"期间西藏地勘局各类地质矿产勘查项目达 378 个，增长了近 8 倍；项目总经费增长了 5 倍多，达 11.19 亿元；积极赢得国家地质投入向西藏大力倾斜，争取国家专门为西藏设立青藏专项，推动我国在西藏建立"国家重要的战略矿产资源储备基地"；积极配合国土资源部和中国地调局工作并取得多项重大成果，领导的项目团队发现了 3 条巨型成矿带、7 个超大型矿床、25 个大型矿床，新增资源量包括铜 3194 万吨、铅锌 1519 万吨、铁矿石 7 亿吨，金 569 吨、银 23015 吨、钼 176 万吨、钨 20 万吨，潜在经济价值 2.7 万亿元，拉动商业勘查 115 亿元、商业融资 200 亿元，西藏地勘局（第二完成单位）建局以来首次获得国家科学技术进步奖特等奖（2011 年度）。

（2）20 世纪 80 年代，在西藏的饮用天然矿泉水资源寻找方面做了大量工作，通过多个泉点调查，发现并主持评价了最稀有的低氘富氢小分子团锂、锶、偏硅酸矿泉水，为打造国家优质矿泉水品牌提供了宝贵的水源地，现已开发成著名矿泉水品牌，取得经济效益近 10 亿元，带动当地就业 1000 余人，培养地质专业技术人才 3000 余人次，社会效益突出。其成果获国土资源部全国地质行业优秀地质找矿项目二等奖。

Awardee of Region Innovation Prize, Dorji

Dorji was born in Gyaca County of Tibet Autonomous Region in September 1953. In August

1978, he graduated from Chengdu Institute of Geology, majoring in regional geological and mineral surveys. He has served as technician, technical director, deputy chief engineer, and chief engineer of the Tibet Geothermal Research Team, chief engineer and director of the Tibet Autonomous Region Geological and Mineral Exploration and Development Bureau, and party secretary of the Tibet Land and Resources Department. In November 2001, he was elected as an academician of the Chinese Academy of Engineering. In April 2003, he was elected as the representative of the 10th National People's Congress. In October 2007, he was elected as the alternate member of the 17th Central Committee. From January 2011 to January 2016, he served as the vice chairman of the Standing Committee of People's Congress of the Tibet Autonomous Region and chief engineer of the Department of Land and Resources of the Autonomous Region. Since July 2017, he started to serve as the Counselor of the People's Government of the Tibet Autonomous Region. He is also the vice chairman of the Tibet Geological Society; a member of the International Geothermal Association; executive deputy director of the China Energy Research Association; a visiting professor and doctoral mentor at the Institute of Mountain Hazards and Environment of the Chinese Academy of Sciences; a visiting professor and doctoral mentor at Chengdu University of Technology; an adjunct professor at Tibet University; Honorary Chairman of the Tibet Association for Science and Technology.

During his 41 years' commitment to geological research, Dorji has made outstanding contributions to geological environment, natural resources, basic geology, etc., and has made a series of pioneering research work.

1. Made major breakthroughs in high-temperature geothermal resources exploration and new energy development in China

He presided over the exploration of high-temperature resources in the deep area of the Yangbajing geothermal field, and discovered high-temperature geothermal wells with more than 10,000 kilowatts single-well capacity, filling the research gap in this field in China.

2. Innovatively propose geological research theory

(1) He discovered cooperatively with relevant experts the world's largest new type of hot spring type cesium-bearing geyserite deposit and presided over its evaluation, which marks the first-time establishment of a new type of caesium deposit, filling a research gap. This discovery won the second prize of the scientific and technological progress from the former Ministry of Geology and Mineral Resources and the second prize of the National Science and Technology Progress Award.

(2) He found zircons dating back to 4.1 billion years ago, which is the oldest nation-wide and second oldest worldwide ancient detrital zircon, providing an important scientific basis for basic geological research.

3. Work to accomplish the establishment of a national resources base

4. Establish the Tibet Plateau innovative talent team

区域创新奖获得者

路 战 远

路战远，1964年7月出生于内蒙古自治区宁城县。2010年毕业于华中科技大学，获博士学位。1985—2003年在内蒙古农业学校工作，任讲师、高级讲师、教务主任、副校长；2003—2006年在内蒙古农牧业机械化研究所工作，任所长、推广研究员；2006—2007年在内蒙古农牧业机械技术推广站工作，任站长、推广研究员；2007—2018年任内蒙古农牧业科学院副院长、研究员；2018年起任内蒙古农牧业科学院院长、研究员。现兼任内蒙古科学技术协会副主席、农业部保护性耕作专家组专家、农业部全程机械化专家指导组专家、中国棉花学会副理事长、河北农业大学和内蒙古大学博士生导师、《北方农业学报》主编等职。

长期从事土壤耕作与作物栽培等研究工作，在农牧交错区农田生态保育和保护性耕作等方面作出了一系列开创性研究工作，为农牧交错区农田生态保护和农业可持续发展作出了重要贡献。

一、研究揭示农牧交错区旱作农田保护性耕作关键因子与作用机理，创新了蓄水保墒与抑制扬尘的关键技术与体系

针对农牧交错区干旱缺水、农田风蚀沙化、尘暴频发、小籽粒种子精量播种难等突出问题，全面系统开展了保护性耕作关键因子与作用机理研究，解析了农牧交错区保护性耕作秸秆覆盖、土壤水分和有机质等关键因子及其互作关系，明确了秸秆覆盖量、留茬高度、带状秸秆覆盖幅宽等技术参数；研究量化了保护性耕作玉米、小麦、杂粮和少耕带作马铃薯等作物种床整备技术指标，创新组合式防壅堵窄开沟、双勺精量排种、多功能联合镇压等关键技术与装置，研制开发了具有区域特色的杂粮、玉米、小麦等免少耕播种系列机具和马铃薯精量播种系列机具20余种；集成建立了以秸秆覆盖与免少耕播种相结合的保护性耕作蓄水保墒与减蒸抑尘的技术体系和配套机具系统。成果应用可增加农田播前土壤含水量 9.3% ～ 25%、减少扬尘 35.9% ～ 68%、年增加土壤有机质含量 0.04% ～ 0.06%。成果有效解决了长期以来一直没有很好解决的农牧交错区小籽粒种子免耕播种难、免耕保苗难和马铃薯等块茎作物无法实施保护性耕作等关键技术难题，为内蒙古乃至我国北方农牧交错区成为保护性耕作主要实施区提供了重要的技术支撑。

二、研究揭示农牧交错区保护性耕作农田杂草发生与演替规律，创新了杂草综合防控技术体系

针对农牧交错区保护性耕作农田区域性杂草发生与危害加重、防除难等瓶颈性技术难题，首次系统研究了农牧交错区保护性耕作对农田杂草种类、发生密度、发生频度、发生时间、优势种群和危害程度等因子的影响及其变量关系，填补了农牧交错区该领域研究空白，提出并建立了保护性耕作农田非生长季除草方法，创新了保护性耕作农田机械除草、化学除草和农艺除草等关键技术，建立了以轮作等农艺措施为基础，机械、化学等除草方法相结合的杂草综合控制技术及体系，杂草防除率达 90% 以上，用药量减少 30% 左右。成果有效解决了保护性耕作农田杂草危害重、防除难和窄行距作物无法机械除草的技术难题。

三、研究突破了以保护生态为基础的农牧交错区少耕带作与抗旱播种保苗关键技术与模式

针对农牧交错区马铃薯等块根块茎作物收获土壤裸露风蚀重、干旱少雨保墒难、作物出苗成苗率低等突出问题，研究揭示了马铃薯等翻耕作物与小麦、燕麦、油菜等留茬免耕作物带状间隔种植的风蚀规律，明确了作物配置、垄向、种植带宽等关键指标，建立了马铃薯种植区少耕带作种植模式；研究阐明了农牧交错区马铃薯等穴播作物与燕麦、油菜等条播作物少耕带作条件下作物出苗期间的降水蓄积量、土壤温度、土壤水分等因子对作物出苗、成苗及作物产量的影响，提出了马铃薯等主要农作物与气候条件、土壤类型、水分条件、种植制度相适应的滴灌补水量化指标，创建了马铃薯等作物抗旱播种保苗关键技术；集成建立了农牧交错区农田主要农作物全程"免少耕全程机械化""小麦/杂粮与马铃薯少耕带作""马铃薯垄（平）作滴灌补水全程机械化"等农艺农机一体化丰产高效技术模式。成果应用可减少农田风蚀 50% 以上、节水 20% ～ 30%、增产 8% 以上，较好地解决了马铃薯等耕翻穴播作物土壤裸露、保护难和作物出苗成苗率低等重大技术问题。

四、研究揭示农牧交错区农田土壤退化成因与地力下降机制和主要农作物水分效应和需肥规律，构建了资源高效种植制度和保育型养地制度，集成建立了不同生态区农田保育与可持续利用技术模式

针对退化农田养分失衡、结构恶化、水肥利用效率低等突出问题，研究揭示了退化农田耕层结构、土壤机械组成、土壤水分、有机质、养分、酶活性等理化性状的变化规律及土壤微生物丰度和多样性的变化规律；阐明了农牧交错区农田土壤退化成因与地力下降机制；揭示了北方农牧交错区退化农田作物水分效应和需肥规律；创新了以农田保土减蚀、增碳培肥、合理耕层构建、水肥高效利用、杂草综合防控为核心的农牧交错区农田生态保育关键技术，确定了不同区域主要作物发展优先序和技术优先序，构建了资源高效种植制度和保育型养地制度；集成建立了大兴安岭沿麓保土增碳丰产高效、西辽河流域地力提升丰产高效、阴山北麓固土减蚀稳产增效、河套灌区水肥统筹绿色高效等农田保育与可持续利用技术模式。成果应用减少风蚀 50% 以上、减少水蚀 60% 以上、作物平均增产 10% 以上，为内蒙古乃至北方农牧交错区探索出了一条农田保护与可持续利用的可行之路。

历经 30 余年的努力，路战远及其团队获国家科技进步奖二等奖 2 项、省部级科技一等奖 5 项；授权国家专利 70 余件，其中发明专利 11 件；制定技术标准 26 项；出版专著或主编著作 14 部，发表论文 150 余篇。先后被授予国家"万人计划"领军人才、全国杰出专业技术人才、"百千万人才工程"国家级人选、国家中青年有突出贡献专家、享受国务院政府特殊津贴专家、全国优秀科技工作者、全国农业科研杰出人才等荣誉称号。培养"百千万人才工程"国家级人选、享受国务院政府特殊津贴专家、全国优秀科技工作者、内蒙古草原英才等人才 20 余人。成果累计推广应用达 1 亿多亩，生态、经济和社会效益显著，为建设我国北方生态屏障、保障国家粮食安全和促进农业可持续发展作出了贡献。

Awardee of Region Innovation Prize，Lu Zhanyuan

Lu Zhanyuan，born in Ningcheng County of Inner Mongolia Autonomous Region in July 1964，is the president and researcher of Inner Mongolia Academy of Agricultural ＆Animal Husbandry Sciences.

Lu has been engaged in soil tillage and crop cultivation for a long time with his team. He has made a series of pioneering research work，and has made important contributions to the farmland ecological protection and conservation，and sustainable agricultural development in the agro-pastoral ecotone in china.

（1）The key factors and action mechanism of conservation tillage in rainfed farmland were revealed，and the key technologies and systems for soil moisture conservation and dust suppression were innovated. Their application can reduce dust by 35.9% ～ 68%.

（2）The regular pattern of occurrence and succession of weeds in conservation tillage farmland was revealed，and integrated weed control technology and system were innovated. Their application can make the weed control rate more than 90%.

（3）Based on farmland ecological protection, the key technologies and models of reduced-tillage zone farming and drought-resistant seedling conservation were broken through. Their application can reduce wind erosion of farmland by more than 50%, save water by 20% ~ 30% and increase production by more than 8%.

（4）The research have revealed the causes of soil degradation, the mechanism of soil fertility decline, the water effect and fertilizer requirement of main crops in the agro-pastoral ecotone, integrated and established a technical model of farmland conservation and sustainable utilization in different ecological areas. Their application can reduce soil wind erosion by more than 50%, increase production by more than 10%.

In short, after more than 30 years of efforts, Dr Lu and his team have attained many kinds of rewards, including two secondary prizes of National Science and Technology Progress Award, five first prizes of provincial and ministerial science and technology progress awards. They also have received 70 national patents(including 11 invention patents), formulated 26 technical standards, and published 14 works and more than 150 papers. That the achievements have contributed to the construction of ecological barriers in northern China, ensuring of national food security and the sustainable agricultural development, which been widely applied in Inner Mongolia over 6.67 million hectares.

区域创新奖获得者

王 维 庆

王维庆，1959 年 5 月出生于新疆维吾尔自治区喀什市。1989 年毕业于浙江大学电机系，获工学硕士学位。1983 年至今在新疆大学任教，先后任电气工程学院副院长、机械工程学院院长、科研处处长、研究生院院长。2002—2010 年兼任西安交通大学博士生导师。其间，2004 年 11 月—2005 年 7 月在德国柏林工业大学做高级访问学者。兼任中国仿真学会电力系统仿真委员会副主任委员，新疆电机工程学会副理事长，新疆新能源产业技术创新联盟理事。作为学科带头人，带领团队获电气工程一级博士点和博士后流动站，"风力发电系统智能控制与并网技术"教育部创新团队（并获滚动支持）。承担国家和省部级项目 30 余项；发表论文 170 余篇、专著 3 部，参编国家标准 1 部；获专利和软件著作权 20 余项；培养博士生、硕士生 97 人，博士后 9 人。先后获全国优秀科技工作者、新疆维吾尔自治区科技进步奖特等奖、新疆维吾尔自治区有突出贡献优秀专家、新疆维吾尔自治区先进工作者、新疆维吾尔自治区优秀教师和天山英才等荣誉称号。

作为我国最早从事风电机组研发的人员之一，在大型风力发电机组关键零部件、整机控制及检测、电能转换和并网送出技术的研究和工程应用方面作出了开创性和引领性的工作。

1. 在国内首次揭示了水平轴、定桨距失速型大型风力发电机组控制机理并提出技术路线图，研制成功国内第一台具有自主知识产权的水平轴、定桨距失速型大型风力发电机组电控系统；主持完成国内第一座大型风电场并网、监控及运行管理系统并产业化

（1）采用现代传感技术和总线结构集散控制方式，提出了大型风电机组双异步电机风速切换设计原理。在国内首次基于大型风力发电机组电控系统各部分分布电容的电磁耦合特性，研发提出了该系统拟制横模、共模干扰的解耦方法，解决了频率高、幅度大的强电磁环境中大型风电机组电控系统电磁兼容和抗干扰的问题。

（2）研制成功我国第一台 600kW 风力发电机组电控系统，达到国内领先水平，填补了国内空白，奠定了我国大型风力发电机组控制机理的基础，使其团队在水平轴、定桨距失速型风力发电机组电控系统和中央监控系统方面处于国内领先水平。

（3）实现当年产品化并应用于金风科技 600/750kW 国产化风力发电机组中，使金风科技的 600kW/750kW/800kW 风力发电机组成为当时国内唯一产品化的具有自主知识产权的风电机组，占领了这个级别的国内市场，实现了引进、消化、吸收和再创新的目标。

相关成果获 2002 年国家科技进步奖二等奖、2000 年新疆维吾尔自治区科技进步奖一等奖。

2. 突破制约我国风电机组的控制技术，形成风电机组仿真建模理论体系，并成功应用于国内第一台拥有自主知识产权的直驱式风力发电机组和电控系统的研制，为我国大型风力发电机组控制技术奠定了基础；在新疆大规模风电开发进程中，主导了兆瓦级单机、集中式和大规模汇集型风电场并网关键技术研究

（1）研发突破了大容量风电机组功率调节技术，提出了大型风电机组桨距优化控制技术及系统参数具体方案，建立了完整的变桨控制动态特性模型，完成三桨叶独立变桨距控制调节策略，实现了平抑载荷波动的有效性。

（2）研发提出了风电机组在大风速区域下的载荷控制技术（暴风控制算法），解决了暴风环境下风电机组的载荷控制问题，提高了切出风速值及机组的发电量。

（3）研发攻克了风电机组高、低电压穿越技术，实现并网型机组在电网短时故障时不脱网，支撑了电网稳定。

（4）研发提出数据挖掘矫正、载荷自适应控制、风电机组检测、风力发电机故障诊断与寿命实时估算、风电场协调控制等技术。突破按不同等级划分进行实时就地自动控制和非实时季节性数据挖掘监控技术，提升了整个风电场风电机组的载荷安全出力、发电量和运行寿命。

（5）研发提出风电场风况短期预估、组合统计模型预测等技术，采用中尺度与微尺度相结合的方法，结合全自动批量模型训练系统，为各风电场提供专用预测模型，实现了对已建和在建风电场发电量的短期预报和调控。

（6）项目成果属国内首创，达到国际先进水平。项目技术于 2011 年年底完成技术转化，于 2012 年应用于 1.5—3MW 直驱式风力发电机组中，降低机组疲劳载荷 >10%，提升单台机组发电量 5% 以上。

相关成果获 2016 年国家科技进步奖二等奖、2013 年新疆维吾尔自治区科技进步奖一等奖。

3. 取得显著的社会经济效益

（1）密切与新疆金风科技股份有限公司、国网新疆电力公司产学研合作，主持完成的国家"九五"重点攻关项目和国家"863 计划"项目成果成功应用于金风科技定桨距、失速型风力发电机组,占领了当时这个级别的国内市场。主持完成的国家"863 计划"项目"大型风电机组独立变桨技术研究与应用""大型风电机组仿真及试验系统开发与研制"及国家自然基金项目"新疆风电场短期发电量预算方法研究"等成果成功应用于风电场,提升了风电场输出功率的稳定性和效益,使大规模风电场群并网成为可能。

（2）基于上述技术成果形成的 1.5—5.0MW 系列风电机组产品成为"十一五"后期和"十二五"期间我国风电装备制造业的主导产品,在全国 200 多座风电场应用推广。近三年累计发电 562.2 亿千瓦时,节约标准煤 2249 万吨,减少有害气体排放 5892.2 万吨,促进了我国风电技术的自主创新与产业化。

Awardee of Region Innovation Prize，Wang Weiqing

Wang Weiqing was born in Kashgar City of Xinjiang Uygur Autonomous Region in May 1959. In 1989，he graduated from the department of electrical engineering of Zhejiang University with a master's degree in engineering. Since 1983，he has been working as a professor and doctoral supervisor in the school of electrical engineering，Xinjiang University. he was been senior visiting scholar from November 2004 to July 2005 at the Technical University of Berlin（Wind energy control technology）with financial support from China Scholarship Council（CSC）. In 2009，he was awarded as the outstanding overseas Returnees of the Xinjiang Uygur Autonomous Region. He is the director of the Engineering Research Center of Education Ministry for Renewable Energy Power Generation and Grid-connected Control，the director of the key laboratory of the Xinjiang Uygur Autonomous Region. From 1998 to March 2004，he was the deputy dean of the school of Electrical Engineering，Xinjiang University. From April 2004 to December 2005，he was the dean of school of mechanical engineering，Xinjiang University. From 2006 to July 2009，he was the director of Scientific Research Department，Xinjiang University. From August 2009 to August 2016，he was the dean of graduate school，Xinjiang University. From 2002 to 2010，he served as doctoral supervisor of Xi'an Jiaotong University. He also serve as deputy chairman of the Power System Simulation Committee of China Simulation Society，deputy chairman of the Xinjiang Electrical Engineering Society，director of the Xinjiang New Energy Industry Technology Innovation Alliance.

Professor Wang Weiqing is one of the earliest personnel engaged in research and development of large-scale wind turbines in China. He has made pioneered research working in the study and engineering applications of key components，control technology and detection，power conversion and grid-connected technology of large-scale wind turbines.

（1）In China，discloses the controlling mechanism of horizontal axis，fixed pitch stall type the large wind power generator the first time and proposed technical roadmap. He has successfully developed the first electric control system for the large wind power generator of horizontal axis, fixed pitch stall type with independent intellectual in China. He hosted the completion and industrialization of first grid connection, monitoring and operation management system of large-scale wind farm in China. He won the second prize of National Science and Technology Progress Award in 2002, the first prize of Science and Technology Progress Award of the Xinjiang Uygur Autonomous Region in 2000.

(2) Breaking through the control technology of China's wind turbines, including independent pitch, storm control, low voltage ride through, wind farm intelligent control, capacity prediction, dynamic physics experiment, wind turbine relay protection. Had solved the key technical problems of wind turbines constrained by human and environmental adaptability forms a wind turbine simulation modelling theory system, and successfully applies the research results to China's first direct-drive wind turbines. Wang Weiqing laid the foundation for China's large-scale wind turbine control technology. In the process of large-scale wind power development in Xinjiang, Wang Weiqing led the research on the key technologies of MW-level single-machine, centralized and large-scale collection wind farms.He won the second prize of National Science and Technology Progress Award in 2016 and the first prize of the Xinjiang Uygur Autonomous Region Science and Technology Progress Award in 2013.

区域创新奖获得者

周 少 奇

周少奇，1965 年 4 月出生于湖南省益阳市。1983—1993 年在大连理工大学化工机械、工程力学、生物化学工程等专业学习，1993 年获工学博士学位；1993—1995 年在华南理工大学发酵工程学科做博士后研究；1995—1997 年在香港大学土木系环境工程学科做博士后研究助理。1997 年起先后在华南理工大学轻工食品学院、造纸与环境工程学院、环境与能源学院工作，1998 年 3 月起任环境科学与工程系创系副主任；2004 年 7 月起创办市政工程专业并任系主任；2002—2003 年挂职任贵州省环境保护局局长助理；2013 年 1 月至今任贵州科学院副院长。其间，2002 年 11 月—2003 年 1 月在 Middlesex 大学做访问教授，2009 年 1 月—7 月在加拿大 Waterloo 大学做高级研究学者。入选国家万人计划领军人才，国务院政府特殊津贴专家，国家绕月探测工程科学应用专家委员会专家，国家"百千万人才工程"一、二层次人才和国家有突出贡献中青年专家，教育部首批新世纪优秀人才，广东省首位环境工程"珠江学者"特聘教授，贵州省百人领军人才，贵州省核心专家。曾获全国化工优秀科技工作者、中国发明人物奖、广东省丁颖科技奖等荣誉称号。获国家科技进步奖二等奖 1 项，中国专利银奖 1 项、优秀奖 2 项，省部级科技奖一等奖 6 项；发表学术论文 370 多篇，主编参编学术著作 9 部；获专利授权 70 多项；培养研究生 150 多名。

周少奇早年从事射流混合反应器、壳体强度和稳定性、高等真菌（灵芝、云芝）发酵液流变力学与灵芝多糖研究，于 1995 年开始从事环境生物技术研究，在生化反应电子计量学、污水生物脱氮除磷理论研究和同步脱氮除磷新技术开发与应用等方面作出了一系列开创性研究。

一、提出生物脱氮电子计量学新方法，创建含氮有机废水生物脱氮新技术

针对污水生物脱氮工艺在进水计量比控制、厌氧／好氧过程互补、好氧／缺氧／厌氧／沉淀设备分离设置方面存在重大缺陷，进而导致反硝化效率严重偏低的突出问题，首先提出生化反应"电子流守恒"原理和生物脱氮电子计量学方法，以微生物生长量为函数研究获得了生物硝化、生物反硝化过程的电子计量方程和系统计量模型18个。其中，获得的反硝化COD/NO_3-N比理论计量模型比环境工程领域120多年来国际著名学者总结理论研究与工程实例获得的唯一经验计量模型提高精度30%以上；同时，首先提出了微生物脱氮除磷过程碳氮磷三要素电子计量方程与计量模型，更新了环境工程污水生物领域的有关基础知识。攻克了本行业依据经验计量模型设计和管理污水生物脱氮过程引起较大误差及过程控制失真的技术难题。

针对我国炼油废水与油田污水处理技术难题，创新了同时硝化反硝化专利技术，率先应用于中国石化广州分公司炼油污水处理技改工程，并广泛推广应用于油田废水、石化废水等处理工程。

针对我国化肥行业含氮污水处理技术难题，与有关龙头企业和骨干企业合作，研究开发氮肥清洁生产与废水处理工艺优化方法，在我国大型化肥生产企业废水处理工程领域获得广泛推广应用。

二、发现反硝化脱氮除磷菌和脱氮除磷新机理，创新城市污水同步脱氮除磷一体化新技术

针对我国城镇污水处理厂普遍存在需要提高总氮、总磷去除率，通过技术改造进行升级提标以达到国家一级A排放标准的技术难题，在生物除磷理论方面突破传统理论通过"厌氧释磷"和"好氧聚磷"两个阶段去除磷的认识，通过16S rDNA克隆基因文库研究，发现传统厌氧/好氧生物除磷工艺中存在反硝化除磷菌DPB，并在广州城市污水处理工程中发现4种可以同时以分子氧、硝态氮、亚硝氮为电子受体的同步脱氮除磷菌，为城市污水同步脱氮除磷工程技改优化应用提供了重要的理论依据。基于反硝化除磷的新机理，针对城市污水混入垃圾渗滤液与粪便污水带来的脱氮除磷难题，深入开展城市污水同步脱氮除磷新工艺的研究与设备开发，构建了城市污水处理单泥系统、双泥膜系统和一体化反硝化除磷系统，创新出改良A^2/O工艺、新型氧化沟工艺、新型UCT工艺等高效同步脱氮除磷专利技术。经工程推广应用表明，一体化反硝化除磷系统在同步脱氮除磷效果方面优于国内外同类技术A^2/O工艺和AB工艺，其总氮与总磷去除率比A^2/O工艺和AB工艺均大幅度提高。通过与设计院及有关企业进行专利实施许可和产学研合作，在我国城镇污水处理工程中获得广泛推广应用。

三、提出厌氧氨氧化协同反硝化脱氮新原理，创新垃圾渗滤液处理新技术

针对垃圾填埋场渗滤液生物处理，特别是其高氨氮含量难以高效处理的世界性难题，提出了厌氧氨氧化与反硝化协同生物脱氮的新技术原理，研发了同时好氧厌氧同步生物脱氮方法，发明了新型的生物反应器，并研发获得了垃圾废水同时好氧厌氧处理高效厌氧氨氧化菌驯化技术，比国内外其他研究小组多数需用220～420天启动厌氧氨氧化过程的时间缩短 4 倍以上。

针对我国普遍采用反渗透、纳滤等膜处理技术处理垃圾渗滤液、进而产生大量浓缩液的重大缺陷，开发出垃圾渗滤液高级氧化深度处理专利技术和垃圾渗滤液提取腐殖酸废水治理方法。垃圾渗滤液的高级氧化处理方法及有关新工艺先后在广州、江门等垃圾填埋场实现工程示范应用，克服了产生垃圾浓缩液的技术难题，出水稳定达到我国同类废水新的一级排放标准，节省了投资及运行成本，经济效益显著。

四、提出我国西部农村污水处理创新技术方案并建设示范工程

针对贵州高原湖泊富营养化控制治理提出的关键技术方案获财政部、环境保护部专项支持，并实现工程推广应用。此外，针对已困扰我国西部典型缺水地区农村给排水一体化处理 60 多年的技术难题，领衔提出技术创新方案，获 2016 年国家首批重点研发计划专项并取得重要成果，已申报国家专利 160 多件，建设了一批示范工程。将为我国西部地区典型的农村污水处理提供重要的科技支撑作用。

Awardee of Region Innovation Prize, Zhou Shaoqi

Zhou Shaoqi was born in Yiyang City of Hunan Province in April 1965. He is the Vice President of Guizhou Academy of Sciences, Professor of South China University of Technology. He received his Ph.D degree from Dalian University of Technology in 1993. Later, he joined South China University of Technology as a post doctorial fellow in fermentation engineering, and as a postdoc Research Associate in environmental engineering at Hongkong University from 1993–1997. He was a visiting professor at Middlesex University funded by the Royal Society of UK in 2002, and a visiting senior research scientist at Waterloo University in Canada in 2009. He received the Ten-thousand People Program: Leading Talent Award in 2016, and was awarded as a Distinguished Professor of Pearl River Scholar in 2009. He became a board member of IWA Anaerobic Digestion China Chapter in 2015. Research interests focus on Environmental biotechnology, Solid waste management and landfill leachate treatment as well as microbial fuel cell, Urban and village/house waste waters treatment technologies, etc. He proposed electronic stoichiometry of biological nitrogen/phosphorus removal including a lot of new derived electronic stoichiometric equations and models, and discovered 4 denitrifying phosphorus bacteria which can use oxygen, nitrate, nitrite as electron acceptor freely. In addition, he has invented a lot of new technologies and apparatus on the basis of the new theory of electronic stoichiometry and the new mechanisms of biological nitrogen/phosphorus removal, and applied in large scale engineering almost all over China. He has gained 1 National Science & Technology Award and 3 National Patent Awards, 7 Provincial 1st class Science & Technology Awards, published over 370 journal papers, 9 books, and applied 117 China patents.

附　　录

APPENDICES

何梁何利基金评选章程

（2007 年 5 月 15 日何梁何利基金信托委员会会议通过）

一、总　则

第一条　何梁何利基金（以下称"本基金"）由何善衡慈善基金会有限公司、梁铢琚博士、何添博士、利国伟博士之伟伦基金有限公司于 1994 年 3 月 30 日捐款成立。2005 年 10 月 12 日经香港高等法院批准。基金捐款人，除了何善衡慈善基金会有限公司及利国伟博士之伟伦基金有限公司外，梁铢琚慈善基金会有限公司和何添基金有限公司各自分别为已故梁铢琚博士及已故何添博士之遗产承办人指定之慈善机构，以便根据本基金信托契约之条款行使有关权力或给予所需批准。

第二条　本基金的宗旨是：

（一）促进中国的科学与技术发展；

（二）奖励取得杰出成就和重大创新的科学技术工作者。

二、评奖条件

第三条　本基金奖励和资助致力于推进中国科学技术取得成就及进步与创新的个人。

第四条　本基金奖励和资助具备下列条件的中华人民共和国公民：

（一）对推动科学技术事业发展有杰出贡献；

（二）热爱祖国，积极为国家现代化建设服务，有高尚的社会公德和职业道德；

（三）在我国科学技术研究院（所）、大专院校、企业以及信托委员会认为适当的其他机构从事科学研究、教学或技术工作已满 5 年。

第五条　获奖候选人须由评选委员会选定的提名人以书面形式推荐。

提名人由科学技术领域具有一定资格的专家包括海外学者组成。

三、奖　项

第六条　本基金设"何梁何利基金科学与技术成就奖""何梁何利基金科学与技术进步奖""何梁何利基金科学与技术创新奖"，每年评奖一次。

第七条　何梁何利基金科学与技术成就奖授予下列杰出科学技术工作者：

（一）长期致力于推进国家科学技术进步，贡献卓著，历史上取得国际高水平学术成就者；

（二）在科学技术前沿，取得重大科技突破，攀登当今科技高峰，领先世界先进水平者；

（三）推进技术创新，建立强大自主知识产权和自主品牌，其产业居于当今世界前列者。

何梁何利基金科学与技术成就奖获奖人每人颁发奖励证书和奖金 100 万港元。

第八条　何梁何利基金科学与技术进步奖授予在特定学科领域取得重大发明、发现和科技成果者，尤其是在近年内有突出贡献者。

何梁何利基金科学与技术进步奖按学科领域分设下列奖项：

（一）数学力学奖

（二）物理学奖

（三）化学奖

（四）天文学奖

（五）气象学奖

（六）地球科学奖

（七）生命科学奖

（八）农学奖

（九）医学、药学奖

（十）古生物学、考古学奖

（十一）机械电力技术奖

（十二）电子信息技术奖

（十三）交通运输技术奖

（十四）冶金材料技术奖

（十五）化学工程技术奖

（十六）资源环保技术奖

（十七）工程建设技术奖

何梁何利基金科学与技术进步奖获奖人每人颁发奖励证书和奖金 20 万港元。

第九条　何梁何利基金科学与技术创新奖授予具有高水平科技成就而通过技术创新和管理创新，创建自主知识产权产业和著名品牌，创造重大经济效益和社会效益的杰出贡献者。

何梁何利基金科学与技术创新奖分设下列奖项：

（一）青年创新奖

（二）产业创新奖

（三）区域创新奖

何梁何利基金科学与技术创新奖获奖人每人颁发奖励证书和奖金 20 万港元。

第十条　本基金每年各奖项名额如下：

何梁何利基金科学与技术成就奖不超过 5 名；何梁何利基金科学与技术进步奖、何梁何利基金科学与技术创新奖总数不超过 65 名（原则上科学与技术进步奖和科学与技术创新奖名额的比例为 3 比 1 至 2 比 1）。而奖金总额不超过该年度信托委员会审议通过的奖金总额。

具体名额根据年度资金运作情况和评选情况确定。

四、评选委员会

第十一条　本基金成立由各相关领域具有高尚道德情操、精深学术造诣、热心科技奖励
　　　　事业的专家组成的评选委员会。

　　　　评选委员会委员经过信托委员会批准、颁发聘任书后，独立行使职能，负责评选工作。

第十二条　评选委员会委员最多不超过 20 人，其中主任一人、副主任二人、秘书长一人，
　　　　由内地学者和海外学者出任。

　　　　评选委员会委员内地学者和海外学者的比例，原则上每四名委员中，内地学者为三
　　　　人，海外学者为一人。

　　　　评选委员会主任、副主任由基金信托契约补充条款规定的信托委员兼任。其中主任
　　　　由补充契约所指明的与科技部有关的信托委员兼任，副主任二人分别由补充契约所
　　　　指明的与教育部有关的信托委员和补充契约所指明的国际学者信托委员兼任。评选
　　　　委员会秘书长由信托委员会任命并征得捐款人同意的人选担任。

　　　　评选委员会委员每三年更换四分之一（不包括主任、副主任及秘书长）。

　　　　此外，评选委员会委员的聘任，贯彻相对稳定和适度更新的原则。其办法由评选委
　　　　员会制定。

　　　　评选委员会办公室设在北京，挂靠科学技术部。

第十三条　评选委员会根据评选工作需要，可组织若干专业评审组、奖项评审组，根据提
　　　　名人的提名推荐材料对被提名人进行初评，产生获奖候选人，提交评选委员会终评。

　　　　专业评审组、奖项评审组的评委由评选委员会任命。

第十四条　本基金各奖项获奖人由评选委员会会议评定。

　　　　何梁何利基金科学与技术进步奖、何梁何利基金科学与技术创新奖的获奖人，由评
　　　　选委员会根据专业评审组、奖项评审组的评选结果，评选审定。

　　　　何梁何利基金科学与技术成就奖获奖人，由评选委员会全体会议根据评选委员提名
　　　　评选产生。评选委员会设立预审小组，必要时对候选人进行考察和听证。

第十五条　评选委员会会议贯彻"公平、公正、公开"原则，实行一人一票制，以无记
　　　　名形式表决确定获奖人。何梁何利基金科学与技术进步奖、何梁何利基金科学与技
　　　　术创新奖的候选人，获半数赞成票为获奖人。何梁何利基金科学与技术成就奖的候
　　　　选人，获三分之二多数赞成票为获奖人。

第十六条　评选委员会在评定获奖人名额时，应适当考虑奖种、学科和区域之间的平衡。

五、授　　奖

第十七条　评选委员会评选结果揭晓前须征求获奖人本人意愿，并通知捐款人及信托委
　　　　员会。遵照捐款人意愿，获奖人应承诺于获奖后，继续在国内从事科学研究和技术

工作不少于三年。

第十八条　本基金每年适当时候举行颁奖仪式，由评选委员会安排向何梁何利基金各奖项获得者颁发证书和奖金，并通过新闻媒体公布获奖人员名单及其主要贡献。

六、出版物和学术会议

第十九条　本基金每年出版介绍获奖人及其主要科学技术成就的出版物。

出版物的编辑、出版工作由评选委员会负责。

第二十条　本基金每年举办学术报告会、研讨会，由评选委员会委员、获奖人代表介绍其学术成就及相关学科领域的进展。

根据基金财政状况，本基金各专业领域专题学术讨论会可在海外举办。

本基金学术报告会、研讨会由评选委员会负责组织。

七、附　　则

第二十一条　本基金评选委员会每年例会一次，总结当年工作，部署下一年度工作，研究和决定重大事宜。

第二十二条　本章程由本基金评选委员会解释。

第二十三条　本章程自 2007 年 5 月 15 日施行。

REGULATIONS OF HO LEUNG HO LEE FOUNDATION ON THE EVALUATION AND EXAMINATION OF ITS PRIZES AND AWARDS

(Adopted at the Meeting of the Board of Trustees on May 15, 2007)

I   General Provisions

Article 1   Ho Leung Ho Lee Foundation (hereinafter referred to as " the Foundation") was established on March 30, 1994 in Hong Kong with funds donated by the S H Ho Foundation Limited, Dr. Leung Kau-Kui, Dr. Ho Tim and Dr. Lee Quo-Wei's Wei Lun Foundation Limited. With the approval of the High Court of Hong Kong, apart from S H Ho Foundation Limited and Wei Lun Foundation Limited (donors of the Foundation), Leung Kau-Kui Foundation Limited and Ho Tim Foundation Limited have respectively been nominated by the estates of the late Dr. Leung Kau-Kui and Dr. Ho Tim to and they can as from October 12, 2005 exercise the powers or give the necessary approvals under the terms of the Foundation's trust deed.

Article 2   Purposes of the Foundation are:

(1) To promote the development of science and technology in China.

(2) To reward the scientific and technical personnel with outstanding achievements and great innovations.

II   Criteria for Awards

Article 3   The Foundation shall grant awards and prizes to individuals who are devoted to the achievements, progress and innovations of China's science and technology.

Article 4   The Foundation shall grant awards and prizes to the citizens of the People's Republic of China who meet the following criteria:

(1) Having made outstanding contributions in promoting the development of science and technology.

(2) Being patriotic, vigorously working for the modernization drive of the country, and preserving lofty social morality and professional ethics.

(3) Being with at least five years of scientific researches, teaching or technical working experience in China's science and technology research institutes, institutions for higher learning and universities, enterprises and other organizations which the Board of Trustees regards as appropriate.

Article 5   Candidates for the awards and prizes of the Foundation shall be recommended in writing by nominators identified by the Selection Board.

Nominators should be qualified experts (including those overseas) in various fields of sciences and technology.

III   Awards and Prizes

Article 6   The Foundation sets three annual prizes. They are the Prize for Scientific and Technological Achievements of Ho Leung Ho Lee Foundation, the Prize for Scientific and Technological Progress of Ho Leung Ho Lee Foundation, and the Prize for Scientific and Technological Innovation of Ho Leung Ho Lee Foundation.

Article 7   The Prize for Scientific and Technological Achievements of Ho Leung Ho Lee Foundation shall be awarded to the outstanding science and technology personnel as follows:

(1) Those who have devoted to scientific and technological progress in China for a long time, having made significant contributions and world-class academic achievements.

(2) Those who have made great breakthroughs in the frontline of science and technology, attaining high levels in science and technology and leading the trend in specific areas in the world.

(3) Those who have made great efforts in pushing forward the technology innovation and have built up powerful self intellectual property and brand of its own so that its industry ranks the top of today's world.

Each winner of the Prize for Scientific and Technological Achievements of Ho Leung Ho Lee Foundation will receive a certificate and the amount of the prize of HK $ 1000000.

Article 8   The Prize for Scientific and Technological Progress of Ho Leung Ho Lee Foundation is for those who have made important inventions, discoveries and achievements in specific subject areas, especially having remarkable contributions in recent years.

The following prizes of the Prize for Scientific and Technological Progress of Ho Leung Ho Lee Foundation are set up by subjects:

(1) Award for Mathematics and Mechanics

(2) Award for Physics

(3) Award for Chemistry

(4) Award for Astronomy

(5) Award for Meteorology

(6) Award for Earth Sciences

(7) Award for Life Sciences

(8) Award for Agronomy

（9）Award for Medical Sciences and Materia Medica

（10）Award for Paleontology and Archaeology

（11）Award for Machinery and Electric Technology

（12）Award for Electronics and Information Technology

（13）Award for Communication and Transportation Technology

（14）Award for Metallurgy and Materials Technology

（15）Award for Chemical Engineering Technology

（16）Award for Resources and Environmental Protection Technology

（17）Award for Engineering and Construction Technology

Each winner of the Prize for Science and Technological Progress of Ho Leung Ho Lee Foundation will be awarded a certificate and the amount of the prize of HK $ 200000.

Article 9   The Prize for Scientific and Technological Innovation of Ho Leung Ho Lee Foundation is for the outstanding contributors who have made high level achievements in science and technology, created industry with self intellectual property and famous brands through technology and management innovation, and thus have created great economic and social benefits for the society.

The following prizes of the Prize for Scientific and Technological Innovation of Ho Leung Ho Lee Foundation are set up:

（1）Award for Youth Innovation

（2）Award for Industrial Innovation

（3）Award for Region Innovation

Each winner of the Prize for Scientific and Technological Innovation of Ho Leung Ho Lee Foundation will be awarded a certificate and the amount of the prize of HK $ 200000.

Article 10   Annual quotas of awardees of each prize of Ho Leung Ho Lee Foundation are as follows:

There should be no more than 5 awardees each year for the Prize for Scientific and Technological Achievements of Ho Leung Ho Lee Foundation; and the total number of the winners of the Prize for Scientific and Technological Progress of Ho Leung Ho Lee Foundation and the Prize for Scientific and Technological Innovation of Ho Leung Ho Lee Foundation should be no more than 65（The proportion of the awardees of the Prize for Scientific and Technological Progress of Ho Leung Ho Lee Foundation and the Prize for Scientific and Technological Innovation of Ho Leung Ho Lee Foundation is in principle from 3 to 1 to 2 to 1）. And the total amount of all the Prizes awarded should not exceed the total amount of prize moneys of the year as approved by the Board of Trustees for that year.

The number of winners of each prize should be decided according to the situation each year of the operation of the Foundation's funds and the results of evaluation and selection for the year.

IV Selection Board

Article 11   A Selection Board shall be constituted under the Foundation, consisting of scholars who are highly respected in ethics, with accomplishments in academic researches and devotion to the work of award of science and technology prizes.

Members of the Selection Board shall independently exercise the powers and are responsible for the evaluation work after they have been appointed with the approval of the Board of Trustees and received the letters of appointment.

Article 12   The total number of the members of the Selection Board should be no more than 20. Among them, there will be one Chair, two Vice Chairs and one Secretary–General. Both local and overseas scholars could be members of the Selection Board.

For every four members of the Selection Board, the ratio between local and overseas scholars should in principle be 3 to 1.

The Chair and the two Vice Chairs of the Selection Board should also be members of the Board of Trustees as stated in the Foundation's Supplemental trust deed. Among them, the Chair should be the member of the Board of Trustees who is related, as stated in the Foundation's Supplemental trust deed, to the Ministry of Science and Technology. And the two Vice Chairs should respectively be the member of the Board of Trustees who is related, as stated in the Foundation's Supplemental trust deed, to the Ministry of Education and the international scholar member of the Board of Trustees as mentioned in the Foundation's Supplemental trust deed.

Secretary General of the Selection Board should be appointed by the Board of Trustees with the agreement of the donors as well.

The members of the Selection Board shall be altered a quarter every 3 years (except Chair, Vice Chair and Secretary General.)

Besides, the appointment of the members of the Selection Board should be in line with the principles of comparative stability and proper renewal. The Selection Board will be responsible for formulation of the ways of selection.

The office of the Selection Board is located in Beijing and affiliated to the Ministry of Science and Technology of China.

Article 13   Several specific professional evaluation panels or prize evaluation panels may be set up under the Selection Board when it is necessary. The first round of evaluation is done according to recommendation materials submitted by the nominators with a candidate list as the results. This list will be submitted to the Selection Board for a final evaluation.

Members of the professional evaluation panels and prize evaluation panels shall be appointed by the Selection Board.

Article 14   Winners of the prizes of the Foundation are evaluated and decided by the Selection Board.

The Selection Board shall evaluate and determine the winners of the Prize for Scientific and Technological Progress of Ho Leung Ho Lee Foundation and the Prize for Scientific and Technological Innovation of Ho Leung Ho Lee Foundation on the basis of results of the work of the professional evaluation panels or the prize evaluation panels.

The Prize for Scientific and Technological Achievements of Ho Leung Ho Lee Foundation should be decided on a plenary meeting of the Selection Board and on the basis of the nomination of the Selection Board. The Selection Board may set up preliminary evaluation panel to exercise the right of examination and hearing of the candidates when necessary.

Article 15　The Selection Board shall work with the principles of "Fairness, Justness and Openness" and "One Member One Vote". Decisions on winners of prizes of the Foundation are made in a way of anonymous ballot by the members of the Selection Board. The endorsement of at least half of the members of the Selection Board is a must for a candidate to win the Prize for Scientific and Technological Progress of Ho Leung Ho Lee Foundation and the Prize for Scientific and Technological Innovation of Ho Leung Ho Lee Foundation; while at least two-third of favorable votes of the total number is a must for candidates to win the Prize for Scientific and Technological Achievements of Ho Leung Ho Lee Foundation.

Article 16　The Selection Board should take the balance between types of prize, between subjects and between regions into consideration in the process of evaluation.

V　Awarding

Article 17　The Selection Board must ask for the winners' willingness prior to any public announcement of the results of evaluation and selection, and notify both the donors and the Board of Trustees. According to the wishes of the donors, the winners are required to stay in China and continue to carry on scientific researches or technological work for no less than 3 years after receiving the prizes.

Article 18　An award granting ceremony will be held each year at a proper time, in which the winners shall be granted with certificates and prizes as arranged by the Selection Board. The list of awardees and their major contributions will be publicized through media.

VI　Publications and Academic Seminars

Article 19　The Foundation shall make a publication yearly to introduce the awardees and their major scientific and technological achievements.

The Selection Board is responsible for editing and publication of the publications.

Article 20　The Foundation shall organize academic seminars every year, in which members of the Selection Board and representatives of the awardees introduce their academic achievements and updated progress in the related areas and make relevant reports where appropriate.

Should the financial situation of the Foundation permits, the academic seminars of specific subjects of the Foundation may be held abroad.

The Selection Board is responsible for the organization of the reports and seminars.

VII Supplementary Provisions

Article 21   The Selection Board of the Foundation holds a meeting annually to summarize the work of the year, to plan the work of the following year and to study and decide on the relevant important issues.

Article 22   The Selection Board of the Foundation shall have the right of explanation of the Articles of this regulation.

Article 23   This regulation becomes effective on May 15, 2007.

关于何梁何利基金获奖科学家
异议处理若干规定

（2009 年 5 月 20 日何梁何利基金信托委员会会议通过）

一、总　　则

为了正确处理对何梁何利基金获奖人提出异议的投诉事件，弘扬科学精神，崇尚科学道德，抵御社会不正之风和科研不端行为，提升何梁何利基金科学与技术奖的权威性和公信力，制定本规定。

二、基本原则

处理对获奖人投诉事件，贯彻以事实为依据，以法律为准绳的原则，遵循科学共同体认同的道德准则，区别情况，妥善处置。

三、受　　理

涉及对获奖科学家主要科技成果评价、知识产权权属以及与奖项有关事项提出异议的署名投诉信件，由评选委员会受理，并调查处理。

匿名投诉信件，原则上不予受理。但涉及获奖人因科研不端行为受到处分、学术资格被取消或与其学术著作、奖项评选相关重要情况的，应由评选委员会跟进调查核实处理。

四、调　　查

评选委员会受理投诉后，由评选委员会秘书长指定评选委员会办公室专人按以下工作程序办理：

1. 将投诉信函复印件送交该获奖人的专业评审组负责人，征求意见。

2. 专业评审组负责人有足够理由认为投诉异议不成立，没有必要调查的，评选委员会秘书长可决定终止处理。

专业评审组负责人认为投诉异议有一定依据，有必要进一步调查的，由评选委员会办公室向获奖人所在部门或单位发函听证。

3. 获奖人所在部门或单位经调查，认为投诉异议不成立或基本不能成立的，应请该单位出具书面意见。评选委员会秘书长可据此决定终止处理。

获奖人所在部门或单位根据投诉认为获奖人涉嫌科研不端行为的，评选委员会应建议该部门或单位根据国家有关规定调查处理，并反馈查处信息。

4. 调查结果应向信托委员会报告。

五、处理决定

获奖人所在部门或单位经调查认定获奖人确属科研不端行为，并作出相应处理的，评选委员会秘书长应当参照《中华人民共和国科学技术进步法》第七十一条规定，提出撤销其奖励决定（草案），经评选委员会主任批准后，提交信托委员会审议。

六、公　　告

因获奖人科研不端行为，撤销其奖励的决定经信托委员会审议通过后，由评选委员会在何梁何利基金年报上公告，并通知本人，返回奖励证书、奖金。

信托委员会对获奖人撤销奖励的决定是终局决定。

七、附　　则

本规定自 2009 年 6 月 1 日起试行。

附:《中华人民共和国科学技术进步法》第七十一条:

"违反本法规定，骗取国家科学技术奖励的，由主管部门依法撤销奖励，追回奖金，并依法给予处分。

违反本法规定，推荐的单位或者个人提供虚假数据、材料，协助他人骗取国家科学技术奖励的，由主管部门给予通报批评；情节严重的，暂停或者取消其推荐资格，并依法给予处分。"

REGULATIONS ON HANDLING THE COMPLAINT LODGED AGAINST THE PRIZE-WINNER WITH HO LEUNG HO LEE FOUNDATION

(Adopted at the Meeting of the Board of Trustees on May 20, 2009)

I   General Principle

For the purpose of handling properly the objection lodged against the prize-winner with Ho Leung Ho Lee Foundation, promoting scientific spirits and upholding scientific ethics, preventing social malpractice or misconduct in scientific research, and improving the public credibility and authority of Ho Leung Ho Lee Foundation with respect to awards for science and technology, the Selection Board hereby formulates the regulations as stipulated below.

II   Basic Principle

The Selection Board shall handle the complaint lodged against any prize-winner in accordance with the principle of taking the facts as the basis and taking the law as the criterion, and deal with each case properly by following the moral standard recognized by the scientific community.

III   Acceptance

For any duly signed letter of objection against a prize-wining scientist with respect to the appraisal of his major scientific and technological achievement, the ownership of intellectual property right and other prize-related matter, the Selection Board shall be responsible for acceptance of the letter of objection and for further investigation and handling thereof.

The Selection Board shall, in principle, not accept a letter of objection written or sent in an anonymous manner. However, if it is mentioned in the letter of objection that, due to misconduct of the prize-winner in the scientific research, the discipline measure is imposed against him, or his academic qualification is cancelled, or there is any other important matter concerning his academic publication and prize selection, such a letter of objection must be accepted by the Selection Board, followed by further investigation, verification and handling.

IV Investigation

Upon acceptance of a letter of objection, the Secretary General of the Selection Board shall designate a special person in the Office of Selection Board to handle the letter of objection according to the procedures as follows:

1. A copy of the letter of complaint shall be sent to the person-in-charge of the specialized evaluation team determining to grant the award to the prize-winner for soliciting his comment.

2. When the person-in-charge of the specialized evaluation team concludes with sufficient reason that the objection cannot be established and it is not necessary to make further investigation, the Secretary General of the Selection Board can make a decision as to terminate the handling of the letter of objection.

When the person-in-charge of the specialized evaluation team deems that the objection can be established on basis of facts but should be proved by further investigation, the office of the Selection Board shall issue a notification to the working unit of the prize-winner to request his presence at a hearing to be held.

3. If the working unit of the prize-winner deems that the objection cannot be established or basically cannot be established after investigation, the working unit is obligated to produce a formal document in writing to state its opinion. Then the Secretary General of the Selection Board has the right to make a decision as to the termination of the handling of the letter of objection.

In case the working unit of the prize-winner deems that the prize-winner commits malpractice or misconduct in proof of the letter of objection, the Selection Board is obligated to propose that the working unit carry out investigation in accordance with government regulations before making a response by sending a feedback to the Selection Board.

4. The investigation results should be reported to Ho Leung Ho Lee Foundation's Board of Trustees.

V Decision

Once the working unit of the prize-winner proves with further investigation that the prize-winner commits malpractice or misconduct, and takes discipline measure against the prize-winner, the Secretary General of the Selection Board should draft a proposal, in accordance with Article 71 of the *Law of the PRC on, Science and Technology Progress*, on withdrawal of the prize awarded to the prize-winner. The proposal needs to be further approved by the Director of the Selection Board before being submitted to Ho Leung Ho Lee Foundation's Board of Trustees for deliberation.

VI Announcement

The Selection Board shall announce its decision with respect to withdrawal of the prize from the prize-winner, due to his malpractice or misconduct, in its annual report with approval of the Ho Leung Ho Lee Foundation's Board of Trustees, and shall notify the prize-winner that the prize and prize-winning certificate are to be cancelled. The decision to withdraw the prize from the prize-winner made by Ho Leung Ho Lee Foundation's Board of Trustees shall be final.

VII Appendix

These regulations shall enter into trial implementation on June 1, 2009.

Appendix: Article 71 of the *Law of the People's Republic of China on Science and Technology Progress* stipulates as follows:

The competent authority shall, in accordance with law, withdraw a prize and a bonus and take disciplinary action against anyone who is engaged in fraudulent practice for winning the National Science and Technology Prize.

For anyone or any working unit, which offers false data, false material, or conspire with others in fraudulent practice for winning the National Science and Technology Prize, the competent authority shall circulate a notice of criticism of such malpractice or misconduct; if the circumstances are serious, the competent authority shall suspend or cancel the working unit's eligibility for recommendation of any prize-winning candidate, and shall punish it in accordance with law.

关于何梁何利基金评选工作
若干问题的说明

何梁何利基金是由香港爱国金融实业家何善衡、梁銶琚先生、何添先生、利国伟先生于 1994 年 3 月 30 日在香港创立的，以奖励中华人民共和国杰出科学技术工作者为宗旨的科技奖励基金。截至 2010 年，已有 901 位获奖科学家获得此项殊荣。经过 16 年的成功实践，何梁何利基金科技奖已经成为我国规模大、层次高、影响广、在国内外享有巨大权威性和公信力的科学技术大奖。为便于科技界、教育界和社会各界进一步了解基金宗旨、基本原则、评选标准和运行机制，在 2010 年 10 月颁奖大会期间，何梁何利基金评选委员会秘书长段瑞春就基金评选章程、评选工作以及社会各界所关心的有关问题，做了如下说明。

一、什么是何梁何利基金评选章程？

何梁何利基金评选章程是评选工作的基本准则。评选章程以基金《信托契约》为依据，由何梁何利基金信托委员会全体会议审议通过和发布。第一部评选章程诞生于 1994 年 3 月 30 日基金成立之时，保障了评选工作从一开始就步入科学、规范、健康的轨道运行。1998 年 5 月 11 日适应香港九七回归和国内形势发展，对评选章程做过一次修订。2007 年 5 月 15 日基金信托委员会会议决定再次修改评选章程，其主要目的，一是根据 2005 年 10 月 12 日香港高等法院批准生效的《补充契约条款》，对评选章程有关条款做相应修改，使之与基金《信托契约》及其《补充契约条款》保持一致。二是将评选委员会适应我国创新国策、改革评选工作的成功经验上升为章程，使之条文化、规范化、制度化，进一步提升各奖项的科学性、权威性。

二、根据《补充契约条款》，评选章程做了哪些重要修改？

何梁何利基金是依据香港法律创立的慈善基金。当初，根据香港普通法原则，实行信任委托制度，由捐款人与信托人签订《信托契约》，经香港终审法院批准成立。信托委员会是基金的最高权力机构，决定基金投资、评选和管理等重大事项。自 1994 年 3 月基金成立以来，当年四位创立者中，梁銶琚先生、何善衡先生、何添先生都在九旬高寿与世长辞。我们永远缅怀他们的崇高精神。由于他们的离去，《信托契约》有关捐款人的权利与义务主体出现缺位，从法律意义上影响到基金决策程序的进行。2005 年 10 月，经香港高等法院批准《信托契约补充条款》将基金"捐款人"统一修订为原捐款人或者其遗产承办人指定的慈善基金，从而实现了捐款人从老一辈爱国金融家向其下一代的平稳过渡。依据此项修订，现基金捐款人为 4 个法人，即何善衡慈善基金有限公司、梁銶琚慈善基金有限公司、何添基金有限公司、利国伟先生和其夫人的伟伦基金有限公司。为此，评选章程也做了相应修改。

三、何梁何利基金奖励对象应当具备什么条件?

何梁何利基金奖励对象为中华人民共和国公民，获奖人应具备下列三个条件：一是对推动科学技术事业发展有杰出贡献；二是热爱祖国，有高尚的社会公德和职业道德；三是在国内从事科研、教学或技术工作已满 5 年。

1994 年 3 月 30 日，何梁何利基金成立时，香港、澳门尚未回归祖国。鉴于当时历史状况，评选章程关于奖励对象为中华人民共和国公民的规定，仅适用祖国内地科技工作者，不包括在香港、澳门地区工作的科技人员。在"一国两制"的原则下，香港和澳门先后于 1997 年 7 月 1 日和 1999 年 12 月 20 日回归祖国。祖国内地与港澳特区科技合作与交流出现崭新局面。而今，香港、澳门特别行政区科技人员，是中华人民共和国公民中的"港人""澳人"，符合章程的要求。为此，自 2007 年起，何梁何利基金奖励对象扩大到符合上述条件的香港特别行政区、澳门特别行政区科学技术人员。

四、现行评选章程对基金奖项结构是如何规定的?

在中央人民政府和香港特区政府的关怀和指导下，16 年来，何梁何利基金已经形成了科学合理的奖项结构和严谨、高效、便捷的评选程序。始终保持客观、公正、权威和具有公信力的评选纪录。现行评选章程规定基金设"科学与技术成就奖""科学与技术进步奖""科学与技术创新奖"。

每年，"科学与技术成就奖"不超过 5 名，授予奖牌、奖金 100 万港元；"科学与技术进步奖"和"科学与技术创新奖"总数不超过 65 名，分别授予相应的奖牌、奖金 20 万港元，其中，"科学与技术进步奖"和"科学与技术创新奖"的数量按 3∶1 至 2∶1 的比例，由评选委员会具体掌握。

五、"科学与技术成就奖"的评选标准是什么?

根据评选章程，符合下列三类条件的杰出科技工作者，均可获得"科学与技术成就奖"。一是长期致力于推进国家科学技术进步，贡献卓著，历史上取得国际高水平学术成就者；二是在科学技术前沿，取得重大科技突破，攀登当今科技高峰，领先世界先进水平者；三是推进技术创新，建立强大自主知识产权和自主品牌，其产业居于当今世界前列者。符合上述标准的获奖人选，既包括毕生奉献我国科技事业、其卓越成就曾达到世界一流水平的资深科学家，也包括以科学研究或技术创新领域的重大突破或突出业绩，使我国取得世界领先地位的中青年杰出人才。在征求意见过程中，我国科技界对此普遍赞同，认为这样修订丝毫没有降低了标准，而是使基金的科技大奖进一步向国际规范靠拢，为在研究开发和创新第一线拔尖人才的脱颖而出注入强大精神动力，也使基金科技奖励更加贴近建设创新型国家的主旋律。

六、"科学与技术进步奖"的评选标准是怎样规定的？

评选章程规定，"科学与技术进步奖"授予在特定学科领域取得重大发明、发现和科技成果者，尤其是在近年内有突出贡献者。需要说明的，一是这里所说的"特定学科"包括：数学力学、物理学、化学、天文学、气象学、地球科学、生命科学、农学、医学和药学、古生物学和考古学、机械电力技术、电子信息技术、交通运输技术、冶金材料技术、化学工程技术、资源环保技术、工程建设技术等17个领域，每一领域设一个奖项。原评选章程用"技术科学奖"涵盖了机电、信息、冶金、材料、工程、环保等技术领域，修订后的章程从学科领域之间平衡考虑，将其分别设立奖项。二是"科学与技术进步奖"评选政策，重在考察被提名人"近年内"的突出贡献。所谓"近年内"是指近10年内。三是随着科学技术飞速发展，新兴学科、交叉学科、边缘学科层出不穷。这些学科的被提名人宜按其最主要成就、最接近学科领域归类。关注新兴、交叉、边缘学科优秀人才，是评选委员会的一项政策。有些确实需要跨学科评议的特殊情况，将作为个案协调处理，但不专门设立新兴学科、交叉学科、边缘学科等奖项。

七、"科学与技术创新奖"的评选标准是怎样规定的？

设立"科学与技术创新奖"是基金评选工作的重要改革。评选章程规定："科学与技术创新奖"授予具有高水平科技成就而通过技术创新和管理创新，创建自主知识产权产业和著名品牌，创造重大经济效益和社会效益的杰出贡献者。这里需要说明的是，创新，是一个经济学的范畴，指的是有明确经济、社会目标的行为。有人解释为"科学思想在市场的首次出现"。何梁何利基金为适应我国提高自主创新能力，建设创新型国家的重大决策设立这个奖项，评选章程所称的"科学与技术创新"，第一，要以高水平的科学技术成就为起点，实现科技成果转化为现实生产力，完成科技产业化的过程。第二，就创新活动而言，是指在高水平科技成就基础上的技术创新和管理创新，包括原始创新、集成创新和在他人先进技术之上的再创新，但应有自主知识产权产业和著名品牌，创造出重大经济效益和社会效益，对于创新成果在教育、节能环保、生态平衡、国家安全、社会公益事业等领域产生的巨大社会效益，将和可计量的经济效益一样，获得评选委员会的认可。第三，任何一项重大创新都是团队作战的成果，"科学与技术创新奖"的得主，可以是发挥核心作用的领军人物，也可以是实现技术突破的关键人物。当然，这里所说的领军人物本身要有科技成就，而不只是行政管理和组织协调工作。

八、怎样理解"科学技术创新奖"所分设的奖项？

根据评选章程，"科学技术创新奖"分设青年创新奖、产业创新奖和区域创新奖等三个奖项。青年创新奖授予在技术创新和管理创新方面业绩突出、年龄不超过 45 周岁的优秀科技人才；区域创新奖授予通过技术创新、管理创新和区域创新，对区域经济发展和技术进步，尤其是对祖国内地、边远、艰苦地区和少数民族地区发展作出突出贡献的人物；产业创新是指通过创新、创业，大幅度推进技术进步和产业升级，包括对传统产业技术改造和新兴产业的腾飞跨越作出贡献的优秀人才。分设上述三个奖项，是评选政策的安排，其本身并不是相互独立的创新门类。因此，"科学技术创新奖"仍然按照创新奖的基本要求统一评选，适当注意三类奖项的结构平衡，不按区域创新奖、产业创新奖、青年创新奖分组切块进行评审。

九、"科学与技术进步奖"和"科学与技术创新奖"评选标准有何差别？

从原则上讲，"科学与技术进步奖"按照学科领域设置，"科学与技术创新奖"基于创新业绩设置，二者有交叉和关联之处，又有重要区别，评选标准的政策取向和侧重有所不同。《评选章程》要求"科学与技术进步奖"获奖人必须是重大发明、发现和科技成果的完成人或主要完成人。而"科学与技术创新奖"的获奖人是在高水平科技成就基础上的创新实践者。前者，重在考察其发明、发现和其他科技成就的水平及其在国内国际的学术地位；而后者，重点考察其产业高端技术创新和管理创新的业绩，包括经济社会效益、自主知识产权和著名品牌建设。当然，"科学与技术创新奖"得主的领军人物本身要有高水平的科技成就，而不只是战略决策、行政管理和组织协调工作。

十、"科学与技术进步奖""科学与技术创新奖"获奖人能否获得"科学与技术成就奖"？

何梁何利基金的宗旨是鼓励我国优秀科学技术工作者，无所畏惧地追求科学真理，勇攀当代科学技术高峰。已经获得"科学与技术进步奖""科学与技术创新奖"的科技工作者，在获奖后，再接再厉，开拓进取，在科学技术前沿取得新的重大科技突破，领先世界先进水平者；或者在产业高端作出新的重大技术创新，建立强大自主知识产权和自主品牌，使得我国产业跃居当今世界前列者；如果在前次获奖后取得的新的杰出成就达到"科学与技术成就奖"标准，可以推荐为"科学与技术成就奖"被提名人的人选，按照《评选章程》规定程序参评，也有望摘取"科学与技术成就奖"的桂冠。

十一、评选委员会按照怎样的程序进行各奖项评选工作？

每年，基金评选委员会按照下列程序开展评选工作：

（一）提名

每年年初，评选委员会向国内外 2000 多位提名人发去提名表，由其提名推荐获奖人选，并于 3 月 31 日前将提名表返回评选委员会。评选办公室将对提名材料进行形式审查、整理、分组、印刷成册。

（二）初评

每年 7 月中旬，评选委员会召开当年专业评审会，进行"科学与技术进步奖""科学与技术创新奖"的初评。其中，"科学与技术进步奖"初评，按照学科设立若干专业评审组进行；"科学与技术创新奖"成立一个由不同行业和领域专家组成的评审组进行初评。经过初评，以无记名投票方式，产生一定差额比例的候选人，提交评选委员会会议终评。

（三）预审

根据《评选章程》，"科学与技术成就奖"候选人由评选委员会委员在初评结束后提名。每年 8 月，评选委员会成立预审小组进行协调、评议，必要时进行考察和听证，产生"科学与技术成就奖"候选人，并形成预审报告，提交评选委员会会议终评。

（四）终评

每年 9 月中旬评选委员会召开全体会议进行终评。对候选人逐一评议，最后，根据基金信托委员会确定的当年获奖名额，进行无记名投票表决。"科学与技术进步奖""科学与技术创新奖"的候选人，获半数以上赞成票为获奖人。"科学与技术成就奖"的候选人，获三分之二多数赞成票为获奖人。

（五）授奖

每年 10 月的适当时候，何梁何利基金举行颁奖大会，向获奖人颁发奖牌、奖金。

十二、何梁何利基金获奖人有哪些权利和义务？

《世界人权宣言》宣布："人人对他所创造的任何科学、文学或艺术成果所产生的精神的和物质的权利，享有受保护的权利"。知识产权是精神权利和经济权利的总和，其本原和第一要义，是给人的智慧、才能和创造性劳动注入强大精神动力。科技奖励是确认和保护精神权利的重要制度，何梁何利基金"科学与技术成就奖""科学与技术进步奖""科学与技术创新奖"获奖人的权利是，享有何梁何利基金获奖科学家的身份权、荣誉权；享有接受何梁何利基金颁发的奖金的权利，该奖金个人所有；有从第二年起成为基金提名人，向基金提名推荐被提名人的权利。根据基金《信托契约》和评选章程，获奖人有义务在获得基金奖励后继续在中华人民共和国从事科学与技术工作不少于三年，为我国科技进步与创新作出更多贡献。

十三、评选委员会委员和专业评委是怎样产生的?

评选委员会是何梁何利基金评选工作的执行机构,通过全体会议审议、决定各奖项获奖人,行使最终评选决定权。根据评选章程,评选委员会由最多不超过20名委员组成。评选委员会主任由科技系统的信托委员担任,副主任委员两人,分别由教育部系统的信托委员和补充契约所指明的国际学者信托委员担任。评选委员会秘书长由信托委员会任命并征得捐款人代表同意的人选担任。

评选委员会委员由信托委员会任命,委员名单通过何梁何利基金出版物、网站公布。

按《评选章程》规定,评选委员会委员的聘任条件是:第一,要具备高尚道德情操,能够公正履行评选委员的职责;第二,要具备精深学术造诣,能够对其所属领域科技成就作出科学性和权威性评价;第三,要热心祖国科技奖励事业,愿意为之作出无私奉献;第四,评选委员会委员的结构配置,原则上每一领域有一名委员,国内评委和海外评委按照三比一的比例安排;第五,评选章程还规定了评选委员会委员的更新和替换制度,以保障评选委员会的生机和活力。

每年7月何梁何利基金召开专业评审会议,进行初评。初评是评选工作的第一道关口。其十多个“科学与技术进步奖”评审组和“科学与技术创新奖”的专业评委,由评选委员会根据工作需要,从250人左右的评审专家库或历年获奖科学家中,按《评选章程》规定的上述条件遴选。

十四、怎样理解基金公平、公正、公开的评选原则?

科学精神的精髓是求实、求是、求真。科技奖励评选工作必须坚持以诚信为本,践行实事求是的方针。何梁何利基金从一开始就贯彻“公平、公正、公开”的评选原则,保持良好的评选记录,得到社会各界的高度评价和充分肯定。所谓公平,体现在所有被提名者,不论职务、职位、学衔、资历,也不论年龄、民族、性别,在评选章程确定的评选标准面前一律平等。所谓公正,是指评选工作严格按照章程确定的评选标准和评选程序进行,无论初评的专业评委,还是终评的评选委员会委员,有权作出独立判断,按一人一票的制度行使表决权,最终依据评委共同体的意志决定获奖人,不受任何单位或个人的干扰。所谓公开,是指何梁何利基金评选章程、评选标准及其解释、评选委员会委员、逐年获奖人材料等,通过年报、网站等向社会公开,接受社会公众的监督和指导。自2006年起,评选委员会在部分省市和部门建立联络员,加强同社会各界的联系。何梁何利基金评选实践经验凝练到一点,就是贯彻“公平、公正、公开”的评选原则,是何梁何利基金的指导方针,是评选委员会的工作纪律,是基金的立业之本、权威之根、公信力之源泉,是一个具有国内和国际影响力的科技大奖的生命线。今后,基金将一如既往恪守“三公”原则,本着对科学负责、对基金负责、对科技共同体负责的精神,做好评选工作，使何梁何利基金科学与技术奖经得起历史的检验。

十五、何梁何利基金有无异议处理程序?

为了弘扬科学精神，崇尚科学道德，抵御社会不正之风和科研不端行为，提升何梁何利基金科学与技术奖的权威性和公信力，基金于2009年5月20日制定并发布了《关于何梁何利基金获奖科学家异议处理若干规定》，自发布之日起试行。

根据该项决定，凡涉及对获奖科学家主要科技成果评价、知识产权权属以及与奖项有关事项提出异议的署名投诉信件，由评选委员会受理，并调查处理。匿名投诉信件，原则上不予受理。但涉及获奖人因科研不端行为受到处分、学术资格被取消或与奖项评选相关重要情况的，应跟进调查核实，酌情处理。

评选委员会的处理原则是，以事实为依据，以法律为准绳，遵循科学共同体认同的道德准则，区别情况，正确处置。经调查，认定获奖人确属科研不端行为，将参照《中华人民共和国科学技术进步法》第七十一条规定，报基金信托委员会审议并作出相应的处分决定，直至公告撤销其奖励的决定，并通知本人，返回奖励证书、奖金。

十六、何梁何利基金未来发展目标是什么?

在中央人民政府和香港特别行政区政府的指导下，在我国科技界、教育界和社会各界的共同努力下，何梁何利基金已经成为我国规模大、权威性高、公信力强的社会力量奖励，成为推进我国科技进步与创新的强大杠杆，在国内外影响和声誉与日俱增。在历年颁奖大会上，党和国家领导人亲临颁奖，发表重要讲话，给予基金同人极大鼓舞和力量。何梁何利基金同人将不负众望，不辱使命，承前肩后，继往开来，在新的起点上总结经验，开拓创新，突出特色，丰富内涵，朝着办成国际一流的科技奖励的方向迈进，为祖国的科技进步和创新，为建设富强民主、文明和谐的社会主义现代化国家而不懈努力!

EXPLANATIONS ON SEVERAL ISSUES ON THE SELECTION WORK OF HO LEUNG HO LEE FOUNDATION

Ho Leung Ho Lee Foundation ("the Foundation") is a scientific and technological award foundation established on March 30, 1994 in Hong Kong by patriotic Hong Kong financial industrialists Ho Sin Hang, Leung Kau-Kui, Ho Tim, Lee Quo-Wei for the purpose of awarding prominent scientific and technological workers of the People's Republic of China. Up to 2010, there were 901 scientists who received this special honor. Within the 16 years of successful practice, HLHL Foundation Scientific and Technological Awards have become major scientific and technological awards of large scale, high standard and extensive influence in China that enjoy enormous prestige and public trust both domestically and abroad. In order for the circle of science and technology, the circle of education, and other various social circles to further understand the Foundation's purpose, basic principles, award selection criteria and operation mechanisms, Mr. Duan Ruichun, secretary general of the Selection Board of HLHL Foundation, made the following explanations during the awards ceremony in October 2010 with respect to the Foundation's selection regulation, selection work and other issues that various social circles are concerned about.

I. What is the Regulation of Ho Leung Ho Lee Foundation on the Selection of the Award Winners of its Prizes?

The Regulation of Ho Leung Ho Lee Foundation on the Selection of the Award Winners of its Prizes ("Selection Regulation") is the fundamental guideline of the award selection work. The Selection Regulation is based on the Foundation's Trust Agreement and deliberated, adopted and published by the plenary meeting of HLHL Foundation Broad of Trustees. The birth of the first selection regulation on March 30, 1994, the very day when the Foundation was established, guaranteed the operation of the selection work in a scientific, regulated and healthy track from the very beginning. On May 11, 1998, a revision was made to the Selection Regulation to adapt to the return of Hong Kong to China and the development of domestic situation. On May 15, 2007, it was resolved at the meeting of the Foundation's Broad of Trustees that another revision would be made to the Selection Regulation. The main purpose of the revision was that, on the one hand, relevant modifications would be made to certain terms and conditions in the Selection Regulation in accordance with the Supplementary Terms to the Trust Agreement which took effect upon approval by the Hong Kong SAR High Court on October 12, 2005 so that the Foundation's Trust Agreement became consistent with its Supplementary Terms to the Trust Agreement while, on the other hand, the successful experience of the Selection Board in adapting to China's national innovation policy and reforming its selection work was elevated to become part of the selection regulation so that the experience was embodied in agreement terms, standards and systems to further improve the scientific and authoritative features of different award categories.

II. What are the Important Modifications to the Selection Regulation Made in Accordance with the Supplementary Terms of the Trust Agreement?

HLHL Foundation is a charity foundation established in accordance with the laws of the Hong Kong SAR. In its early days, the trust system was established in accordance with the principles in Hong Kong's common law and the foundation was established upon the approval of the Hong Kong Supreme Court after the donors and the trustees signed the Trust Agreement. The Board of Trustees is the supreme body of power of the Foundation that decides on major matters of the foundation in investment, award selection and management. After the foundation was established in March 1994, Mr. Ho Sin Hang, Mr. Leung Kau-Kui and Mr. Ho Tim of the four founders, whose sublime and noble spirits we will all cherish forever, passed away in their nineties. Due to their decease, the main parties to the rights and obligations of donors in the Trust Agreement became absent, which affected the operation of the Foundation's decision-making procedures in terms of law. In October 2005, it was uniformly revised in the Supplementary Terms of the Trust Agreement, upon the approval of the Hong Kong SAR High Court, that the "donors" of the Foundation became the charity foundations designated by the original donors or their estate administrator. Thus a peaceful and smooth transition was achieved with respect to donors from the old generation patriotic financers to the charity foundations run by their next generation. According to the revision, the current donors of the Foundation are four legal persons, namely the S. H. Ho Foundation Limited, the Leung Kau-Kui Foundation Limited, the Ho Tim Foundation Limited, and the Wei Lun Foundation Limited of Mr. Lee Quo-Wei and his wife. And the relevant modifications were made to the Selection Regulation accordingly.

III. What Conditions Need the Winners of the Awards of HLHL Foundation Have?

The winners of the awards of HLHL Foundation shall be the citizens of the People's Republic of China. And they also need to meet the following three conditions: First, they shall have made prominent contributions in the development of the undertakings in science and technology. Second, they shall love the motherland and exhibit noble social ethics and good professional ethics. Third, they shall have engaged in scientific and technological research work, teaching work or technical work for no less than five years in China.

When HLHL Foundation was established on March 30, 1994, Hong Kong and Macao were not returned to the motherland yet. In view of the historical situation then, the provision in the Selection Regulation that the winners of the awards shall be citizens of the People's Republic of China only applied to scientific and technological workers in China's mainland and scientific and technological workers in Hong Kong and Macao were excluded. Then Hong Kong and Macao were returned to the motherland under the principle of "one country, two systems" respectively on July 1st, 1997 and December 20, 1999. And a brand new situation emerged in the cooperation and exchange between the mainland of China and the Hong Kong and Macao SARs. Now, the scientific and technological workers in the Hong Kong and Macao SARs are "Hong Kong people" and "Macao people" among the citizens of the People's Republic of China and thus meet the conditions in the Selection Regulation. Therefore, the scope of the scientists eligible to the awards of HLHL Foundation was expanded from 2007 to include scientific and technological personnel in the Hong Kong and Macao SARs who meet the above conditions.

IV. What are the Provisions on the Structure of the Award Categories in the Prevailing Selection Regulation?

Under the care and guidance of the Central People's Government and the government of the Hong Kong SAR, HLHL Foundation has formed during 16 years a scientific and rational structure of the award categories and a selection regulation of meticulousness, high efficiency, convenience and swiftness. It has always retained its objective, fair, authoritative selection performance and won good public trust. As provided in the prevailing Selection Regulation, the Foundation sets up the Prize for Scientific and Technological Achievements, the Prize for Scientific and Technological Progress, and the Prize for Scientific and Technological Innovation.

Each year there will be no more than five winners of the Prize for Scientific and Technological Achievements. Each of them will be given a medal and a prize of HKMYM one million. The total number of the winners of the Prize for Scientific and Technological Progress and the Prize for Scientific and Technological Innovation will not exceed 65. Each winner will be given a corresponding medal and a prize of HKMYM 200000. Among these, the proportion of the winners of the Prize for Scientific and Technological Progress to those of the Prize for Scientific and Technological Innovation will range from 3 : 1 to 2 : 1. The proportion will be determined by the Selection Board on the basis of specific situation.

V. What are the Selection Criteria on the Prize for Scientific and Technological Achievements?

According to the Selection Regulation, all outstanding scientific and technological workers who meet the following three conditions are eligible to be honored with the Prize for Scientific and Technological Achievements. The first condition is that the scientist has been committed for a long time to promoting the scientific and technological achievements of the state in China and he or she has made eminent contribution and obtained high-level international academic achievements in his career. The second condition is that the scientist has obtained major scientific and technological breakthroughs in the frontiers of science and technology, mounted the peak of the science and technology of the present age, and obtained achievements of a world-leading standard. Third, the scientist has promoted technological innovation and established powerful independently-owned intellectual property and brand. And the industry in which the scientist works is one of the leading industries in the world. The candidates who meet the above standards include both senior scientists who have devoted their whole life to Chinese scientific and technological undertakings and obtained eminent achievements that were once first-rate in the world and youth and middle-aged outstanding talents who have made major breakthroughs or prominent achievements in the area of scientific and technological research and technical innovation so that China got a world-leading position in the area. During the process of opinion solicitation, the Chinese scientific and technological circle expressed general approval of the revision and indicated that such revision lowered the standard by not a slight bit while pushing the Foundation's awards one step further and closer to international standards. It injected powerful spiritual impetus for top-level talents to excel in the frontline of research and development and innovation. The revision also drew the Foundation's scientific and technological awards more closer to the mainstream ideology of building an innovative country.

VI. What are the Provisions on the Selection Criteria of the Prize for Scientific and Technological Progress?

It is provided in the Selection Regulation that the Prize for Scientific and Technological Progress will be honored to scientists who have made major inventions, discoveries and scientific and technological results in particular disciplinary areas, particularly those who have made prominent contributions in recent years. First, it needs to be noted that the "particular disciplines" stated here include 17 disciplines, namely mathematics and mechanics, physics, chemistry, astronomy, meteorology, earth sciences, life sciences, agronomy, medical sciences and materia medica, paleontology and archeology, technology of machinery and electronics, information technology, communication and transportation technology, metallurgical materials technology, chemical engineering technology, resources and environment protection technology, and engineering and construction technology. One award category is established for each of these areas. In the original selection regulation, the Award of Technical Sciences is set up to cover various technical areas including machinery, electronics, information, metallurgy, material science, engineering and environment protection. The revised procedure sets up different award categories for these areas out of the consideration on the balance between various disciplinary areas. Second, the selection policy on the Prize for Scientific and Technological Progress focuses on examining and reviewing the prominent contribution of the nominees "within recent years". And "within recent years" refers to within the recent ten years. Third, as emerging disciplines, interdisciplines, and fringe disciplines come up one after another with the rapid development of science and technology, the nominees from these disciplines should desirably be classified according to their most important achievements and the closest disciplines to which these belong. To pay more attention to the excellent talents from emerging disciplines, interdisciplines and fringe disciplines is one policy of the Selection Board. The special cases that truly need cross-disciplinary review and deliberation will be processed through coordination as separate cases. But no prize category will be established particularly for emerging disciplines, interdisciplines and fringe disciplines.

VII. What are the Provisions on the Selection Criteria of the Prize for Scientific and Technological Innovation?

Setting up the Prize for Scientific and Technological Innovation is an important reform of the Foundation's selection work. It is provided in the Selection Regulation that " the Prize for Scientific and Technological Innovation will be awarded to scientists who have high-level scientific and technological accomplishments and who have established an industry with independently-owned intellectual property and famous brand, created significant economic and social benefits, and made prominent contribution". It needs to be noted here that, as a term in economics, innovation refers to acts with specific economic and social goals. Some people defines it as the "first presence of an idea in science on the market". HLHL Foundation set up the innovation award to adapt to China's important decision to improve the ability to independent innovation and build an innovative country. For the purpose of the Selection Regulation, to make "scientific and technological innovation" first needs to make high-level scientific and technological achievements as its starting point to realize the transformation of scientific and technological achievements into real productive force and complete the process of scientific and technological industrialization. Second, innovation activities refer to technological and managerial innovations on the basis of high-level scientific and technological achievements. These include original innovation, integration innovation and re-innovation on the basis of other people's advanced technology. And such innovations should create independently-owned intellectual properties and famous brands and create significant economic and social benefits. Besides, the Selection Board also accepts and approves, in the same way as measurable economic benefits, the enormous social benefits created by innovation results in the areas of education, energy preservation and environment protection, ecological balance, national security, and social public interest undertakings. Third, as any major innovation is the result of teamwork, the winner of the Prize for Scientific and Technological Innovation may be either a leading person that plays the key role or a key person who has achieved technical breakthroughs. Naturally, the leading person here needs to have his or her own scientific and technological accomplishments in addition to conducting administrative management, organization and coordination work.

VIII. How should the Award Categories Set Up in the Prize for Scientific and Technological Innovation be Understood?

In accordance with the Selection Regulation, the Prize for Scientific and Technological Innovation includes three award categories of the Award for Youth Innovation, the Award for Region Innovation and the Award for Industrial Innovation. The Award for Youth Innovation will be given to excellent scientific and technological talents not older than 45 years old who have achieved prominent performance in technical and managerial innovation. The Award for Region Innovation will be given to people who have made prominent contributions to regional economic development and technological progress through technical, managerial and regional innovations, particularly those who have made contributions to China's inland, remote regions, regions of harsh conditions, and regions of ethic minorities. The Prize for Industrial Innovation will be given to excellent talents who have made contributions through innovation and entrepreneurship to greatly promote technical progress and industrial upgrading, which include both the technical transformation of traditional industries and the leap-forwards of emerging industries. The above three award categories are set up according to the arrangement in selection policy. These do not define mutually-independent types of innovation. Therefore, the selection of the winners of the Prize for Scientific and Technological Innovation will be conducted as a whole part in accordance with the basic requirements on the Prize while proper attention will be paid to retain the structural balance between these three award categories. Selection and evaluation will not be conducted in a manner that the Award for Region Innovation, the Award for Industrial Innovation and the Award for Youth Innovation are separated and form different groups.

IX. What are the Differences in the Selection Criteria of the Prize for Scientific and Technological Progress and the Prize for Scientific and Technological Innovation?

In principle, the Prize for Scientific and Technological Progress has award categories set up in accordance with different disciplines while the Prize for Scientific and Technological Innovation has award categories based on innovation results. The two prizes have overlaps and connections while there are important differences between them. And the policy orientations and stresses in their selection criteria are also different. The Selection Regulation requires that the winners of the Prize for Scientific and Technological Achievements must be completers or major completers of major inventions, discoveries and scientific and technological research results while the winners of the Prize for Scientific and Technological Innovation are scientists in innovative practices on the basis of high-level scientific and technological achievements. The former focuses on examining the standard and value of a scientist's invention, discovery or other scientific and technological achievement and its domestic and international academic status. The latter focuses on examining a person's performance in high-end industrial technical and managerial innovations, including economic and social benefits, independently-owned intellectual properties and building of famous brands. Naturally, the winners of the Prize for Scientific and Technological Innovations need to have high-level scientific and technological achievements as leading persons in addition to just conducting strategic decision making, administrative management, organization and coordination work.

X. Can the Winners of the Prize for Scientific and Technological Progress and the Prize for Scientific and Technological Innovation Be Honored with the Prize for Scientific and Technological Achievements?

The purpose of HLHL Foundation is to encourage excellent Chinese scientific and technological workers to dauntlessly pursue the truth of science and courageously mount the peaks in modern science and technology. The scientific and technological workers who have won the Prize for Scientific and Technological Progress and the Prize for Scientific and Technological Innovation may continue to forge ahead and break new grounds. And they may achieve new important breakthroughs in the frontiers of science and technology and lead in the cutting edge area of the world. Or they may make new important technical innovations in the high-end areas of an industry and create powerful independent intellectual properties and independent brands so that China's relevant industries become industrial leaders in the world. If such scientists' new outstanding achievements obtained after the previous prize winning meet the criteria for the Prize for Scientific and Technological Achievement, these scientists may be recommended as candidates to be nominated to the Prize for Scientific and Technological Achievements. They will participate in the evaluation in accordance with the procedures as provided in the Selection Regulation. And it is hopeful that they may become the laureates of the Prize for Scientific and Technological Achievements.

XI. In Accordance with What Procedures Will the Selection Board Conduct the Selection Work for Various Award Categories?

Each year, the Foundation's Selection Board will carry out selection work in accordance with the following procedure:

A. Nomination. In the beginning of each year, the Selection Board will send nomination forms to over 2000 domestic and foreign nominators. The nominators will recommend candidates for award winners and return the nomination form to the Selection Board by March 31st. The Selection Office will conduct the formal examination, arranging, assorting, and printing of the nomination materials and bind them into booklets.

B. Preliminary Evaluation. In the middle of July each year, the Selection Board will hold the year's specialized evaluation meeting and conduct the preliminary evaluation for the Prize of Scientific and Technological Progress and the Prize for Scientific and Technological Innovation. In the preliminary evaluation, that of the Prize for Scientific and Technological Progress will be conducted with a number of specialized evaluation groups formed according to different disciplines. The preliminary evaluation of the Prize for Scientific and Technological Innovation will be conducted by an evaluation group consisting of experts from different industries and areas. After the preliminary evaluation, candidates will be determined with a proportion of competitive selection by means of secret ballot and submitted to the meeting of the Selection Board for final evaluation.

C. Preliminary Review. In accordance with the Selection Regulation, the candidates of the Prize for Scientific and Technological Achievements will be nominated by the members of the Selection Board upon the conclusion of the preliminary evaluation. Each August, the Selection Board will form a preliminary evaluation group to conduct coordination and evaluation. Inspection tours and hearings will be made when necessary. Then the candidates for the Prize for Scientific and Technological Achievements will be determined and a preliminary review report will be prepared and submitted to the meeting of the Selection Board for final evaluation.

D. Final Evaluation. In the middle of September each year, the Selection Board will hold a plenary meeting to conduct final evaluation. Candidates will be evaluated one by one. And finally a secret ballot will be made on the selection in accordance with the numbers of prize winners of the year determined by the Trust Board of the Foundation. The candidates for the Prize for Scientific and Technological Progress and the Prize for Scientific and Technological Innovation will become prize winners with over half of the votes in favor. The candidates for the Prize for Scientific and Technological Achievements will become prize winners with over two thirds of the votes in favor.

E. Award Ceremony. At a proper time in October each year, HLHL Foundation will hold an award ceremony to present medals and prizes to the winners.

XII. What Are the Rights and Obligations of the Winners of the Awards of HLHL Foundation?

The *Universal Declaration of Human Rights* states that "Everyone has the right to the protection of the moral and material interests resulting from any scientific, literary or artistic production of which he is the author. " Intellectual property rights are the sum of both spiritual and economic rights. Its origin and primary significance is to inject powerful spiritual drive to people's wisdom, talent and creative labor. Scientific and technological awards are important systems to recognize and protect spiritual rights. The rights of the winners of the Prize of Scientific and Technological Achievements, the Prize for Scientific and Technological Progress, and the Prize for Scientific and Technological Innovation of HLHL Foundation are the enjoyment of the right of status and the right of honor of the prize-winning scientists of HLHL Foundation, the enjoyment of the right to accept the prize money granted by HLHL Foundation which shall be owned personally by the prize winners, and the right to become a nominator of the Foundation from the year next to the prize winning to recommend nominees to the Foundation. In accordance with the Foundation's Trust Agreement and Selection Regulation, the prize winner is obligated to continue to engage in scientific and technological work in the People's Republic of China for three years after prize winning so as to make more contribution to China's scientific and technological advancement and innovation.

XIII. How are the Members of the Selection Board and the Specialized Evaluators Selected?

The Selection Board is the implementing body of the selection work of HLHL Foundation. It conducts deliberation through plenary meeting, decides on the winners of the award categories, and exercises the right of decision in final evaluation. In accordance with the Selection Regulation, the Selection Board consists of no more than twenty members at the most. The chairman of the Selection Board shall be a member of the Board of Trustees for the circle of science and technology. The two vice chairmen of the board shall be a member of the Board of Trustees from the bodies under the Ministry of Education and a member of the Board of Trustees who is an international scholar as specified in the Supplementary Terms to the Trust Agreement. The secretary general of the Selection Boards shall be appointed by the Board of Trustees upon the consent of the representatives of the donors.

The members of the Selection Board are appointed by the Board of Trustees. And the list of such members will be published through the publications and website of HLHL Foundation.

As provided in the Selection Regulation, the conditions for the appointment of a member of the Selection Board are: First, the person needs to have noble ethics and the ability to fairly perform the duties of the member of the Selection Board. Second, the person needs to have sophisticated academic accomplishment and the ability to make scientific and authoritative evaluation on the scientific and technological achievements in his or her own specialized field. Third, the person needs to have enthusiasm on the motherland's undertakings in scientific and technological awards and the willingness to make selfless contributions to these undertakings. Fourth, with respect to the structural distribution of the members of the Selection Board, there shall be one member from each area in principle and the proportion between domestic and overseas members shall be 3 : 1. Fifth, the Selection Regulation provides for the renewal and replacement system of the members of the Selection Board so as to ensure the liveliness and vigor of the board.

Each July, HLHL Foundation holds a specialized evaluation meeting to conduct the preliminary evaluation. The preliminary evaluation is the very first step in the selection work. About a dozen of evaluation groups for the Prize for Scientific and Technological Progress and the specialized evaluators of the Prize for Scientific and Technological Innovation will be selected by the Selection Board on the basis of working needs and in accordance with the above conditions as provided in the Selection Regulation from an evaluation expert pool containing about 250 persons or the prize winners in previous years.

XIV. How should People Understand the Foundation's Selection Principles of Fairness, Justice and Openness?

The essence of the scientific spirit is to be practical, honest and truth-seeking. The selection work for the scientific and technological awards must adhere to the principle of sincerity and follow the guideline of doing things with a realistic and pragmatic approach. HLHL Foundation persistently carries out the selection principle of fairness, justice and openness from the very beginning. It retains good selection records and wins high praises and full recognition from various social circles. The principle of fairness is embodied in the provision that all the nominees, regardless of their jobs, positions, academic titles or work experiences and also their age, ethnic group or gender, are equal with respect to the selection criteria determined in the Selection Regulation. The principle of justice refers to the provision that the selection work is carried out strictly in accordance with the selection criteria and procedures determined in accordance with the Selection Regulation. Any person as either a specialized evaluator in the preliminary evaluation or a member of the Selection Board in final evaluation has the right to make independent judgment and exercise the right to vote under the system of one vote for one person. The prize winners are eventually determined according to the common will of all the evaluators free from the intervention of any entity or individual. The principle of openness refers to the practice that HLHL Foundation's Selection Regulation, Selection Criteria, and their explanations and the information about the members of the Selection Board and the prize winners of different years are published to the society through annual report and website to receive supervision and guidance from the public in the society. From 2006, the Selection Board has appointed liaison persons in some governmental departments, provinces and cities to strengthen its contact with various social circles. One viewpoint that can summarize the practical experience of the award selection of HLHL Foundation is to carry out the selection principle of "fairness, justice and openness." It is the guideline of HLHL Foundation, the working discipline of the Selection Board, and the cornerstone of the Foundation, the root of its authoritativeness and the source of its public trust. It is the lifeline of this major scientific and technological award with both domestic and international influence. From now on, the Foundation will adhere to this three-word principle as always. It will carry out the selection work well with the spirit of being responsible to science, to the Foundation, and to the scientific and technological community so that the scientific and technological awards of HLHL Foundation can stand the test of the history.

XV. Does HLHL Foundation Have Dispute Handling Procedures?

With a view to carrying forward the spirit of the science, advocating the ethics of the science, guarding against the unhealthy tendencies in the society and the improper conducts in scientific and technological research, and enhancing the authoritativeness and public trust of HLHL Foundation's scientific and technological awards, the Foundation formulated and published on May 20th, 2009 *Several Provisions on Handling the Disputes on the Prize-Winning Scientists of Ho Leung Ho Lee Foundation*. It took effect from the date of publication.

In accordance with the resolution on the document, the Selection Board will accept, investigate and handle all the signed complaint letters on the disputes with respect to the evaluation of the main scientific and technological research results, the ownership of relevant intellectual properties, and the matters about award categories related to a prize-winning scientist. In principle, anonymous complaint letters will not be accepted and handled. However, where such anonymous complaint letters involve the information that a prize winner has been punished due to improper conducts in scientific and technological research, that his academic title or qualification was cancelled, or other information related to the award evaluation, follow-up action shall be taken to investigate and verify. Such disputes shall then be handled according to actual situation.

The complaint handling principle of the Selection Board is to take facts as the basis and the law as the criterion, follow the ethical principles commonly accepted by the science community, distinguish different situations, and handle correctly. Where it is determined upon investigation that a prize winner really involves in improper conducts in scientific and technological research, the case will be referred to the Board of Trustees of the Foundation for deliberation with reference to the provisions in Article 71 of the *Law of the People's Republic of China on*, *Science and Technology Progress*. The board will make resolutions on corresponding punishment up to that of a public announcement to cancel its reward. The person involved will be notified of the decision and required to return his certificate and prize money.

XVI. What are the Goals of HLHL Foundation on Its Future Development?

Under the guidance of the Central People's Government and the government of the Hong Kong SAR and with the joint efforts of China's scientific and technological circle, education circle and various social circles, HLHL Foundation has already become an awarding organization founded with social resources that is of large scale, high authoritativeness, and strong public trust in China. It becomes a powerful lever to push forward China's scientific and technological advancement and innovation. Its domestic and foreign influence and reputation also grow constantly. China's state and CPC leaders attended in person the award ceremonies in the previous years. They presented the awards and delivered important speeches to give great encouragement and power to our colleagues working with the Foundation. The people of HLHL Foundation will live up to the expectations of the people and their own commitment. They will build on the past and usher in the future. They will summarize their experiences and move on from a new starting point. They will explore and innovate, highlight the Foundation's features, enrich its connotations, and advance in the direction of making it an internationally first-rate scientific and technological award. They will work hard and relentlessly for the motherland's scientific and technological advancement and innovation and for building China into a wealthy, democratic, civilized and harmonious socialist modern country!

关于何梁何利基金（香港）北京代表处公告

（2019 年 11 月 20 日北京市公安局批准）

何梁何利基金是香港爱国金融家何善衡、梁铢琚、何添、利国伟先生基于崇尚科学、振兴中华的热忱，各捐资 1 亿港元于 1994 年 3 月 30 日在香港注册成立的社会公益性慈善基金。其宗旨是奖励中华人民共和国杰出科学技术工作者，服务祖国科技进步与创新伟业。

根据《中华人民共和国境外非政府组织管理法》，经申请，并经北京市公安局批准，何梁何利基金（香港）代表处自 2019 年 11 月 20 日在北京宣告成立。

何梁何利基金（香港）代表处负责基金在中国境内开展活动，执行评选委员会指定提名、初评、终评和颁奖大会等日常事务。举办基金学术论坛、图片展。出版《何梁何利奖》等刊物。

特此公告。

何梁何利基金（香港）北京代表处

2020 年 1 月 1 日

PUBLIC ANNOUNCEMENT OF THE BEIJING REPRESENTATIVE OFFICE OF THE HO LEUNG HO LEE FOUNDATION (HONG KONG)

(Approved by Beijing Municipal Public Security Bureau on November 20, 2019)

With their fervor for advocating science and rejuvenating the Chinese nation, four patriotic financial industrialists in Hong Kong—Mr. Ho Sin–Hang, Mr. Leung Kau–kui, Mr. Ho Tim and Mr. Lee Quo–Wei—each donated 100 million HK dollars to register the establishment of the Ho Leung Ho Lee Foundation in Hong Kong on March 30, 1994. The Ho Leung Ho Lee Foundation is aimed to reward the outstanding science and technology workers of the People's Republic of China and to serve the great undertaking of advancing scientific and technological progress and innovation in the motherland.

The Ho Leung Ho Lee Foundation submitted an application in accordance with *The Law of the People's Republic of China on Administration of Activities of Overseas Nongovernmental Organizations in the Mainland of China*. With the approval of the application by the Beijing Municipal Public Security Bureau, the Beijing Representative Office of the Ho Leung Ho Lee Foundation (Hong Kong) was announced to be established on November 20, 2019 in Beijing.

The Beijing Representative Office of the Ho Leung Ho Lee Foundation (Hong Kong) is responsible for conducting activities of the Ho Leung Ho Lee Foundation in the mainland of China, and handling day–to–day affairs of the Selection Board of Ho Leung Ho Lee Foundation such as designating nominees, holding preliminary and final evaluations, and holding the awarding ceremony of the Ho Leung Ho Lee Foundation. It is also responsible for organizing academic forum and photo exhibition of the Ho Leung Ho Lee Foundation, and publishing periodicals including the *Ho Leung Ho Lee Prize*.

The public announcement is hereby given.

Beijing Representative Office of the
Ho Leung Ho Lee Foundation (Hong Kong)
January 1, 2020

何梁何利基金捐款人简历

捐款者何善衡慈善基金会有限公司之创办人

何 善 衡

何善衡博士，1900年出生，广东番禺市人。

何博士于1933年创办香港恒生银号，其后又创办恒昌企业及大昌贸易行。1952年恒生银号改为有限公司，1959年改称恒生银行，何氏一直担任董事长一职。1983年，于恒生银行成立50周年时，何氏因年事关系，改任恒生银行名誉董事长至病逝。

何博士经营之业务包括银行、贸易、信托、财务、酒店、保险、地产、船务、投资等。

何博士热心慈善公益不遗余力。1970年设立何善衡慈善基金会，资助国内外慈善事业，包括地方建设、教育、医疗、科学等，帮助社会造就人才，尤其对广州市及其家乡一带贡献很多。1978年创办恒生商学书院，免费提供教学，并曾任多所学校校董。1971年获香港中文大学荣誉社会科学博士衔，1983年获香港大学荣誉法律博士衔，1990年及1995年分别获广州市中山大学荣誉顾问衔及名誉博士学位，1993年获广州市荣誉市民及番禺市荣誉市民称谓。

何善衡博士于1997年12月4日在香港病逝，享年97岁。

梁 铢 琚

梁铢琚博士，1903年出生，广东顺德人。

梁博士为恒昌企业之创办人，曾任恒生银行董事、大昌贸易行副董事长，亦为美丽华酒店企业有限公司、富丽华酒店有限公司、Milford国际投资有限公司等董事以及恒生商学书院校董等。

梁博士早年在穗、港、澳等地经营银号和贸易，为大昌贸易行创办人之一，为工作经常往返国内各大商埠及海外大城市，或开设分行，或推进业务，并与合伙股东制订运作规章，积极培育人才；梁博士领导华商参与国际贸易，并于20世纪60年代协助香港政府重新厘定米业政策，对香港的安定繁荣有卓越贡献。

梁博士宅心仁厚，精于事业，淡薄声名，热心公益。数十年来对社会福利、教育、医疗事业捐助良多，堪称楷模。较为显著者包括捐款建成纪念其先父之圣高隆庞女修会梁式芝书院，纪念其先母之保良局梁周顺琴学校，香港大学梁铢琚楼，香港中文大学梁铢琚楼，香港浸会学院"梁铢琚汉语中心"，岭南学院梁铢琚楼，广州中山大学捐建两千两百座位的梁铢琚堂与梁李秀娱图书馆，赞助杨振宁博士倡议之中山大学高级学术研究中心基金会及中国教育交流协会留学名额，为清华大学设立"梁铢琚博士图书基金"，中国人民解放军第四军医大学"梁铢琚脑研究中心"，清华大学建筑馆——梁铢琚楼。

在香港的其他教育捐助包括：顺德联谊总会梁铢琚中学，顺德联谊总会梁李秀娱幼稚园（屯门），顺德联谊总会梁李秀娱幼稚园（沙田），香港励志会梁李秀娱小学，恒生商学书院，劳工子弟学校新校，九龙乐善堂陈祖泽学校礼堂，乐善堂梁铢琚学校，乐善堂梁铢琚书院，香港大学黄丽松学术基金，香港女童军总会沙田扬坑营地及梁李秀娱花园；在医疗卫生方面包括：医务卫生署土瓜湾顺德联谊总会梁铢琚诊所，香港防癌会，香港放射诊断科医生协会，玛丽医院"梁铢琚糖尿病中心"，玛丽医院放射学图书博物馆教学资料和医院员工的福利，香港大学医院在山东省为胃癌研究工作经费，支持张力正医生在葛量洪医院的心脏病手术和医疗的发展经费及捐助圣保禄医院设立心脏中心并以"梁铢琚心脏中心"命名；在社会福利捐献包括：九龙乐善堂梁铢琚敬老之家，东区妇女福利会梁李秀娱晚晴中心，香港明爱，西区少年警讯活动及跑马地鹅颈桥区街坊福利会等；向宗教团体的捐助包括：资助基督教"突破机构"开设青年村——信息站，赞助"志莲净苑"重建基金及大屿山"宝莲禅寺"筹募兴建天坛大佛基金等。

多年来，梁博士对家乡顺德的地方建设、科技教育、医疗事业亦大量资助，其中包括捐资成立国家级重点中学梁铢琚中学，中学的科学楼并增置教学仪器，北头学校，梁铢琚图书馆及图书，增设杏坛医院230张病床、独立手术室及分科设备仪器等，杏坛康乐活动中心，北头大会堂及北头老人康乐中心，北头乡每户开建水井一口，修葺北头主路及河道两岸，北头乡蚕房四座，梁铢琚夫人保健中心（即妇产幼儿医院），梁铢琚夫人幼儿园及梁铢琚福利基金会。

1987年梁博士荣获香港中文大学颁授荣誉社会科学博士学位，1990年被广州中山大学聘为名誉顾问，1992年获顺德市（今顺德区）颁授为首位荣誉市民，1994年国务院学位委员会批准清华大学授予梁博士名誉博士学位；同年4月，国务院总理李鹏为梁博士题词"热心公益，发展教育"，以赞扬其贡献。1995年6月21日，香港大学向已故梁铢琚博士追授名誉法学博士文凭。

在海外方而，梁博士亦曾捐助英国牛津大学、苏格兰Aberdeen大学医学院与加拿大多伦多颐康护理中心。

梁铢琚博士于1994年11月10日在香港病逝，享年91岁。

何　　添

　　何添博士于 1933 年加入香港恒生银行有限公司（前为恒生银号），于 1953 年任董事兼总经理，1967—1979 年任恒生银行副董事长。何添博士于 2004 年 4 月退任恒生银行董事，同时获该行委任为名誉资深顾问。何添博士曾任多个上市公司董事职位，包括美丽华酒店企业有限公司（董事长）、新世界发展有限公司、新鸿基地产有限公司、熊谷组（香港）有限公司及景福集团有限公司。

　　何添博士积极参与公职服务，他为香港中文大学联合书院永久校董、香港中文大学校董会校董、恒生商学书院校董、邓肇坚何添慈善基金创办人之一、香港何氏宗亲总会永久会长、旅港番禺会所永久名誉会长及金银业贸易场永远名誉会长。

　　何添博士于 1982 年获香港中文大学颁授荣誉社会科学博士学位；1997 年获香港城市大学颁授名誉工商管理学博士学位；1999 年获香港大学颁授荣誉法律博士学位；于 1988 年、1993 年、1995 年及 2004 年分别获广州市、番禺市、顺德市及佛山市授予荣誉市民的称号；又于 1996 年 11 月出任中华人民共和国香港特别行政区第一届政府推选委员会委员。

　　何添博士于 2004 年 11 月 6 日在香港病逝，享年 95 岁。

捐款者伟伦基金有限公司之创办人
利　国　伟

　　利国伟博士于 1946 年加入香港恒生银行有限公司（前为恒生银号），1959 年 12 月任该行董事，1976 年 1 月任副董事长，1983—1996 年 2 月做执行董事长，1996 年 3 月至 1997 年 12 月任非执行董事长，1998 年 1 月至 2004 年 4 月任名誉董事长，退任后续任名誉资深顾问。

　　在公职方面，利国伟博士 1963—1982 年为香港中文大学司库，1982—1997 年为该大学校董会主席，并于 1994 年 11 月 30 日起被该校委为终身校董。利博士亦曾先后任香港李宝椿联合世界书院创校主席及名誉主席。此外，亦曾任江门市五邑大学名誉校长。

　　利国伟博士曾先后任香港行政局议员 7 年，立法局议员 10 年，银行业务咨询委员会委员 14 年，教育委员会主席 7 年，教育统筹委员会主席 5 年。

利国伟博士历年获香港及海外多所大学颁授荣誉博士学位，这些学校分别为香港中文大学（1972）、英国赫尔大学（University of Hull）（1985）、英国伯明翰大学（University of Birmingham）（1989）、香港大学及香港城市理工学院（即现时之香港城市大学）（1990）、香港理工学院（即现时之香港理工大学）及香港浸会学院（即现时之香港浸会大学）（1992）、英国伦敦市政厅大学（London Guildhall University）（1993）、清华大学及香港公开进修学院（即现时之香港公开大学）（1995）。利博士于 1971 年及 1995 年分别获选为英国银行学会及美国塔夫斯大学（Tufts University）院士，并于 1991 年、1993 年、1995 年、1996 年及 2003 年分别获选为英国牛津大学圣休学院（St Hugh's College, Oxford University）、爱丁堡皇家医学院（Royal College of Physicians of Edinburgh）、香港心脏专科学院、香港内科医学院以及英国剑桥李约瑟研究所荣誉院士，并于 1993 年获广州市政府、开平市政府及江门市政府颁授荣誉市民名衔。此外，利博士在南华早报及敦豪国际（香港）有限公司主办之 1994 年香港商业奖中获商业成就奖。利博士于 1995—2003 年受聘为中国老教授协会名誉会长，并于 1997 年荣获香港特别行政区政府颁授"大紫荆勋章"，2006 年获香港证券专业学院授予荣誉会员衔。

多年来，利国伟博士对其原籍之开平地方建设、教育及医疗事务多所资助，对江门市亦捐赠不少。此外，对清华大学、上海市和广州市之其他机构亦分别作出捐献。

利国伟博士于 2013 年 8 月 10 日在香港病逝，享年 95 岁。

BRIEF INTRODUCTION TO THE DONORS TO
HO LEUNG HO LEE FOUNDATION

Brief Biography of Dr. S. H. Ho

Dr. S. H. Ho, the founder of the S. H. Ho Foundation Ltd. which donated to Ho Leung Ho Lee Foundation, born in 1900, was a native of Panyu, Guangdong Province. He cofounded Hang Seng Ngan Ho in Hong Kong in 1933 and later, the Hang Chong Investment Co Ltd. and the Dah Chong Hong Ltd. In 1952, Hang Seng Ngan Ho was incorporated and in 1959, was renamed Hang Seng Bank Ltd. From 1960 until 1983, Dr. Ho served as Chairman of the Bank. In 1983, on the 50th anniversary of the Bank, he became its Honorary Chairman until he passed away.

Dr. Ho was involved in a wide range of businesses, including banking, trade, trusteeship, financing, hotels, insurance, property, shipping and investment.

Dr. Ho was a philanthropist who was committed to promoting charitable causes. In 1970, he founded the S. H. Ho Foundation Ltd to support charitable causes in China and overseas, including regional construction, education, medical services, scientific research and the training of new talent. His contributions to Guangzhou and his homeland were particularly notable. In 1978, he founded the Hang Seng School of Commerce to provide free education to aspiring youths. He also sat as director on many school boards. In 1971, he was conferred the Honorary Degree of Doctor of Social Science by The Chinese University of Hong Kong and in 1983, an Honorary Degree of Doctor of Laws by The University of Hong Kong. In 1990, he became an Honorary Adviser to the Zhongshan University in Guangzhou and was conferred the Honorary Doctorate's degree by that University in 1995. He was made an Honorary Citizen of Guangzhou and of Panyu in 1993.

Dr. S. H. Ho passed away peacefully in Hong Kong on December 4, 1997 at the age of 97.

Brief Biography of Dr. Leung Kau-Kui

The late Dr. Leung Kau-Kui was born in 1903, a native of the City of Shunde in Guangdong Province. Dr. Leung made his mark in the businesses of foreign exchange and trading in Guangzhou, Hong Kong and Macau early in his career. He was a pioneer in leading Chinese businessmen to participate in international trades.

Throughout his career, Dr. Leung held directorships in various companies. He was a director of the Hang Seng Bank, founder of Hang Chong Investment Co. Ltd., and one of the founders and Vice-Chairman of the Dah Chong Hong Ltd. —a leading Chinese-owned trading firm in Hong Kong during the colonial days. He was also a director of Miramar Hotel and Investment Co. Ltd. Furama Hotel Co. Ltd., Milford (International) Investment Co. Ltd., and a director of the Hang Seng School of Commerce.

Dr. Leung travelled regularly and extensively to cities in China and overseas to set up branches for Dah Chong Hong Ltd. as well as to promote and develop businesses for his partners. During the 60's, he helped to restructure the import procedures of rice to Hong Kong from Thailand contributing significantly to the stability and prosperity of Hong Kong.

Benevolent, enterprising and self-effacing, Dr. Leung was a committed contributor to charitable causes. He gave generously to education, medical social services and religious organisations. Among the charitable causes which he had supported were: the Missionary Sisters St. Columban Leung Shek Chee College in memory of his late father, the Po Leung Kuk Leung Chou Shun Kam Primary School in memory of his late mother, The University of Hong Kong's KK Leung Building, The Chinese University of Hong Kong's Leung Kau-Kui Building, Lingnan College's Leung Kau-Kui Building, the Hong Kong Baptist College's (now the Hong Kong Baptist University) School of Continuing Education Leung Kau-Kui Hanyu Institute, K. K. Leung Architectural Building of Beijing's Tsinghua University, Guangzhou's Zhongshan University's Leung Kau-Kui Hall and Leung Lee Sau Yu Library, and The K. K. Leung Brain Research Centre of the Fourth Military Medical University in Xian, China. He also sponsored the Foundation of Zhongshan University Advanced Research Centre and the China Educational Exchange Association's Scholarships for Overseas Studies, both of which were promoted by Professor Yang Chen Ning. He also set up the Book Foundation of Dr. Leung Kau-Kui for Tsinghua University.

In Hong Kong, his other contributions were supports given to: Shun Tak Fraternal Association Leung Kau-Kui College, Shun Tak Fraternal Association Leung Lee Sau Yu Kindergarten (Tuen Mun), Shun Tak Fraternal Association Leung Lee Sau Yu Kindergarten (Shatin), The Endeavourers Leung Lee Sau Yu Memorial Primary School, Hang Seng School of Commerce, the assembly hall of Lok Sin Tong Chan Cho Chak Primary School, Lok Sin Tong Leung Kau-Kui Primary School, Lok Sin Tong Leung Kau-Kui College, Dr. Raymond Huang Foundation of the University of Hong Kong, S. T. F. A. Leung Kau-Kui Clinic of the Medical and Health Department, The Hong Kong Anti-Cancer Society, Queen Mary Hospital's Leung Kau-Kui Diabetes Centre and donations to upgrade the Radiology Library/Museum as well as teaching materials and staff welfare of the Hospital. He also contributed to the Department of Medicine of the University of Hong Kong to do research work on gastric cancer in Shandong Province, China. Dr. Leung also made generous contributions to the religions bodies, which included assisting the Christian Break-through Organization in establishing and donating to the Youth Village-Information Centre, redevelopment foundation of the Buddhist Chi Lin Nunnery, as well as the construction fund of the Buddha Statue at Po Lin Monastery on Lantau Island.

Dr. Leung was generous and zealous in promoting education in science and technology and medical services in his hometown, Shunde. In particular, he was the first donor working to improve the public amenities of his native Beitou Village. Notable projects which he supported in Shunde included multipurpose halls, hospitals, child care and nursery centres, schools, kindergartens, libraries, sports and recreational centres as well as welfare institutions.

Dr. Leung received an Honorary Degree of Doctor of Social Sciences from The Chinese University of Hong Kong in 1987 and became an Honorary Adviser to Guangzhou's Zhongshan University in 1990. In 1992, the government of Shunde named him an Honorary Citizen. He was conferred an Honorary Doctorate by Tsinghua University in 1994. In April 1994, Premier Li Peng praised him for his enthusiastic support of charitable causes and development of education in China.

Dr. Leung had also donated to overseas institutions such as the Oxford University of United Kingdom, the medical school of Aberdeen University in Scotland, and the Yee Hong Geriatric Centre in Toronto, Canada.

Dr. Leung passed away peacefully in Hong Kong on November 10, 1994 at the age of 91.

Brief Biography of Dr. Ho Tim

Dr. Ho Tim joined Hang Seng Bank Ltd (formerly Hang Seng Ngan Ho) in Hong Kong in 1933, was appointed its Director and General Manager in 1953 and Vice-Chairman from 1967 to 1979. In April 2004, he retired from the Board of Hang Seng Bank Limited and was named one of the Bank's Honorary Senior Advisers. Dr. Ho held directorships in a number of listed companies. He was the Chairman of Miramar Hotel and Investment Co. Ltd.; a Director of New World Development Co. Ltd., Sun Hung Kai Properties Ltd., Kumagai Gumi (Hong Kong) Ltd. and King Fook Holdings Ltd.

Dr. Ho was active in public service. He was a Permanent Member of the Board of Trustees of the United College of The Chinese University of Hong Kong, a Council Member of The Chinese University of Hong Kong, a Board Member of the Hang Seng School of Commerce, one of the founders of the Tang Shiu Kin and Ho Tim Charitable Fund, Permanent President of the Ho's Clansmen Association Ltd., Honorary President of the Panyu District Association of Hong Kong and Honorary Permanent President of the Chinese Gold & Silver Exchange Society.

In 1982, The Chinese University of Hong Kong conferred on Dr. Ho the Honorary Degree of Doctor of Social Science; in 1997, an Honorary Doctorate Degree of Business Administration by The City University of Hong Kong; and in 1999, an Honorary Degree of Doctor of Laws by The University of Hong Kong. He was made an Honorary Citizen of Guangzhou, Panyu, Shunde and Foshan in 1988, 1993, 1995 and 2004 respectively by the respective municipal governments. He was appointed a member of the Selection Committee of the First Government of the Hong Kong

Special Administrative Region of the People's Republic of China in November 1996.

Dr. Ho Tim passed away peacefully in Hong Kong on November 6, 2004 at the age of 95.

Brief Biography of Dr. Lee Quo-Wei

Dr. Lee Quo-Wei, the founder of Wei Lun Foundation Limited which donated to Ho Leung Ho Lee Foundation, joined Hang Seng Bank (formerly Hang Seng Ngan Ho) in Hong Kong in 1946. He was appointed a Director of the Bank in December 1959 and elected Vice-Chairman in January 1976. He became Executive Chairman of the Bank from 1983 until February 1996; non-executive Chairman from March 1996 to December 1997. He was appointed Honorary Senior Advisor of the Bank after his appointment as Honorary Chairman from January 1998 to April 2004.

Dr. Lee was well-known for his active involvement in public services. He had been Treasurer of the Chinese University of Hong Kong from 1963 to 1982, the Chairman of the Council of the University from 1982 to 1997 and a Life Member of the Council of the University since 30 November 1994. He was the Founding Chairman and later the Honorary Chairman of the Li Po Chun United World College of Hong Kong as well as the Honorary President of Jiangmen's Wuyi University.

He was a member of the Executive Council in Hong Kong for 7 years and a member of the Legislative Council for 10 years. He was also a member of the Banking Advisory Committee for 14 years, Chairman of the Board of Education for 7 years and Chairman of the Education Commission for 5 years.

Several universities in Hong Kong and overseas had conferred Honorary Doctorate Degrees on Dr Lee, including The Chinese University of Hong Kong in 1972, University of Hull (United Kingdom) in 1985, University of Birmingham (United Kingdom) in 1989, University of Hong Kong in 1990, City Polytechnic of Hong Kong (presently known as the City University of Hong Kong) in 1990, Hong Kong Polytechnic (now the Hong Kong Polytechnic University) and Hong Kong Baptist College (now the Hong Kong Baptist University) in 1972, London Guildhall University (United Kingdom) in 1993, Tsinghua University (Beijing of China) and the Open Learning Institute (now the Open University of Hong Kong) in 1995. Dr Lee was also elected to a fellowship of the Chartered Institute of Bankers, London in 1971 and Tufts University (USA) in 1995 as well as honorary fellowships of St Hugh's College, Oxford University; Royal College of Physicians of Edinburgh; Hong Kong College of Cardiology; and Hong Kong College of Physicians; and Needham Research Institute, Cambridge in 1991, 1993, 1995, 1996 and 2003 respectively. In 1993, he was made an Honorary Citizen of Guangzhou, Kaiping and Jiangmen by the three municipal governments. In the 1994 South China Morning Post/DHL Hong Kong Business Awards, he was awarded Businessman of the year. Dr Lee had been engaged Honorary President of

China Senior Professors Association from 1995 to 2003. In July 1997, he was awarded the Grand Bauhinia Medal by the Hong Kong Special Administrative Region Government. In 2006, he was elected Honorary Fellow for the year by the Hong Kong Securities Institute.

Over the years, Dr Lee had donated generously to his homeland Kaiping, helping to improve infrastructure, education and medical services. He had also made significant contributions to Jiangmen. In addition, he had made donations to Tsinghua University in Beijing and other institutions in the cities of Shanghai and Guangzhou.

Dr Lee Quo-Wei passed away peacefully in Hong Kong on August 10, 2013 at the age of 95.

何梁何利基金信托人简历

朱 丽 兰

朱丽兰，女，1935年8月出生于上海。教授，原科学技术部部长，现任全国人大常委会委员、全国人大教科文卫委员会主任委员。曾就读于上海中西小学，毕业于第三女中。1956年在苏联敖德萨大学高分子物理化学专业学习，1961年获优秀毕业生文凭。回国后在中国科学院化学研究所工作到1986年。长期从事高分子反应动力学、高分子材料剖析及结构表征研究。所承担的高分子材料剖析、性能结构形态关系的研究项目曾分别获国家级重大科研成果奖及应用成果奖，多次在国内外发表学术论文。曾任中国科学院化学研究所研究室主任和所长职务。

1979—1980年，在德国费拉堡大学高分子化学研究所做访问学者。在科研工作中，发展了一种新的染色技术用于制备样品，被称为一种突破，在国内外同行中享有较高声誉。

1986—2001年，曾任国家科委副主任、常务副主任、科学技术部部长。任国家科委、科技部领导期间，组织制定并实施了国家高技术研究发展计划（"863"计划）、国家发展基础研究的攀登计划以及高技术产业化的火炬计划等。倡导和推行新的专家管理机制，提出了一系列适应当代高技术发展规律并结合中国国情的管理理论与政策、方法，出版了专著《当代高技术与发展战略》《发展与挑战》等，并获中国材料研究学会成就奖。由于在推动国际科技合作以及促进中国国家高技术研究发展与产业化方面成绩卓著，1993年获美洲中国工程师协会颁发的杰出服务奖；1998年获德国联邦总统星级大十字勋章。

朱丽兰曾任中国工程院主席团顾问，中国科学院学部主席团顾问，国家科技领导小组成员，中央农村工作领导小组成员，国家信息化领导小组成员，国家奖励委员会主任委员等职。现任中国化学会常务理事会理事，中国对外友好协会常务理事，中国自然辩证法研究会理事，中国材料研究学会理事，并被聘为北京理工大学、国家行政学院、清华大学、中国科学院化学研究所兼职教授。

朱丽兰是国际欧亚科学院院士、亚太材料科学院院士。

高 迎 欣

高迎欣现为中国银行（香港）有限公司（"中银香港"）副董事长兼总裁以及战略及预算委员会委员。曾于 2007 年 5 月至 2015 年 3 月任中银香港执行董事，2015 年 3 月至 2017 年 12 月任中银香港非执行董事和风险委员会委员，自 2018 年 1 月起调任中银香港执行董事。

高迎欣于 1986 年加入中国银行。自 2015 年 5 月至 2018 年 1 月担任中国银行副行长，2016 年 12 月至 2018 年 1 月担任中国银行执行董事，并曾在中国银行集团境内外多家机构担任不同职务，包括中国银行总行公司业务部总经理、中银国际总裁兼首席运营官等。2005 年 2 月至 2015 年 3 月任中银香港副总裁（企业银行）。目前兼任中银香港集团内多项职务，包括中银保险（国际）控股有限公司董事长、中银集团人寿保险有限公司董事长以及中银香港慈善基金董事长。高迎欣现任香港特别行政区多项公职，包括香港中国企业协会会长、香港中资银行业协会会长，外汇基金咨询委员会成员、银行业务咨询委员会成员，香港银行同业结算有限公司主席，香港交易及结算所有限公司风险管理委员会成员，香港特区人力资源规划委员会委员，香港银行学会副会长等。

高迎欣于 1986 年毕业于华东理工大学，获工学硕士学位。

杜 占 元

杜占元，1962 年 7 月生，湖南华容人。1985 年 7 月参加工作。美国马萨诸塞大学植物与土壤科学系植物生理化学专业毕业，研究生学历，哲学博士学位，农艺师。

现任教育部副部长、党组成员。

1978—1982 年，湖南农学院基础课部生理生化专业学生；1982—1985 年，北京农业大学农学系植物生理生化专业硕士研究生；1985—1989 年，国家科委中国农村技术开发中心农业处干部、负责人；1989—1993 年，美国马萨诸塞大学植物与土壤科学系植物生理生化专业博士研究生；1993—1994 年，国家科委综合计划司计划处干部、主任科员；1994—1997 年，国家科委综合计划司计划处副处长（其间：1996—1997 年，在美国杜克大学法学院和商学院进修科技政策与商业管理）；1997—1998 年，国家科委综合计划司计划处处长；1998—2000 年，科技部发展计划司计划协调处、成果处处长；2000—2001 年，科技部发展计划司副司长；2001—2006 年，科技部发展计划司司长（其间：2003—2004 年在中央党校一年制中青年干部培训班学习）；2006—2008 年，科技部农村科技司司长；2008—2010 年，科技部副部长、党组成员；2010 年起任教育部副部长、党组成员。

郑 慧 敏

郑慧敏女士为恒生银行副董事长兼行政总裁、恒生银行（中国）及恒生集团内若干附属公司之董事长、恒生指数顾问委员会主席、澳洲 Treasury Wine Estates Limited（富邑葡萄酒集团）独立非执行董事以及何梁何利基金信托委员会委员。郑慧敏亦为汇丰控股集团总经理及香港上海汇丰银行董事。

郑慧敏于 1999 年加入汇丰集团，曾出任个人理财服务及市场推广业务多个要职。2007 年获委任为香港个人理财服务主管；2009 年为亚太区个人理财服务董事；2010 年为亚太区零售银行及财富管理业务主管。2014 年被委任为汇丰集团环球零售银行业务主管，至 2017 年出任恒生银行副董事长兼行政总裁。

郑慧敏目前亦出任下列机构的职务：
- 香港恒生大学校董会主席
- 香港大学校董
- 香港公益金董事及执行委员会委员
- 江苏省港商投资企业服务协会荣誉会长
- 中国银联国际顾问
- 第十二届江苏省政协委员
- 中国（广东）自由贸易试验区深圳前海蛇口片区暨深圳市前海深港现代服务业合作区咨询委员会委员
- 香港银行学会副会长

其过往职务包括：
- 美国花旗银行市场总监
- 香港按揭证券有限公司董事

• 汇丰集团多间公司董事

郑慧敏毕业于香港大学并取得社会科学学士学位，为 Beta Gamma Sigma 香港大学分会终身荣誉会员。

沈 祖 尧

沈祖尧，1959 年出生。1983 年取得香港大学内外全科医学士学位，1992 年获得加拿大卡尔加里大学生命科学博士学位并于 1997 年获得香港中文大学医学博士学位。沈祖尧为中国工程院院士，英国爱丁堡、格拉斯哥及伦敦皇家内科医学院院士，美国肠胃病学学院院士，澳洲皇家内科医学院院士，香港内科医学院院士及香港医学专科学院院士及香港科学院创会院士。

曾任香港中文大学医学院内科学系讲师、内科及药物治疗学系系主任、医学院副院长，逸夫书院院长等职，并于 2010—2017 年，担任香港中文大学校长。

为肠胃研究权威，研究对象包括肠道出血、幽门螺杆菌、消化性溃疡、乙型肝炎和大肠癌，其研究成果为世界肠胃病的防治带来了重大影响及改变。2004 年，他带领由 15 个亚太国家的专家组成的团队开展了大肠癌筛查研究，为筛查制定了清晰的规范，并在亚太地区推广大肠癌筛查。此外，还积极开展科研，著作甚丰。他在国际期刊发表逾千篇科研文章，写作逾 15 本书籍，并为逾 15 本著名期刊担任评审。

现任香港中文大学莫庆尧医学讲座教授、中大消化疾病研究所主任及消化疾病研究国家重点实验室（香港中文大学）主任。

BRIEF INTRODUCTION TO THE TRUSTEES OF
HO LEUNG HO LEE FOUNDATION

Brief Biography of Professor Zhu Lilan

Professor Zhu Lilan, female, born in Shanghai in August 1935, is the member of the Standing Committee of the National People's Congress, the director of the Science, Education, Culture and Health Commission of the National People's Congress, former minister of the Ministry of Science and Technology of China. From 1956 to 1961, Professor Zhu studied in the Aodesa University of former Soviet Union majoring in macromolecule physical chemistry. After graduated from the university as an excellent student, Professor Zhu worked in the Institute of Chemistry, Chinese Academy of Sciences till 1986. For a long time, Professor Zhu had been conducted the research of macromolecule reactivity dynamics, macromolecule material analysis and structure token. The research project had got the national award of Grand Research Achievements and Award of Application Achievements. During this period, Professor Zhu served as the director of the research department and the director of the Institute of Chemistry, Chinese Academy of Sciences.

From 1979 to 1980, Professor Zhu was a visiting scholar in macromolecule institute in Fleberg University in Germany. In her research, she developed a kind of new dyeing technique for the sample producing, which was considered a break through at that time and won high reputation in the research circle.

From 1986 to 2001, Professor Zhu was appointed vice-minister of the State Science and Technology Commission and minister of the Ministry of Science and Technology of China. During this period, Professor Zhu organized the formulating and implementation of the National High-Tech Development Plan (863 Plan), National Climbing Plan for the Basic Research, and Torch Program for the High-Tech Industrialization. Professor Zhu advocated and implemented the new expertise management mechanism, put forward a series of management theories and policies which suit to the development of high-tech and the situation of China, published her monograph *High-tech*, *Development Strategy in the Contemporary Era*, *Development and Challenge*. Owing to her outstanding contribution to promoting international science and technology cooperation and the development of China's high-tech research and industrialization, Professor Zhu was awarded the Outstanding Service Prize in 1993 by the American Association of Chinese Engineers, and the Germany Federal President Star Great Cross Medal in 1998.

Professor Zhu has been the counselor of Chinese Academy of Engineering Presidium, the counselor of Chinese Academy of Science Presidium, the member of State Science and Education Steering Group, member of Central Rural Work Steering Group, member of State Informationalization Steering Group, director-commissioner of State Award Commission. Professor Zhu is now the member of China Chemistry Society Administrative Council, the administrative member of the board of the Association of China Foreign Friendship Relations, the member of board of China Nat-ural Dialectic Seminar, the director of China Material Seminar. Professor Zhu is also the concurrent Professors of Beijing University of Science and Technology, National Administration College, Tsinghua University, Chemistry Institute of Chinese Academy of Sciences. Professor Zhu is the academician of International Europe and Asia Academy of Science, and the academician of Asian and Pacific Material Academy of Science.

Brief Biography of Mr. Gao Yingxin

Mr. Gao Yingxin is the Vice Chairman, Chief Executive, and a member of the Strategy and Budget Committee of Bank of China (Hong Kong) Limited ("BOCHK"). He was Executive Director of BOCHK from May 2007 to March 2015, as well as Non-executive Director and a member of the Risk Committee of BOCHK from March 2015 to December 2017. He has been re-designated as Executive Director of BOCHK since January 2018.

Mr. Gao joined Bank of China Limited ("BOC") in 1986. He was Executive Vice President of BOC from May 2015 to January 2018, Executive Director of BOC from December 2016 to January 2018. He has held a number of positions in various domestic and overseas institutions of BOC Group, including General Manager of Corporate Banking at BOC Head Office, and President and Chief Operating Officer of BOC International Holdings Limited, among others. Mr Gao was Deputy Chief Executive (Corporate Banking) of BOCHK from February 2005 to March 2015. He also holds other roles with BOCHK Group currently, including Chairman of BOC Insurance (International) Holdings Company Limited, Chairman of BOC Group Life Assurance Company Limited and Chairman of BOCHK Charitable Foundation. Mr Gao holds a number of public offices in Hong Kong. He serves as Chairman of both the Hong Kong Chinese Enterprises Association and the Chinese Banking Association of Hong Kong, and sits on the Exchange Fund Advisory Committee and the Banking Advisory Committee. He is also Chairman of Hong Kong Interbank Clearing Limited, a member of both the Risk Management Committee of Hong Kong Exchanges and Clearing Limited, and Human Resources Planning Commission of the Hong Kong Special Administrative Region, as well as Vice President of The Hong Kong Institute of Bankers, etc.

Mr Gao graduated from the East China University of Science and Technology with a Master's Degree in Engineering in 1986.

Brief Biography of Mr. Du Zhanyuan

Du Zhanyuan, born in July 1962 in Huarong, Hunan Province, started to be employed in July 1985. He graduated from the specialty of plant biology and biochemistry in the Department of Plant and Soil Sciences in the University of Massachusetts in the USA. He has postgraduate education and holds the titles of Ph. D. and agronomist.

He is currently vice minister of education of China and member of the ministry's CPC committee.

1978—1982, student in the specialty of biology and biochemistry of the department of basic courses in the Hunan College of Agriculture;

1982—1985, postgraduate of master program of the specialty of plant biology and biochemistry in the Department of Agriculture in the Beijing Agricultural University;

1985—1989, cadre and person-in-charge of the section of agriculture in the China Rural Technology Department Center of the State Science and Technology Commission;

1989—1993, postgraduate of doctorate program in the specialty of plant biology and biochemistry in the Department of Plant and Soil Sciences of the University of Massachusetts, USA;

1993—1994, cadre and principal staff member of the planning section in the Department of Comprehensive Planning of the State Science and Technology Commission;

1994—1997, deputy chief of the planning section in the Department of Comprehensive Plan-ning of the State Science and Technology Commission (During the period of 1996—1997 in this period, he studied science and technology policies and business administration in the Schools of Law and Business in the Duke University, USA);

1997—1998, chief of the planning section in the Department of Comprehensive Planning of the State Science and Technology Commission;

1998—2000, chief of sections of planning and coordination and of research results in the Department of Development and Planning of the Ministry of Science and Technology;

2000—2001, deputy director of the Department of Development and Planning in the Ministry of Science and Technology;

2001—2006, director of the Department of Development and Planning in the Ministry of Science and Technology (During the period of 2003—2004, he studied in the one-year middle-aged and young cadre training program in the Party School of the CPC Central Committee);

2006—2008, director of the Department of Rural Science and Technology in the Ministry of Science and Technology;

2008—2010, vice minister of science and technology and member of the ministry's CPC committee;

In 2010, vice minister of education and member of the ministry's CPC committee.

Brief Biography of Ms Louisa Cheang

Ms Louisa Cheang is Vice-Chairman and Chief Executive of Hang Seng Bank, and Chairman of Hang Seng Bank (China) and various subsidiaries in Hang Seng Group. She is Chairman of Hang Seng Index Advisory Committee of Hang Seng Indexes, an Independent Non-executive Director of Treasury Wine Estates Limited, Australia and a Member of the Board of Trustees of the Ho Leung Ho Lee Foundation. She is also a Group General Manager of HSBC and a Director of The Hongkong and Shanghai Banking Corporation.

Ms Cheang joined HSBC in 1999, and has worked across a wide range of Personal Financial Services and Marketing positions. She was appointed Head of Personal Financial Services, Hong Kong in 2007; Regional Director of Personal Financial Services, Asia Pacific in 2009; and Regional Head of Retail Banking and Wealth Management, Asia Pacific in 2010. Ms Cheang became Group Head of Retail Banking, HSBC in 2014 prior to her appointment as Vice-Chairman and Chief Executive of Hang Seng Bank in 2017.

Ms Cheang currently also holds the following appointments:
- Chairman of the Board of Governors of The Hang Seng University of Hong Kong
- Member of the Court of The University of Hong Kong
- Board Member and Member of Executive Committee of The Community Chest of Hong Kong
- Honorary President of Jiangsu Service Association for Hong Kong Enterprise Investment
- International Advisor of China Union Pay
- Member of The Twelfth Jiangsu Provincial Committee of the Chinese People's Political Consultative Conference
- Member of the Consulting Committee of Qianhai & Shekou Area of Shenzhen, China (Guangdong) Pilot Free Trade Zone, and Qianhai Shenzhen-Hong Kong Modern Service Industry Cooperation Zone of Shenzhen
- Vice President of The Hong Kong Institute of Bankers

Her previous appointments include:
- Marketing Director of Citibank N.A.
- Director of The Hong Kong Mortgage Corporation Limited
- Director of various subsidiaries in HSBC

Ms Cheang graduated from The University of Hong Kong receiving a Bachelor of Social Sciences degree. She was made a Chapter Honoree of Beta Gamma Sigma of The University of Hong Kong Chapter.

Brief Biography of Joseph Jao-Yiu Sung

Joseph Jao-yiu Sung was born in 1959. He received his medical degree (MB BS) from The University of Hong Kong in 1983, and conferred Ph.D in biomedical sciences by the University of Calgary in 1992 and MD by The Chinese University of Hong Kong (CUHK) in 1997. He is an Academician of the Chinese Academy of Engineering of the People's Republic of China and holds fellowships from the Royal Colleges of Physicians of Edinburgh, Glasgow, London, and Australia, the American College of Gastroenterology, the American Gastroenterological Association, the Hong Kong College of Physicians, the Hong Kong Academy of Medicine and Hong Kong Academy of Sciences (ASHK).

He joined the CUHK's Department of Medicine as Lecturer in 1992, and became Chairman of Department of Medicine and Therapeutics (1999—2010), Associate Dean (Clinical)(2002—2004), Associate Dean (General Affairs) (2004—2009) of the Faculty of Medicine, Head of Shaw College (2009—2010) and the Vice-Chancellor and President of CUHK (2010—2017).

A world-renowned scientist in Gastroenterology and Hepatology, Professor Sung's research interests include intestinal bleeding, Helicobacter Pylori, peptic ulcer, hepatitis B, and colorectal cancer. Professor Sung, together with his research team, has pioneered several projects, the results of which have a major impact on and have changed the practice of gastroenterology worldwide. He led a group of 15 Asia-Pacific countries to launch colorectal cancer screening research in 2004 and laid down clear guidelines and promoted colorectal screenings in the region. A tireless prolific researcher, Professor Sung has published over 1000 scientific articles in international journals, authored more than 15 books, and refereed for more than 15 prestigious journals.

He is currently Mok Hing Yiu Professor of Medicine, Director of Institute of Digestive Disease of CUHK and Director of State Key Laboratory of Digestive Disease (CUHK).

何梁何利基金评选委员会成员简历

评选委员会主任
朱 丽 兰

朱丽兰,女,1935年8月出生,浙江湖州人,教授。现任中国发明协会理事长,澳门特别行政区科技奖励委员会主任。曾任国家科委副主任(1986年)、国家科学技术部部长(1998年),全国人大常委会教科文卫委员会主任委员(2001年),中国工程院主席团顾问,中国科学院学部主席团顾问,国家科教领导小组成员,国家科技奖励委员会主任委员,澳门特别行政区科学技术委员会顾问等职。

在中国科学院化学所从事高分子材料剖析及结构形态表征、反应动力学研究期间,承担了多项国家、国防重点科研攻关项目,曾获国家级、省部级重大科研成果奖及应用成果奖。担任全国人大常委会教科文卫委员会主任委员期间,负责组织完成《科技进步法》《义务教育法》的修订和实施;组织实施一批关系到社会、民生、科技、文化、卫生等重要法律的立法调研与修法任务,为法制建设奠定重要基础。

发表了多篇有关高技术发展现状及对策和管理方面的文章,出版了《当代高技术与发展战略》《发展与挑战》等专著。曾获中国材料研究学会成就奖。由于在推动中国高技术发展及国际科技合作方面成绩显著,获美洲中国工程师协会颁发的杰出服务奖、德国总统颁发的德意志联邦共和国大十字勋章、乌克兰总统二级勋章。

评选委员会副主任
杜 占 元

杜占元,1962年7月出生。先后就读于湖南农业大学、中国农业大学并获得学士学位和硕士学位;1993

年在美国马萨诸塞大学植物与土壤科学系植物生理生化专业获得博士学位。长期在国家科技部、教育部工作，曾任科技部副部长，现任教育部副部长。

在农业生物领域具有很深的科研造诣，在植物生理研究的国际刊物上发表论文若干篇，并曾获得美国东北园艺学会研究生优秀论文奖第一名。对科技管理和技术创新经济方面有深入研究，在科技部任职期间，曾参与国家"十五""十一五"科技发展规划以及科技支撑计划的制订等。在国内科技管理刊物和报纸上发表论文多篇，并合作编著了《中小企业与技术创新》和《中国制造业发展报告》等学术型专著，对国家科技战略和国际学术前沿有全面深刻的了解和把握。近年来，在研究推动高校科技、研究生教育、教育信息化等方面做了大量工作。

任教育部副部长期间，主要分管高校科技、学位管理与研究生教育、教育信息化等工作，对科技管理工作有着深入的研究，在科技工作、高层次人才培养、教育信息化等方面具备丰富的管理经验。

评选委员会副主任
沈 祖 尧

沈祖尧，1959年出生。1983年取得香港大学内外全科医学士学位，1992年获得加拿大卡尔加里大学生命科学博士学位并于1997年获得香港中文大学医学博士学位。沈祖尧为中国工程院院士，英国爱丁堡、格拉斯哥及伦敦皇家内科医学院院士，美国肠胃病学学院院士，澳洲皇家内科医学院院士，香港内科医学院院士及香港医学专科学院院士及香港科学院创会院士。

曾任香港中文大学医学院内科学系讲师、内科及药物治疗学系系主任、医学院副院长，逸夫书院院长等职，并于2010—2017年担任香港中文大学校长。

为肠胃研究权威，研究对象包括肠道出血、幽门螺杆菌、消化性溃疡、乙型肝炎和大肠癌，其研究成果为世界肠胃病的防治带来了重大影响及改变。2004年，他带领由15个亚太国家的专家组成的团队开展了大肠癌筛查研究，为筛查制定了清晰的规范，并在亚太地区推广大肠癌筛查。此外，还积极开展科研，著作甚丰。他在国际期刊发表逾千篇科研文章，写作逾15本书籍，并为逾15本著名期刊担任评审。

现任香港中文大学莫庆尧医学讲座教授、中大消化疾病研究所主任及消化疾病研究国家重点实验室（香港中文大学）主任。

评选委员会秘书长
段 瑞 春

段瑞春，1943年2月出生。上海交通大学工学学士，中国科学院研究生院理学硕士，北京大学法学硕士；20世纪90年代，任国家科委政策法规与体制改革司司长、国务院知识产权办公会议办公室主任，2000—2007年任国务院国有重点大型企业监事会主席。现任中国科学技术法学会会长、中国产学研合作促进会常务副会长。

我国知识产权、科技政策和企业创新领域著名专家，具有自然科学、经济管理和法律科学复合型知识结构。曾主持起草我国《技术合同法》《科学技术进步法》《国家科技奖励条例》等法律法规；参加多项知识产权法律的制定和修改工作；担任中美、中欧、中俄科技合作知识产权谈判首席代表、中国"入世"知识产权谈判主要代表；《国家知识产权战略》总报告评审组组长；何梁何利基金《信托契约》《评选章程》主要制定者之一。

其研究成果于1992年获得国家科委科技进步奖一等奖、1993年获得国家科技进步奖二等奖，均为第一完成人。2004年获我国技术市场建设功勋奖，2008年获中国科技法学杰出贡献奖。撰写出版《国际合作与知识产权》《技术合同原理与实践》《技术创新读本》《科技政策多维思考》等多部著作。

评选委员会委员
马 永 生

马永生，1961年10月生于内蒙古自治区呼和浩特市。石油地质学家、沉积学家。1980年至1990年先后就读于中国地质大学（原武汉地质学院）和中国地质科学院，获博士学位。现任中国石化集团公司副总经理、总地质师。2009年当选中国工程院院士。

长期从事中国油气资源勘探理论研究和生产实践，在中国海相碳酸盐岩油气勘探理论和技术方面取得了多项创新性成果，成功指导发现了普光、元坝等多个大型、特大型天然气田，为国家重大工程"川气东送"提供了扎实的资源基础。他在非常规天然气领域的前瞻性研究，为中国第一个页岩气田——涪陵页岩气田的发现作出了重要贡献。他的科研成果对缓解我国天然气供需矛盾、发展地区经济与环境保护起到了重要的促进作用。

获国家科技进步奖一等奖 2 项；2007 年获何梁何利科学与技术成就奖，同年获第十次李四光地质科学奖；2013 年被评为国家首批"万人计划"杰出人才。由于他在石油工业界的杰出成果，2017 年国际小行星中心将国际编号为 210292 号小行星命名为"马永生星"。

评选委员会委员
王 小 凡

王小凡，著名癌症生物学家。1955 年出生于乌鲁木齐市，1982 年毕业于武汉大学生物化学专业，同年考入中国科学院遗传研究所，并在当年举办的首届"中美生物化学联合招生项目"（CUSBEA）中取得第一名的成绩赴美留学。1986 年获加州大学洛杉矶分校博士学位，之后在麻省理工学院师从癌症生物学家 Robert A. Weinberg 从事博士后研究。1992 年被聘为杜克大学药理学和肿瘤生物学系助理教授，成为最早在杜克大学执教的华人教授之一。1998 年成为终身教授，2003 年晋升为正教授。现任杜克大学医学中心药理学和肿瘤生物学 Donald and Elizabeth Cooke 终身讲席教授。

王小凡在细胞信号转导、DNA 损伤与修复、癌症转移分子机制、肿瘤微环境等多个领域均有重要学术贡献，尤其在 TGF-β 相关研究领域取得了令人瞩目的成绩。先后发表了 100 多篇学术论文，其中在 *Cell*、*Nature*、*Science*、*Cancer Cell*、*Nature Cell Biology* 等高水平杂志上发表论文 20 余篇。王小凡长期坚持通过多种渠道为中国的教育科技事业建言献策，推动、促成了一系列改善中国教育科研环境的政策制度，目前担任中国国务院侨办海外专家咨询委员会委员。

评选委员会委员
朱 道 本

朱道本，1942年8月出生于上海，原籍浙江杭州。有机化学、物理化学家，中国科学院化学研究所研究员，1997年10月当选为中国科学院院士。

1965年毕业于华东化工学院，1968年华东化工学院有机系研究生学习后到中国科学院化学研究所工作。曾任中国科学院化学研究所副所长、所长、中国化学会理事长、国家自然科学基金会副主任。现任中国科学院学术委员会副主任、中国科学院有机固体重点实验室主任等职。

20世纪70年代开始有机固体领域的研究，在有机晶体的电导、铁磁性、分子薄膜与器件、C60及其衍生物的结构性能等研究都引起了国际同行的关注。发表论文500余篇，研究成果曾获国家自然科学奖二等奖4项，中国科学院自然科学奖二等奖2项。

评选委员会委员
杨 祖 佑

杨祖佑，1940年出生。获美国康奈尔大学博士学位。先后任普度大学航空宇宙工程系主任，工学院院长；曾兼任美国国家科学基金会智能制造工程中心共同主任，同时任阿姆斯特朗（首位登陆月球者）杰出宇航讲座教授。现任美国圣塔芭芭拉加州大学校长（1994年始任），美国国家工程院院士，美国航天、机械学会Fellow，中国工程院海外院士。兼任美、中、印、日、加"三十米望远镜"计划（简称"TMT"计划）主席，太平洋滨42所大学联盟主席（包括北大、清华、复旦、科大、浙大、南京），美国总统科学奖章评委，科维理科学基金会理事，曾任美国大学联盟（AAU，包括62所顶尖研究型大学）主席，芬兰千禧科技奖评委。共获7所大学荣誉博士。

长期致力于教学及科研。从事宇航结构、颤振、控制转型至地震、制造、材料（LED）及生物工程等方面的研究，亲任博士论文主席指导60篇，发表期刊论文200余篇，学术会议论文 200 余篇，有限元教科书 1 本（被 40 余所美国大学采用，有中文、日文版）。

曾获 2008 年美国航天学会结构、振动、材料奖（SDM Award），美国工程教育学会最高李梅金质奖章以及十余次最佳教学奖。

评选委员会委员
杨 纲 凯

杨纲凯，1948 年 7 月生于上海市。自 1973 年起任职香港中文大学，曾任物理系主任、理学院院长、研究院院长、副校长。现任香港中文大学敬文书院院长、物理系教授，香港特别行政区教育统筹委员会委员、课程发展议会主席。曾任香港特别行政区大学教育资助委员会委员及香港研究资助局主席，亚太物理联会秘书长、副会长。1965—1972 年就读于美国加州理工学院，主修物理，1969 年获学士学位，1972 年获博士学位。1972—1973 年在美国普林斯顿大学从事教学及研究。

长期从事理论物理学研究，包括基本粒子、场论、高能唯象、耗散系统及其本征态展开，对光学、引力波等开放系统的应用作出贡献，其主要研究成果载于有关国际杂志，包括 Microscopic derivation of the Helmholtz force density，Phys Rev Lett 47，77；Late time tail of wave propagation on curved spacetime，Phys Rev Lett 74，2414；Quasinormal mode expansion for linearized waves in gravitational systems，Phys Rev Lett 74，4588；Quasinormal modes of dirty black holes，Phys Rev Lett 78，289 等。1999 年被选为美国物理学会院士，2004 年被选为国际欧亚科学院院士。

评选委员会委员
张 立 同

张立同，女，1938 年 4 月出生于重庆，著名航空航天材料专家。1961 年毕业于西北工业大学。1989—

1991 年在美国 NASA 空间结构材料商业发展中心作高级访问学者。现任西北工业大学教授、博士生导师、超高温结构复合材料技术国家重点实验室学术委员会副主任。1995 年当选中国工程院院士。

致力于航空航天材料及其制造技术研究，在薄壁复杂高温合金和铝合金铸件的无余量熔模精密铸造技术及其理论基础研究中取得丰硕成果。揭示了叶片变形规律、粗糙度形成规律和陶瓷型壳中温和高温软化变形机理。创新发展了高温合金无余量熔模铸造技术、铝合金石膏型熔模铸造技术、高温合金熔模铸造用中温和高温抗蠕变陶瓷型壳材料、高温合金泡沫陶瓷过滤净化材料技术等。相关成果成功用于航空发动机和飞机构件生产中。

突破大型空间站用陶瓷基复合材料技术，建立了具有自主知识产权的制造工艺、制造设备与材料环境性能考核三个技术平台，打破了国际技术封锁。

获国家技术发明奖一等奖 1 项，国家科技进步奖一、二、三等奖 4 项，国家级教学成果奖二等奖 1 项，获授权国家发明专利 64 项。

评选委员会委员
张 恭 庆

张恭庆，1936 年 5 月 29 日出生于上海。1959 年毕业于北京大学数学系，毕业后留校工作至今。1978 年作为我国改革开放后第一批赴美访问学者赴美进修。现为北京大学教授、中国科学院院士、发展中国家（第三世界）科学院院士、高校数学研究与人才培养中心主任，还担任多个国际核心刊物的编委。

著名数学家。发展无穷维 Morse 理论为临界点理论的统一框架，并首次将其应用于偏微分方程的多解问题，其著作成为该领域的基本文献。发展了集值映射的拓扑度理论以及不可微泛函的临界点理论，使之成为研究数学物理方程以及非光滑力学中的一类自由边界问题的有效方法。

曾荣获全国科技大会奖（1978）、国家自然科学奖三等奖（1982）、国家自然科学奖二等奖（1987）、陈省身数学奖（1986）、有突出贡献的中青年科学家（1984）、第三世界科学院数学奖（1993）、华罗庚数学奖（2009）、北京大学国华奖、方正教学特等奖（2011）等。

评选委员会委员
陈 佳 洱

陈佳洱，1934 年 10 月 1 日出生于上海。中国科学院院士、第三世界科学院院士。现任北京大学物理学教授，国家重点基础研究计划（"973"计划）专家顾问组副组长，国际科联中国协调委员会副主席等职。

曾任北京大学校长和研究生院院长、国家自然科学基金委员会主任、中国科学院数理学部主任和中科院主席团成员以及中科院研究生院物理科学学院院长等职。

长期致力于低能粒子加速器及其应用的教学与科研工作，善于把握学科前沿发展与国家需求的结合，前瞻性地部署物理研究与人才培养，开拓发展我国的射频超导加速器、超灵敏加速器质谱计、射频四极场加速器、高压静电加速器等，是我国低能粒子加速器的奠基者和领头人之一。

陈佳洱长期在北京大学和国家自然科学基金委等单位担任领导工作，并曾担任国家中长期科技规划领导小组成员等职，为我国科学技术中长期规划的制订与相关的科教事业的发展作出了重要贡献。

评选委员会委员
郝 吉 明

郝吉明，1946 年 8 月出生于山东省，著名环境工程专家。1970 年毕业于清华大学，1981 年获清华大学硕士学位，1984 年获美国辛辛那提大学博士学位。现任清华大学教授、博士生导师、教学委员会副主任、环境科学与工程研究院院长，兼任国家环境咨询委员会委员、中国环境与发展国际合作委员会委员。2005 年当选中国工程院院士，2018 年当选美国国家工程院外籍院士。

致力于中国空气污染控制研究 40 余年，主要研究领域为能源与环境、大气污染控制工程。主持全国酸沉降控制规划与对策研究，划定酸雨和二氧化硫控制区，被国务院采纳实施，为确定我国酸雨防治对策起到主导作用。建立了城市机动车污染控制规划方法，推动了我国机动车污染控制进程。深入开展大气复合污染特征、成因及控制策略研究，发展了特大城市空气质量改善的理论与技术方法，推动我国区域性大气复合污染的联防联控。长期开展大气污染控制关键技术研究，在燃煤烟气除尘脱硫脱硝、机动车污染控制等领域作出贡献。

获国家科技进步奖一等奖 1 项、二等奖 2 项，国家自然科学二等奖和国家技术发明二等奖各 1 项，国家教学成果一等奖 2 项。2006 年获国家教学名师称号，获 2015 年度哈根－斯密特清洁空气奖及 2016 年 IBM 全球杰出学者奖。

评选委员会委员
钱 绍 钧

钱绍钧，1934 年出生于浙江平湖。1951 年考入清华大学物理系，后在北京俄语专科学校和北京大学物理系、物理研究室（现技术物理系）学习。现任原总装备部科技委顾问，研究员，中国工程院院士。曾任核试验基地副司令员、司令员，国防科工委科技委常任委员。

长期从事核试验放射化学诊断工作，参与了由原子弹到氢弹、由大气层到地下的一系列核试验，建立完善多项诊断方法和技术，显著提升测量精度。多次参加国防科技和武器装备发展战略研究，参与组织国家中长期科学技术发展规划专题研究。指导开展国防应用基础研究，努力促进与国家基础研究的协调链接。指导军用核技术发展，长期跟踪研究国际态势及主要国家政策演变，参与军备控制研究和"全面禁止核试验条约"谈判。

出版译著 1 部，主编专著 2 部，撰写科技论文和重要科技档案多篇，获国家科技进步奖特等奖、二等奖各 1 项，国家发明奖二等奖、三等奖各 1 项，军队科技进步奖多项。

评选委员会委员
倪　军

　　倪军，1961 年 11 月出生于青海，著名制造科学专家。1982 年获上海交通大学学士学位。1984 年和 1987 年分别获得美国威斯康星大学硕士和博士学位。1987 年起在美国密歇根大学任教至今。现为美国密歇根大学吴贤铭制造科学冠名教授及机械工程系终身教授；上海交通大学校长特聘顾问、交大密西根学院荣誉院长，并同时担任美国密西根大学吴贤铭制造研究中心主任及美国国家科学基金会产学研"智能维护系统中心"共同主任。倪军教授目前担任世界经济论坛（达沃斯论坛）未来制造委员会主席。

　　曾担任美国国家科学基金会"可重组制造系统中心"执行主任及美国国家科学基金会产学研"制造质量测量与控制中心"主任。倪军教授主要从事先进制造科学领域中智能制造技术的研究，包括基于工业大数据分析和人工智能技术在精密质量控制、制造过程效率优化、重大装备的可靠性和健康预测管理、智能维护系统等研究。他的研究成果在众多工业领域得到成功应用。

　　倪军教授获得 40 多项学术成就奖。2013 年获中华人民共和国国际科技合作奖；1994 年获克林顿颁发的美国总统教授奖；2013 年获国际制造工程师协会金奖，是该奖 1955 年设立之后首位获此殊荣的华人学者；2009 年获美国机械工程学会 William T. Ennor 最高制造技术奖；2002 年当选为美国制造工程师学会 FELLOW；2004 年当选为美国机械工程学会 FELLOW；1991 年获国际制造工程师学会杰出制造工程师奖。

评选委员会委员
高　文

　　高文，1956 年出生。1988 年获哈尔滨工业大学计算机应用博士学位，1991 年获日本东京大学电子学博士学位。北京大学信息学院教授，博导。2011 年当选中国工程院院士。

　　主要研究领域为数字媒体技术。长期以来从事计算机视觉、模式识别与图像处理、多媒体数据压缩、多模式接口以及虚拟现实等的研究，在视频编码与分析、手语识别与合成、人脸识别、数字图书馆等领域有精深造诣。主持"973"计划（首席）、"863"计划、国家自然科学基金等国家级项目二十余项；担任数字音视频编解码技术标准（AVS）工作组组长，为视频编码国家标准与国际标准的创立和推广作出主要贡献。曾任 IEEE ICME 2007 和 ACM MM 2009 旗舰会议主席。

有科学著作 5 部，在国际期刊上发表论文百余篇。作为第一完成人，在视频编码与系统等研究领域成果曾 5 次获得国家科技进步奖二等奖，1 次获国家技术发明奖二等奖。

评选委员会委员
桑 国 卫

桑国卫，1941 年 11 月出生，浙江湖州人。临床药理学家，中国工程院院士。中国药学会理事长，"十一五""十二五""十三五"国家"重大新药创制"重大专项技术总师，工信部"医药工业'十三五'发展规划"专家咨询委员会主任，中国药品生物制品检定所资深研究员，上海中医药大学名誉校长。曾任十一届全国人大常委会副委员长、农工民主党中央主席。

对长效注射与口服甾体避孕药及抗孕激素的药代动力学、种族差异及临床药理学做了系统研究，取得多项重大成果。近年来，在新药的安全性评价、质量控制和临床试验等方面进行了卓有成效的工作，为加强我国 GLP、GCP 平台建设作出了重要贡献。

获全国科技大会奖 2 项，国家科学技术进步奖二等奖 3 项，部委级科技进步奖一等奖 1 项、二等奖 4 项。1997 年获何梁何利科学与技术进步奖（医学药学奖）。2008 年获吴阶平—保罗·杨森奖特殊贡献奖。2014 年获国际药学联合会药学科学终身成就奖。

评选委员会委员
曹 雪 涛

曹雪涛，1964年7月出生，山东济南人。1990年毕业于第二军医大学。现为中国医学科学院院长、中国工程院院士、医学免疫学国家重点实验室主任，兼任中国免疫学会理事长、全球慢性疾病防控联盟主席、亚洲大洋洲免疫学会联盟主席等。担任 *Cell* 等杂志编委。

主要从事天然免疫识别及其免疫调节的基础研究、肿瘤免疫治疗应用性研究。发现了具有重要免疫调控功能的树突状细胞新型亚群；独立发现了22种免疫相关分子；系统研究了天然免疫识别与干扰素产生调控的新机制；探讨了表观分子在炎症与肿瘤发生发展中的作用；建立了肿瘤免疫治疗新途径并开展了临床试验。

以第一完成人获国家自然科学奖二等奖1项，中华医学科技奖一等奖1项，军队科技进步奖一等奖1项，上海市自然科学奖一等奖3项，已获得国家发明专利16项，获得2个国家Ⅱ类新药证书。研究成果入选2011年中国十大科技进展。获得光华工程奖、长江学者成就奖、中国青年科学家奖、中国十大杰出青年等。以通讯作者发表SCI收录论文220余篇，包括 *Cell*、*Science*、*Nature Immunology*、*Cancer Cell*、*Immunity* 等。论文被SCI他引5600多次；编写和共同主编专著8部；培养的博士生中有11名获得全国百篇优秀博士论文。

评选委员会委员
程　　序

程序，1944年出生，江苏无锡人。1965年毕业于北京农业大学（现中国农业大学）农学系，后入中国农业科学院作物育种栽培研究所从事研究工作。现为中国农业大学教授，博导。曾就职于北京市农科院、农业部等单位。主要研究方向为可持续农业与农村发展、农业生态与生态农业以及生物能源等。

曾主持农业现代化规律和实验基地建设（实验基

地：北京市房山区窦店村）以及生态农业两个研究项目。1985 年率先引进农业可持续发展的理论，此后开始研究中国条件下农业可持续发展的途径。重点放在农牧交错生态脆弱带的生态恢复途径，以及探索可持续的集约化农业模式的研究两个方面。

作为第一完成人，先后被授予北京市科技进步奖一等奖及国家星火科技奖（等同科技进步奖）一等奖。累计获省部级科技进步奖二、三等奖 7 项，1988 年被批准为国家级有突出贡献的中青年专家。

著有《可持续农业导论》和《中国可持续发展总纲第 13 卷：中国农业与可持续发展》两部专著。

评选委员会委员
曾 庆 存

曾庆存，1935 年 5 月出生于广东省阳江市（原阳江县）。1956 年毕业于北京大学物理系。1961 年在苏联科学院应用地球物理研究所获副博士（现称博士即 Ph. D.）学位。回国后先后在中国科学院地球物理研究所和大气物理研究所工作。1980 年当选中国科学院院士。现为中国科学院大气物理研究所研究员。

主要研究领域为大气科学和地球流体力学。致力于大气环流和地球流体动力学基础理论和数值模式及模拟、地球系统动力学模式、数值天气预报和气候预测理论、气候动力学和季风理论、大气边界层动力学、卫星遥感理论方法、应用数学和计算数学以及自然控制论等的研究工作。在国际上最早提出半隐式差分法和平方守恒格式，最早成功将原始方程应用于实际数值天气预告（1961）和研制成大气海洋耦合模式并用作跨季度气候预测（1990，1994），提出系统的卫星大气遥感理论（1974）以及自然控制论理论方法（1995）。

曾获国家自然科学奖二等奖 2 项和三等奖 1 项，中国科学院自然科学奖一等奖 6 项和杰出贡献奖 1 项。出版专著包括《大气红外遥测原理》《数值天气预报的数学物理基础》《短期数值气候预测原理》《千里黄云——东亚沙尘暴研究》等。发表学术文章约百篇。

BRIEF INTRODUCTION TO THE MEMBERS OF THE SELECTION BOARD OF HO LEUNG HO LEE FOUNDATION

Zhu Lilan, Director of the Selection Board

Zhu Lilan, female, was born in August 1935 and is of the origin of Huzhou, Zhejiang Province. At present, she is the Chairman of the China Association of Inventions and the Chairman of the Committee of Science and Technology Awards of Macau Special Administrative Region. She was the vice-minister of the State Science and Technology Commission (1986), the Minister of the Ministry of Science and Technology (1998), the Director of the Education, Science, Culture and Public Health Committee of the National People's Congress (2001), the counselor of Chinese Academy of Engineering Presidium, the Advisor of the Presidential Committee of CAS Academic Board, the Member of the State Leading Group of Science, Technology and Education, the Director of the State Committee of Science and Technology Awards and the Advisor of the Macao Science and Technology Council.

When analyzing polymer materials and researching morphological structure and reaction dynamics in the Institute of Chemistry of the Chinese Academy of Sciences, Zhu Lilan undertook several national and national defense key science and technological projects and was granted the statelevel and provincelevel significant scientific and technological result awards and application result awards. When being the Director of the Education, Science, Culture and Public Health Committee of the National People's Congress, she organized the amendments to and implementation of the Science and Technology Progress Law and the Compulsory Education Law; and organized a series of investigations for making the laws and amending the important laws concerning such matters as society, people's life, science and technology, culture and health, which has provided an important basis for legal construction.

Zhu Lilan has published several articles and books on the status quo of hi-tech development and the corresponding strategies and management measures, including *Modern Hi-tech. Development Strategy in the Contemporary Era* and *Development and Challenge*. She was granted the Achievement Award by the Chinese Materials Research Society. Thanks to her significant contribution to the development of China's hi-tech development and international scientific and technological cooperation, Zhu Lilan obtained the Distinguished Service Award granted by the Chinese Institute of Engineers, USA, the Grand Cross Medal of the Federal Republic of Germany granted by German President and the Medal No. 2 of Ukraine President.

Du Zhanyuan, Deputy Director of the Selection Board

Du Zhanyuan was born in July 1962. He got his bachelor's degree from Hunan Agricultural University and master's degree from China Agricultural University. He got his doctoral degree on Plant Physiology & Biochemistry from the Plant & Soil Science Department of University of Massachusetts in the US in 1993. He worked for the Ministry of Science and Technology and the Ministry of Education of the People's Republic of China and served as Deputy Minister of the Ministry of Science and Technology. He is now Deputy Minister of the Ministry of Education.

He is well established in the field of agriculture & biology and has published several essays on plant physiology in international science journals. He won the top award during an essay competition for postgraduates of the Northeast Horticultural Society in the U.S. He has conducted indepth study of science and technology management and technological innovation economy. During his tenure at the Ministry of Science and Technology, he participated in the formulation of the 10th and 11th Scientific and Technological Development Plans and Technological Cornerstone Plans. He has also published numerous essays in Chinese magazines, journals and newspapers on the subject of science management and coauthored academic monographs such as *Small and Medium-Sized Enterprises and Technological Innovation and China Development Report on Manufacturing Industry.* He has full knowledge and deep understanding of China's national science and technology strategies and the cutting edge development of international academia. In recent years, he has been dedicated himself to promoting technology in higher education institutions, development of postgraduate education and application of information technology in education.

As Deputy Minister of the Ministry of Education, his responsibilities cover science and technology in higher education institutions, degree management and postgraduate education and application of information technology in education. He has conducted in-depth research programs on science and technology management with rich managerial experience in the areas of science and technology, cultivation of high-caliber talent and application of information technology in education.

Joseph Jao-Yiu Sung, Vice Director of the Selection Board

Joseph Jao-yiu Sung was born in 1959. He received his medical degree (MB BS) from The University of Hong Kong in 1983, and conferred PhD in biomedical sciences by the University of Calgary in 1992 and MD by The Chinese University of Hong Kong (CUHK) in 1997. He is an Academician of the Chinese Academy of Engineering of the People's Republic of China and holds fellowships from the Royal Colleges of Physicians of Edinburgh, Glasgow, London, and Australia, the American College of Gastroenterology, the American Gastroenterological Association, the Hong Kong College of Physicians, the Hong Kong Academy of Medicine and Hong Kong Academy of Sciences (ASHK).

He joined the CUHK's Department of Medicine as Lecturer in 1992, and became Chairman of Department of Medicine and Therapeutics (1999—2010), Associate Dean (Clinical)(2002—2004), Associate Dean (General Affairs) (2004—2009) of the Faculty of Medicine, Head of Shaw College (2009—2010) and the Vice-Chancellor and President of CUHK (2010—2017).

A world-renowned scientist in Gastroenterology and Hepatology, Professor Sung's research interests include intestinal bleeding, Helicobacter Pylori, peptic ulcer, hepatitis B, and colorectal cancer. Professor Sung, together with his research team, has pioneered several projects, the results of which have a major impact on and have changed the practice of gastroenterology worldwide. He led a group of 15 Asia-Pacific countries to launch colorectal cancer screening research in 2004 and laid down clear guidelines and promoted colorectal screenings in the region. A tireless prolific researcher, Professor Sung has published over 1000 scientific articles in international journals, authored more than 15 books, and refereed for more than 15 prestigious journals.

He is currently Mok Hing Yiu Professor of Medicine, Director of Institute of Digestive Disease of CUHK and Director of State Key Laboratory of Digestive Disease (CUHK).

Duan Ruichun, Secretary-General of the Selection Board

Duan Ruichun, born in February 1943, is a bachelor of engineer from Shanghai Jiaotong University, a master of science from Graduate University of Chinese Academy of Science and a master of law from Peking University. In the 1990s, he was the Director of the Policy, Law and System Reform Department of the State Science and Technology Commission and the Director of the Intellectual Property Working Meeting Office of the State Council. From 2000 to 2007, he was the Chairman of the Board of Supervisors for Key Large State-Owned Enterprises of the State Council. At present, Duan Ruichun is the Chairman of the China Association for Science and Technology and the permanent vice chairman of the China Association for Promotion of Cooperation among Industries, Universities & Research Institutes.

As a famous expert in China's intellectual property rights, scientific and technological policies and enterprise innovation, Duan Ruichun possesses interdisciplinary knowledge in natural science, economic management and legal science. He has led the drafting of many Chinese laws and regulations such as the Technology Contract Law, the Scientific and Technological Progress Law and the Regulation on National Awards for Science and Technology; he has participated in drafting of and amendments to many laws on intellectual property rights; he was the chief representative of the Intellectual Property Negotiations for Scientific and Technological Cooperation between China and the United States and the main representative of intellectual property negotiations in the process of China's entry into WTO; he was the Leader of the Review Team of the general report of the National IP Strategy; and he was one of the main person formulating the Trust Deed and the Selection Articles of the Ho Leung Ho Lee Foundation.

Due to his research results, Duan Ruichun was granted the first prize of the Science and Technology Progress Award by the State Science and Technology Commission in 1992 and granted the second prize of the Science and Technology Progress Award in 1993. He was granted the recognition award of China's technology market in 2004 and the significant contribution award of the China Law Association on Science and Technology in 2008. He has written and published several books such as *International Cooperation and Intellectual Property Rights*, *Principles and Practice of Technology Contracts*, *Guidelines on Technology Innovation* and *Multi-Dimensional Thinking of Scientific and Technological Policies*.

Ma Yongsheng, Member of the Selection Board

Ma Yongsheng, a petroleum geologist and sedimentologist, was born in Hohhot City of Inner Mongolia in October 1961. He obtained his bachelor's and master's degrees from China University of Geosciences (previously known as Wuhan College of Geology) and received his Ph.D. from Chinese Academy of Geological Sciences in 1990. He is now the Vice President and Chief Geologist of China Petroleum & Chemical Corporation (Sinopec Group). He has been elected as academician of Chinese Academy of Engineering in 2009.

Over the past few decades, he devoted his career to the research and application of the petroleum and natural gas exploration theory. He has made great contributions to the marine carbonates hydrocarbon exploration theory with a number of leading technological and theoretical achievements. For instance, he led the successful discovery of several giant natural gas reservoirs in China, such as the Puguang and Yuanba gas fields, establishing solid foundations for the Sichuan-to-East China Gas Transmission Project. His pioneering research in unconventional natural gas contributed significantly to the discovery of Fuling shale gas field in Chongqing, China's first large-scale shale gas field. His research accomplishments have also remarkably facilitated the mitigation of natural gas supply-demand imbalance, as well as the promotion of regional economy and environmental protection in China.

Ma has won the 1st Prize of the National Science & Technology Progress Award twice. In 2007, he won the Scientific & Technological Achievements Award granted by the Ho Leung Ho Lee Foundation. In the same year, he won Li Siguang Geoscience Prize for the 10th time. In 2013, he was selected as one of China's first six outstanding scientists supported by the National Ten-Thousand Talents Program. For his distinguished achievement in the petroleum industry, the Minor

Planet Center named No. 210292 asteroid officially after him as "Ma Yongsheng Planet" in 2017.

Wang Xiaofan, Member of the Selection Board

Wang Xiaofan is a renowned cancer biologist. He was born in Urumqi in 1955.

In 1982, he graduated from Wuhan University after completing an undergraduate program in biological chemistry, and was admitted into the Institute of Genetics, the Chinese Academy of Sciences.

In the same year, he ranked the highest in the first China–United States Biochemistry Examination and Application (CUSBEA) and went to the U.S. to pursue further studies.

In 1986, he obtained the doctoral degree from the University of California, Los Angeles (UCLA) . Later he engaged in post–doctoral study by following Robert A. Weinberg, an eminent cancer biologist, at Massachusetts Institute of Technology (MIT) .

In 1992, he was engaged as an assistant professor by the Department of Pharmacology and Tumor Biology at Duke University, becoming one of the earliest Chinese professors who taught at Duke University.

He became a tenure–track professor in 1998 and was promoted to be a full professor in 2003.

He is the Donald and Elizabeth Cooke Professor of Cancer Research at the Department of Pharmacology and Cancer Biology, School of Medicine, Duke University.

Professor Wang Xiaofan has made important academic contributions in many fields including cell signal transduction, repair of DNA damage, molecular mechanism of cancer metastasis and tumor microenvironment. In particular, he has made eye–catching achievements in the field related to TGF–β. He has published more than 100 academic papers, of which more than 20 were published in high–level academic periodicals such as *Cell, Nature, Science, Cancer Cell* and *Nature Cell Biology*.

Over a long period of time, professor Wang Xiaofan has insisted on offering advice and putting forward suggestions on education and science and technology undertakings in China through various channels. He has promoted or brought about a series of policies and systems for improving the environment of education and scientific research in China. He currently serves as a member of the Overseas Expert Consultant Committee of Overseas Chinese Affairs Office of the State Council.

Zhu Daoben, Member of the Selection Board

Zhu Daoben, born in Shanghai in August 1942, came from Hangzhou, Zhejiang Province. As an organic and physical chemist, he is a researcher from the Institute of Chemistry of the Chinese Academy of Sciences. In October 1997, He was elected as an academician of the Chinese Academy of Sciences.

He graduated from East China Institute of Chemical Technology in 1965 and completed his postgraduate program at the Organic Chemistry Department of the Institute in 1968. Then he began his career at the Institute of Chemistry of the Chinese Academy of Sciences. Throughout his career, he has served as Deputy Director and Director of the Institute of Chemistry, Director-general of Chinese Chemical Society and Deputy Director of the National Natural Science Foundation. Currently, he is Vice Director of the Academic Committee of the Chinese Academy of Sciences and Director of the Key Laboratory of Organic Solids.

Since 1970s, Zhu has been involved in the research of organic solids and attracted international attention in the fields of conductance of organic crystal, ferromagnetism, molecular membranes and devices, structure performance of C60 and its derivatives. He has published over 500 papers. His research findings have won four National Natural Science Awards (Grade II) and two Natural Science Awards (Grade II) of the Chinese Academy of Sciences.

Henry T. Yang, Member of the Selection Board

Henry T. Yang was born in 1940. He obtained a Ph.D. from Cornell University. He has served as Dean of the Aerospace Engineering Department and Head of the Engineering College of Purdue University. He used to be a co-director of the Smart Manufacturing Engineering center of the National Science Foundation (U. S.) and an outstanding professor of Armstrong (the first Moon lander) Astronautics Lectures. Currently, he is President of University of California Santa Barbara (since 1994), an academician of American Academy of Engineering, a fellow of both American Institute of Aeronautics and Astronautics and American Society of Mechanical Engineers, an overseas academician of Chinese Academy of Engineering and an academician of the Taiwan Academia Sinica. He is the chairman of the Thirty-metre Telescope Program (TMT Program) jointly sponsored by the United States, China, India, Japan and Canada. He is the chairman of the Association of Pacific Rim 42 Universities (including Peking University, Tsinghua University, Fudan University, University of Science and Technology of China, Zhejiang University and Nanjing University), a member of the Selection Board of the United States Presidential Medal of Science and a member of council of the Kavli Foundation. He used to be the Chairman of Association of American Universities (AAU) that consists of 62 top universities and a member of the Selection Board of Finnish Millennium Technology Grand Prize. He has been conferred seven honorary doctoral degrees.

He has been involved in teaching and research in aerospace structure, oscillation, control transition to earthquake, manufacturing, material (LED) and biological engineering. He has served as doctoral supervisor for sixty dissertations. He has published over 200 papers in journals, over 200 papers for academic conferences and one textbook on finite element (used by over forty American universities and translated into Chinese and Japanese).

He won the SDM Award granted by the American Institute of Aeronautics and Astronautics in 2008. He won Benjamin Garver Lamme Gold Metal, the highest one granted by the American Society for Engineering Education, and over ten excellent awards for education.

Kenneth Young, Member of the Selection Board

Born in July 1948 in Shanghai, Kenneth Young has been working at The Chinese University of Hong Kong (CUHK) since 1973, and has held the position of Chairman of the Department of Physics, Dean of the Faculty of Science, Dean of the Graduate School and Pro-Vice-Chancellor/Vice-President. At present, Kenneth Young is Master of the CW Chu College and professor of physics at CUHK. He is also a member of the Education Commission (EC) and the Chairman of the Curriculum Development Council of the Hong Kong SAR. He was a member of the Hong Kong University Grants Committee and Chairman its Research Grants Council. He was the Secretary and later Vice-President of the Association of Asia Pacific Physical Societies. Kenneth Young studied at the California Institute of Technology from 1965 to 1972 and obtained the BS in physics in 1969 and the Ph.D. in physics and mathematics in 1972. He was engaged in teaching and research at Princeton University from 1972 to 1973.

Kenneth Young has been engaged in physics research for a long time, on topics including elementary particles, field theory, high energy phenomenology, dissipation system and their eigenfunctions expansion, with applications to such open systems as optics and gravitational waves. Some of his publications include "Microscopic derivation of the Helmholtz force density", Phys Rev Lett 47, 77; "Late time tail of wave propagation on curved spacetime", Phys Rev Lett 74, 2414; "Quasinormal mode expansion for linearized waves in gravitational systems", Phys Rev Lett 74, 4588; "Quasinormal modes of dirty black holes", Phys Rev Lett 78, 289. Kenneth Young was elected as a Fellow of the American Physical Society in 1999 and an academician of International Eurasian Academy of Science in 2004.

Zhang Litong, Member of the Selection Board

Zhang Litong, female, born in Chongqing in April of 1938, is a famous expert in aerospace materials. She graduated from Northwestern Polytechnical University in 1961. She was a senior visiting scholar in the Business Development Center of Spatial Structure Materials of NASA of the US from April 1989 to January 1991. Now, she acts as a professor and doctoral supervisor of Northwestern Polytechnical University and the deputy director of the Academic Committee of National Key Laboratory on Ultra-temperature Structure Composite Material Technology. She was elected as an academician of the Chinese Academy of Engineering in 1995.

She has been devoting himself to the research of aerospace materials and the technologies of manufacturing aerospace materials for many years and has achieved abundant research results in marginless melted module precise casting technologies and their fundamental theory research of thin-wall complex high-temperature alloy and aluminum alloy castings. She reveals the blade deformation rules, roughness generation rules and middle/high-temperature softening deformation mechanism of ceramic shells. Through independent innovation, she develops marginless melted module casting technology of high-temperature alloy, plaster-mold melted module casting technology of aluminum alloy, technology of middle/high-temperature creep-resisting ceramic shell materials for melted module casting of high-temperature alloy, and technology of foamed ceramic filtering and purifying materials for high-temperature alloy. Relevant achievements have been applied to production of aero-engines and aircraft components successfully.

After returning to China, she establishes three technology platforms with independent intellectual property rights (manufacturing process, manufacturing equipment and material and environment performance assessment), breaking international blockade on technologies.

She was awarded with one first-class prize of National Award for Technological Invention, four first-class, second-class and third-class prizes of National Award for Scientific and Technological Progress, one second-class prize of State-level Teaching Award. She is authorized with 64 national invention patents.

Zhang Gongqing, Member of the Selection Board

Zhang Gongqing was born on May 29, 1936 in Shanghai. After he graduated from the Department of Mathematics of Peking University in 1959 he worked in his university. In the year of 1978, as one of the first visiting scholars since the reform and opening-up, he made further study in the United States. Now he is a professor of Peking University, an academician of Chinese Academy of Sciences, an academician of the Academy of Sciences for the Developing World, the Director of the Research and Talent Training Center for Teaching and Learning Mathematics in Universities and Colleges, and he also serves as a member in the editorial board of many international core academic journals.

As a famous mathematician, he develops infinite dimensional Morse theory into a unified framework of the critical point theory, and is the first one to employ Morse theory as a tool to study multiple solutions to partial differential equations. His monograph is the fundamental literature of the related field. He also develops the topological degree theory of set-valued mappings and the critical point theory of non-differential functional, making them a kind of free boundary problem in the study on equations of mathematical physics and on non-smooth mechanics.

He won the Award of National Science & Technology Conference (1978), the third prize of the State Natural Sciences Award (1982), the second prize of the State Natural Sciences Award (1987), Chen Xingshen Mathematics Prize (1986), the title of the Young Scientist with Outstanding Contributions (1984), the Third World Academy of Sciences Award in Mathematics (1993), Hua Luogeng Mathematics Prize (2009), Guohua Award of Peking University, and Special Award for Teaching presented by Founder Group (2011), etc.

Chen Jiaer, Member of the Selection Board

Chen Jiaer, born on October 1, 1934 in Shanghai, is an academician of Chinese Academy of Sciences, an academician of the Academy of Sciences for the Developing World. He is currently a professor of physics at Peking University, the vice director of the Advisory Group of the National Basic Research Program of China (or 973 Program), and the vice chairman of the China Coordination Committee of the International Council of Scientific Unions.

He was the president of the Peking University and the dean of the Graduate School of Peking University, the director of the Committee of the National Natural Sciences Foundation, the director of the Division of Mathematics and Physics of the Chinese Academy of Sciences (CAS), a member of the CAS presidium, and the dean of the School of Physics of the Graduate University of CAS.

For a long time he has been devoting himself to the teaching and scientific research of the low-energy particle accelerator and its application. He is good at combining the cutting-edge development of an academic subject with national demands and planning the research in physics and talent training in a forward-looking way. He pioneered the development of RF superconducting accelerator, ultra-sensitive accelerator mass spectrometry, RF quadrupole field accelerator and electrostatic accelerator in China. He is a founder and one of the leaders in researching and developing low-energy particle accelerator in China.

Chen Jiaer was a long-time leader in Peking University and the Committee of the National Natural Science Foundation, and was also a member of the Leadership Group of Medium and Long Term Planning for Development of Science and Technology. He made important contribution to the formulation of the National Medium and Long Term Planning of Development of Science and Technology and the development of relevant science and education causes in China.

Hao Jiming, Member of the Selection Board

Hao Jiming, a well-known expert in environmental engineering, was born in Shandong Province in August 1946. He graduated from Tsinghua University in 1970. He earned a master degree from Tsinghua University in 1981, and obtained a Ph.D. from University of Cincinnati in 1984. At Tsinghua University, he is a professor, tutor for doctoral candidates, deputy director of the teaching committee, and director of the Research Institute of Environmental Science and Engineering. He is also a member on the National Environmental Consultation Committee and China Council for International Cooperation on Environment and Development. He was elected as academician of the Chinese Academy of Engineering in 2005, and was elected as foreign academician of the National Academy of Engineering in the U.S. in 2018.

Hao Jiming has dedicated himself to the research in controlling air pollution in China for more than 40 years. His main fields of research include energy and environment, and air pollution control engineering. He is in charge of national acid deposition control planning and the research in countermeasures against acid deposition. His research result on dividing the areas for controlling acid rain and carbon dioxide has been adopted by the State Council, playing a guiding role in formulating China's policies on preventing and treating acid rain pollution. He has developed the planning and methods for controlling pollution caused by motor-driven vehicles in urban areas, promoting the control of the pollution caused by motor-driven vehicles in China. He has conducted in-depth research in the characteristics, causes and control policy on air compound pollution, further developed the theoretical and technological methods on improving the air quality in mega cities, and promoted the joint efforts to prevent and control the regional air compound pollution in China. He has conducted the research in the key technologies for controlling air pollution for a long period of time, and has made contributions in the fields such as dust control, desulfurization and denitration in coal-fired flue gas, and control of the pollution caused by motor-driven vehicles.

Hao Jiming won one first-prize and two second prizes of National Award for Scientific and Technological Progress, one second prize of National Award for Natural Science and two second prizes of National Award for Technical Invention, and two first prizes of National Award in Teaching Achievement. He was granted the title of national famous teacher in 2006. He won the Haagen-Smit Clean Air Award in 2015, and the IBM Global Faculty Award in 2016.

Qian Shaojun, Member of the Selection Board

Qian Shaojun was born in 1934 in Pinghu, Zhejiang Province. In 1951, he was admitted to the Department of Physics of Tsinghua University, and later studied Beijing Russian Language College, Department of Physics and the Research Section of Physics (now the Department of Technical Physics) of Peking University. He currently works as a consultant and research fellow of the Committee of Science and Technology of General Armament Department of the PLA, a research fellow and an academician of the Chinese Academy of Engineering. He used to be the deputy commander and the commander of the Nuclear Test Base, and was a standing member of the Committee of Science and Technology in the State Commission of Science and Technology for National Defense Industry.

He has been long engaged in the radiochemical diagnostic work of nuclear test and participated in a series of atomic bomb and hydrogen bomb nuclear tests conducted in the atmosphere or underground, in which he remarkably enhanced the measurement accuracy by establishing and improving many diagnostic approach and technology. For many times he took part in the study on the development strategy of science and technology and weaponry and equipment for national defence and participated in organizing the special research in national medium and long term scientific and technical development planning. He guided the basic study on applying research results in national defense, and worked hard to make such basic study consistent with the national basic research programs. He was put in charge of developing nuclear technology for military use, kept track of long-term changes with international situations and the policy evolvement of some leading nations, and instructed and took part in the study of arms control. He participated in the negotiation of the Comprehensive Nuclear Test Ban Treaty and guided the preparatory work for the performance of the treaty after it was signed.

His published works include a translated work, two monographs, wrote many scientific and technical papers and important scientific and technical articles for archival purpose. He won the Top Prize of the State Scientific and Technological Progress Award and the second prize of the State Scientific and Technological Progress Award once, the second prize of the State Award for Inventions and the third prize of the State Award for Inventions once, and the Military Progress Prize in Science and Technology many times.

Ni Jun, Member of the Selection Board

Ni Jun was born in Qinghai Province in November 1961. He is the Shien-Ming (Sam) Wu Collegiate Professor of Manufacturing Science and Professor of Mechanical Engineering at the University of Michigan, USA. He is the director of the Wu Manufacturing Research Center and the co-director of a National Science Foundation sponsored Industry/University Cooperative Research Center for Intelligent Maintenance Systems at the University of Michigan. Professor Ni served as the founding Dean of the University of Michigan – Shanghai Jiao Tong University Joint Institute located in Shanghai, China and is currently the Honorary Dean and Special Advisor to the President of Shanghai Jiao Tong University. Professor Ni is currently the Chairman of Global Future Council on Production at the World Economic Forum. Professor Ni served as the Deputy Director of the National Science Foundation Engineering Research Center for Reconfigurable Manufacturing Systems, and the Director of a National Science Foundation sponsored Industry/University Cooperative Research Center for Dimensional Measurement and Control in Manufacturing.

Professor Ni's research covers many topics in advanced manufacturing, including smart manufacturing technologies, and applications of industrial big data analytics and artificial intelligence in quality assurance, precision manufacturing, and intelligent maintenance systems. His research has been successfully applied by various industrial companies.

Selected honors and awards that Professor Ni received are 2013 International Science and Technology Cooperation Award from the President of People's Republic of China, 2013 Gold Medal from Society of Manufacturing Engineers, 2009 Ennor Manufacturing Technology Award from American Society of Mechanical Engineers, and 1994 Presidential Faculty Fellows Award from President Clinton. He is an elected Fellow of International Society of Engineering Asset Management, International Society for Nano-manufacturing, American Society of Mechanical Engineers, and Society of Manufacturing Engineers.

Gao Wen, Member of the Selection Board

Gao Wen was born in 1956. He received his doctorate in computer application from Harbin Institute of Technology in 1988, and earned a doctorate in electronics in Tokyo University in 1991. Now he is a professor of the School of Information of Peking University, tutor for doctoral candidates. In 2011, he was elected the academician of the Chinese Academy of Engineering.

His main area of research is digital media technology. He has long been engaged in the research in many fields including computer vision, pattern recognition and image processing, Multimedia data compression, and multi-model interface and virtual reality. He is a scientist of profound accomplishments in video coding and analysis, sign language recognition and synthesis, human face identification, and digital library. He was put in charge of more than twenty state-level research programs like 973 program (chief leader), 863 program and programs of the National Natural Science Foundation. He served as the leader of the Audio Video Coding Standard (AVS) Workgroup, making main contribution to the establishment and popularization of the international standards with independent intellectual property of China. He was the president of the Flagship Conference of the IEEE ICME 2007 and ACM MM 2009.

He completed five scientific monographs and has more than one hundred papers published in international academic periodicals. As the main participant in completing the research project of video coding and system, he won the second prize of the State Scientific and Technological Progress Award for five times and the second prize of the State Technological Invention Award for one time for his achievements in this regard.

Sang Guowei, Member of the Selection Board

Sang Guowei was born in Huzhou, Zhejiang in November 1941. He is a clinical pharmacologist, an academician of the Chinese Academy of Engineering, Chairman of Chinese Pharmaceutical Association, Chief Engineer for the important specific techniques for the national "development of important new medicines" in the "11th Five-Year Plan", "12th Five-Year Plan" and "13th Five-Year Plan". He is also the director of the Expert Consultation Committee of the "Development Program of the Pharmaceuticals Industry in the 13th Five-Year Plan" of the Ministry of Industry and Information Technology, senior research fellow of National Institute for the Control of Pharmaceutical and Biological Products (NICPBP), honorary president of Shanghai University of Traditional Chinese Medicine (SHUTCM), and was the vice chairman of the 11th National People's Congress Standing Committee, and chairman of Chinese Peasants' and Workers' Democratic Party.

He has systematically studied the pharmacokinetics, race differences and clinical pharmacology of steroidal contraceptives and antiprogestogens for long-acting injection and for oral taking, and made a number of important achievements. He has done fruitful work in terms of safety evaluation, quality control and clinical trial etc. for new drugs in recent years, and has made great contributions in strengthening China's construction of the GLP and GCP platforms.

He has won two National Scientific Conference Awards (in 1978), three Second Prizes of National Science and Technology Progress Award (in 1987, 1997 and 2008), one First Prize and four Second Prizes of Science and Technology Progress Award at the ministerial and commission levels, the Science and Technology Awards of the Ho Leung Ho Lee Foundation in 1997 (Medical-Pharmaceutical Award), the Special Contribution Award of the Wu Jieping-Paul Janssen Medical-Pharmaceutical Award in 2008, and the Lifetime Achievement Award in Pharmacy Science of the Federation International Pharmaceutical (FIP) in 2014.

Cao Xuetao, Member of the Selection Board

Cao Xuetao, was born in July 1964 in Jinan City, Shandong Province. In 1990, he graduated from the Second Military Medical University. He is the President of Chinese Academy of Medical Sciences (CAMS), member of the Chinese Academy of Engineering, and the Director of National

Key Laboratory of Medical Immunology. Concurrently he is the President of the Chinese Society for Immunology, Chairperson of Global Alliance of Chronic Diseases (GACD), and President of the Federation of Immunological Societies of Asia-Oceania (FIMSA). He also serves as a member of the editorial board of magazines including Cell.

He is mainly engaged in fundamental research on innate immune recognition and relevant immune regulation, and applicability research on tumor immunotherapy. He has found a new dendritic cell (DC) subset with an important immune regulation function, independently identified 22 immune-related molecules, systematically studied innate immune recognition and the new mechanism for interferon production regulation, explored apparent molecular action on inflammation and cancer development and progression, established new approaches for tumor immunotherapy, and carried out relevant clinical trials.

He won the second-class prize of National Science and Technology Awards as the primary participant of a research project, a first-class prize of Chinese Medical Science and Technology Awards, a first-class prize of Military Science and Technology Progress Awards, three first-class prizes of Shanghai Science and Technology Progress Awards. He has obtained 16 national invention patents and two national category-II new medicine certificates. His research result was selected as one of the top ten results representing the scientific and technological progress in China in 2011. He was presented with Guanghua Engineering Science and Technology Award, Cheng Kong Scholar Achievement Award, China Young Scientist Award, and others. As corresponding author, he published over 220 papers in SCI-cited journals including Cell, Science, Nature Immunology, Cancer Cell, Immunity and others. His papers have been non-self-cited for over 5600 times in SCI-cited journals; he has written and served as a co-chief-editor for eight monographs. Of all the doctoral candidates under his tutorship, 11 have been presented with the awards of "national 100 excellent dissertations for doctoral degrees."

Cheng Xu, Member of the Selection Board

Cheng Xu, born in 1944, is of the origin of Wuxi, Jiangsu Province. He graduated from the Department of Agronomy of Beijing Agricultural University (Now China Agricultural University), later he worked in the Institute of Crop Breeding and Cultivation of the Chinese Academy of Agricultural Science. He is currently a professor of the China Agricultural University, and a tutor for doctoral candidates. He worked in the Beijing Academy of Agricultural Science and the Ministry of Agriculture. His major fields of research include sustainable agriculture and rural development, agricultural ecology and ecological agriculture.

He was put in charge of two research projects: one is the construction of the Agricultural Modernization and Experimental Base (location: Doudian village, Fangshan County, Beijing) and the other is Ecological Agriculture Program. In 1985, he took the lead in introducing the theory of sustainable agricultural development. From then on he started to study the way to realize sustainable agricultural development in China. He focused his research on the ecological restoration in the fragile farming–pastoral transitional zones and the exploration of the sustainable intensive agriculture.

As the main participant in completing the research project, he won the first prize of the Beijing Science and Technology Progress Awards and the first prize of the National Sparkle Technology Award (equivalent to Science and Technology Progress Award). He was totally presented with seven second or third prizes of science and technology progress awards at provincial and ministerial level. In 1988, he was approved as a National Young & Middle–Aged Expert with Outstanding Contribution.

His works include *An Introduction to Sustainable Agriculture* and *General Program on Sustainable Development in China Volume* 13: *Agriculture in China and the Sustainable Development.*

Zeng Qingcun, Member of the Selection Board

Zeng Qingcun, born in May 1935 in Yangjiang County of Guangdong Province, graduated from the Department of Physics of Peking University in 1956. In 1961, he completed his Licentiate (namely Ph. D now) in the Institute of Applied Geophysics of the Soviet Academy of Science. After he returned to China he worked in the Institute of Geophysics and then the Institute of Atmospheric Physics of the Chinese Academy of Sciences (CAS). He was elected as an academician of the Chinese Academy of Sciences in 1980. Currently he is a research fellow of the Institute of Atmospheric physics of the CAS.

His major research field includes atmospheric sciences and geophysical fluid dynamics. He has been devoting himself to the study of the basic theory and numerical model and simulation of general atmospheric circulation and fluid dynamics, earth system dynamics model, numerical weather prediction and climatic prediction theory, climate dynamics and monsoon theory, dynamics of atmospheric boundary layer, theoretical method of satellite remote sensing, applied mathematics and numerical mathematics, and natural cybernetics. He is the first one in the world to put forward half–implicit difference scheme and square conservative scheme, applied the original equation into the actual numerical climate prediction (1961), developed the marine–atmosphere coupled mode for the extra–seasonal climate predictions (1990, 1994), and put forward the systematic theory of satellite remote sensing (1974) and the Theoretical method of natural control (1995).

He won the second prize of the State Natural Sciences Award twice and the third prize of the State Natural Sciences Awards once, the first prize of the Natural Science Award of the CAS six times and Outstanding Contribution Award once. His monographs include *Principles of the Atmospheric Remote Sensing in Infrared*, *Mathematical Physics Foundations of the Numerical Weather Prediction*, *Principles of the Short−term Numerical Climatic Prediction*, *Yellow Clouds Stretching Thousands of Miles—The research on Dust−storm in East Asia*. He has also published hundreds of academic articles.